2010 NAEYC STANDARDS
Initial and Advanced Early Childhood Professional Preparation Programs
Correlations with Chapter Content

These NAEYC Standards provide the foundation for accreditation of early childhood programs in higher education.

Standards		Chapters
Standard 1:	**Promoting Child Development and Learning**	
1a:	Knowing and understanding young children's characteristics and needs.	2, 3, 5, 6, 7, 8, 9, 10, 11, 12, 13
1b:	Knowing and understanding the multiple influences on early development and learning.	2, 3, 5, 6, 7, 8, 9, 10, 11, 12, 13
1c:	Using developmental knowledge to create healthy, respectful, supportive, and challenging learning environments for young children.	1, 3, 4, 5, 6, 7, 8, 9, 10, 11, 12
Standard 2:	**Building Family and Community Relationships**	
2a:	Knowing about and understanding diverse family and community relationships.	7, 12, 14
2b:	Supporting and engaging families and communities through respectful, reciprocal relationships.	7, 14
2c:	Involving families and communities in young children's development and learning.	7, 8, 11, 14
Standard 3:	**Observing, Documenting, and Assessing to Support Young Children and Families**	
3a:	Understanding the goals, benefits, and uses of assessment.	6
3b:	Knowing about and using observation, documentation, and other appropriate assessment tools and approaches.	6
3c:	Understanding and practicing responsible assessment to promote positive outcomes for each child.	6
3d:	Knowing about assessment partnerships with families and with professional colleagues to build effective learning environments.	14
Standard 4:	**Using Developmentally Effective Approaches**	
4a:	Understanding positive relationships and supportive interactions as the foundation of their work with young children.	1, 2, 3, 5, 8, 9, 10, 11, 12, 13
4b:	Knowing and understanding effective strategies and tools for early education.	1, 2, 3, 5, 8, 9, 10, 11, 12, 13
4c:	Using a broad repertoire of developmentally appropriate teaching/learning approaches.	1, 2, 3, 4, 5, 8, 9, 10, 11, 12, 13

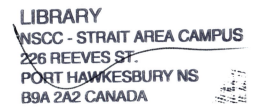

Standards	Chapters
Standard 5: Using Content Knowledge to Build Meaningful Curriculum	
5a: Understanding content knowledge and resources in academic disciplines: language and literacy, the arts – music, creative movement, dance, drama, visual arts; mathematics; science, physical activity, physical education, health and safety; and social studies.	4, 8, 9, 10, 11, 13
5b: Knowing and using the central concepts, inquiry tools, and structures of content areas or academic disciplines.	8, 9, 10, 11, 13
5c: Using own knowledge, appropriate early learning standards, and other resources to design, implement, and evaluate developmentally meaningful and challenging curriculum for each child.	2, 8, 9, 10, 11, 13
Standard 6: Becoming a Professional	
6a: Identifying and involving oneself with the early childhood field.	3, 5, 15
6b: Knowing about and upholding ethical standards and other early childhood professional guidelines.	6, 14, 15
6c: Engaging in continuous, collaborative learning to inform practice.	15
6d: Integrating knowledgeable, reflective, and critical perspectives on early education.	3, 5, 15
6e: Engaging in informed advocacy for young children and the early childhood profession.	3, 5, 14, 15
Standard 7: Early Childhood Field Experiences	
7a: Opportunities to observe and practice in early childhood age groups.	6
7b: Opportunities to observe and practice in two of the three main types of early education settings (early school grades, child care centers and homes, Head Start programs).	1

SECOND EDITION

Strategies for Including Children with Special Needs in Early Childhood Settings

Ruth E. Cook, Ph.D.

Anne Marie Richardson-Gibbs, M.A.

Laurie Nielsen Dotson, M.A.

CENGAGE
Learning·

Australia • Brazil • Mexico • Singapore • United Kingdom • United States

Strategies for Including Children with Special Needs in Early Childhood Settings, **Second Edition**
Ruth E. Cook, Anne Marie Richardson-Gibbs, Laurie Nielsen Dotson

Senior Product Director: Marta Lee-Perriard

Senior Product Manager: Cheri-Ann Nakamaru

Associate Content Developer: Jessica Alderman

Senior Digital Content Specialist: Jaclyn Hermesmeyer

Marketing Manager: Andrew Miller

Content Project Manager: Samen Iqbal

Art Director: Helen Bruno

Manufacturing Planner: Doug Bertke

Production and Composition: MPS Limited

Photo Researcher: Lumina Datamatics

Text Researcher: Lumina Datamatics

Cover and Text Designer: Lisa Buckley

Cover Image: Charles Barry

For product information and technology assistance, contact us at **Cengage Learning Customer & Sales Support, 1-800-354-9706.**

For permission to use material from this text or product, submit all requests online at **www.cengage.com/permissions.** Further permissions questions can be e-mailed to **permissionrequest@cengage.com.**

Library of Congress Control Number: 2016946788

Student Edition:
ISBN: 978-1-305-96069-5

Loose-leaf Edition:
ISBN: 978-1-305-96071-8

Cengage Learning
20 Channel Center Street
Boston, MA 02210
USA

Cengage Learning is a leading provider of customized learning solutions with employees residing in nearly 40 different countries and sales in more than 125 countries around the world. Find your local representative at **www.cengage.com.**

Cengage Learning products are represented in Canada by Nelson Education, Ltd.

To learn more about Cengage Learning Solutions, visit **www.cengage.com.**

Purchase any of our products at your local college store or at our preferred online store **www.cengagebrain.com.**

Printed in the United States of America
Print Number: 01   Print Year: 2016

Contents

CHAPTER 3

Adaptations for Children with Specific Disabilities   31

CHAPTER 4

Arranging the Physical Environment to Support the Inclusion of Children with Special Needs 58

CHAPTER 5

Preventing and Managing Challenging Behaviors   74

PART 2 • Adapting Daily Activities in Inclusive Early Childhood Settings

CHAPTER 6

Monitoring Individual Child Progress 95

CHAPTER 7

Managing Arrival, Departure, and Other Transitions 110

CHAPTER 8

Engaging Children with Special Needs in Free Play 122

Circle Time, including Music and Rhythm Activities 141

Strategies for Including Children with Special Needs in Early Childhood Settings, 2nd edition, is intended to be a resource to early childhood educators working in a variety of community-based settings, including child care, Head Start, and preschool programs in which young children with special needs are included. Changes in the federal special education law, or *IDEIA*, have strengthened the mandate for inclusion of young children with special needs in typical and natural environments where they have opportunities to interact with their peers and to participate as equal members of their community. This access to inclusive environments is a precious, hard-fought right.

As access to community-based settings increases, the responsibility for meeting the needs of young children with special needs is no longer the exclusive purview of special educators and therapists. It is increasingly shifting to early childhood educators. This practical, hands-on guide includes ideas for accommodating young children with disabilities in all areas of curriculum. Adaptations are offered by activity, rather than by disability, within natural environments. Focus is on embedding instruction within daily routines. Chapters are short with lots of examples given for working with a variety of common disabilities such as cerebral palsy, Down syndrome, autism, visual impairment, hearing loss, and behavioral challenges. The book includes a balance of text, photos, and graphics.

This is an immediately applicable resource that can provide both an introduction to working with young children with special needs for students in early childhood education, as well as a usable resource and problem-solving guide for early childhood education practitioners and paraprofessionals. Families with a young child placed in an inclusive setting, disability specialists, therapists, and early childhood special education personnel who provide inclusion support to young children with special needs will appreciate the practicality of this text.

Conceptual Approach

As access to inclusive environments becomes more widely available, and more and more young children with special needs (including children with significant and complex needs) are served in early childhood settings, teacher trainers in the field of disability and early childhood special education have an obligation. They must provide training and resources to early childhood educators that will enable them to expand their skill base and confidence in working with young children who have significant learning and behavior challenges.

This book assumes that readers already have a solid base of knowledge about child development and, at least, a beginning-level experience in early childhood education. This is an important assumption because effective early childhood *special* education must be built upon this foundation. Such a knowledge base includes understanding child development across the domains of social and emotional development, language and cognition, adaptive (self-help) skills, and emergent literacy. It also includes a solid knowledge of developmentally appropriate practice and a strong commitment to understanding and meeting the needs of children and families from culturally diverse backgrounds. Without this essential foundation, professionals with early childhood education cannot effectively meet the needs of children with disabilities.

The content and scope of this book are far from exhaustive. Rather, this guide is intended as an immediately useful introduction to understanding and accommodating young children with special needs in group settings. It includes an introduction to the nature of specific disabilities, useful teaching strategies, planning and intervention supports in daily activities, and an approach to working with families, paraeducators, and specialists. Emphasis is placed on providing the supports necessary to ensure access and full participation in classrooms and programs.

Organization

The book is organized in three parts. Part 1, *Special Education Foundations: Understanding Special Needs and Universal Instructional Strategies*, includes basic information related to working with children with special needs and sets the stage for the provision of supports that will maximize participation in activities embedded within the daily routine. Chapter 1 offers an overview of the significant legislation and defining features and benefits of inclusion, and discusses service-delivery models. Chapter 2 describes numerous essential instructional strategies that will enhance the learning of all children. Chapter 3 includes basic descriptions of some of the most challenging disabilities, including Down syndrome, autism, visual impairment, hearing loss, and cerebral palsy. Chapter 4 discusses considerations for designing the classroom environment in ways that best meet the needs of children who have various types of disabilities. Chapter 5 provides a basic understanding of behavior challenges in children with special needs and an overview of practical strategies and techniques for both preventing behavior challenges and managing them once they occur. Part 1 ends with Chapter 6 on monitoring children's progress. It explains the Individualized Family Service Plan (IFSP) and the Individualized Education Program (IEP), and provides simple suggestions for ongoing monitoring of children's progress toward specific goals and objectives.

Part 2, *Adapting Daily Activities in Inclusive Early Childhood Settings*, includes several chapters devoted to the particular challenges posed by different daily activities. These include arrival/departure and transitions (Chapter 7), free play (Chapter 8), circle time (Chapter 9), tabletop activities (Chapter 10), outside activities (Chapter 11), mealtimes (Chapter 12), and emergent literacy activities (Chapter 13). Each chapter provides general suggestions for designing these activities in ways that will be most supportive of children with special needs. Included are notes, labeled *Helpful Hints*, related to special adaptations for children with specific disabilities.

Part 3, *Working with the Early Childhood Special Education Team*, includes two chapters. Chapter 14 provides early childhood educators with important information about the challenges that parents and caregivers of children with special needs often face. It addresses the importance of establishing partnerships with families. Chapter 15 describes the roles and contributions of specialists and therapists. It discusses the ways in which paraeducators and one-to-one assistants can best support children with disabilities. Also included in this chapter is a brief overview of collaborative teaming and problem-solving processes.

Special Features and Updates

- Chapter-at-a-Glance introductions highlight key points.
- Chapters align with relevant *NAEYC Standards for Initial Early Childhood Professional Development* and *DEC Recommended Practices in Early Intervention/Early Childhood Special Education*.

- Learning objectives focus attention and guide student learning.
- Colorful photos and attractive color design make the book more visually exciting.
- Definition and use of person-first terminology throughout reinforces the inclusive spirit of the text.
- Numerous new strategies for adapting materials, routines, and activities accommodate the needs of a variety of young children with special needs in inclusive settings.
- Real-life examples illustrate key points.
- Web Links provide sites with useful related information.
- Considerations to facilitate diversity awareness are provided.
- Helpful Hints address challenges and adaptations specific to different disabilities.
- Read–Reflect–Discuss scenarios illustrate key ideas.
- Resources, references, and key terms (defined in a glossary at the end of the text) are included.
- Adaptation checklists adapted from CARA's Kit are provided.
- The appendices include a Developmental Skills Reference Chart, updated examples of blank educational forms for quick utilization, and samples of an adapted lesson plan and an Individualized Education Program.
- MindTap for Education is a fully customizable online learning platform with interactive content designed to help students learn effectively and prepare them for success in the classroom. Through activities based on real-life teaching situations, MindTap elevates students' thinking by giving them experiences in applying concepts, practicing skills, and evaluating decisions, guiding them to become reflective educators.

Chapter-by-Chapter Changes

The second edition of *Strategies for Including Children with Special Needs in Early Childhood Settings* has been significantly updated since it was first published in 2001. The most notable changes have been listed here by chapter:

Chapter 1 (*The Origins and Dimensions of Quality Inclusion*): The introduction from the prior edition has been expanded significantly to create a brand new first chapter. It gives readers a working definition of quality inclusion, paving the way for the strategies in the rest of the text. It also covers the major legislation that governs the ways inclusion is implemented in classrooms, and the various delivery support models that can be used to best assist children with special needs.

Chapter 2 (*Instructional Strategies Supporting the Inclusion of Young Children with Special Needs*): A new section has been added that includes alignment with CARA's Kit on how to determine the level of support to provide each child with special needs. Two new tools, everyday adaptation materials and the EESS acronym, are introduced to help facilitate inclusion.

Chapter 3 (*Adaptations for Children with Specific Disabilities*): Updates in this chapter bring the use of terminology and classifications of various disabilities in line with recommended practices.

Chapter 4 (*Arranging the Physical Environment to Support the Inclusion of Children with Special Needs*): Considerations when planning a technology activity area along with reference to the NAEYC recommendations and a useful early childhood technology evaluation toolkit enrich this chapter. Increased attention has been given to the value of outdoor play areas as evidenced in a garden "project" and the provision of guidelines for designing outdoor environments.

Chapter 5 (*Preventing and Managing Challenging Behaviors*): This chapter has been aligned with the Center on the Social and Emotional Foundations for Early Learning (CSEFEL). Greater emphasis is given to the prevention of challenging behaviors. A section has been added on understanding and effectively working with English language learners. Examples of a functional behavior assessment and positive behavior support plan have been included to accompany the scenario about Frederika.

Chapter 6 (*Monitoring Individual Child Progress*): Emphasis on embedding goals and objectives into naturally occurring daily opportunities is now considered to be necessary before progress can be monitored. Strategies for providing the prompts necessary to help children be successful are also included. Many of the data collection charts have been updated and an IFSP/IEP summary handout has been created.

Chapter 7 (*Managing Arrival, Departure, and Other Transitions*): Information has been expanded on learning opportunities and successful strategies for departure and transitions. A new helpful hint discusses ways to enhance the home-to-school connection. A discussion on the importance of visual cues was created as well as a new figure summarizing all of the adaptations discussed in the chapter.

Chapter 8 (*Engaging Children with Special Needs in Free Play*): Expanded information on engaging children in free play and examples have been inserted throughout this chapter. New information on making adaptations using the EESS acronym, open-ended and close-ended toys, and using different types of toys to meet diverse learners' needs is included. The closing figure summarizes all the adaptations discussed.

Chapter 9 (*Circle Time, including Music and Rhythm Activities*): This redesigned chapter combines the "Circle Time" and "Music and Rhythm Activities" chapters from the previous edition. There are new sections on types of circle time activities, adaptations for children with special needs, and key dimensions to consider during circle time.

Chapter 10 (*Tabletop Activities*): This chapter places more emphasis on all tabletop activities, hence the title change. It includes a new section on enhancing and embedding early math skills within tabletop activities. Adaptations using the EESS acronym and levels of support are discussed while the chapter closes with a summary of all the adaptations.

Chapter 11(*Outside Play*): Information has been expanded to provide strategies for access and participation of all children with disabilities outside of their classroom. Additional content supports motor planning and perceptual motor development. Added are two sections that encourage peers to play with children with disabilities and suggest intentional planning of outside activities using a portable inclusion cart.

Chapter 12 (*Mealtimes*): Snack time has been expanded to include all mealtimes. Added are new pictures and discussions of special equipment and adaptations that can facilitate development of independence and communication skills at mealtimes.

Chapter 13 (*Supporting Language and Emergent Literacy in Children with Special Needs*): The discussion of the relationship between language and literacy has been enriched. There are new sections on how to adapt books, technology apps to support communication and literacy, and books about diversity. Attention is given to how to make adaptations to support language and literacy development, including visual supports that are durable.

Chapter 14 (*Communicating and Collaborating with Families*): Understanding families' emotional reactions has been updated and expanded to include the involvement of fathers, concerns of siblings, and attention to diversity. New forms to assist families and prepare practitioners for collaborative team meetings are available.

Chapter 15 (*Collaborating with Disability Specialists and Paraprofessionals*): The final chapter, again, emphasizes the need for collaborative team efforts. As inclusive specialists are in greater demand, reflections of a current inclusion specialist offer insight into both the potential and the responsibilities of the position.

Accompanying Teaching and Learning Resources

MindTap™: The Personal Learning Experience

MindTap Education for *Strategies for Including Children with Special Needs in Early Childhood Settings,* 2nd edition, represents a new approach to teaching and learning. A highly personalized, fully customizable learning platform with an integrated eportfolio, MindTap helps students to elevate thinking by guiding them to:

- Know, remember, and understand concepts critical to becoming a great practitioner;
- Apply concepts, create curriculum and tools, and demonstrate performance and competency in key areas in the course, including national and state education standards;
- Prepare artifacts for the portfolio and eventual state licensure, to launch a successful professional career; and
- Develop the habits to become a reflective practitioner.

As students move through each chapter's Learning Path, they engage in a scaffolded learning experience, designed to move them up Bloom's taxonomy, from lower- to higher-order thinking skills. The Learning Path enables preservice students to develop these skills and gain confidence by:

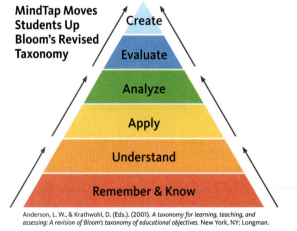

Anderson, L. W., & Krathwohl, D. (Eds.). (2001). *A taxonomy for learning, teaching, and assessing: A revision of Bloom's taxonomy of educational objectives.* New York, NY: Longman.

- Engaging them with chapter topics and activating their prior knowledge by watching and answering questions about authentic videos of teachers teaching and children learning in real classrooms;
- Checking their comprehension and understanding through Did You Get It? assessments, with varied question types that are autograded for instant feedback;
- Applying concepts through mini-case scenarios—students analyze typical teaching and learning situations, and then create a reasoned response to the issue(s) presented in the scenario; and
- Reflecting about and justifying the choices they made within the teaching scenario problem.

MindTap helps instructors facilitate better outcomes by evaluating how future teachers plan and teach lessons in ways that make content clear and help diverse students learn, assessing the effectiveness of their teaching practice, and adjusting teaching as needed. MindTap enables instructors to facilitate better outcomes by:

- Making grades visible in real time through the Student Progress App so students and instructors always have access to current standings in the class.
- Using the Outcome Library to embed national education standards and align them to student learning activities, and also allowing instructors to add their state's standards or any other desired outcome.
- Allowing instructors to generate reports on students' performance with the click of a mouse against any standards or outcomes that are in their Mind Tap course.
- Giving instructors the ability to assess students on state standards or other local outcomes by editing existing or creating their own MindTap activities, and then by aligning those activities to any state or other outcomes that the instructor has added to the MindTap Outcome Library.

MindTap Education for *Strategies for Including Children with Special Needs in Early Childhood Settings,* 2nd edition, helps instructors easily set their course because it integrates into their existing Learning Management System and saves instructors time by allowing them to fully customize any aspect of the learning path.

Instructors can change the order of the student learning activities, hide activities they don't want for the course, and—most importantly—create custom assessments and add any standards, outcomes, or content they do want (for example, YouTube videos, Google docs). Learn more at www.cengage.com/mindtap.

Online Instructor's Manual

The instructor's manual contains a variety of resources to aid instructors in preparing and presenting text material in a manner that meets their personal preferences and course needs. It presents chapter-by-chapter suggestions and resources to enhance and facilitate learning.

Online Test Bank

The test bank contains objective and essay questions to challenge your students and assess their learning.

Cengage Learning Testing Powered by Cognero

The test bank also is available through Cognero, a flexible, online system that allows you to author, edit, and manage test bank content, as well as create multiple test versions in an instant. You can deliver tests from your school's learning management system, your classroom, or wherever you want.

Online PowerPoint Lecture Slides

These vibrant, Microsoft PowerPoint lecture slides for each chapter assist you with your lecture by providing concept coverage using images, figures, and tables directly from the textbook!

Acknowledgments

First and foremost, we would like to acknowledge the children, families, and dedicated early childhood educators who have helped us understand the challenges of disabilities and allowed us to practice providing the supports and accommodations encouraged throughout this text. More specifically, we would like to thank such individuals from the El Monte City School District Head Start and State Preschool programs, Centro de Niños Padres at California State University at Los Angeles, the Mount Saint Mary's Child Development Center in Los Angeles, and the Southern Illinois University Child Development Center in Edwardsville, Illinois. Special gratitude is extended to the administrators, staff, children, and families of Parkway Child Development Center and Kiddo Land Learning Center for their contributions to the adaptive teaching strategies and photos included throughout the book.

Over the years, an incredible number of students, colleagues, friends, and family have influenced our thinking and had faith in our ability to produce a practical, hands-on guide with strategies that could truly support the successful inclusion of young children with a variety of disabilities. Among them is Abby Wang, a young woman with Down syndrome, who graduated from Centro de Niños Padres 26 years ago. We are grateful that she has not only provided friendship, but she also personalized the education process for a person with disabilities.

Others include Kathy Lewis, who shared valuable knowledge through the years while developing the Parkway inclusion program, and Moon and Yang Chia from Kiddo Land Learning Center whose camaraderie and support were inspiring. We wish to acknowledge and thank photographer Chuck Berry for the colorful photos that enrich this edition throughout, and Betty Tseng for the delightful adapted lesson plan found in the appendices.

As authors, we want to express appreciation to our colleagues and students, through the years, who have motivated us to continue to seek ways to foster inclusive education. Not only have we been writing in support of inclusion, but we have also been fortunate to be involved in such local initiatives as *Project Support* at Cal State, Los Angeles, and the *Inclusion Collaborative* of Santa Clara County under the extremely able leadership of Janice Battaglia. These incredible, innovative initiatives involving a diversity of agencies give us hope that we are progressing toward equal opportunity for all. We are extremely grateful to these and other similar projects for stepping up to support equal access for ALL children and youth.

The individual who was primarily responsible for the first edition of this book is Dr. M. Diane Klein who has also inspired and contributed to this new edition. Her background in speech pathology and audiology was indispensable to Chapter 13. We are eternally grateful to her for sharing her expertise and the wisdom she gained while serving as a professor of early childhood special education at Cal State, Los Angeles; being the executive director of Centro de Niños Padres; and initiating *Project Support,* which served to model support of young children with disabilities. We sincerely thank her for her mentorship, wisdom, and collegiality. Without her, this book would not exist.

The authors would like to send special appreciation to the significant others in their lives who provide the continual support necessary to complete the tasks involved in producing such a text. Specifically, eternal gratitude goes to Curtis Cook and Kenny Dotson who were there every step of the way. We also want to extend sincere appreciation to Jessica Alderman, whose patience and guidance throughout has been invaluable, and to Samen Iqbal and Jill Traut for their assistance throughout the production process.

Lastly, the authors would like to thank those who took the time to review portions of our new manuscript, which provided useful feedback during the revision process:

Dr. Michael A. Barla
Fontbonne University

Diane Bordenave
Southern University at New Orleans

Deborah Bruns
Southern Illinois University, Carbondale

Penny P. Craven
Mississippi State University

Jenny Fererro
Palomar College

Janet Filer
University of Central Arkansas

Linda S. Hensel
Concordia University Wisconsin

Martha Howard
Tennessee Technological University

Priya Lalvani
Montclair State University

About the Authors

Ruth E. Cook, PhD, is a professor emeritus and was director of special education, at Santa Clara University in Santa Clara, California. Formerly, she was also the director of two inclusive campus preschool programs, one at Mount Saint Mary's University in Los Angeles and the other at Southern Illinois University at Edwardsville. These experiences prompted her to be the lead author of *Adapting Early Childhood Curricula for Children with Special Needs,* now in its 9th edition. Beginning in 1982, it helped set the stage for inclusion of young children in early childhood settings. Currently, she is an instructor in the EPIC (Education Preparation for Inclusive Classrooms) program at the Santa Clara County Office of Education, which she helped originate. This program offers credentials that create teachers prepared to service birth to 5-year-olds with disabilities and those in K-12 who have moderate to severe disabilities.

Anne Marie Richardson-Gibbs, MA, is an inclusion specialist working with preschoolers, transitional kindergarteners, and kindergarteners with special needs enrolled in early childhood programs and elementary schools in El Monte, California. She was a program specialist for the California Department of Education SEEDS Project, providing technical assistance to early intervention and preschool programs throughout the state. She was also the program director of Centro de Niños y Padres, an early intervention program at Cal State University, Los Angeles, for eight years. During this time, she pioneered a consultant position providing inclusion support for young children with disabilities in inclusive settings.

Laurie Nielsen Dotson, MA, is an adjunct faculty of child development at Mission College in Santa Clara, California. She was the former inclusion training specialist for Santa Clara County Office of Education, providing inclusion coaching and professional development trainings to school districts, preschools, and community agencies. She is cross-trained in early childhood education and early childhood special educatton. Laurie is not only a special educator, but is also a person living with a disability who has made accommodations and adaptations to her life. It is interesting to note that Mrs. Dotson used assistive technology, in the form of a voice recognition system, as an alternative form of writing for many of the updates in this edition.

CHAPTER 1

The Origin and Dimensions of Quality Inclusion

LEARNING OBJECTIVES

After studying this chapter, you will be able to:

LO 1-1: Explain significant legislation that influences special education and inclusion policy.

LO 1-2: Summarize three defining features of high-quality inclusion in early childhood education.

LO 1-3: Describe the dimensions and variations of inclusion supports.

LO 1-4: Compare and contrast the different ways supports and services can be delivered.

LO 1-5: Recognize and discuss the benefits of inclusion.

The following NAEYC Standards and DEC Recommended Practices are addressed in this chapter:

naeyc

Standard 1: Promoting Child Development and Learning
Standard 4: Using Developmentally Effective Approaches
Standard 7: Early Childhood Field Experiences

DEC

Practice 2: Environment
Practice 4: Instruction
Practice 5: Interaction
Practice 6: Teaming and Collaboration

This chapter explains the foundation and rationale for inclusion of children with and without disabilities together in settings where ALL belong and ALL are welcome:

- Significant legislation and policies have paved the way for inclusion.

- High-quality service delivery requires a shift in service delivery that provides the support necessary to enable access and participation of all children.

- The keys to successful inclusion are effective models of service delivery and support.

- Inclusion support and delivery models vary considerably and are only limited by educators' knowledge and creativity as well as the extent of collaboration within the environment.

- Although inclusion of children is not without its challenges, there are many evidence-based benefits.

Introduction

It is the purpose of this book to focus primarily on strategies and supports that will enable *all* children to fully participate in natural settings and to develop their full potential. The authors realize that effective inclusion also requires collaborative, supportive partnerships with families and colleagues. This chapter explains the foundation and rationale of inclusion where children with and without disabilities play and learn together in a setting where *all* belong and *all* are welcomed. Significant laws, legislation, and policies have paved the way for inclusion. However, successful inclusion relies on a shared definition and a variety of supports and delivery models that will be discussed.

1-1 Historical Overview of Special Education Law and Inclusion

Since 1975, with the passage of Public Law 94-142 (the Education for all Handicapped Children Act), the United States has had laws in place that mandate educational services for school-age children with disabilities. In 1986, Public Law 99-457 (Education of the Handicapped Act Amendments) extended this law to include preschool-age children and encouraged states to develop comprehensive services for infants from birth to age three. In 1990, the 1975 law was further amended, and the name was changed to the **Individuals with Disabilities Education Act (IDEA)**, which replaced the term *handicapped children* with the "person-first" phrase *individuals with disabilities*. This was a

Photo 1-1 All children with and without disabilities play and learn together in inclusive classrooms.

very small change with a very big impact. The federal government was acknowledging that a person with a disability should be recognized as a whole person and not just his/her disability. This concept is called **person-first terminology (PFT)**, which places the person ahead of the disability as a reminder that a disability is only one characteristic of a person. Figure 1-1 provides some examples.

Beginning with the IDEA amendments in 1990, a series of additional amendments were made. One of the early amendments in 1991, Public Law 102-119, required infants and toddlers to have services delivered in normalized settings. "To the maximum extent appropriate," young children with disabilities were to be served in **natural environments** such as their home, community early care, and educational settings where children without disabilities are participating. Thus, this law extended the requirement of placement in the least restrictive environment to young children. The **least restrictive environment** means that, to the greatest extent possible, children with disabilities must be educated alongside and with children who do not have identified disabilities. In other words, placement in the general education classroom must be considered first, with appropriate support services, before considering a segregated special education classroom.

As a result, infants, toddlers, and preschoolers, regardless of their disability, will increasingly be served in nonspecial education settings. Families have gradually realized that their children have the right to receive appropriate services to address the needs created by their disabilities in typical community-based environments. In 2004, IDEA was again amended by Public Law 108-446, under what is now called Individuals with Disabilities Education Improvement Act (IDEIA). One major change makes it possible for young children to receive services without requiring a more specific diagnosis than *developmentally delayed*. It is expected that many children will progress enough through early intervention services that a more specific diagnosis can be avoided or delayed.

WEBLINK

For more information on person-first terminology, see the website *Disability Is Natural* at www.disabilityisnatural.com.

Use terms that show respect and acceptance for all by placing the person ahead of the disability.

Say: *a student with an intellectual disability*
Instead of: *an intellectually disabled student*

Say: *a boy with autism*
Instead of: *an autistic boy*

Say: *students in special education*
Instead of: *special education students*

Figure 1-1 Person-First Terminology

1-1a Americans with Disabilities Act: Provision of Equal Opportunity for All

In 1990, another law was passed that had a major impact on educating children in child care centers. The **Americans with Disabilities Act (ADA)**, amended in 2008, assures reasonable accommodations for all individuals with disabilities. This includes the right of **access** and accommodation in preschool and child care centers. The ADA requires that child care centers provided by government agencies cannot discriminate against people with disabilities based solely on their disability. These agencies, as well as private child care centers and home-based centers, need to provide equal opportunity to all. They must provide reasonable accommodations and cannot exclude children with disabilities unless their presence would pose a direct threat to the health or safety of others or require a fundamental alteration of the program. The only exceptions are child care centers run by religious organizations. There are frequently asked questions that help child care centers determine their role in complying with ADA law. See Appendix A for a summary of several of the most pertinent questions. Figure 1-2 provides a summary of relevant federal legislation. It should be noted, however, that even though legislation mandates services in natural environments considered to be the least restrictive environments for young children, the term *inclusion* is not specifically included in the law.

1-1b Head Start

As noted in Figure 1-2, Head Start, a federal early education program, was mandated to develop inclusive practices as early as 1972. Since then, many programs have provided the least restrictive environment for a minimum of 10 percent of their population who were required to be children with disabilities. As a result, Head Start was at the forefront of the inclusion effort because it started inclusion even before rights of access and accommodations in child care centers were established for children through the

1968 *Public Law 90-538: Handicapped Children's Early Education Assistance Act* Established experimental early education programs through Handicapped Children's Early Education Program (HCEEP).

1972 *Public Law 92-424: Economic Opportunity Act Amendments* Established preschool mandate that required that not less than 10 percent of the total number of Head Start placements be reserved for children with disabilities.

1975 *Public Law 94-142: Education for All Handicapped Children Act* Provided free appropriate public education to all school-age children (preschool services not mandated).

1986 *Public Law 99-457: Education of the Handicapped Act Amendments of 1986* Extended Pub. L. No. 94-142 to include three- to five-year-olds; provided incentives to states to develop comprehensive systems of services for infants and toddlers from birth to three with disabilities and their families.

1990 *Public Law 101-336: The Americans with Disabilities Act (ADA)* Assures full civil rights to individuals with disabilities, including access and accommodations in preschools and child care centers.

1990 *Public Law 101-476: Individuals with Disabilities Education Act (IDEA)* Reauthorization of Pub. L. No. 94-142. Uses "person-first" language, that is, "individuals with..." rather than "handicapped."

1991 *Public Law 102-119: Individuals with Disabilities Education Act Amendments of 1991.* "To the maximum extent appropriate," children are to be in natural environments in which children without disabilities participate.

1997 *Public Law 105-17: Individuals with Disabilities Education Act Amendments of 1997* Reauthorization of IDEA. Preschool services continues to be included under Part B; infants and toddlers included under Part C. Strengthens mandates for inclusion in the least restrictive environment for preschoolers and provision in "natural environments" for infants and toddlers. It also strengthened the recognition of families as integral partners in the early intervention process. States could now use the term developmentally delayed for young children.

2004 *Public Law 108-446: Individuals with Disabilities Education Improvement Act (IDEIA) of 2004* Reauthorization of IDEA. Parents now have a right to mediation for dispute resolution.

2007 *Public law 110-134: Head Start Act* Reauthorization of the Head Start Act. Further aligned Head Start with IDEA to ensure that children with disabilities have an individualized education program (IEP) or individualized family service plan (IFSP) as defined by IDEA regulations.

2008 *Public Law 110-325: The Americans with Disabilities Amendments Act (ADAAA) of 2008* To restore the intent of Pub. L. No. 101-336 Americans with Disability Act. Broadens the definition of disability and expands the categories of major life activities.

Figure 1-2 Key Legislation Affecting Young Children with Disabilities

WEBLINK

For more information on Head Start's commitment see http://depts.washington.edu/hscenter/.

Americans with Disabilities Act in 1990. Moreover, Head Start has removed barriers to make it easier for children with disabilities to receive services. For example, Head Start has often made provisions for families of children with disabilities to receive services even if the family's income is over the poverty guidelines. In addition, Head Start is providing training to its staff on evidence-based instructional strategies to include students with disabilities through its Head Start Center for Inclusion.

> "Early childhood inclusion embodies the values, policies, and practices that support the right of every infant and young child and his or her family, regardless of ability, to participate in a broad range of activities and contexts as full members of families, communities, and society. The desired results of inclusive experiences for children with and without disabilities and their families include a sense of belonging and membership, positive social relationships and friendships, and development and learning to reach their full potential. The defining features of inclusion that can be used to identify high-quality early childhood programs and services are access, participation, and supports" (p. 2).

Figure 1-3 Definition of Early Childhood Inclusion (DEC/NAEYC. (2009). *Early childhood inclusion: A joint position statement of the Division of Early Childhood (DEC) and the National Association for the Education of Young Children (NAEYC)*. Chapel Hill: University of North Carolina, FPG Child Development Institute.)

1-1c A Major Shift in Service Delivery

Serving young children in the least restrictive and natural environments requires a major shift in the roles and responsibilities of professionals and in how early intervention and special education services are delivered. This shift also creates the potential for increasing the responsibility of child care workers and early childhood educators for the early care and education of children with significant needs and challenges. Many early childhood personnel, whose jobs are already extremely demanding, may not feel ready to take on this new role. Chapter 2 will help professionals create a framework on which to build the foundation for providing the support necessary to enable effective inclusion of children with disabilities. A definition of effective inclusion is included in Figure 1-3.

1-2 Defining Features of High-Quality Early Childhood Inclusion

According to the joint position paper by DEC/NAEYC (2009), there are three defining features of **high-quality early childhood inclusion**:

- **Access**. Children with disabilities need to have access to the classroom, the curriculum, and to the materials and equipment. They need to be able to approach and obtain classroom materials, learning centers, and activities. Most of the time, access can be accomplished by providing simple adaptations. This book will offer simple strategies to facilitate inclusion that use materials and activities found in most classrooms and that can be embedded in daily routines.
- **Participation**. Children with disabilities need to be full participating members in their families, communities, and society. To ensure full **participation** in the classroom, some children might need more than simple adaptations. Hence, teachers will need to use a wide range of strategies, including more intensive interventions in the forms of technology, specialized equipment, and scaffolding for children with disabilities to learn and participate in all activities at their own level.
- **Supports**. High-quality inclusion requires supports for families and staff from all levels, including administrators and specialists. Supports and policies should include not only professional development regarding inclusive best practice, but also strategies for collaboration and cooperation. Without these essential elements, success may be elusive. In addition, programs should make provisions to maximize staff competency and seek guidance from relevant early learning standards.

Reflecting on the three defining features of high-quality inclusion—access, participation, and supports—programs can use this information to improve their current inclusive practices. Some early childhood programs request that children with disabilities be "ready" to be enrolled. Being "ready" probably means that children with disabilities do everything the same as everyone else in the classroom or that children can handle most activities without supports and adaptations. This is not the point of inclusion. The least restrictive environment (LRE) and the previous inclusion definition require the teachers to make the necessary supports and adaptations to serve not only children with disabilities, but all children. Therefore, it's not the children who need to be "ready"; it's the teachers. This book is a resource to help educators get ready by gaining the necessary knowledge, skills, and dispositions to support all children. The next section will briefly explore the different dimensions of inclusion support.

1-3 Dimensions of Inclusion Support

One of the pleasures of working in the fields of early childhood education and early childhood special education is the opportunity to create programs and classrooms that support inclusion and full participation of young children with special needs and their same-age peers without disabilities. The vision of this book is to provide knowledge and motivation for early childhood educators to create and implement effective and creative individualized supports that enable all young children to be the enthusiastic learners they are capable of being! However, simply being committed to creating inclusive environments does not guarantee successful inclusion.

The key word here is *supports*. All too often, inclusive placements fail because key players have not collaboratively designed effective strategies to support all children's participation. Each child with so-called "special needs" can be viewed as a unique mosaic of strengths, challenges, and learning styles. His or her learning success and joyful participation in the classroom depend on our creation of the configuration of supports that effectively facilitate the child's learning, participation, and social interaction. These supports ensure that each child with special needs has access and participation in the core curriculum, as well as opportunities for development of true friendships and social skills.

Successful inclusion depends not simply on what services are provided, or who provides them. Although specific therapies and services (for example, behavior therapy, speech/language interventions, physical therapy, and so on) address disability-specific challenges, they do not directly target the children's success as full participants in the inclusive environment. Successful inclusion *support* enables children to become full participants in the early education classroom or program.

Photo 1-2 Everyone participates and is supported to run the race in his or her own way in this inclusion classroom.

1-4 Delivery of Supports and Services in Inclusive Preschool Settings

There is no definitive or most successful model of inclusion support. There are many possibilities, limited only by educators' knowledge and creativity, and by the extent of **collaboration** between the classroom team and support providers. The following material describes some of the dimensions and variations of inclusion supports and service delivery models.

1-4a Direct versus Indirect (Consultative) Supports

The services listed earlier such as speech and occupational therapy are **direct services** in which the service provider interacts directly with a student. However, services can also be provided *indirectly* via **consultation**. The following scenario describes an example of **indirect services**:

> The teachers in an inclusive Head Start program are concerned about how to encourage communicative interaction with a young child with complex disabilities. A speech-language pathologist (SLP) carefully observes and interacts with the child in different activities, records the child's communicative behaviors, and discusses the child's strengths and needs with the classroom teacher and with parents. After observing the child and engaging in conversation with parents and teachers, the SLP makes specific recommendations and provides written notes describing strategies the adults might embed within daily routines. The SLP agrees to meet again with the adults in two weeks, and to observe the child again at that time.

In this scenario the SLP as "consultant" shares information and strategies with the teacher (who might be considered the "consultee"). The teacher receives information and suggestions from the consultant, which the teacher then uses on behalf of the child. Thus, the consultant in this case provides *indirect* support to the child. Ideally, service providers who typically work *directly* with the child (such as physical therapists or behavioral interventionists) will *also* provide indirect support via consultation by sharing results and strategies with the child's teacher, parents, and other service providers.

Within the field of education, regardless of whether services are direct or indirect, the ideal relationships among adults on behalf of children with special needs are those that are truly *collaborative*. To the extent there is real two-way sharing of strategies, results, ideas, and so on, the consultation becomes collaborative consultation, which can be very effective.

1-4b Collaboration: The Key to Successful Inclusion

Services for young children with special needs, direct or indirect, must be collaborative. Still relevant today is the definition of **collaborative consultation** offered by Heron and Harris (2001): "An interactive process that enables people with diverse expertise to generate creative solutions to mutually defined problems: It often produces solutions that are different from those that individual team members would produce independently" (p. 567). For further understanding of the importance and potential of collaboration, see Friend and Cook (2013).

Whether we are considering inclusion supports provided by specialists in the inclusive classroom or the daily problem solving of a classroom team of teachers and their paraprofessional assistants, administrators, parents, and specialists, the key to success with any team is the ongoing use of collaborative strategies in everyday interactions among adults. Particularly important to inclusion success are collaboration, communication, and buy-in from key administrators. For a discussion of administrator perspectives and challenges related to preschool inclusion, see Richardson-Gibbs and Klein (2014).

An additional key concept is the notion of problem solving. A **problem-solving approach** assumes that challenges will naturally arise in the endeavor of inclusion of children with special/unique needs within the typical early childhood classroom. It also assumes that a collaborative problem-solving approach will not only solve problems, but will also often generate creative solutions and more effective programs for all children and adults. Collaborative consultation is not "unidirectional," as in the case of a service provider whose approach is to say, "I'm the expert. Let me tell you how to do this." Rather, the therapist would discuss and demonstrate his or her ideas and suggestions, and then ask the teacher and other team members to describe their own ideas and experiences with that child.

1-4c Pull-Out versus Push-In

Another important consideration in designing inclusion supports is *where* support is provided. The terms *pull-out* and *push-in* are sometimes used. For example, using a **pull-out model**, an SLP or occupational therapist may remove a child from the classroom to provide intervention or assessment. This may be deemed necessary because of the need for quiet, space, or equipment, and so on. However, a **push-in model**, in which services are provided *within* the classroom, can have many advantages. For example, the service provider gains a much better understanding of the curriculum and behavioral demands on the target child, as well as whether the student is generalizing skills and interactions with peers, and also whether the goals and strategies are the appropriate ones for functioning in the classroom environment.

Regardless of setting, it is critical that collaborative communication take place among all key players. The service provider must somehow share strategies and progress notes with the classroom teacher. Effective inclusion support and collaboration require that service providers communicate with classroom teachers and staff in ways that ensure that skills can be encouraged and practiced *between therapy sessions*, not just when the service provider is directly interacting with the child. Very little skill building can occur within a 30-minute once-per-week pull-out session. It will require follow-through of teachers and staff (and parents) *between* visits, as well as providing feedback to the service provider, that will bring about true collaboration and child progress.

1-4d Examples of Inclusion Support "Models"

To date, there are no generally accepted standards or guidelines for whether, when, and how inclusion support is to be provided. Just as with IFSPs and IEPs, the particular model of support should also be individualized, keeping in mind several factors such as the strengths and needs of the children, the preferences of the family, characteristics of the setting, and the resources available. The following discusses some service-delivery models.

Itinerant Model. In the previous example, the SLP service provider uses an itinerant direct service model. An **itinerant** is not permanently assigned to one classroom, but travels from site to site to deliver services. An itinerant may provide direct services, or ideally, may incorporate *collaborative consultation* by using demonstration and problem solving with teachers and the classroom staff. This is referred to as an *itinerant consultation model*.

An *itinerant consultation inclusion support model* can be very effective. In this model a skilled early childhood special educator (ECSE) travels from site to site to provide itinerant consultation to teachers and staff on behalf of the children with special needs who are included in the program. This model requires that the early childhood special educator has expert knowledge of early childhood development, disability characteristics and learning styles, and a range of specific intervention and teaching techniques for addressing specific challenges, as well as excellent collaborative consultation skills, of course. (See Richardson-Gibbs and Klein [2014] for a detailed description of important consultant skills and activities used in a collaborative consultation model of support.) This model of inclusion support can be very cost effective. A skilled ECSE consultant can serve 20 or more students using an itinerant model across three or four sites.

One-to-One Paraprofessional. Probably the most widely used inclusion support model is the assignment of a **one-to-one paraprofessional** to provide constant observation and support to a single child. Although there are circumstances in which this may be the best accommodation for supporting a particular child, this approach should be used with caution. Such arrangements, if not supervised carefully, can have disadvantages. For example, Giangreco and colleagues (2010) noted there has been concern that classroom assistants might spend too much time in close proximity to students. If not managed properly, this can result in the child developing an extreme dependency upon the aide, and may interfere with the development of peer social skills, and so on. Even so, earlier research found that instructional assistants can facilitate inclusive practices when they interact frequently with *all* students and when independence is promoted by limiting the amount of direct instruction provided to children with disabilities (Hill, 2003).

Specific strategies for avoiding common problems in using one-to-one inclusion support include supervision of one-to-one support providers, clarification of specific roles as team members, and the skills and commitment to encourage children's independence. It is also recommended that whenever feasible, aides be hired for groups of children rather than for an individual child. Guidelines can be developed to ensure fading of prompts, the use of natural supports such as peer support, avoidance of hovering, and clarification of role responsibilities. Mutual training of paraprofessionals and their supervisors can go a long way toward role clarification and collaboration.

Co-teaching. Another common model of inclusion support is referred to as a **co-teaching model**. In this model a group of children without disabilities and their teacher are combined in the same classroom with a group of children who have disabilities and a special education teacher. (This model is also referred to as a "blended model" because it blends two classes into one.) Although each co-teacher may have expertise and strength in different areas of curriculum and child characteristics, they must collaborate and problem-solve together throughout the day. Ideally, both teachers are equally invested in learning outcomes for all children, while at the same time using their own unique expertise. There are many ways to structure the roles and responsibilities of each teacher. The goal is for the two teachers to achieve a true collaborative partnership. It is particularly important that co-teachers each see themselves as responsible for *all* children in the classroom, not just "their" children. For this model to be effective, sufficient planning time and administrative support is essential to ensure that both the general educator and the special educator are equally involved in all aspects of the teaching process.

WEBLINK

To fully understand how co-teaching isn't just taking turns, see Anne Beninghof's episode of the Transformative Principal podcast found through her website www.ideasforeducators.com.

1-5 Benefits of Inclusion

Inclusion has been shown to have many benefits for children with and without disabilities. A thorough joint report from the U.S. Department of Health and Human Services (HHS) and the Department of Education (ED) presents a summary of over 50 studies describing the benefits of including young children with disabilities with

Preschool years bring awareness of likenesses and differences. It is critical to foster all children's desires to be exactly who they are no matter how much they are alike or different from anyone around them. In addition, it is essential to encourage all to accept their differences—whatever they are: hair color, height, weight, size of nose, and so on.

After all, disabilities are just differences. As Kathie Snow reminds us: A disability "is just a body part that works differently." For a better understanding of how we can help young children build respect for all, see the article *Same and Different: Respect for All* by going to www.disabilityisnatural.com/same-different.html.

Photo 1-3 Inclusive classrooms encourage children without disabilities to better understand and accept diversity, disability, and differences.

their peers without disabilities (HHS & ED, 2015). A sample of these findings includes the following:

- Individualized supports in the form of research-based strategies can be successfully implemented in the inclusive environment.
- Significant progress and gains with learning can be made even by children with intense needs due to significant disabilities. Some studies have reported *greater* gains in inclusive settings than in segregated settings, particularly in the areas of cognition and communication skills.
- More progress can be made with skills in the areas of cognition, communication, and social- emotional development (for example, friendships and social skills) compared to children who are in special education programs only.

Research also suggests that the best outcomes are more likely to be achieved when children with disabilities begin inclusive education early and continue with high-quality inclusion through their school years:

- The students who spent more time in general education classrooms were more likely to have fewer absences, to have higher reading and math test scores, and have a higher chance of future employment and future earnings than those who spent less time in general education classrooms.

Studies show that children *without* disabilities in inclusive early childhood settings:

- Can show attitudinal changes such as an increase in compassion, empathy, and understanding of diversity and disability.
- Can benefit from having developmental specialists on site who can provide individual supports that could help a variety of children in the classroom and assistance when needed for unidentified delays or disabilities.

Summary

Inclusion is about belonging and membership in a community. The philosophy of this book is that children with disabilities should feel welcomed and valued as participating members of a group while receiving expert services and instruction. Legislation such as the Individuals with Disabilities Education Act (IDEA) and Americans with Disability Act (ADA) protect this right for children with disabilities. Although high-quality early childhood inclusion practices have long been advocated, successful implementation continues to be refined and still remains out of reach for some. This chapter explained the factors that make up high-quality early childhood inclusion, a variety of inclusion supports and service delivery models, and the benefits of inclusion.

Read–Reflect–Discuss
Welcoming Patricia

Marianne, a director of a neighborhood child care center, was excited to meet her potential new student, Patricia. When Patricia and her mother, Joyce, walked into the classroom, Marianne was a bit surprised to learn that Patricia was a little girl with Down syndrome. Marianne was concerned because, as a new director, she had never been responsible for a child with Down syndrome before. Nonetheless, she quickly tried to cover her surprise and bent down to introduce herself to Patricia. The child smiled at her and waved hello. They entered the four-year-old classroom where Patricia immediately went over to the dramatic play area and picked up a baby doll. Once Patricia was comfortable and playing, Marianne and Joyce sat at a table in the back of the classroom to talk. Joyce explained that she was looking for a part-time child care program as Patricia goes to a special education program in the afternoon. Marianne asked Joyce some questions about the special education program and then she asked what Patricia likes to do when in the special education program. Then, she asked Joyce to describe her daughter's needs and if there were any special considerations that should be kept in mind. Joyce thoughtfully provided the following description.

Patricia just turned four years old and learned to walk one year ago. She needs a little bit of help navigating play structures as sometimes she walks up the steps holding the rail and sometimes she crawls. At that point, Marianne decided that it would be a good idea to have Joyce and Patricia stay while the classroom went outside so she could observe Patricia's motor skills to determine how much support she would need and if she had enough staff. Joyce expressed concern that her daughter wears diapers and was wondering if that was okay. Marianne thought about that and explained that the four-year-old classroom does not have a diaper-changing table, but that it is right next to the three-year-old classroom that does have one. Marianne would have to talk to the staff to discuss creative ways to supervise the classroom while Patricia gets her diaper changed. They discussed actually placing Patricia in the younger classroom, but decided that she should stay with her same-age peers.

Joyce also explained that Patricia has a few single words and uses several different signs and gestures. Joyce handed Marianne a three-page worksheet with pictures describing the signs that Patricia knows. Though the staff does not know sign language, the signs, thought Marianne, seemed pretty easy to learn. In the meantime, Patricia seemed very comfortable in the room exploring many toys and even went and sat down for some of the circle time. When the classroom went outside, Marianne was pleased to discover that the other children were very accommodating. They made sure not to bump into Patricia as she slowly climbed the structure. Also, two students waited at the top and encouraged Patricia to keep going. A staff person stayed fairly close to the structure as Patricia needed help sitting on her bottom to go down the slide. Marianne saw that even when Patricia was not on the climbing structure, the staff stayed fairly close to make sure all children were safe.

Upon reflection, Marianne's general feeling was that the special needs of Patricia were relatively easily accommodated with some creative thinking and help from the mother, such as the sign language handout. She explained to the mom that the staff has not been trained to work with a child who has Down syndrome, but that she was sure that they would be willing to learn. Joyce said, "that's okay, when I had Patricia, I wasn't trained either."

Read–Reflect–Discuss Questions

1. Identify the factors in Appendix A that Marianne took into consideration to ensure that she was complying with the Americans with Disability Act.
2. Based on Appendix A, what other questions would be helpful to ask to understand Patricia's needs?
3. Thinking ahead, what are some of the benefits and challenges that might arise from including Patricia?

Key Terms

access

Americans with
    Disabilities Act (ADA)

collaboration

collaborative
    consultation

consultation

co-teaching model

direct services

high-quality early
    childhood inclusion

inclusion

indirect services

Individuals with
    Disabilities Education
    Act (IDEA)

itinerant

least restrictive
    environment (LRE)

natural environments

one-to-one
    paraprofessional

participation

person-first
    terminology (PFT)

problem-solving
    approach

pull-out model

push-in model

supports

Helpful Resources

The Council for Exceptional Children (CEC)

www.cec.sped.org

This organization provides policy and advocacy regarding educational concerns for individuals with disabilities as well as professional standards and professional development in the field of special education. CEC has journals specific to special education: *Exceptional Children* and *Teaching Exceptional Children*.

The Division for Early Childhood (DEC)

www.dec-sped.org

This is focused primarily on children birth through age eight who have disabilities or are at risk for developmental delays. Of special interest are their position statements, recommended practices for early childhood special education, and the journal, *Young Exceptional Children*.

National Association of the Education of Young Children (NAEYC)

www.naeyc.org

This organization promotes high-quality early learning through developmentally appropriate practice, policy, and research, as well as professional and educational standards in the field of early childhood education for all children birth through age eight. Of special interest is their journal, *Young Children*.

National Center for Infants, Toddlers, and Families

www.zerotothree.org

This website furthers the organization's mission of promoting the healthy social, emotional, and intellectual development of infants and toddlers by supporting and strengthening families, communities, and those who work on their behalf. Of special interest is their journal, *Zero to Three*.

National Early Childhood Technical Assistance Center

www.nectac.org

This website provides a link to a resource especially designed to make services and systems available throughout the country to assist infants, toddlers, and preschool-age children with disabilities and their families.

The Child Care Law Center

childcarelaw.org

This website provides legal information to child care providers, families, and advocates about state and federal laws and regulations related to child care.

United States Department of Education

www.ed.gov

This website has links to the Office of Special Education Programs, which provides information about special education laws. It provides links to the Office of Early Learning for children birth through third grade including children with disabilities.

Wrightslaw

www.Wrightslaw.com

This is the leading website providing reliable, accurate information about special education law and advocacy. It includes articles, case studies, and a variety of free resources.

CHAPTER 2

Instructional Strategies Supporting the Inclusion of Young Children with Special Needs

LEARNING OBJECTIVES

After studying this chapter, you will be able to:

LO 2-1: Discuss adaptations and accommodations used to facilitate access to general curriculum.

LO 2-2: Explain the specific challenges related to getting and retaining attention, and how to use a high-preference inventory to identify motivators.

LO 2-3: Describe the zone of proximal development and how scaffolding can be used effectively.

LO 2-4: Explain two essential strategies for fostering repetition and routine.

LO 2-5: Provide an example of a task analysis that includes the sequence of observable behavioral steps necessary to complete a self-help task.

LO 2-6: Give examples of adult communicative strategies that have been demonstrated to support the development of language and cognition.

LO 2-7: List strategies that are effective in preventing challenging behaviors.

LO 2-8: Discuss universal instructional strategies well enough to consider making adaptations to accommodate specific disabilities.

The following NAEYC Standards and DEC Recommended Practices are addressed in this chapter:

naeyc

Standard 1: Promoting Child Development and Learning
Standard 4: Using Developmentally Effective Approaches
Standard 5: Using Content Knowledge to Build Meaningful Curriculum

DEC

Practice 2: Environment
Practice 4: Instruction
Practice 5: Interaction
Practice 6: Teaming and Collaboration

A number of strategies that are universal and, thus, can be used effectively with any child with special needs, will be discussed in this chapter:

- **Accommodations and modifications.** Inclusion is facilitated by adaptations that provide children with disabilities the support needed to access the general curriculum.

- **Levels of support**. The amount and type of support given to children can influence their ability to gain confidence and independence.

- **Using everyday materials.** Many adaptations to materials and toys can be easily made by using everyday materials that are found in most preschool classrooms.

- **Getting children's attention.** The role of motivation and the importance of identifying high-preference activities are essential factors in optimizing learning for children with special needs.

- **Working in the learning zone.** The use of social mediation of the environment (for example, *scaffolding*) can help guide teachers in providing just the right amount of support.

- **Doing it again and again.** Repetition, routines, and predictable environments are key to learning and successful inclusion of young children with special needs.

- **Teaching one step at a time.** Perhaps one of the most tested strategies for helping children learn is the use of task analysis to break skills into small steps.

- **Talking to children.** The role of adult language input and communicative interactions in supporting the development of language and cognition is well documented. These strategies must be built into the curriculum and must be part of the child's ongoing experience.

- **Using an ounce of prevention.** The development of many challenging behaviors can be minimized by understanding and using a variety of preventative strategies.

Introduction

The field of early childhood special education embraces the philosophy of developmentally appropriate experiences in the least restrictive environment. However, experience has shown us that to ensure success, general early childhood education (ECE) teachers and early childhood special educators (ECSE) must all learn the specific strategies and techniques necessary for accommodating and supporting children with special needs in community-based settings.

This chapter will present an overview of these techniques and strategies. ECE teachers will discover that although the focus of this book is on meeting the needs of children with special needs, many of the practices described will also significantly enhance the development of *all* children. ECE teachers will also realize that as a result of their training and experience and their dedication to children and families, they have already developed many of the skills and strategies described in this book.

Perhaps the greatest difference between ECE and ECSE is the extent to which teachers play an active and direct role as intervenors or social mediators of children's experiences. The role of ECE teachers tends to focus on organizing and managing the environment and materials while encouraging children to participate in those environments. To ensure that children with special needs fully benefit from the early childhood environment, teachers may need to orchestrate children's experiences more directly. For some ECE teachers this may require taking a more active role than they otherwise might.

2-1 Adaptation Strategies: The Bridge to Facilitating Inclusion

As stated earlier, the law requires that students with disabilities have the right to access and participate in general education curriculum (which includes appropriate supports and services, as well as accommodations and modifications to ensure access and progress). *General curriculum* is defined as the same curriculum that students without disabilities are using. It should be noted, however, that in the United States, there is no official preschool general education curriculum because public schools are not required to serve preschool children without disabilities. This creates a significant challenge for many school districts to find or create appropriate ECE settings in which to include preschoolers with special needs.

Furthermore, as stated in the Division for Early Childhood-National Association for the Education of Young Children (DEC/NAEYC) inclusion definition, students need to have a sense of belonging and membership by having access to all the classroom areas, materials, and activities. Lastly, the specific guideline of *teaching to enhance development and learning* within developmentally appropriate practice (DAP) states that teachers' skills "include the ability to adapt curriculum, activities, and materials to ensure full participation of *all* children" (2009, p. 18).

It is important to note that the term *adaptation* does not appear in IDEA law. **Adaptation** is used here and elsewhere to refer to the broad range of ways in which curriculum goals, activities, and materials can be changed and individualized to ensure a child's participation and learning in the general education classroom. Two terms referring to such adaptations are used in the law: *accommodations* and *modifications*. Although the law doesn't actually define them, the two terms tend to be used interchangeably. However, there are distinctions between them, discussed as follows.

The term **accommodation** is more likely to be used in reference to something a child uses to participate in the same activities as typical children, and achieve and demonstrate classroom goals. Accommodations may include using equipment like a wheelchair or walker for a child who is not ambulatory, attaching a specially designed paintbrush to a child's hand with Velcro, and using assistive technology to enable a child to communicate or turn on a battery-operated toy. Accommodations may also refer to a change in the larger environment (or program policies) that removes barriers and allows comfortable access to an environment. Such accommodations include adding access ramps, rearranging the space in a classroom, providing a one-to-one aide to keep a child from running away, placing high-contrast markers to help a child identify certain materials, breaking a task into small steps for a child with a cognitive disability, or reducing the ambient noise in a classroom to accommodate the needs of a child wearing a hearing aid or a child who is sensitive to certain sounds. Accommodating the students' disability characteristics and challenges enables them to demonstrate skills in specific goal areas, interact successfully with peers, and access the curriculum, materials, and learning environments.

The term **modification** may refer to changing the *curriculum* goals in some way. For example, for a child with a more complex intellectual disability, a modified writing goal could be drawing lines and circles with crayons, markers, or a paintbrush, or perhaps learning to write just the first letter of his name, rather than independently writing his entire name.

These kinds of modifications and accommodations will be critically important to many children with special needs. Without them, some children will not thrive in an inclusive classroom. However, their effectiveness may totally depend on careful planning that provides them just at the right time.

2-1a Levels of Support

When providing adaptations to students, teachers need to consider the level of support that is given to students while remembering that the goal is to help students become as independent as possible. Making appropriate adaptations helps students become more independent with the **least amount of help** from the teacher. Often, the use of physical assistance represents the **most amount of help**, and may actually *increase* the child's dependence. Physical assistance takes many forms. For example, an adult does an activity for a student, or provides "hand-over-hand" assistance by placing a hand over the child's hand to do an activity, or physically manipulates the child's body. Using physical assistance is not necessarily an incorrect strategy, especially for children whose needs definitely require physical assistance. However, this is not usually necessary. Physical assistance could be an overused strategy in some classrooms and may encourage dependence.

Determining the Levels of Support. The authors of *CARA's Kit: Creating Adaptations for Routines and Activities* (Milbourne & Campbell, 2007) offer a way to help teachers determine how to use the least amount of help. They discuss four other adaptations to try before teachers provide physical assistance:

- **Adapt the environment** by removing barriers or providing visual supports. Instead of holding the child's hand to get from circle time to the sink, enhance the environment by placing tape on the floor so the child can independently follow the line to wash hands.
- **Adapt the activity and routine** by making a change with circle time, classroom schedule, transitions, and other classroom activities. Provide two shorter circle times throughout the day instead of one long circle time if children have difficulty attending.
- **Adapt the materials** by making changes to the classroom materials and toys to make it easier to access them and participate. Simplify puzzles by having larger knobs or stabilize puzzles by placing a shelf liner underneath.
- **Adapt the requirements or instruction** by simplifying directions, reducing the number of steps in the instructions or providing instructions in a different way with pictures, real objects, or photographs. During snack time, have a picture that shows the children how many of each food to take: 2 crackers and 2 apples. Figure 2-1 provides four questions that should be considered before providing supports.

1. Specifically, what behavior is the student exhibiting?	2. What is the preferred behavior that you want the child *to do*? State positively and specifically.

Goal: Before using physical assistance to support the preferred behavior, try first using the least amount of help by asking, *what else can we do*? Physical assistance should be used only when you have tried everything else.

WHAT ELSE CAN WE DO?

LEVELS OF HELP

How can we change or adapt the environment?	How can we change or adapt the activity or routine?

Least

How can we change or adapt the materials?	How can we change or adapt the requirements or instructions?

CAUTION Use physical assistance cautiously and only as a last resort!

Most

Figure 2-1 Determining the Level of Support

⌄⌄ **Professional Resource Download**

Felt	Cardboard	Variety of different tapes
Trays	File folders	Variety of different binder clips
Rulers	Index cards	Velcro strips and dots
Glue gun	Highlighters	Black permanent markers
Shelf liner	Pipe cleaners	Foam sheets and curlers
Shoelaces	Rubber bands	High-contrast laminated sheets
Glue sticks	Contact paper	Small wooden blocks
Clipboards	Popsicle sticks	Sticky notes and dots
Pom-poms	Sheet protectors	Alphabet and number strips

Figure 2-2 Examples of Everyday Materials Used for Making Adaptations

2-1b Tools that Facilitate Adaptations

Effective inclusion supports can be simply made from materials in most classrooms. In addition to the levels of support discussed previously, two more tools can help teachers facilitate adaptations: everyday materials and the *EESS* acronym.

Everyday Materials. Planning for adaptations requires having materials on hand that can be easily retrieved when children are having difficulty in the classroom. Preschool classrooms are well stocked with common frequently used materials that can be used to make adaptations (see Figure 2-2). It can be helpful to have these materials all in the same place so that staff can easily access them when needed. For example, a child might be having difficulty stringing beads. By the time the teacher walks around the classroom looking in different cupboards for the masking tape to enlarge the tip of the string, the child has become even more frustrated and has walked away from the activity. It's a good recommendation to have these materials in the same place so staff can easily access them and make adaptations right on the spot to support the child. Placing them in a clear tub or bag can further help staff quickly see where the materials are as can be seen in Photo 2-1.

Photo 2-1 Storing everyday materials in a clear bin makes them easily visible and accessible.

EESS Acronym: The Purpose of Adaptations. When making adaptations for children with special needs, it is important to understand the purpose of each adaptation. The main purpose is to *make it easier* for children to access classroom materials, activities, instruction, and the environment as independently as possible. Luongo and Kearns (2015) have identified four strategies that help assist teachers with making adaptations: **enlarge, enhance, stabilize**, and **simplify**. Putting these words together in an acronym, **EESS**, helps teachers to remember how to make activities "easier" for students to access and participate. Figure 2-3 shows how using everyday materials such as Velcro, a glue gun, and foam can make activities easier for students while demonstrating the purpose of each adaptation using EESS.

The use of adaptations in the environment can almost be like having the support of another teacher in the classroom. In other words, the use of photos, icons, picture schedules, color-coding strategies, classroom arrangements, and so on can provide *environmental supports* that cue and reinforce the behaviors targeted by the teacher. Whenever one staff person must leave to

Enlarge the writing utensil with foam and red tape. Enlarge the slider by putting a small slice in the foam block so it fits over the slider and glue with glue gun. Makes it easier to grasp and manipulate.

Enhance the puzzle by gluing matching colored construction paper into puzzle slots. This makes it easier to match the pieces.

Stabilize the lotto game pieces to the board with Velcro so that they do not move around. Stabilize the board itself by placing the black shelf liner under it.

Simplify the shape sorter by reducing the number of holes from five to three. Use yellow construction paper and tape to cover the more difficult star and cross holes

Figure 2-3 Purpose of the Adaptation

physically support a student, less supervision is available. So, instead of having a staff person physically involved in helping a child wash his or her hands, we can adapt the environment by using a visual support for the routine of hand washing. The poster shown in Photo 2-2 serves as a visual support to teach the individual steps of washing one's hands.

The staff person can introduce the adaptation, teach each step, and then gradually decrease their support until the student can function independently. This visual support can actually help *all* students through the transition of hand washing as it outlines the steps and expectations. The staff will put energy and time into teaching the steps in the beginning until the children learn how to wash their hands independently, which is still less time in the long run than physically assisting with hand washing on a daily basis. It's important to mention that not all children with disabilities will become independent hand washers. If children indeed need physical assistance, they

Photo 2-2 Providing a visual support helps teach the individual steps of hand washing.

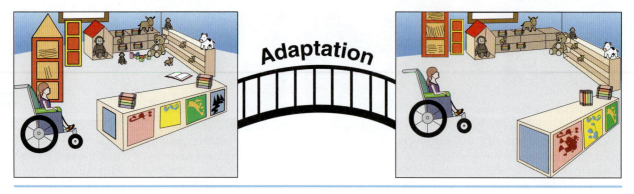

Figure 2-4 Enlarging the entrance is the adaptation that functions as a bridge to independent access and participation.

can be encouraged to do some of the steps independently. For instance, they can throw the paper towel away.

Implementing adaptations by using the tools of everyday materials with EESS and providing the right level of support will help students independently access the materials, activities, and the environment in the classroom. When children have better access because their individual needs are being met, then they will be able to fully participate at their own level. Therefore, adaptations function as a *bridge* that helps children with special needs access the curriculum and become full participating members in the classroom. Figure 2-4 illustrates the provision of access to an activity.

2-2 Universal Teaching Strategies: Specific Challenges

Children cannot learn if they are not paying attention and are not engaged. Children pay attention to things that interest them. As seen in Photo 2-3, one of the challenges of working with children with special needs is that it is sometimes difficult to identify what motivates them.

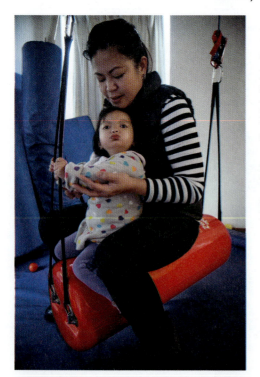

Photo 2-3 This parent encourages her child to be engaged in the activity of swinging.

2-2a Getting Their Attention

Some children (children on the autism spectrum, or those who have complex sensory challenges, such as deaf-blindness) may be interested in objects and sensations that are not typically appealing to other children. For example, a child may engage in repetitive sensory experiences, such as watching a flickering light or rocking back and forth, or may become very attached to a piece of material or an unusual object.

Other children, such as those with cognitive delays, may be interested in activities appropriate for much younger children, such as throwing, banging, or mouthing objects. Still others may have difficulty sustaining attention long enough to become engaged and motivated by an activity. Following are some examples of behaviors that can be of concern:

- Not looking directly at a toy or event. They may use peripheral rather than central vision, thus giving the impression of not visually attending.
- Not reaching or pointing, even though they are interested. This could be due to motor difficulties and/or visual impairment.
- Not smiling often or having minimal facial expression (referred to as "flat affect"). This may be a characteristic of children who have very low muscle tone or visual impairment, or it may be a symptom of an emotional disorder. Other children may lack a social smile, but may smile unpredictably. This is sometimes a characteristic of children with autism.

Activity/Item/Person	Response to Presentation	Response to Removal
1. Singing his favorite song	Became very still	Cried
2. Placed on tricycle	Smiled, rocked a bit	No response
3. Grandmother enters room	Raised arms	Cried when she left room
4. Placed on potty	Cried	Stopped crying

Figure 2-5 Preference Inventory

2-2b Conducting a High-Preference Inventory

As a result of these kinds of differences, it may be helpful for ECE teachers to identify motivators for a specific child by conducting a **high-preference inventory**. Information for the inventory is collected via a number of sources, including caregiver interviews and direct observations of a child at the center. Figure 2-5 illustrates an example of an inventory recording sheet.

2-2c Unique Ways of Expressing Interest and Attention

An advantage of conducting the high-preference inventory, in addition to identifying motivating objects and activities, is that it provides an opportunity to carefully observe and better understand a child's unique ways of expressing interest and attention. A child may:

- become very still and quiet when she is interested in something but may not be looking at or even facing the object.
- flap arms and hands excitedly when interested in something.
- stiffen and extend arms and legs, or turn head away even though she is interested. In other children this reaction may be a sign of rejection or disinterest. The story of Jorge provides an example.

Jorge's Music

Jorge does not talk and has little facial expression. Mrs. Muniz, his teacher, is concerned because he does not seem to enjoy any of the activities in the child care center. She asked the ECSE consultant for some help in motivating Jorge. The consultant joined Mrs. Muniz in carefully observing Jorge several times during the day.

They noticed that when someone turned on the tape player during free play and again during song time, Jorge stiffened a bit and extended his arms. Mrs. Muniz said she always assumed that he was uncomfortable when he did this. They decided to check with Jorge's mother. They learned from her that this extension is often an indication of excitement or pleasure. The mother also commented that Jorge loves listening to CDs when his older sister is home.

This helped Mrs. Muniz realize that music was one of Jorge's passions. She was able not only to acknowledge this and increase opportunities for him to listen to music, but she could use music as a reward for Jorge's participation in other activities, such as finger painting, which he had previously resisted. Gradually, Mrs. Muniz realized that Jorge was becoming interested in many more activities.

In seeking the attention of young children in today's diverse society, it is important to be aware of cultural differences in responsiveness to adults. For example, eye contact has different interpretations among cultural groups. Western cultures have fairly similar social expectations where eye contact is appropriate and expected. In Ghana, young children are taught not to look at adults because doing so is considered to be an act of defiance. African American children may have been taught to lower their eyes as a show of respect. Cultural expectations differ, as well, when it comes to touching, personal space, hand and arm gestures, head movements, and facial expressions. The following resource from "The Provider's Guide to Quality & Culture" offers additional awareness when it comes to cultural expectations of nonverbal communication: http://erc.msh.org/mainpage .cfm?file=4.6.0.htm&module=provider.

2-3 Working in the Learning Zone: Understanding the Zone of Proximal Development

One theory that has proven helpful in working with young children with special needs has to do with the importance of assisting children's learning through social mediation of the environment. The Russian psychologist L. S. Vygotsky developed the concept of the **zone of proximal development (ZPD)** (Vygotsky, 1980). Explained simply, this is the range of performance within which children can function if they have support from another individual. As portrayed in Figure 2-6, area A would be the range within which a child can function independently and does not need assistance. Area C is probably much too difficult for a child; in this range the child would need almost total support to perform the task. Area B is the range within which the child can achieve *with some support*. After receiving such support, the child can eventually advance to independence, and the zone of proximal development would move along the continuum to a level of greater difficulty.

Area A	Area B	Area C
Child can perform task independently; no support needed	Adult assistance most effective within this range	Task is too difficult for the child; total support needed

Figure 2-6 The Zone of Proximal Development

2-3a Scaffolding

The term used to refer to the provision of just the right amount of support within the zone is **scaffolding** (Bruner, 1982). The term is derived from the structure that supports a painter or window washer working on a tall building. The scaffold is the support necessary for a worker to perform successfully. Adults who can read children's cues can determine just the right amount and type of support necessary for children to perform a task. Adults then gradually reduce this support until the child can perform independently. The example of Jason may help demonstrate this concept.

Jason's Puzzle

Jason can independently complete his shape puzzle, which contains just three separate noninterlocking shapes: a square, a circle, and a triangle. He is interested in another puzzle that has pieces in the shape of a simple scene containing a tree, a house, and a car. He tries to do this puzzle but is unsuccessful because he is not used to placing the pieces in just the right position relative to other pieces. His teacher notices his frustration and moves in to assist him:

- She scaffolds and mediates this experience by helping him rotate the pieces slightly so they will fit.
- She does this several times, waiting each time to see at what point he needs assistance.
- She gradually reduces her assistance until he can perform this new puzzle independently.

Many teachers scaffold each day without giving it much thought. They already use this technique to help children learn difficult tasks. By being more aware of scaffolding as a specific strategy and matching it carefully to the child's existing skill, it can be very effective as a support for a child with special needs.

Photo 2-4 Children clean up after snack time.

2-4 Doing it Again and Again: The Importance of Repetition and Routine

Two strategies, predictable routines and planned transitions, can foster a learning environment for children with special needs.

2-4a Creating Predictable Routines

For children with special needs, consistency in daily routines makes it much easier to learn than a chaotic, unpredictable schedule. In addition, unpredictable environments may contribute to children's anxiety and insecurity. This is true not only for children with special needs but also for children who have been in unstable or abusive home situations.

Similarly, frequent repetition of activities develops a sense of comfortable familiarity and mastery, which not only helps children learn, but also builds self-esteem. Examples of repetition and other strategies used to develop vocabulary and sentence structure are found in Figure 2-8 later in this chapter.

All children are most successful when experiencing a predictable routine that is consistent and varies only when there is a special event or activity. Novel events are best appreciated against a backdrop of familiar routine. The following is an example of a daily schedule that works well for a half-day structured toddler program:

9:00 Arrival and free play
9:40 Cleanup
9:45 Opening circle and welcome song
10:00 Rhythm/dancing activity
10:10 Art centers
10:30 Outside activity
10:50 Toileting and hand washing
11:05 Snack
11:20 Cleanup, tooth brushing
11:40 Goodbye circle
11:50 Departure

2-4b Planning Transitions

Also important are clear cues that signal transitions from one activity to the next. Children with special needs often find transitions stressful and difficult. They may be unsure about what is happening next. They may have difficulty stopping an enjoyable activity. They may find the relative *busyness* of a transition frightening.

Creating routines for transitions can be helpful for children who have difficulty with transitions from one activity to another. These examples of consistent cues may help create transition routines:

- Give a five-minute and/or one-minute warning.
- Provide a visual cue or picture of the next activity.
- Play the song "Hi ho, hi ho, it's off to work we go" when transitioning to centers.
- Ring a bell to signal the end of outside play.
- Sing a goodbye song before going to cubbies to prepare for departure.

2-5 One Step at a Time: Making Skills Easier to Learn Through Task Analysis

Skills and tasks that seem simple for children without disabilities may be too complex for children who have special needs. This does not mean they cannot learn the task; it simply means the task needs to be broken down into smaller steps. The strategy of **task analysis** can often be helpful. Task analysis is particularly beneficial in teaching skills that can be analyzed into a sequence of observable behavioral steps.

2-5a Analyzing the Sequence

Most children have little difficulty learning to dispose of their empty lunch containers and utensils in the trash or sink. However, for some children with special needs, this may be difficult to learn. Simple repetition of the task each day may not be sufficient learning support. The teacher can perform a simple task analysis of the sequence of behaviors, sometimes referred to as a **behavior chain**, as shown in Figure 2-7.

The more severe the disability, the smaller the steps may need to be. For example, Step 2 above may need to be broken into separate training for each item—the cup, spoon, and napkin.

2-5b Training Each Step

The teacher teaches one step at a time, using the principles of scaffolding and the zone of proximal development for each step. Sometimes it is effective to begin by teaching the *last* step and working backward, referred to as **backward chaining**. These steps refer to the previous example:

1. **First training objective:** The teacher provides total assistance to get the child over to the sink and then encourages the child to place washable items in the sink by herself and then move away from the sink to the bathroom.
2. **Second training objective:** After the child learns to do this, she is taught to sort the paper items from the washable items, place them in the trash, and then proceed to the sink.
3. **Third training objective:** Once she is handling the tasks in the second objective independently, the teacher works on getting the child to walk without assistance from the table to the trash, while carrying her utensils. The child then independently completes the steps in the first and second objectives, thus completing the chain.

Depending on the nature of the child's special needs, she may never be able to perform some steps in a behavior sequence independently without some kind of assistance or environmental adaptation. The teacher will work with the disability specialist to modify the task to achieve maximum independence for the child with minimum demands on the teacher.

Step 1: Stand up from table; push chair in.

Step 2: Pile empty cup, spoon, and napkin on plate.

Step 3: Carry items to trash container.

Step 4: Place paper items (napkin and plate) in trash.

Step 5: Move to sink.

Step 6: Place washable items (spoon and cup) in sink.

Step 7: Walk to bathroom.

Figure 2-7 Task Analysis: Taking Dishes to the Sink

2-6 Talking to Children Makes a Difference

One of the most interesting discoveries in recent years is the extent to which adult communication can play an important role in children's development. For children with learning challenges, adult communicative input can often make or break the child's chances for optimizing learning potential. The following adult communicative strategies have been demonstrated to support the development of language and cognition in young children.

2-6a Follow the Child's Lead

Probably the single most important communication strategy is to respond to the child's attempts to communicate and to talk about things that interest the child, as this interaction demonstrates:

> **Child (tugging at teacher's sleeve):** Buh! Buh!
> **Teacher (not understanding):** What, Shelley? What are you trying to tell me?
> Child points to a bluebird sitting on the windowsill.
> **Teacher:** Oh! You see the bird. It's a bluebird. He likes to sit on our windowsill.

2-6b Use Progressive Matching

Progressive matching, also called *expansion,* is a simple strategy based on the principle that children learn best from an adult language model that is just slightly more complex than the children's current capabilities. For example, if a child is just beginning to use two-word combinations, the adult uses simple, short sentences and phrases. If a child is using simple sentences, the adult can model more complex structures. The adult can also add more information in addition to modeling slightly more complex structure. This is referred to as **expatiation**, or **semantic extension**:

> **Child:** Bird window.
> **Teacher:** Yes. The bird is in the window!
> **Child:** Rock sinking. Rock too heavy?
> **Teacher:** Do you think the rock is sinking *because* it's too heavy?

2-6c Use Labels and Specific Descriptors

Children readily develop vocabulary and concepts when they hear the specific names of things, actions, and characteristics. Compare these two examples. Each teacher is commenting on a child's attempt to brush a doll's hair:

> **Ms. Jones:** Oh she looks very pretty now, doesn't she? How nicely you're doing that!
> **Mr. Ramirez:** Oh I see you're *brushing* the *baby's* hair. Her *hair* looks very pretty now that you've *brushed* it.

Note that Ms. Jones, while following the child's lead and talking about what the child is interested in, does not use specific vocabulary. She does not label key actions and objects. Mr. Ramirez, on the other hand, specifically labels the most salient aspects of the child's activity: *brush, baby,* and *hair.* This is sometimes referred to as **mapping language onto experience**. In this way the child not only learns key vocabulary and concepts, but also learns that language is a way of representing the world around us in precise ways, like a road map. This in turn supports the child's cognitive development by helping her develop complex internal representations of complex relationships among objects, events, and characteristics.

2-6d Repeat Key Words and Phrases

All individuals, young and old, need some degree of repetition when learning a new task or word. Children with special needs often need many more repetitions than their same-aged peers. Thus it is important for teachers to develop the habit of repeating key words and phrases to assist children in processing and remembering what is said.

> **Teacher (talking about the body parts of a baby chick):** Here is the chick's mouth. We call this a beak. A beak. The chick's mouth is called a beak.
> **Child:** A buh?
> **Teacher:** That's right. Beak. It's a beak.

2-6e Use Appropriate Pacing

Pacing refers to the rate of speaking and the length of pause between sentences. Teachers who vary their pace can create different moods and add interest to their spoken language. Many children with disabilities have difficulty processing rapidly incoming information. Their comprehension and interest can often be enhanced by slowing down the pacing of complex or new information.

We vary widely in how fast we speak. Some people just naturally talk quickly, while others may speak very slowly. Teachers may wish to record themselves to determine whether their typical speaking rate in the classroom is unusually fast. If so, they can assist young children with language learning difficulties—as well as children whose first language is not English—by simply slowing down their speaking rate.

2-6f Give Children Ample Time to Respond

This strategy is somewhat related to pacing. Many children with special needs not only have difficulty processing what they hear, but they may also need more time to organize and encode what they want to say. A common phenomenon observed among children with special needs is called **learned helplessness**. This refers to a pattern of extreme passivity and lack of initiative. Children may develop this characteristic for many reasons. A common reason is that some adults find it difficult to restrain themselves. Instead, they might rush to help instead of giving the child a chance to be independent in caring for themselves. Often, sufficient time is not allowed for children to respond.

2-6g Create the Need to Communicate

Children with limited or no communication skills must be motivated to communicate. One simple way to do this is to create a situation in which the child must initiate communication in some way to obtain something she wants. For example, a favorite toy or music tape can be kept out of the child's reach. The child must learn to initiate a request for the desired object.

An even simpler technique is called a **request for more strategy**. The teacher simply interrupts a pleasurable activity, such as swinging or listening to music, and waits for the child to respond, using prompts and cues if necessary. The following examples illustrate this strategy.

Jessica and Pokémon Creating a Need to Communicate

Jessica has Down syndrome and does not use speech. She is able to make a few noises and she can point and use directed eye gaze. Her mother reports that she loves watching *Pokémon* on TV at home. The teacher usually makes sure to give Jessica the Pokémon puzzle during free play times. Jessica has mastered this puzzle, and it is clearly one of her preferred toys. The teachers decide to encourage Jessica to communicate more by leaving the puzzle in view, but on a shelf Jessica cannot reach. Initially the teacher shows Jessica where the puzzle is and prompts her to point and vocalize to get the puzzle. The next time Jessica wants the puzzle, the teacher waits and does not prompt her. Jessica walks to the teacher, makes a sound to get her attention, then points to the puzzle. The teacher responds quickly, saying, "Oh, Jessica, you want the Pokémon puzzle. Let me get it for you."

Developing Vocabulary and Concepts

Follow the child's lead: Talk about and elaborate upon what the child is interested in.

Use appropriate pacing and rate of speaking: Some children have difficulty processing rapid speech. Some adults may need to slow down a bit.

Encourage conversational turn-taking: Be sure to wait long enough to give the child plenty of time to respond to your comments or questions.

Carefully label things and actions: "We call that a *taxi*" and "See how I'm *copying* the letter."

Carefully describe characteristics of things and events at developmental level of the child: "You have five big blocks in your tower, and one tiny one on top!"

Use repetition and redundancy: "You have five blocks in your tower. Five blocks: one, two, three, four, five. Can you count the five blocks?"

For more advanced children ask open-ended questions: "Why did that fall down?" "How can we fix it?" Closed questions: "What is that called?" "What color is that?"

Encourage understanding of relationships between events and effects: "What do you think will happen if we add the water now? Yes, if we add the water, then it will bubble up." "The paint turned orange because we added the red to the yellow."

Developing Sentence Structure

Model "expansions" of child's utterance: Produce a slightly longer, more complex version of what the child said. For example, the child says "Johnny ball?" Teacher responds, "Yes, that is Johnny's ball."

Model complex sentence structure: "If we add another block, then it will fall down." "After we eat lunch, then we will go outside." "The paint dried out because we left the top off."

Figure 2-8 Strategies to Develop Vocabulary and Sentence Structure

Interrupting the Ride

Juan Carlos loves being pushed in the swing at the park. The teacher helps him get seated into the swing and starts pushing him. Suddenly the teacher stops the swing. She then waits until Juan Carlos indicates he wants more swinging by saying, "Go!" The teacher then says, "Oh, you want to swing some more? Okay, here we go." And she starts pushing the swing again. Eventually, by using this technique on a regular basis, the teacher helps Juan Carlos learn to use a short sentence, "More swing please," rather than just a single word.

2-7 Using an Ounce of Prevention: Managing Challenging Behavior

The most common child characteristic that results in failed placements in inclusive settings is disruptive behavior. (Chapter 5 will address this topic in some detail.) Although any child can develop challenging behaviors, children with special needs may present these sorts of behaviors more often. Characteristics of certain disabilities may be more likely to lead to the development of behavior challenges if they are not handled effectively. Children who have neurological impairments or attention deficits may have difficulty learning to regulate impulses and control aggression. Children with autism may be highly sensitive to certain sounds or to overly stimulating environments in general, and may have a tantrum or run away in an attempt to escape this sensory overload.

2-7a Strategies to Head Off Behavior Challenges

Certain preventive strategies can be incorporated into any classroom. Although these strategies will not prevent all behavior challenges, they will go a long way in minimizing the development of these behaviors. These preventive strategies include many of the strategies already discussed in this chapter:

- Using a consistent, predictable schedule with clear transition cues
- Allowing adequate time to complete tasks
- Reducing frustration tolerance by breaking new or difficult tasks into small steps
- Identifying triggers such as loud music or being crowded by other children
- Reducing sensory overload
- Providing some alternative communication mode such as pictures or signs for a child who cannot express wants and needs
- Establishing and enforcing consistent, clear rules (preferably no more than three or four), with consistent consequences
- Providing extra attention and adult support *before* a child demands it or engages in inappropriate behavior

Some children with disabilities may develop challenging behaviors despite these measures, and some may enter your classroom with already well-established behavior challenges. For these children, various strategies and interventions may be necessary. But for many children "an ounce of prevention" is definitely more effective than "a pound of cure"!

2-8 Instructional Strategies for Children with Mild to Moderate Disabilities

Chapter 3 will deal with the characteristics and needs of children with specific types of disabilities, often referred to as **low-incidence disabilities** because they affect relatively small proportions of the population. Such disabilities as visual impairment, hearing loss, severe cognitive disability, or autism often present unique and complex challenges. Though the incidence rate of autism is increasing, it is still considered to be a low-incidence disability under IDEA.

It should be noted, however, that many—perhaps most—children with special needs who are included in early childhood settings can be characterized as having **high-incidence disabilities**, sometimes referred to as **mild to moderate disabilities**. These occur with greater frequency but tend to require less intensive interventions. Mild to moderate disabilities include such characteristics as attention deficit disorders, mild cognitive/intellectual disability, mild speech and language delay, and noncompliant behaviors.

For children with mild to moderate disabilities, careful and thoughtful implementation of the strategies described in this chapter will often be sufficient to support their successful inclusion in the early childhood setting. The addition of frequent and careful observation of the child's behavior in light of specific goals and objectives can ensure not only access to the inclusive environment but also the successful achievement of desired outcomes for that child.

Summary

The adaptation and universal instructional strategies included in this chapter can assist and enhance the learning of *all* young children. For children who have special needs, these strategies are essential supports for efficient learning. For children with mild to moderate disabilities, careful use of these strategies may be sufficient to support their successful inclusion in the early childhood classroom. For children with low-incidence disabilities who have more significant challenges, these strategies are necessary but not sufficient. The next chapter will present an overview of the characteristics of specific disabilities and some additional strategies that may be useful to early childhood educators who find these children included in their classroom or program.

Read–Reflect–Discuss
Helping Manuel Adjust

When Mrs. Jackson learned that a child with special needs would be placed in her Head Start classroom, she was not concerned. Manuel was described as a "four-year-old child with Down syndrome, recently placed in foster care." Mrs. Jackson had worked with two other children who had Down syndrome and found them to be delightful. They were easygoing and affectionate.

After Manuel's first week in her classroom, however, Mrs. Jackson began to worry. Manuel was unexpectedly active and aggressive. His only word was "No!" which he used often as he pushed away any child who came within reach. His favorite activities seemed to be playing in water—wherever he could find it, especially in the toilet!—and dumping things out of containers.

Mrs. Jackson contacted the Head Start special needs coordinator for her program and asked for some assistance. After observing Manuel in the classroom and at home, Mrs. Jackson, the special needs coordinator, and the foster mother arranged a meeting to talk about possible interventions. The foster mother indicated that Manuel had only been with her for a month; his biological mother had recently been incarcerated for selling drugs, and no other family members were available to care for Manuel.

Several changes were identified that Mrs. Jackson could fairly easily incorporate into her classroom. Because she realized Manuel was dealing with many unexpected changes in his life, her first goal was to increase the predictability of the daily schedule. She tried to be a bit more consistent about the sequence of the major activities of the day, and she was careful to signal clearly the end of one activity and the transition to a new activity. She also assigned the assistant who seemed to have the best relationship with Manuel to be his primary caregiver. These adaptations created a safer environment for Manuel and seemed to reduce his overall levels of anxiety and aggression.

Another strategy incorporated his *high-preference activities* of water play and dumping. When Mrs. Jackson read Manuel's file, she realized that his developmental level was below that of a two-year-old and that the activities that motivated him were not so atypical when viewed in that light. She began to use the water table more often in the classroom and outside activities. She tried to think of center activities that could incorporate water in more appropriate ways, such as food coloring, soap and water, and water and cornstarch. Mrs. Jackson also asked an older child to help Manuel learn to play dump truck. This involved loading a large dump truck with Legos, pushing the truck a little ways, then dumping the plastic building blocks into a container. A volunteer helped encourage the peer helper to repeat this activity over and over until Manuel began to be able to do it himself—loading and driving the truck to the container, not just dumping its contents. Initially Manuel would only do the dumping. By beginning at this level, the volunteer and the peer were able to scaffold the activity until Manuel could do it independently.

These strategies provided more opportunities for Manuel to focus on the same activities in which the other children were participating. Because he was highly motivated by the activities, he gradually became less bothered by other children in his space. Within a month he was no longer aggressive with the other children and seemed well settled into the daily routine. Staff then began focusing on his needs in the area of language development. Mrs. Jackson reminded them to emphasize and label key words, especially the words for things that interested him most, and repeat the words in short sentences or phrases. Manuel began immediately to try to imitate the key words and gradually began using the words spontaneously, especially to request a favorite food or toy.

Read–Reflect–Discuss Questions

1. What aspects in Manuel's life created challenges for his adjustment to the Head Start center?
2. What steps could Mrs. Jackson take in the future when new children are referred to her program to make their transition to the center-based program easier?
3. What instructional strategies did Mrs. Jackson use? Can you think of additional strategies or adaptations that might be helpful for Manuel?

Key Terms

accommodation

adaptation

backward chaining

behavior chain

EESS

expatiation

high-incidence
  disabilities

high-preference inventory

learned helplessness

least amount of help

low-incidence disabilities

mapping language
  onto experience

mild to moderate
  disabilities

modification

most amount of help

pacing

progressive matching

request-for-more strategy

scaffolding

semantic extension

task analysis

zone of proximal
  development (ZPD)

Helpful Resources

CARA's Kit

Campbell, P. H., Kennedy, A. A., & Milbourne, S. A. (2012). *CARA's kit for toddlers.* Baltimore, MD: Brookes Publishing Co.

Milbourne, S. A., & Campbell, P. H. (2007) *CARA's kit: Creating adaptations for routines and activities.* Philadelphia, PA: Child and Family Studies Research Programs, Thomas Jefferson University.

Both spiral-bound guidebooks come with a multimedia CD-ROM and explain how to make adaptations in inclusive preschool and toddler classrooms.

ConnectABILITY.ca

connectability.ca/category/kids

This website has a wealth of information about how to adapt and accommodate for children with special needs. There are variety of links to videos about adaptations, fact sheets about disabilities, visual engine to make visual supports, and supported inclusion.

The Early Childhood Technical Assistance Center (ECTA Center)

www.ectacenter.org

This national website has many resources for topics such as inclusion, DEC recommended practices, early intervention, and implementation of best practice.

Special Quest Multimedia Training Library

www.specialquest.org/pdf/pre_incl_pkg.pdf

This website has a variety of training videos and resources to support inclusion for young children birth through age five with disabilities and their families.

CHAPTER 3

Adaptations for Children with Specific Disabilities

LEARNING OBJECTIVES

After studying this chapter, you will be able to:

LO 3-1: Discuss relevant strategies for supporting children with Down syndrome.

LO 3-2: Describe the challenges and available intervention approaches for children with autism.

LO 3-3: Explain some of the characteristics of children with motor impairments, and ways to encourage their participation.

LO 3-4: Discuss the characteristics and recommended strategies for working with children with visual impairments.

LO 3-5: Describe the different types of hearing loss, preferred communication modes, and effective teaching strategies for children with hearing loss.

LO 3-6: Clarify the difference between high- and low-incidence disabilities.

The following NAEYC Standards and DEC Recommended Practices are addressed in this chapter:

naeyc

Standard 1: Promoting Child Development and Learning
Standard 4: Using Developmentally Effective Approaches
Standard 6: Becoming a Professional

DEC

Practice 2: Environment
Practice 4: Instruction

In this chapter we will discuss strategies and adaptations for use with children with specific mild to severe disabilities:

- **Moderate to severe intellectual disabilities.** One of the most common intellectual disabilities is Down syndrome. Children with Down syndrome have identifiable physical features. Early developmental progression has much in common with children who do not have disabilities, but milestones are achieved at a much slower pace.

- **Autism spectrum disorder (ASD).** ASD is characterized by atypical social and communicative behaviors. Children with autism often avoid social interaction or have difficulty with appropriate social-pragmatic skills. Many children with ASD may be hypersensitive to sound and touch.

- **Visual impairment and blindness.** Children with visual impairment may range from having very limited vision (for example, blindness with light perception only) to having some functional vision under certain conditions or within a very circumscribed visual field. Visual impairment restricts the development of mobility and the understanding of many concepts.

- **Hearing impairment.** Children with mild to moderate hearing impairment can usually be accommodated in an inclusive setting with simple adaptations and a good understanding of the components and function of the hearing aid. Children with more severe losses will require a team approach. The ECE teacher will need to be informed as to the preferred mode of communication, which is typically speech, but in some cases will be sign language. Increasingly, infants and young children with significant hearing loss receive cochlear implants.

- **Orthopedic impairment.** The most common **orthopedic impairment** is cerebral palsy, which interferes in various ways with children's voluntary muscle movement and postural control. ECE teachers will need to obtain information from disability specialists such as a physical therapist who can demonstrate how to position the child for maximum comfort and performance and ways to adapt toys and utensils.

- **High-incidence disabilities.** High-incidence disabilities occur with greater frequency than other conditions and are often characterized by less intensive needs. These include children at risk for a learning disability, children who have speech or language impairment, and children with mild intellectual disabilities.

Introduction

While the teaching strategies described in Chapter 2 will be useful with all children, many children have special needs that require specific adaptations. It is imperative that the ECE professional initially obtain the services of the appropriate disability specialist to understand the specific dimensions of the child's disability. However, access to these specialists is often limited. Thus, the information presented in this chapter will identify some of the most critical needs and strategies for use with children with the following conditions: Down syndrome, visual impairment, hearing impairment, cerebral palsy, and autism. Although our major categories correspond to federal definitions and there are many other specific disabilities and conditions, we focus on some of the most common.

The first section describes the *low-incidence disabilities* most likely to be represented in inclusive settings. These disabilities are readily diagnosed early in life and have many clear and distinct characteristics. They often require the support of a number of specialists. High-incidence disabilities, such as learning disabilities and speech and language delays may be more common, but are often more difficult to diagnose as they may have less distinct characteristics. A section at the end of this chapter includes a brief discussion of high-incidence disabilities.

3-1 Children with Down Syndrome: A Common Example of Intellectual Disabilities

Children who have **intellectual disabilities** or delays are developmentally younger than their chronological age. Thus, their reasoning ability, language skills, emotional and behavioral maturity, and independence may be like that of a much younger child. One of the most common disorders characterized by intellectual disability is **Down syndrome**. According to the National Down Syndrome Society, although children with Down syndrome typically demonstrate cognitive delays, these cognitive challenges are often mitigated by the many strengths and talents they exhibit. These children often have notable strengths in social skills, visual memory, and musical talent. Though speech and language skills are typically delayed, the effective use of visual supports such as picture communication systems are common and effective. Also, various technology apps for electronic devices including iPads and mobile phones are widely used with great benefit. Strengths in the area of visual processing are well documented (Hodapp & Ly, 2003).

3-1a Physical and Health Characteristics

The following briefly address characteristics of children with Down syndrome.

Physical Features. Because this is a chromosomal condition, children with Down syndrome typically present identifiable physical features. These usually (but not always) include short stature, low muscle tone (hypotonia), loose joint ligaments that sometimes make arms and legs seem floppy, and short fingers with atypical crease patterns in the palms of the hands.

Motor. Though gross motor development is typically somewhat delayed as a result of low muscle tone, most children with Down syndrome walk by age two years.

Health Concerns. Children who have Down syndrome are more likely to have certain health problems. These sometimes include heart malformations, frequent upper respiratory infections, chronic mouth breathing, and mild to moderate hearing loss.

A rare but dangerous condition that is more common in children with Down syndrome than in the general population is **spinal subluxation**. This is a partial dislocation of one of the upper spinal vertebrae. The condition exists in approximately 15 percent of children who have Down syndrome. In approximately 1 percent of these children, the dislocation leads to a serious condition of spinal cord compression. Even though it is rare, teachers should be aware of the symptoms of this spinal cord compression:

- Head tilt to one side
- Increased clumsiness
- Limping or refusal to walk
- Weakness of one arm

Some medical professionals suggest that every child who has Down syndrome should be x-rayed to determine whether spinal subluxation—and thus the potential for spinal compression—exists (Roizen, 2013). In the absence of this diagnostic information, teachers may want to limit gymnastic activities such as somersaults.

Cognition. Although the *average* range of cognitive ability for children with Down syndrome is in the moderate range, it should be noted that there is a very wide range of cognitive levels in this population, from severe to mild cognitive disability. Perhaps the most notable recent development in our understanding of teaching and learning in this population is the increasing emphasis on literacy development (Bird & Buckley, 2001). Particularly interesting are reports of young children with Down syndrome achieving sight word vocabularies commensurate with their same-aged peers. Also, reports of reading development actually support the development of speech and language skills, rather than the other way around, as is the conventional wisdom (Buckley, 2002).

Angie is an attractive young woman in her early 20s. She has Down syndrome. Throughout her schooling she attended special education classes for children with significant disabilities. In high school her curriculum was focused on "functional" skills such as self-management and basic communication, though her speech intelligibility was limited. Fortunately, Angie had received some early training in American Sign Language that supplemented her communication to some extent. In her teens she became very interested in signing the letters of the alphabet, which inspired her mastery of printing and spelling important words. Interestingly, without receiving any speech/language therapy, her speech intelligibility began to improve. It is quite possible that this improvement was the result of Angie's knowledge of letters and spelling. One can only imagine how much more Angie might have accomplished had she been viewed in her early years as a potential reader!

Social. Children with Down syndrome are often responsive and prefer social interactions over interactions with objects. Because of these social characteristics, children with Down syndrome are often very successful in inclusive settings, particularly when provided with appropriate curriculum adaptations and modifications.

Learning Style. Children with Down syndrome achieve many of the same developmental milestones as children without disabilities; however, they usually do so at a slower pace. In addition, their rate of response is often slower than children without disabilities. Thus, teachers may need to provide longer wait times. Children may also need many repetitions to master a task. Particularly important, as already mentioned, is the need for teachers to take advantage of these children's strengths in visual processing given they usually have relatively weaker abilities in auditory processing and memory.

Additionally, children with Down syndrome often demonstrate low **task persistence** as they do not tend to stick with tasks they start. They are more likely to be motivated by the praise and encouragement of their significant others (for example, a teacher or parent) rather than by task mastery and achievement.

3-1b Teaching Strategies

Given that children with Down syndrome usually have mild or moderate intellectual disabilities, the following strategies can be very effective.

Pacing. It is helpful for teachers to slow down the pace of activities in the classroom. Although this may not be necessary for every activity, if a child with Down syndrome appears to be having difficulty learning a particular task or routine, slowing down your demonstration or presentation will help the child learn the task more easily.

Pacing involves both the rate of speaking and moving—how fast a teacher talks or performs a task or activity—as well as how long the teacher *waits* for children to respond or complete a task. One teacher made the following comment: "Counting

---

Helpful Hint

A slower pace can be a helpful strategy for many children, not just children with Down syndrome. For example, children who are learning English as a second language will comprehend better and learn English faster if the teacher avoids speaking with a rapid pace. Similarly, children who have learning disabilities and language delays may also benefit from a slower speech rate. In addition, pausing and waiting gives children time to process the request and formulate an answer or action.

to five silently before giving the child a prompt or providing assistance really has helped me slow down and give kids plenty of time to respond."

Task Analysis. It is important to break tasks into small steps (as discussed in Chapter 2) and assist children in learning one step at a time.

Jose Learns to Clean Up after Snack

Jose is having trouble cleaning up his dishes after snack time. He plays with leftover food, and because he likes playing in water, he goes directly to the sink rather than throwing paper items in the trash. His teacher, Mr. Chee, has to help him with nearly every step each day. Mr. Chee can first do a task analysis. This involves analyzing the task into its component parts or steps. These would include:

1. Piling up the dishes on his tray
2. Standing up
3. Picking up the tray
4. Walking to the counter
5. Placing the tray on the counter
6. Throwing paper items in the trash
7. Placing dishes in the sink
8. Placing the tray on the stack

By learning one step at time, Jose will eventually be able to complete the entire task on his own.

Helpful Hint

It is often more effective to start at the *end* of the sequence and work backward. In Jose's example, Mr. Chee would begin working on teaching Jose to place the tray on the stack of trays first, then work on placing the dishes in the sink, and so on, until he can do the whole sequence.

Repetition. One of the most effective, yet simplest, techniques for supporting the learning of children with cognitive disabilities is repetition. Simply repeating key words or movements an extra time or two can significantly increase a child's opportunity to learn. Compare the two samples that follow. Two different teachers describe what happens when water is added to flour.

Use of Repetition   Comparing Mrs. Moore and Mrs. Reston

Mrs. Moore: Look. When you pour the water in, it gets really sticky. See? OK, does someone else want a turn mixing the dough?

Mrs. Reston: First *pour* the *water* into the *flour.* OK, you *poured* the *water* into the *flour.* Now feel how *sticky* it is. The *water* and the *flour* are *sticky* now. You *poured* the *water* into the *flour* and made *sticky dough!*

Although the content of the two comments is similar, Mrs. Reston's language includes more repetition and recasting of the key words describing the activity.

3-2 Children with Autism

Autism offers significant challenges to educators and families alike. It was thought to be a rare disorder. However, the numbers continue to increase, suggesting that it is essential that early childhood educators be prepared to support and include children on the autism spectrum. It is interesting to note that autism is much more prevalent in boys.

Since Leo Kanner first identified the disorder in the 1930s, there have been numerous theories about its cause. Early on, it was considered a psychiatric disorder with an emotional origin. Specifically, it was often theorized that rejecting caregivers caused autism. This theory has been clearly debunked, along with the theory that autism is caused by vaccinations. Today, as a result of several different research efforts related to the neurophysiology of the disorder, we realize that autism is related to atypical structure and/or neural transmission processes of the brain. However, the exact nature of these central nervous system differences—as well as the causes—are still not well understood.

Even more painful for families, the best intervention methods for children with autism are also not well understood. In recent years, we have seen a virtual explosion of treatment approaches. The following presents characteristics of autism, current theory about the neurological basis of the disorder, and some consistently effective intervention strategies.

3-2a Characteristics of Autism

The hallmark of the disorder is a pervasive failure of the development of social communication. The most recent *Diagnostic and Statistical Manual of Mental Disorders* (American Psychiatric Association, 2013) now classifies autistic disorders under the overarching category of autism spectrum disorder (ASD). Common to all of the individuals on this broad spectrum is the poor development of social skills. Although we will not go into detail here regarding the diagnostic criteria, it is important to note that to be diagnosed with autism, a child must exhibit significant delay in social communication and symbolic skills prior to the age of three years and must demonstrate characteristics in the following three areas: (1) significant delay or inappropriate use of language; (2) failure to develop normal social relationships and interactions; and (3) demonstration of obsessive or ritualistic, repetitive behaviors such as spinning objects or insistence on exact repetitions of sequences of nonfunctional behavior. One currently accepted theory is that many children with autism demonstrate *neurological hyperresponsivity*. They are also described as having extremely acute sensory abilities, particularly in the areas of hearing and touch. Thus, they are **hypersensitive** to certain sensations. For example, sounds that may be barely audible to most individuals, such as a faraway siren, may be distracting or irritating. Moderately loud sounds, such as a typical preschool classroom, are often painful or overwhelming to children with autism. This sensitivity may extend to the area of touch. A child may find the tags on the inside of his shirt to be unbearable. As a result of this tactile defensiveness, an infant with autism quickly finds ways to avoid certain kinds of touch. He may not mold easily to his mother's body when held. As he gets older, he may constantly move away from potential body contact.

Most children with autism avoid making direct eye contact. They prefer to use their peripheral vision. As a result they often appear not to be paying attention because they do not look directly at the object or person.

One of the ironic and mysterious characteristics of children with autism is that although they avoid some sensations, they might have an intense craving for other sensations—particularly when they have control over them. For example, a certain type of sensory craving may lead a child to stare at bright lights, listen obsessively to a certain song, or engage in continuous self-stimulatory or self-injurious behavior. Such behaviors might be considered to be obsessive or ritualistic, repetitive behaviors.

Children with autism are also described as having serious motor planning difficulties. They have difficulty initiating behavior. They also have a hard time changing a behavior once it is under way. Children with autism use few nonverbal communication gestures, such as pointing, directed reaching, or facial expressions. Figure 3-1 summarizes common characteristics of autism.

3-2b Intervention/Treatment Approaches

A complete inventory of even the most common treatment approaches is far too lengthy to include here. These treatments range from drugs and special diets to specific auditory training regimens to behavior modification. It is extremely important to remember that no two individuals on the spectrum seem to have identical symptoms. A symptom may be mild in one child and severe in another. Children with

- Avoidance of social interaction, or inappropriate social interaction: may avoid eye gaze, walk away when approached, or approach/touch adult as an inanimate object rather than a person
- Inability to establish *joint reference,* or shared attention, directed by an adult, to an object or event
- Absence of language, or use of bizarre or nonfunctional language; use of *echolalia,* repetition of same phrase or sentence over and over; use of unusual sounds
- Hypersensitivity to certain sensory stimuli, especially sound and touch: may seek to avoid or escape; may refuse to touch certain textures; may appear *not* to hear; may cover ears or scream in response to certain sounds; may notice sounds too quiet for anyone else to hear
- Insistence on sameness: may react with extreme anxiety or agitation when daily schedule or physical environment is changed
- Repetitious, self-stimulatory behavior, such as spinning toy car wheels, twirling piece of string or a bent stick, rocking, and hand flapping
- Preference for use of peripheral (side) vision rather than direct eye gaze, especially when looking at people
- Noncompliant behavior
- Poor self-help skills, though not due to motor problems
- More common in boys than girls

Figure 3-1 Common Characteristics of Children with Autism

autism vary widely in abilities and, thus, vary widely in the number and nature of supports they need. Some display incredible strengths, especially in rote memory, visual memory, and visual processing. Many have very special interests that draw their attention. A few of the most common strategies that can be used to build on their strengths are described here.

Applied Behavior Analysis. **Applied behavior analysis (ABA)** is probably the most widely known approach to intervention. This teaching approach involves observation, assessment, task analysis, systematic teaching of skills, and ongoing data collection to monitor progress. Of the ABA approaches, the Lovaas **discrete trial approach** is, perhaps, the most highly researched and accepted approach. This traditional behavioral approach is highly structured and often uses tangible reinforcers (for example, candy or tokens) for specific behavior (for example, eye contact or naming objects). The discrete trial approach typically requires approximately 20 to 40 hours a week of intensive one-on-one specific response training and is found to be most effective when begun before 30 months of age (MacDonald et al., 2014).

Functional Behavior Analysis. Employing a different behavioral approach, educators using **functional behavior analysis** carefully analyze a child's current behavior repertoire to determine if her behavior is getting her what she wants. If not, she is taught more appropriate functional behaviors, particularly focusing on language and social skills (Koegel & LaZebnik, 2005).

Pivotal Response Teaching. **Pivotal Response Teaching (PRT)** is a systematical application of the principles of ABA. It builds on the interests of the child and seems to be particularly effective with the development of communication, play, and social behaviors. Research suggests that it can be highly effective when implemented before the age of five. The treatment is performed in the natural environment, is highly intensive, and uses items that are age appropriate and reinforcing to the child. It avoids negative interactions and focuses on four pivotal areas of development: motivation, response to multiple cues, self-initiation, and self-management (Koegel & Koegel, 2012).

TEACCH. The Treatment and Education of Autistic and Communication Handicapped Children (TEACCH) model is a specially designed, highly structured, classroom program that specifically adapts the activities and the physical structure and organization of the classroom to mitigate those factors that interfere with learning. It supports the development of appropriate behavior and communication patterns and teaches basic academic skills (Mesibov, Shea, & Schopler, 2004).

Sensory Integration Therapy. This model first assesses the extent to which sensory processing and integration difficulties are interfering with normal development. **Sensory integration therapy** then implements specific therapeutic procedures to ameliorate abnormalities in sensory integration. This approach should be planned and carried out only by a trained sensory integration (SI) therapist, most often an occupational therapist (Ayres, 2005).

Floor Time. This approach, developed by child psychiatrist Stanley Greenspan, is becoming increasingly popular among early interventionists working with two- and three-year-olds who demonstrate difficulties with self-regulation and symptoms of autism. **Floor time** focuses on the interactive relationship between a caregiver and child, attempting to enhance and increase turn-taking and responsive interaction cycles through open-ended play activities (Greenspan & Weider, 2006).

PECS (Picture Exchange Communication System). As already mentioned, children with autism often handle visual/graphic information more easily than auditory/verbal information. One successful approach to developing communication behaviors is the use of the **picture exchange communication system (PECS)** further described in Chapter 13. This fairly simple approach requires children to select a picture card, approach the adult, and hand the adult the card to make a request or comment. This approach has several advantages for children with autism:

- It focuses on *functional* communication.
- It requires little interaction and exchange.
- It relies more on visual information than on auditory.
- It provides an acceptable replacement behavior for children whose communicative behaviors have become disruptive and inappropriate.

The many other approaches to autism are too numerous to mention here. Unfortunately, there is no *magic bullet* or cure, and there is much disagreement among professionals as to the most effective intervention.

3-2c Behavior Challenges in Children with Autism

Although the social communication difficulties are at the core of the disability of autism, the characteristic most likely to interfere with successful inclusion is inappropriate behavior. Often because of the communication difficulty and/or hypersensitivity to certain stimuli, children with autism may present extremely challenging behaviors. Examples of these behaviors include:

- Repetitive, self-stimulatory actions such as rocking, spinning, and hand flapping (Occasionally these behaviors may involve self-mutilation, such as head banging or skin picking.)
- Rigid, ritualistic patterns such as touching all the pictures on the wall upon arrival at school or racing along the playground fence in a repeated pattern
- Absence of social responsiveness and extreme difficulty with compliance
- Escape behaviors such as running away (with little warning), crawling into small spaces, covering ears, and screaming

In addition, the topic of behavior management is addressed in Chapter 5 of this book.

3-2d Teaching Strategies for Children with Autism Spectrum Disorders

The following strategies have proven to be consistently helpful for early childhood teachers in managing the behavior of all children:

Work Closely with the Child's Family. Typically, parents of children with autism are extremely well informed about the disorder as well as the specific characteristics of their children.

Complete a High-Preference Inventory. Interview the child's parents to determine those objects and activities that the child really likes or dislikes. Often these may be unusual fixations—either positive or negative. It is important for the teacher to understand the child's fears and cravings. (Recall that we discussed high-preference inventories in Chapter 2; see Figure 2-5 for an example.)

Jason's Unexplained Tantrums

In a discussion with Jason's mother, his teacher, Rhonda, was surprised to learn that Jason has an extreme fear of fans or anything that sounds like a fan. This helped her realize that Jason's seemingly random temper might be related to the air conditioner turning on in the classroom. Jason's mother also told Rhonda that although Jason is very sensitive to light touch or tickling, that he often finds a deep massaging type of touch on his back or arms very calming.

Create a Well-Organized, Predictable Classroom. This is probably the single most important strategy. Areas of the classroom should be well marked. Children on the autism spectrum have difficulty transitioning between activities. Therefore, the daily routines should be consistent and displayed clearly via a sequence of pictures or photos in the front of the room as a visual schedule. Children should be encouraged to check their schedule regularly to predict what comes next. Changes in routine can be very upsetting. If a routine must be changed, more time should be allowed and a warning given.

Transitions from one activity to the next should be very clear and handled in a predictable manner. Giving children a "warning" lets them know that they will need to stop their current activity soon. For example, use visual supports such as a red "stop" sign to signal the need to stop one activity, and a green sign, with a photo representing the next activity, to begin another. It often helps to provide an object for the child to carry that signifies the next activity like a book to carry to the library corner. Waiting periods can be filled with songs or other activities to sustain engagement.

Try to Reduce the Noise Level of the Classroom to the Extent Possible. High levels of noise interfere significantly with learning. If the room is highly resonant, consider adding area rugs and wall hangings made of absorbent materials or fabric to dampen the sound. Avoid meaningless background music. Given that some children are hypersensitive to even small noises and others seem not to hear anything going on around them, the use of sounds to signal transitions from one activity to another can be ineffective. Familiar songs may be useful if used consistently to assist with transitions between activities.

Use Firm Pressure Touch When Touching the Child Rather than Light Touch. Although light, fleeting touch may be annoying to children with autism, firm pressure, especially applied to the chest and back, may be calming or at least easier to tolerate. Provide some kind of anticipatory cue so children know you are going to touch them and are not startled by the contact.

Be Consistent about Consequences for Unacceptable Behavior. For example, if a child bites other children, all staff should respond to this behavior in the same way, such as promptly removing the child from the play area. Even more importantly, try to determine exactly what triggers the behavior and change the environment to reduce the likelihood of reoccurrence.

Use Visual Communication Systems. Many children with autism respond better to visual stimuli such as pictures or printed words rather than to speech. Pictures can be used during transitions to cue what is happening next. Pictures can also be used by the child to indicate wants and needs. Additional suggestions are found in Chapter 13.

Speak in a Quiet Voice. Some children with autism are particularly sensitive to certain voice qualities or too loud speech. Loud shrill voices may be particularly annoying.

Request Support from Specialists. In addition to support from an early childhood special educator, in some cases it may be helpful to obtain specialized support. A **behavior specialist** may be able to determine the cause of and interventions for certain disruptive behaviors. In some cases an evaluation by a sensory integration therapist (usually an occupational therapist) may be helpful in understanding sensory overload and processing problems. See Chapter 15 for a more complete discussion on consulting specialists.

3-3 Children with Cerebral Palsy and Other Motor Impairments

Cerebral palsy is a neurological disorder that significantly affects a child's ability to control movement. It is generally the result of some insult to the brain that occurs either in utero or at the time of birth.

3-3a Characteristics of Children with Cerebral Palsy (CP)

Cerebral palsy is the most common motor disability among children of all ages. A continuum of motor dysfunction due to insult to the brain may include a child with clumsy and awkward movements on one end, and a child with CP who has severe impairments on the other. The following discusses general characteristics of children with mild, moderate, and severe CP.

Persistence of Primitive Reflexes. One of the reasons children with cerebral palsy have difficulty controlling their voluntary movements is that involuntary movements and postures caused by certain reflexes persist and cannot be overridden by voluntary movement. An example of such a persistent reflex would be the *rooting reflex*. This reflex enables an infant to automatically turn to the mother's breast when that side of the face is stimulated. Although this reflex is helpful to newborns, it normally disappears as higher-level control centers of the brain take over and establish voluntary patterns, such as grasping a bottle at midline.

A child who has cerebral palsy, however, may continue to reflexively turn his head to the side touched well past infancy. Thus, if you are helping a child eat and touch the side of his face to move it toward midline, he will actually resist your touch and turn toward the side you are touching rather than to midline. It is easy to mistake the child's resistance for rejection or noncompliance. It is important to realize the child has no control over this movement.

Another common reflex pattern seen in children who have cerebral palsy is referred to as the **asymmetric tonic neck reflex (ATNR)** (see Figure 3-2). This reflex

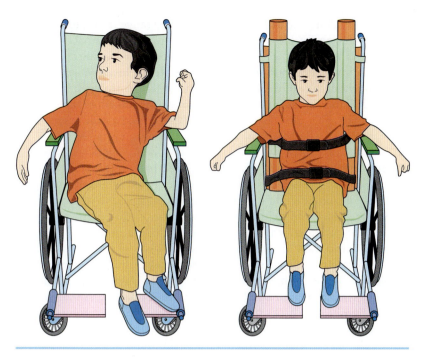

Figure 3-2 Positioning to Inhibit Asymmetric Tonic Neck Reflex

is triggered by certain movements of the head and neck and results in a sort of *fencing* position with the arm and leg on one side of the body flexed, and the other arm and leg extended. Positioning to inhibit this reflex is essential because the ATNR inhibits voluntary use of arms and hands and interferes with trunk control and stability. Be sure to check with a physical therapist and parent regarding how to position the child to inhibit this reflex.

Thus, a child with cerebral palsy has difficulty initiating and controlling voluntary movements, as well as difficulty *inhibiting* involuntary movements as reflected in the example of Chung Lee.

Chung Lee's ATNR

Chung Lee has cerebral palsy. She is included in a Head Start program. Her teacher, Ms. Torelli, noticed that at lunchtime, Chung Lee often turned her head away from the assistant feeding her. Ms. Torelli assumed that this meant Chung Lee wasn't hungry.

However, after talking with her physical therapist, Ms. Torelli realized that this was a reflex that occurred when Chung Lee tried to move her head forward and open her mouth. The physical therapist showed Ms. Torelli how to position Chung Lee and stabilize her head to avoid the head-turning reflex (ATNR). This intervention was successful and allowed Chung Lee to eat more easily.

Muscle Tone. The movements of children with cerebral palsy may be either **hypotonic** or **hypertonic**. These terms refer to the tone of the muscles. Muscles described as low tone or floppy are hypotonic. They lack strength, and intense movements of any duration are difficult. Muscles that are tense often cause the limbs to either extend or contract into extreme positions. Muscles with increased tone or tension are hypertonic. Many children with cerebral palsy actually demonstrate both high and low tone in different parts of their body. Also, some children have constantly alternating tone, which produces a sort of writhing movement. This is referred to as **athetosis**.

The extent to which cerebral palsy interferes with a child's development of movement, or **motor control**, depends upon the severity of the condition and the affected parts of the body. Thus, the degree of disability may range from mild involvement, which may be most noticeable in fine motor tasks, to involvement of both upper and lower extremities as well as the neck and trunk. If only the legs are affected and not the upper body, the condition is referred to as **diplegia**. Involvement of both arms and legs on only one side of the body is referred to as **hemiplegia**. Involvement of the trunk and all four limbs is referred to as **quadriplegia**. When there is severe involvement of both arms and legs, the child is likely to need a wide range of adaptive equipment, such as a wheelchair, other adapted seating, and standers.

Mobility and Postural Control. Two areas related to a child's motor control difficulty must be understood: mobility and postural control. **Mobility** is a child's ability to move his body, either to ambulate from one place to another or to move and manipulate objects by using his arms and hands. Specialists and therapists frequently refer to children who are ambulatory or non-ambulatory. Children who are **ambulatory** can walk unassisted, whereas children who are **non-ambulatory** need the assistance of a device such as a wheelchair or walker. **Postural control** refers to a child's ability to maintain a stable position. Achieving a stable position often requires environmental adaptations such as special chairs that support the optimal position of the child's body. If the child is not in a secure, comfortable, balanced position, she is not free to work on controlling body movements or to pay attention to things going on around her. Her energy and attention are focused on maintaining balance.

Also important is positioning the child in ways that will inhibit certain primitive reflex patterns such as ATNR. Persistence of positions caused by these reflexes will be detrimental to the child because they may place extra stress on certain joints or muscles, or they may result in maladaptive compensatory movements or postures.

Early childhood teachers must work closely with a physical therapist or an educational specialist in the area of physical disabilities to determine the child's positioning and equipment needs. Parents are also helpful resources regarding these adaptations.

Nutrition. Providing adequate nutrition may be a challenge for children with severe physical disabilities. Because of fine motor difficulties, children may have trouble eating independently. Poorly developed chewing and swallowing patterns may interfere with eating certain textures of food. A child with cerebral palsy cannot swallow correctly if the head is tilted back. The head should be in a neutral position or slightly forward. Finally, children with cerebral palsy may experience frequent stomach upset and constipation.

Cognitive Level. Cognitive abilities in children with cerebral palsy can range from severe impairment of overall cognitive ability to normal intellectual function. Cognitive level may be difficult to assess accurately in children who have cerebral palsy. This is primarily due to significant limitations of both spoken language and nonverbal communication such as pointing, nodding, and use of facial expressions. Without some reliable means of communication, it is very difficult to assess cognitive skills accurately. Parents are often the most knowledgeable regarding cognitive skills of young children with cerebral palsy. The early childhood educator can make certain informal observations that may provide clues as to cognitive level in the preschool-age child who has severe cerebral palsy. For example, a sense of humor, quick social response, learning something after only a few repetitions, and use of directed eye gaze to communicate wants and needs may be indicators of cognitive ability. It is crucial that teachers not associate severe motor involvement with low cognitive ability. It is possible for children with severe spastic quadriplegia who have very little voluntary muscle control to be extremely bright.

Even when cognitive level is normal, a child with cerebral palsy may have learning disabilities related to perceptual difficulties, such as auditory and visual processing difficulties or visual–motor (eye–hand) coordination problems.

Communication Skills. This is often the most important area of support and intervention for children who have cerebral palsy. If the motor involvement interferes with the intelligible production of speech, it is essential that some form of **augmentative or alternative communication (AAC)** be established. Parents and some professionals may believe that use of an AAC system, such as a communication board, interferes with the child's development of speech. In fact, just the opposite may be the case. Speech development can be enhanced by providing an alternative means of communication. With today's proliferation of electronic, computerized devices, many inexpensive sources of assistive technology can support play activities and communication for children with significant motor impairments (see Chapter 13 for additional information).

It is critical that early childhood teachers work closely with other specialists (such as a speech and language specialist, physical therapist, or physical disabilities itinerant teacher) to design an AAC system. If no resources appear to be immediately available, teachers can develop simple communication systems, such as picture cards, that take advantage of a child's existing repertoire of voluntary movements. Such movements might include directed eye gaze, reaching, or pointing with the head.

3-3b Teaching Considerations for Children with Motor Disabilities

These strategies apply to children with cerebral palsy and those with other significant motor disorders.

Provide Ample Wait Time for Child to Respond. Children with cerebral palsy often have difficulty organizing a response. For example, if you ask a child to point to the toy he wants, it may take him quite a long time to respond even if he understands the task. If the teacher assumes that the child cannot respond or has not understood and does not offer enough time for the child to respond, he will soon become discouraged and stop trying to respond (learned helplessness).

Be Aware of Involuntary Movements. It is important to understand that some of the child's movements may be unintentional. For example, as the child attempts to open her mouth to vocalize, this may trigger an involuntary reflex of turning her head to the side. It may appear that she is trying to avoid looking at you. You may not realize that she is trying to vocalize, but she is unable to inhibit other movements. Sometimes proper positioning will help the child inhibit these extraneous movements. Consult with a physical therapist or educational specialist about positioning and other strategies for each child.

Position the Child for Maximum Participation. Consultation with physical and occupational therapists will be important to determine the positions and adaptive equipment that may be necessary to ensure that the child can participate in early childhood activities. Figure 3-3 is an example of the use of adaptive equipment to increase participation.

Enable the Child to Participate in Some Way in All Activities. As a general rule, children should be positioned so that hips and knees are bent at 90-degree angles,

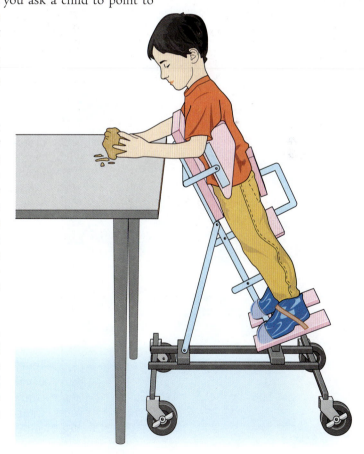

Figure 3-3 Child Placed in Stander to Increase his Ability to Participate in Tabletop Activity

Photo 3-1 This child is seated in a stable position with simple adaptations.

Photo 3-2 Here a child is using a switch to access the computer.

feet are not dangling but resting flat on some surface, and the child is seated squarely on buttocks not on the tail bone. A child seated in a stable position is shown in Photo 3-1. For some children, shoulders and head may also need stabilization or support.

It is important to figure out some way for a child with a severe physical disability to participate and not just observe activities. One way of participating is to allow the child to activate a switch to turn on a battery-operated toy or food blender. Not only does this allow the child to participate more actively, but it also provides important switch activation practice for eventually operating a computer or electronic communication device. See Photo 3-2 for an example of a switch.

The child can also point to a card indicating the song or storybook he would like during circle time. Again, this not only aids participation but also supports the development of literacy skills. Jenny's example demonstrates both of these strategies.

Jenny's Favorite Song

Jenny has spastic quadriplegia. As a result she has limited voluntary control of her arms and legs, and she cannot speak. She has fairly good control of her head, and she often uses directed eye gaze to indicate what she wants. At music time her teacher presents choices of three songs. Picture cards representing the song choices are attached with Velcro to a large board. When it is Jenny's turn to choose a song, she simply uses her eye gaze to select a song card. The cards are spaced far enough apart so that it is easy to determine which one Jenny is indicating.

Her favorite song is "The Wheels on the Bus." She especially likes the verse "The horn on the bus goes *beep beep beep.*" Because Jenny has fairly good head control, her physical disabilities consultant suggests constructing a head switch that allows Jenny to turn on a music player by simply moving her head to the right. The music player has a loop tape that repeats the sound of a loud horn going "beep beep beep" each time the switch is activated. Now when the children get to Jenny's favorite verse of the song, Jenny can independently make an important contribution. Jenny is a participating member in this activity even though her physical ability is extremely limited. The other children think the loud beeping of the music player is great fun. They are also learning to read the names of the songs printed on each card.

Teach Classmates How to Assist. Given that playmates are usually eager to help, it is important to teach them how to encourage rather than "take over." Model how to ask if the child wants help first. Then, help the playmate to accept "no" without getting their feelings hurt. Encourage playmates to find ways to be inclusive. For example, if it is time to bring toys in from the yard, playmates can fill the basket on the walker. The child with the physical disability can then lead the way toward the classroom.

3-4 Children with Visual Impairment

Although inclusion of a child with total blindness may be rare, children with low vision or whose visual impairment is combined with other disabilities are increasingly participating in inclusive settings. Visual impairment is a technical and complex field that requires the expertise of a visual impairment (VI) consultant. However, early childhood educators should find the following foundational information helpful.

3-4a Characteristics of Visual Impairment

There are many types of visual impairment. This may be the child's only disability or it may accompany other conditions, such as Down syndrome or cerebral palsy. Diseases of the eye and various visual conditions affect not only visual acuity (that is, how accurately the child can see at close and far ranges) but also may affect the visual field (where the child can see). For example, one child may see only a narrow central field (tunnel vision, discussed later in the chapter), while another child may use peripheral vision, and yet another can see only an area in one corner of the visual field. See Figure 3-4.

The itinerant vision specialist can conduct a functional vision assessment. This assessment provides information regarding how the child is actually using his or her vision. The results of the functional vision assessment will provide the teacher with information and recommendations about such things as:

- Optimal distance of objects
- Visual field preference
- Use of light sources
- Color preferences
- Creation of optimal contrasts

It is important to realize that few individuals are totally blind. Nearly all children who have visual impairment have some usable vision. These children are referred to as having **low vision**. Even children with total blindness may see shadows and

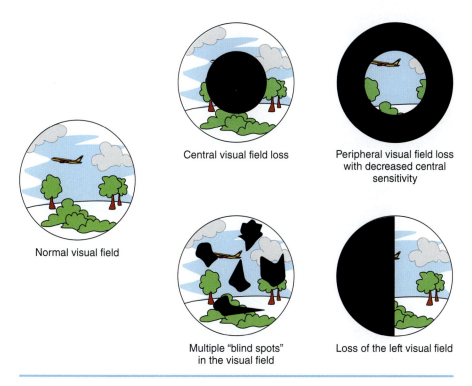

Normal visual field

Central visual field loss

Peripheral visual field loss with decreased central sensitivity

Multiple "blind spots" in the visual field

Loss of the left visual field

Figure 3-4 Examples of Restricted Visual Fields

movement. Furthermore, children can *learn* to use their residual sight just as children who have hearing loss can learn to use their residual hearing. When visual information is consistently paired with other sensations such as touch or sound, the vision may eventually acquire meaning. Umberto's example demonstrates this possibility.

Umberto Learns to Use His Vision

Umberto has a significant visual impairment. He has light perception and vaguely perceives shapes. Umberto's mother has told the teacher that his favorite food is bananas. His mother often sends a small container of mashed bananas in his lunch. The teacher asks his mother to send the whole banana, rather than mashing it ahead of time. Each time Umberto has a banana, his teacher shows him the banana before peeling and mashing it. The first few times she shows him the banana, it appears as a meaningless blotch of yellow. But each time the banana is presented, Umberto holds it and feels his teacher peel it. He smells it, tastes it, and hears the word *banana*. Eventually he can actually recognize the banana, and he has a very thorough understanding of all its characteristics.

3-4b General Categories of Visual Impairment

The pathology and characteristics of all types of visual impairment are much too extensive to describe here. However, early childhood educators should be aware of the difference between total blindness and low vision, as well as the condition referred to as **cortical visual impairment**.

Only about 25 percent of all individuals who have visual impairment are totally blind. Another 25 percent have some light perception. The remaining 50 percent have enough usable vision that they can see large print with proper enhancement. Thus they are said to have low vision (Chen, 2014).

Total Blindness. Although individuals who are *legally blind* may have considerable vision, the educational definition of *total blindness* refers to a total absence of vision or the ability to perceive only light (Hunt & Marshall, 2012). Such individuals learn primarily through other senses, such as hearing and touch.

Low Vision. Children who have low vision have some residual vision that can become functional with proper intervention, adaptation, and training. In addition to using a variety of sensory cues, a child who has low vision will also learn how to use and enhance residual vision. Early childhood educators can work closely with a VI specialist to learn about specific strategies, such as lighting and contrast, and adaptive equipment (for example, print enlargers).

Cortical Visual Impairment. Some children with severe neurological disorders may have a complex condition known as cortical visual impairment. This condition often accompanies multiple disabilities, including seizure disorders and cerebral palsy. In this case the problem is not with the structure and function of the eye itself but rather with the brain's ability to process and make sense of incoming visual information. It is a common misconception that this condition cannot be improved. These children often have some fleeting functional vision; however, it is somewhat unpredictable.

3-4c Strategies for Working with Children with Visual Impairments

Children with visual impairments exhibit a wide range of cognitive and intellectual abilities. Their potential may be underestimated because they miss so much incidental learning, which can have a significant impact on their development. It is important to be optimistic and utilize the following strategies.

Use of Sensory Cues. Children who are blind or who have only light perception must rely on other sensory cues for information about objects and experiences. Most useful sensory cues should be offered *prior* to an event to help the child *anticipate it.* For example, prior to presenting the child with finger paint, it might be helpful for the child to smell the paint and hear the teacher repeat "finger paint."

The most common cues are **auditory cues** and **tactile cues**. Most teachers are intuitively aware of the need to use verbal and sound cues for children with visual disabilities and to provide opportunities for the child to touch and feel various properties of an object. However, it is also important to be aware of other important sensory cues.

Olfactory cues. These are cues related to the odor or fragrance of an object. It is important to realize that *all* objects have an odor. Thus you can encourage the child to smell any object to obtain additional information about that object. For example, encourage the child to smell food items, paints, lotions, and flowers. Equally important might be the opportunity to smell such less fragrant items as dirt, paper towels, soiled clothing, and the fish bowl!

Kinesthetic cues. These cues incorporate movement. For example, before placing a child in a swing, tell him what you're about to do and then move him in a brief swinging motion before placing him in the swing. If you want the child to begin finger painting, you could move his hands in circles on the paper before giving him the paint.

Strategies to Enhance Low Vision. Using lighting, contrast, distance, and position to optimal effect can help make the most of low vision.

Lighting. Use of proper lighting can enhance vision. Should the object be lit from behind or from the side? Which lighting is best—natural, incandescent, or fluorescent? Is the child light-sensitive, in which case she might do better in low-light conditions using a spotlight on the object? These are questions that can best be answered in consultation with a vision specialist. For children who are not light-sensitive, Figure 3-5 lists some specific suggestions for enhancing illumination.

Contrast. Maximum contrast helps children with low vision optimize their functional use of sight. For example, dark-colored objects should be placed on a light background, such as a dark blue bowl on a white place mat. Place light-colored objects on dark backgrounds; for example, a white and yellow jack-in-the-box can be placed on a black blanket on the floor. See Photo 3-3 for examples of visual contrast.

---

1. Avoid creating glare or light directed at child's face.
2. When interacting with an adult, the child's back should be toward the light source so the adult's face is illuminated.
3. Overhead lighting in the classroom should be bright.
4. Lighter-colored walls maximize light.
5. It may be helpful to illuminate play materials directly.

Note: Always consult a vision specialist to determine best adaptations. (For example, some children with visual impairment are extremely sensitive to light, and these suggestions may not be appropriate.)

Figure 3-5 Tips for Adapting Illumination for Children with Low Vision. (Adapted from Dotie-Kwan (2000), Project Support.)

Photo 3-3 This tray and place setting provide an example of visual contrast.

Distance and position. If a child is nearsighted, objects need to be brought closer to the child, and printed material needs to be enlarged. For a child who has a narrow visual field, or **tunnel vision**, it may be easier to see objects that are farther away; the child may see small objects and pictures better than larger ones (Chen, 2014). The optimal position of objects and materials will depend on the nature of a child's field loss.

Use of Hand-Over-Hand Guidance. Use of hand-over-hand or hand-under-hand techniques is common when working with children with limited vision (Chen, 2014). With **hand-over-hand guidance**, the adult manipulates the child's hands to perform a task such as using a marking pen. **Hand-under-hand guidance**, on the other hand, may be more effective for children who resist having their hands manipulated or who are tactually defensive, such as for a task like pushing a button. See Figure 3-6 for examples.

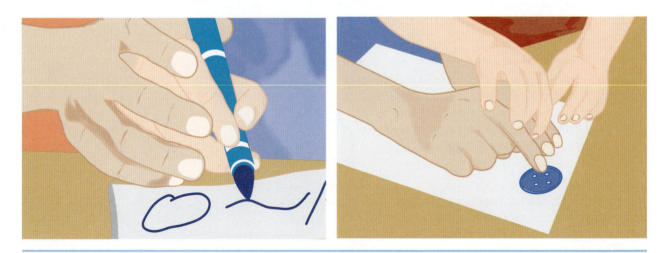

Figure 3-6 Hand-over-Hand and Hand-under-Hand Guidance

Whenever adaptations for children are being considered, early childhood educators must include families fully to be certain that all adaptations are consistent with family values. For example, conflicts may arise along the continuum from nurturance to independence. Given that a central feature of early childhood education is the development of independence, some families may feel that their central values are being questioned. Many parents see their role as one of continuing to nurture and protect during the early childhood years. Their vigilance may be heightened given that preschool may be the child's first experience with "strangers" in an environment away from family (Lynch & Hanson, 2011).

Real Objects in Meaningful Contexts. Keep in mind that children with low vision and children who are blind will have difficulty understanding *replicas* of real things. For example, understanding that a stuffed animal is a representation of a real animal is a slow process. If a child is unfamiliar with real cats, it will be impossible for him to understand what a toy cat is. Also, functional contexts will offer the most meaning for a child with a visual impairment. Introduce new words and concepts in natural and logical situations first. For example, trying to pretend to wash dishes or put a doll to bed in dramatic play will not be meaningful if the child has never washed dishes or experienced putting a real baby to bed.

Strategies for Working with Children Who Have Cortical Visual Impairment. Strategies that may be helpful for children with cortical visual impairment are quite different from those used with children with low vision. For example, these children may actually see better with their peripheral vision rather than central vision. Thus, they may see objects better by looking *away* from them rather than directly at them. Chen (2014) also suggests the following strategies for children with cortical blindness:

- Reduce multisensory stimulation, allowing children to concentrate on the visual input.
- Allow children to touch objects while looking at them.
- Place objects far apart; avoid visual crowding.
- Bring objects fairly close to the child.
- Use contrasting colors, especially yellow and red (rather than black and white) to highlight objects.
- Understand that a child may be able to use peripheral vision more effectively than central vision.

3-5 Children with Hearing Impairment

Many young children have some degree of hearing loss. Hearing losses vary in severity, ranging from mild to profound, and in type of loss (for example, a loss due to some obstruction in the middle ear versus damage to the auditory nerve). Children with mild to moderate hearing loss can usually be accommodated in the early childhood setting with fairly simple adaptations related to using visual cues, seating the child close to the speaker, and learning how to perform daily checks on the function of the child's hearing aid. Working closely with the child's parents is essential. Children with more severe hearing loss will need greater support in the ECE setting. ECE teachers will need to obtain important information and assistance from not only parents, but also perhaps from an audiologist and a speech pathologist or teacher of the deaf. It should be noted that IDEIA uses the term *hearing impairment* to denote individuals with hearing losses. However, given that many in the deaf community do not view hearing loss as disabling, we are choosing to use the term *loss* instead of *impairment*. The following summarizes some of the key issues in working with children with hearing loss.

3-5a Understanding Different Types of Hearing Loss

To understand the type of hearing loss a child has, we must consider:

- The *severity* or extent of the loss, which is measured in **decibels**, a measure of loudness.
- The *pitch range* or **frequencies** (for example, high or low) most affected.
- The site along the auditory pathway that causes the loss (the bones of the middle ear, the cochlea, or the nerve that connects the ear to the brain.)

Information regarding the type of hearing loss a child has can be obtained from the child's parent, from an audiogram often included in the child's file, or from the child's audiologist.

Loudness Threshold and Pitch Range. Very few children are totally deaf. Most children with hearing loss have some **residual hearing**. It is important to ask certain questions about this residual hearing. Is it in the high frequencies or low frequencies? Figure 3-7 provides information about the intensity (or loudness) and the frequency range (pitch) of common environmental sounds. For example, the roar of a truck is a fairly loud, low-frequency sound at around 100 decibels. A whisper, on the other hand, is fairly quiet at less than 30 decibels but is a higher-pitch sound. A rock band is in the middle of the pitch range, but is very loud at 110 decibels.

Also, what is the **threshold** of this hearing? In other words, how loud does a sound have to be for a child to hear it? Figure 3-8 presents an audiogram on which a child's hearing threshold is recorded for each pitch, with the lowest pitch (250 Hz) on the left and the highest pitch (8,000 Hz) on the right.

Note that this child has near normal hearing in both ears for low-pitch sounds, but hearing thresholds are much worse in the higher frequencies, especially in the right ear (marked with a circle).

Helpful Hint

The average conversational voice is at about 50 to 60 decibels. The quietest sound most individuals can detect is around 0 to 10 decibels, and the pain threshold is around 120 decibels.

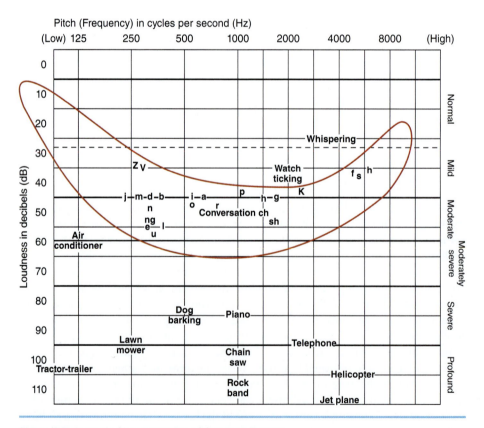

Figure 3-7 Acoustic Characteristics of Common Sounds

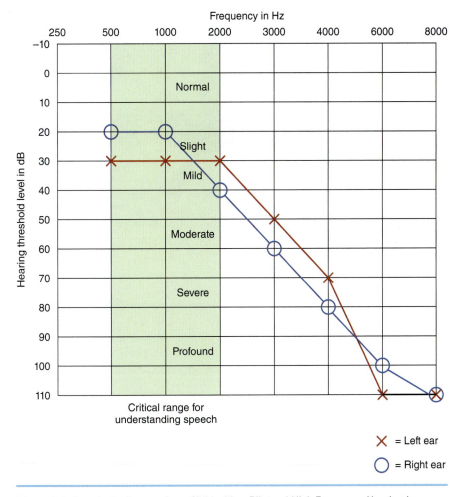

Audiogram

Frequency in Hz

Hearing threshold level in dB

Normal
Slight
Mild
Moderate
Severe
Profound

Critical range for
understanding speech

X = Left ear
◯ = Right ear

Figure 3-8 Sample Audiogram for a Child with a Bilateral High-Frequency Hearing Loss

Most children with a significant hearing loss wear a hearing aid. The audiological report will contain information regarding the child's **aided hearing**, or how well the child hears with the hearing aid on. With the hearing aid on, the child may have significantly improved thresholds for loudness but may still experience significant distortion of sounds. This will be particularly true if the child has significantly worse hearing in the high frequencies than the low, as compared with a child who has a more *flat* audiogram, with the loss about the same for all pitches. When sounds are distorted, they remain unclear even when they are made louder.

Conductive versus Sensorineural Hearing Loss. The audiological report will also indicate whether the child has a **conductive hearing loss** or a **sensorineural hearing loss**. This difference is related to where the problem is that has caused the hearing loss. Figure 3-9 is a diagram of the hearing mechanism.

A problem or obstruction in the outer or middle ear will cause a conductive loss. Examples of conditions that cause conductive loss include:

- Middle ear infections
- Ruptured tympanic membrane (ear drum)
- Otosclerosis (calcification of the middle ear bones)
- Foreign objects placed in the ear canal
- Congenital atresia, or narrowing of the ear canal

Conductive losses are never at the profound level of severity. Usually a conductive loss will not exceed around 60 decibels. Also, conductive losses can often be

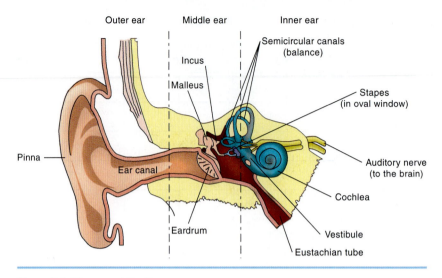

Figure 3-9 Diagram of the Ear

improved through surgery, such as replacing bones in the middle ear, or medication, including antibiotics for an ear infection.

Losses that result from problems in the cochlea in the inner ear or along the auditory nerve that leads to the auditory areas in the temporal lobe of the brain are referred to as *sensorineural*. Common causes of sensorineural hearing losses in children include:

- Diseases such as meningitis or cytomegalovirus (CMV)
- Heredity
- Ototoxic drugs, such as high doses of aspirin
- Head injury that severs the auditory nerve

For the most part sensorineural losses are permanent, although more children are receiving **cochlear implants**. Not long ago, this surgical procedure, which implants an electronic device that approximates certain functions of the cochlea, was considered quite experimental. Today, it has become a widely performed procedure with younger and younger children. The performance of children with cochlear implants as shown in Figure 3-10 is often impressive (Hunt & Marshall, 2012).

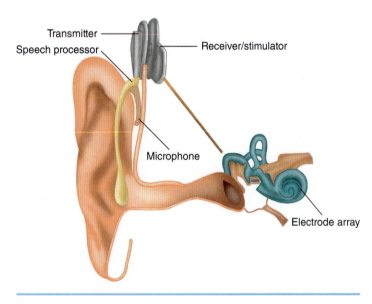

Figure 3-10 A Cochlear Implant

3-5b Issues Related to Preferred Communication Modes: Signing versus Speech

For as long as there have been individuals with hearing loss, there has been controversy about the best communication system to use. Put simply, some people believe that children with hearing loss must live in a *hearing world* and thus must learn speech or *spoken English* as their primary mode of communication. Others strongly believe that sign language should be taught as the primary language of people with significant hearing loss. In the past, many children with hearing loss had great difficulty learning spoken English. Thus, proponents of manual communication systems, such as sign language, argued that the opportunity to learn an effective communication system should not be delayed or compromised by struggling to learn speech when American Sign Language, the sign system preferred by most members of the deaf community, could be learned early and with little difficulty, if children have good models.

It is critical that the ECE staff discuss the approach being used by the child's family. If the family is using an **oral approach**, procedures for enhancing speech development and use of residual hearing, or a cochlear implant, should be incorporated into the classroom. If the family prefers a **manual approach**, the ECE staff will need to learn a basic signing vocabulary. Some families will prefer a **total communication approach**, which attempts to combine the two approaches.

3-5c Learning Styles and Characteristics of Children with Hearing Loss

Characteristics and thus learning styles of children with hearing loss vary considerably. A significant percentage of children have one or more additional, educationally significant challenges, such as the following.

Language Development. For children with significant hearing loss the greatest challenge is in the area of the development of communication skills, including both receptive and expressive language. In the early years the development of symbolic communication is often significantly delayed, unless the child has been exposed to sign language from an early age. The development of language and literacy will continue to be major challenges throughout the school years. Again, the child who has received a cochlear implant and who receives intensive auditory training has the potential to develop good spoken language.

Cognitive Skills. Children whose only disability is hearing loss do not have impairment of cognitive skills. However, some children have multiple disabilities, including hearing loss. When this is the case, significant cognitive delay may be compounded by the hearing loss. One key to informal assessment of cognitive abilities in a child with hearing loss is to observe carefully the child's play and problem-solving skills. It is important not to confuse language skills with cognitive skills. Children will demonstrate normal play activities in those areas that do not require language, such as block building and drawing. Also, children who have significant hearing loss but normal cognition will often find effective nonverbal ways of communicating through gestures and facial expression.

Social Skills. Because of the typical delay in speech and language, social skills may be affected at the preschool level. ECE teachers can significantly alleviate this problem by explaining the nature of the child's communication difficulty, by teaching a basic sign vocabulary to hearing peers in the class, and by encouraging participation of hearing peers in the activities preferred by the child with a hearing loss.

3-5d Teaching Strategies for Children with Hearing Loss

The following strategies can aid in teaching children with hearing loss:

- **Seat the child close to the sound source.** Make sure the child is positioned near the teacher, the stereo speaker, or musical instruments. If the child hears better from one ear, then be certain that ear is closest to the sound source.
- **Help the child develop residual hearing.** Identify interesting environmental sounds, such as an airplane, telephone ringing, and air conditioner.
- **Make sure the child can see your face.** Don't cover your mouth with your hand. Be aware of potential lighting glare, which might interfere with the child's sight. Finally, face the child, preferably at eye level.
- **Speak clearly at a good volume.** However, do not exaggerate your speech.

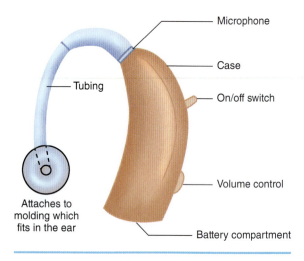

Figure 3-11 Components of a Behind-the-Ear Hearing Aid

Labels on figure: Microphone, Case, On/off switch, Volume control, Battery compartment, Tubing, Attaches to molding which fits in the ear

- **Use the child's name to get his attention.** You may also need to touch the child. Wait for him to be looking at you before giving directions.
- **Work collaboratively with families.** Also, consult with other professionals, including an audiologist, speech pathologist, and/or deaf and hard-of-hearing specialist.
- **Include visual and tactile cues.** These cues will assist the child's comprehension of language. Also when possible, demonstrate what you want the child to do.
- **Learn about the child's hearing aid.** It is critical that early childhood educators obtain training related to the child's hearing aid (see Figure 3-11). Parents are often good resources for the following information:
  - How to set the hearing aid controls
  - How to check the battery and function of the aid
  - How to clean the ear mold
  - How to insert the aid in the child's ear
  - How to assist the child in managing his hearing aid independently
  - How to help children with cochlear implants
- **Make sure you and other speakers are close enough.** Be aware that the farther a speaker is from a hearing aid, the more distorted (that is, less clear) the speech signal will be.
- **Reduce ambient noise.** Be aware of the effect of the acoustics in your room. Rooms that are highly *resonant* tend to create difficult auditory environments for children with hearing aids. Use rugs, cloth wall hangings, and soft furniture to reduce resonance. Also, wherever possible, eliminate or reduce background (ambient) noise such as fans, music, and traffic. (As noted earlier, noise mitigation is important for all learners!) See a list of tips in Figure 3-12 for including children with hearing loss in large group activities.

- Use music! Even silent children will often vocalize during music and singing.
- Use music with heavy bass sound; vibro-tactile, low pitch is easier to hear and sense.
- Use preferential seating for children to make the most use of their hearing.
- Seat children away from ongoing noises such as heaters, electrical equipment, and outdoor windows, so that hearing aids don't pick up on this ambient noise.

Figure 3-12 Tips for Including Children with Hearing Loss in Large Group Activities

3-6 High-Incidence Disabilities

The disabilities described so far in this chapter are considered *low-incidence disabilities* because they occur relatively rarely in the general population. Although children with low-incidence disabilities may be less common in the ECE classroom, they often present significant challenges and have distinct needs and characteristics.

More common are the *high-incidence disabilities,* which are more prevalent and are often considered to be *milder,* requiring less intense interventions. However, this is not always the case.

Some high-incidence disabilities (for example, learning disabilities and attention deficit disorder) present a greater diagnostic challenge and are often not identified until the child approaches school age. Although characteristics of these disabilities often overlap and may be much more variable and more difficult to define, the following is a simplified attempt at characterizing them.

3-6a Learning Disability

The term **learning disability** covers a wide range of neurologically based difficulties or *brain differences* that affect the ways in which a child processes and organizes visual and auditory information. These neurological differences can interfere significantly with learning to read and write. Most professionals are uncomfortable with the use of this term prior to school age because interference with academic performance is considered part of the definition. The federal definition of *learning disability* requires that there be a *discrepancy* between intellectual ability and academic achievement (Hunt & Marshall, 2012).

Children with learning disabilities often have difficulties with impulse control and behavior regulation, difficulty sustaining and focusing attention, and difficulty with language development. Children with learning disabilities often demonstrate inconsistent and variable skills and performance. For example, they may have great difficulty in one skill area, but excel in another. Or, they may perform a task perfectly one day, and appear to have forgotten it the next.

It is important to determine each child's unique learning and processing characteristics. That is, via conversations with parents and specialists, try to determine which learning modes (for example, visual, auditory, tactile) the child prefers, as well as whether the child finds certain situations or sensory experiences stressful. It will also be important to determine the effects of any medications the child may be taking.

3-6b Speech and Language Impairment

Language skills refer to the ability to learn vocabulary, to put words together into complete sentences, and to understand when others speak. Children with language disorders may also have difficulty with **pragmatics**, or the appropriate and effective use of language in social communication. **Speech skills** refer to the ability to produce the sounds, or **phonemes**, that make up words. Although many children have difficulty with both speech and language, it is possible to have difficulty with just one or the other. In early childhood it is sometimes difficult to differentiate between speech and language *delays,* which suggest that a child may eventually catch up, versus speech and language *disorders,* which require intensive speech or language therapy.

Teachers must realize that children who attempt to communicate but who cannot make themselves understood can experience a great deal of frustration. As a result children may develop behavior challenges, either as an attempt to communicate their needs or simply as an expression of frustration. When the child's speech is extremely difficult to understand, teachers may find it may be helpful to use some nonverbal strategies suggested in other chapters to reduce frustration. (See, for example, suggestions regarding AAC earlier in this chapter and the use of picture communication in this chapter and Chapter 13.)

In Chapter 2, the strategies for communicative interactions include some of the most effective and easily implemented strategies that ECE teachers can use to support and enhance language development, such as following a child's lead, expanding and recasting the child's utterance, and repetition of key words. Speech disorders require therapeutic interventions with a speech-language specialist. Simple strategies that can support a speech specialist's efforts include phoneme awareness activities, avoidance of overly rapid speech rate, teacher's repetition of key words, and rhyming and sound imitation games.

Summary

Children can experience learning and developmental challenges from a number of different causes. Many conditions and anomalies create challenges for young children and their caregivers. This chapter has attempted to familiarize early childhood educators with the characteristics most frequently associated with certain disabilities.

Read–Reflect–Discuss
Ryan Goes to Preschool

Ryan is four years old, and today will be his first day at the Learning Together Children's Center. Ryan has been diagnosed with autism spectrum disorder (ASD), and has received several in-home therapies (speech therapy, occupational therapy, and consultation for behavior management). This is his first day in a group setting. Ryan is an only child, and his mother, Carmen, has been anxious for him to have experiences with children without disabilities. However, she also has concerns about the challenges he may face.

As is common for children on the autism spectrum, Ryan has significantly delayed speech and language skills. He uses spoken language only to request favorite foods (Cheerios and french fries) and to express resistance or rejection by saying "No no no." He has also had a history of severe temper tantrums, but, with the assistance of a behavior specialist, these outbursts have become rare.

Despite her son's challenges, Carmen believes Ryan is very smart. He can use his iPad and other electronic devices much better than she can. And he already recognizes the letters of the alphabet. He plays with plastic letters, and can point to the correct letters when Carmen names them. Carmen is convinced he is ready for school.

On Ryan's first day, Carmen is anxious, but confident that this will be a great experience for Ryan. Ryan seemed to sense Carmen's positive anticipation, and was smiling as he noticed the huge letters above the school entryway. As they enter the busy classroom, Ryan immediately pulls away and runs back out the door. Carmen did not expect this.

Read–Reflect–Discuss Questions

1. What are Ryan's strengths?
2. What might explain Ryan's running away?
3. What classroom practices and teaching strategies might work for Ryan?

Key Terms

aided hearing

ambulatory

applied behavior analysis (ABA)

asymmetric tonic neck reflex (ATNR)

athetosis

auditory cues

augmentative or alternative communication (AAC)

behavior specialist

cochlear implant

conductive hearing loss

cortical visual impairment

decibels

diplegia

discrete trial approach

Down syndrome

floor time

frequencies

functional behavior analysis

hand-over-hand guidance

hand-under-hand guidance

hemiplegia

hypersensitive

hypertonic

hypotonic

intellectual disabilities

language skills

learning disability

low vision

manual approach

mobility

motor control

non-ambulatory

oral approach

orthopedic impairment

phonemes

picture exchange communication system (PECS)

Pivotal Response Teaching (PRT)

postural control

pragmatics

residual hearing

quadriplegia

sensorineural hearing loss

sensory integration therapy

speech skills

spinal subluxation

tactile cues

task persistence

threshold

total communication approach

tunnel vision

Helpful Resources

Curricula

Blind Children's Center. *First steps: A handbook for teaching young children who are visually impaired.* Retrieved from www.blindchildrenscenter,mycafecommerce.com/product/first-steps.

Bricker, D. D., & Waddell, M. (2007). *AEPS curriculum for three to six years.* Baltimore, MD: Paul H. Brookes.

Johnson-Martin, N. M., Hacker, B. J., & Attermeier, S. M. (2004). *The Carolina curriculum for preschoolers with special needs.* Baltimore, MD: Paul H. Brookes.

VORT Corporation. (2010). *HELP 3-6 curriculum guide.* Palo Alto, CA.

Organizations

American Foundation for the Blind, www.afb.org
Council on Education of the Deaf, www.councilondeafed.org
Down Syndrome Education International, www.dseinternational.org
Epilepsy Foundation, www.epilepsy.com
National Association for Down Syndrome, www.nads.org
National Down Syndrome Society, www.ndss.org
National Organization for Rare Diseases (NORD), www.rarediseases.org
Special Education Resources on the Internet, www.seriweb.com
United Cerebral Palsy, www.ucp.org

Catalogs for Adaptive Equipment and Toys

AbleNet, Inc., 2625 Patton Road, Roseville, MN 55113-1308, (800) 322-0956, www.ablenetinc.com

Let's play: Guide to toys for children with special needs, BrainLine, WETA, 2775 South Quincy Street, Arlington, VA 22206, (703) 998-2020, www.brainline.org

Rifton Equipment, P.O. Box 260, Rifton, NY 12471-0260, (800) 571-8198, www.rifton.com

Tumble Forms, Patterson Medical, (800) 323-5547, tumbleforms.com

Arranging the Physical Environment to Support the Inclusion of Children with Special Needs

LEARNING OBJECTIVES

After studying this chapter, you will be able to:

LO 4-1: Describe the primary concerns to be taken into account when creating optimal environments for young children with and without disabilities.

LO 4-2: Discuss considerations that should be given to planning for the best use of space within the environment.

LO 4-3: Create developmentally appropriate and accessible activity areas or learning centers that will support inclusion of children with a variety of disabilities.

LO 4-4: Explain criteria essential to choosing and arranging materials that are responsive to individual developmental levels and needs.

LO 4-5: Elaborate on factors to be noted when designing specific activity centers.

The following NAEYC Standards and DEC Recommended Practices are addressed in this chapter:

naeyc

Standard 1: Promoting Child Development and Learning
Standard 4: Using Developmentally Effective Approaches
Standard 5: Using Content Knowledge to Build Meaningful Curriculum

DEC

Practice 2: Environment
Practice 4: Instruction
Practice 5: Interaction

In this chapter, we will discuss how arranging the physical environment can positively or negatively affect children's learning and behavior:

Children with special needs need to feel physically and emotionally safe. This requires creating environments that are easily accessible and free of hazards (particularly for children who are visually impaired or who have significant motor disabilities). Daily schedules and environments should be predictable and allow as much independence as possible:

- **Arrangement of the physical environment can support independent access.** To accommodate adaptive or supportive equipment such as wheelchairs, the available physical space must be carefully arranged so that children have access to each and every area of the room.

- **Floor plans require careful consideration.** For example, some children may need access to an enclosed space. Floor plans should minimize clutter and include clearly marked boundaries; they must accommodate adaptive equipment.

- **Activity areas must include materials appropriate for children with different types of disabilities.** For example, materials must appeal to children functioning at developmentally young levels and toys and tools that are interesting and motivating to children with motor and sensory disabilities.

Introduction

Even if you are working in a center or classroom where the environment has already been arranged, take time to study that environment to determine if it is appropriate to accommodate young children with special needs. Remember that how an environment is arranged can determine how behavior within that environment is managed. Time spent thoughtfully arranging space and materials may prevent time lost and stress spent later on managing negative child behaviors.

4-1 Creating a Safe Environment

In creating the most positive environment possible, the arrangement of the elements within a learning environment should promote two features: *safety* and *independent access*.

4-1a Psychological Safety

Children must be and feel both physically and psychologically safe. Early childhood educators are sometimes tuned in to ensuring physical safety while they may give less attention to psychological safety. Experienced educators observe that children who do not feel safe will test the limits until they understand the organization and limits of their environment. Therefore, arrangement of space and materials must have order and stability.

These elements contribute to the predictability children need to feel safe. For example, if objects are kept in the same place every day, children feel secure in knowing where to find and where to return materials. Just consider how anxious anyone feels when something is not in its expected place. Remember how you feel as you search for your keys? When changes must be made, they should be made gradually. Adults should acquaint children with visual impairments regarding changes as soon as they occur.

4-1b Physical Safety

Creating physically safe environments for children with special needs may require specific considerations:

- Children who are unstable and fall easily need to be able to rely on sturdy and stable furniture. Thus, shelves and cabinets may need to be secured.
- Sharp corners can be adapted with rubber or foam edges.

- Some outdoor play areas may need rubber matting.
- Handrails may need to be added for children with unsteady gaits and for children with low vision.
- Obstacles in main traffic ways need to be clearly marked for children with low vision. For example, you can place duct tape with a black and white checkerboard pattern on a post that children must walk around.
- Curbs and steps must also be clearly marked for children with low vision.
- Cords, wires, and plugs must be out of children's reach.

4-1c Encouraging Independent Access

To accommodate adaptive or supportive equipment such as wheelchairs that may be necessary to facilitate inclusion, the available physical space must be carefully arranged. However, it is important not to *overadapt*. Making only necessary adaptations will minimize the focus on children's disabilities and encourage all children to learn to navigate around the normal barriers of a natural setting.

Spaces must be designed and materials selected that invite children to become *independently* and *actively involved* with their environment. Walkways must be wide enough for children who use wheelchairs or crutches to have access to each activity area provided. Watson and McCathren (2009) provide a checklist that can be easily accessed to determine if any early childhood program is ready to include children with special needs (see Weblink). Early childhood programs can use this tool to assess their curricula, physical space, and guidance techniques with specific questions about readiness for children with physical disabilities, hearing loss, visual impairments, communication and language disorders, intellectual disabilities, and sensory integration concerns.

Architectural Considerations. Examples of some of the architectural considerations to ensure safety and independent access are doors, ramps, toilets, chairs, and tables.

- *Doors.* Doors can be difficult for many young children to open. When children with physical disabilities are included, ease of opening, closing, and holding doors open may be a significant problem. Also, they may need to be wider than standard doors to accommodate wheelchairs.
- *Ramps.* When more than one wheelchair is to be accommodated, ramps wide enough to allow two chairs to pass are ideal. The slope of any ramps will need to be somewhat less steep than those designed for adults.
- *Toilets.* Toilet seats should be at variable heights. Toilet stalls need to be more than 36 inches wide to facilitate transfers from wheelchairs to toilets. It may be necessary to adapt a potty chair or toilet for a child with a disability.
- *Handrails.* Children with disabilities can benefit from handrails to help stabilize their body as they move from one activity to the next. Handrails are frequently used next to toilets and sinks. Photo 4-1 shows an example of handrails next to the sink.
- *Table height and seating.* For many children with special needs, adaptations may be needed in table height and seating to ensure proper positioning. Children may need smaller chairs so their feet can touch the

Photo 4-1 A handrail helps children stabilize themselves while using the sink.

floor; children with low muscle tone may need armrests and back support. Although seating adaptations may require extra effort initially, the payoff will be increased participation and comfort for children. Photos 4-2 and 4-3 demonstrate examples of effective seating adaptations. If children are allowed to stand while doing tabletop activities, they can have the freedom to move their wiggly bodies while focusing on activities. This adaptation might help children who have high energy levels and attention difficulties.

Often, adapting the physical environment in even small ways can increase independence for children who have special needs. This in turn reduces the burden on staff to provide individual assistance. An important goal for children with special needs is physical independence. This independence will also help prepare children to function successfully in future learning environments.

4-2 Floor Plan Considerations for Children with Special Needs

Although it is not necessary to create totally unique or adapted environments to include children with special needs, certain challenges may be of more frequent concern with this population. The following issues may be important considerations for some children.

4-2a Need for Quiet Area

Many children with special needs, especially children with autism, have low thresholds of tolerance for noisy and/or crowded busy environments. Providing a quiet area where children can be somewhat isolated and where the noise is damped can offer brief respites. There should always be a safe, comfortable area that children may seek out when they need or want to be alone. Children can be taught to take themselves to this private corner when they begin to feel overwhelmed. A staff member should monitor a child's behavior at all times while she is in the quiet area and can assist the child in developing self-control by letting her decide when she is ready to rejoin the group.

4-2b Avoidance of Large Open Areas

Some children with special needs may be overwhelmed by environments that seem disorganized and confusing. Divide large rooms into specific areas for activities, and clearly mark the boundaries of those areas with dividers, shelves, and other furniture and equipment. See the section later in this chapter on "Planning Activity Areas" for additional ideas. Photo 4-4 shows activity areas separated by clear boundaries.

Photo 4-2 Adapting table height and seating increases independence for children with special needs.

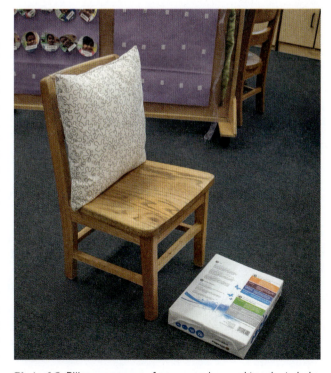

Photo 4-3 Pillows or reams of paper can be used to adapt chairs and ensure proper positioning.

Photo 4-4 Arranging furniture and chairs to create clear boundaries helps organize the environment for children.

4-2c Consideration of Some Children's Preference for Enclosed Space

Some children prefer a more enclosed, small space in which to play. It is helpful to arrange at least one area that is enclosed on at least three sides. However, the enclosure should not be more than about two feet in height to allow easy viewing of the area.

4-2d Need for Acoustic Adaptations

Highly resonant, noisy environments may create significant stress for many children with special needs—and many adults as well! This can interfere with children's ability to pay attention, and can increase irritability, behavior challenges and aggression. Sound can be dampened by use of acoustic tile, rugs, materials hung from the ceiling, and fabrics and artwork on the walls. Many classrooms have background music while children play. However, music can create unwanted reactions such as lack of concentration with some children. Children with special needs should be observed to see if they get anxious or agitated when music is on. If so, it would be a good idea to keep the music off.

4-2e Visually Simple Presentation of Materials to Reduce Clutter

Children who appear to be unable to choose activities or seem to be at loose ends may be reacting to too much clutter or to disorganized presentation of toys and materials. The following are examples of suggestions that may make it easier for children to select materials:

- Store items in a consistent place.
- Group similar items together on shelves.
- Allow empty space between items (children with visual processing difficulties or low vision may not recognize items that are jammed together).
- Use pictures to clearly label containers of manipulatives, or small toys and objects that aid in the development of fine motor skills.

4-3 Planning Activity Areas for Children with Special Needs

Activity areas are spaces within the room designed to facilitate different types of activities ranging from a small group of tabletop games to more robust activities such as block building and pretend play. Differential design will encourage children to learn that different behaviors are expected in various settings and that as activity demands change, so should behavior. Too much open space invites running and wandering around. Too much clutter is difficult for children who have trouble focusing.

Children tend to become more readily engaged in activities when the space is arranged into well-defined areas of activity. Well-defined activity areas have visible boundaries, surfaces to accommodate the activity, and adequate space for display of materials and storage. Instead of encircling all activity areas with bookcases and storage units, more creative boundaries can be used. For instance, fluid boundaries might include the use of canopies, streamers, mobiles, carpeting, colored tape, or different colored surfaces. Whatever the cues that designate different areas, they must be clear and consistent, and they should be of sufficient contrast to attract the notice of a child with visual impairments.

One goal should be to achieve an appropriate *balance* of activity areas suited to the developmental levels, skills, and interests of all children. Arrangement of the activity areas will also need to take into consideration the daily schedule. For example, if children are to participate in several small tabletop activities at once, then several areas with tables will be necessary.

Versatile materials such as paints, clay, musical instruments, blocks, or a combination of materials may offer a broad continuum of possible adaptations to meet the needs of children at different developmental levels. Materials should be displayed at a height accessible to children.

The following considerations are recommended in arranging each activity center: a library corner, art and water play area, tabletop manipulatives center, building area, and dramatic play area.

4-3a Library Corner

This quiet, calm area might be carpeted, offer large pillows, and feature a variety of literacy materials. Some sturdy infant/toddler books must be included along with talking books, pop-up books, adapted books, and copies of books used at group story time. The library corner also might include writing paper, magic markers, envelopes, stickers, a toy mailbox, and a blackboard. Some preschools offer a separate "writing area" with these supplies available for children during work or choice time.

4-3b Art and Water Play Area

A *messy* center for art activities and water play might include easels, a sand/water table, and storage for paper and art materials. Easily cleaned flooring is a must. Even children with severe disabilities often enjoy water play; they like feeling running water on their hands and the soothing activities of filling and pouring. In the sand table, hiding and finding objects and burying their hands can engage young children. Be aware of small objects that may present choking hazards to children with developmental delays who may still put things in their mouths.

4-3c Tabletop Manipulatives Center

A manipulatives play center features a table and shelves to hold well-marked containers of puzzles, small toys, and manipulatives. Initially children with severe disabilities may prefer to *dump and fill* in this area; they may not be able to play appropriately with small **manipulatives** or materials that can be handled and put together such as puzzles and blocks without specific training and facilitation. Be sure to include a variety of empty containers for this purpose, such as jars with lids, cylinders, dump trucks, and buckets. Children can then put items in the containers and take them back out rather than assembling them to create a finished product. Again, because developmentally young children may put small items in their mouths, some children will need to be closely supervised when they play in this area.

4-3d Building Area

Children with special needs often enjoy stacking and knocking down block towers (or knocking down towers that others have stacked!). The instant effect of the falling blocks can be quite motivating. This activity can provide opportunities for motor development and development of social skills such as turn-taking and respecting other children's creations. Another engaging activity is building ramps and letting cars and balls roll down the ramp. The greater the effect at the bottom of the ramp, the more interesting it is. Block building is a noisy activity and, naturally, needs to be kept away from activities requiring concentration such as the library area.

4-3e Dramatic Play Area

A dramatic play center may offer dress-up items, especially skirts with elastic waists, adult shoes, hats, and purses. These items can provide opportunities for staff to help children with disabilities practice dressing skills. Clothing should be easy to put on, take off, and fasten. Dress-up clothes may need to be adapted with Velcro, larger buttons, and pull rings or tabs for zippers. A mirror should be nearby. Dolls, doll beds, baby bottles, a high chair, a small rocking chair, and housekeeping toys (stove, dishes, pots and pans, and brooms) are some of the easiest toys for very developmentally young children to use to begin pretend play scenarios. Include items that represent home life within various cultures. However, limiting the number of items in this area can help children play more meaningfully. Too many dishes, pretend food objects, and so on, often lead to children simply dumping items and not engaging in meaningful pretend play. Remember, dramatic play can also be noisy, so placing it near the block area is not unusual.

4-3f Technology Center

Computers have, increasingly, come to be expected in preschool classrooms. In fact, the National Association for the Education of Young Children (NAEYC) and the Fred Rogers Center provided a position statement in 2012 on the use of technology and young children. This position statement can be accessed at www.naeyc.org

Photo 4-5 Computer time should be a shared learning activity.

/content/technology-and-young-children. It acknowledges that, if used wisely, technology and media can support learning and the development of relationships both with adults and their peers. The authors also recommend that for preschoolers, screen time should be fewer than 30 minutes per day for each child in a half-day program and less than one hour a day for each child in full-day programs.

It is clear that effective use of technology only comes about with careful planning and guidance of developmentally appropriate practices. Use of technology and media should not replace other essential activities such as creative play, exploration, physical activity, conversation, outdoor experience, or any other typical preschool experience. Most of all, involvement with technology and media should not become an isolated activity. Two child seats should be placed in front of each computer and an adult chair should be nearby. Monitors must be at children's eye level and accessible from wheelchairs, if necessary. Computers should be placed close enough to one another to encourage interaction and sharing of ideas among children. Unlike adults or older children, the goal for computer use is not to perform a particular task, but to learn. It is an activity. As shown in Photo 4-5, it is a chance for at least two children to explore, to converse, and to take turns.

Training for both teachers and children is essential, software must be of high quality, and teachers must carefully consider and set limits for children's use of technology. Fortunately, McManis and Parks (2011) reviewed the literature and produced the Early Childhood Educational Technology Evaluation Toolkit. This toolkit can be used by individual teachers—or, better yet, by a team dedicated to selecting developmentally appropriate technology.

WEBLINK

The Early Childhood Educational Technology Evaluation Toolkit can be accessed at https://s3.amazonaws.com/upload.hatchearlychildhood.com/ebooks/Hatch-evaluating-technology-ebook-sm.pdf.

4-4 Arranging Materials within Activity Areas

The level of child involvement in activities is influenced by the arrangement of materials and space within activity areas. All children must have access to enter and exit each area as well as access to all materials. Activity areas that are well defined, neat, and clean tend to invite use and cleanup at the end of an activity. Clearly labeled shelves and containers using photos and words contribute to effective cleanup times and encourage both matching (object to photo) and emerging literacy (identifying letters and words).

4-4a Visibility and Consistency

Visibility and consistency of materials help to stimulate children's interest. Toys and materials should be consistently available and placed in the same location to allow children repeated access to materials so they can practice emerging skills. However, periodically changing a few items can stimulate interest and promote new skills.

Large items can be stored on open shelves while small items such as cubes or crayons should be in containers on the open shelves. The teacher should seek to find out how a setting appears at the child's level. Are there interesting items for children to see and touch? Are some of the materials and toys accessible to a child who is minimally mobile?

4-4b Accessibility

Familiar items found in homes should be included along with commercially available educational materials. This is particularly important for children whose home culture differs from that of the center.

Accessible materials that are easy to take out and store are more likely to be used and returned than less accessible items. Arrange materials so that they can be easily viewed, taken from shelves and storage units, and returned to their proper place.

4-4c Labeling

Picture labels on shelves and toy containers facilitate proper placement of items and prereading skills. The pictures on original toy boxes can provide wonderful and inexpensive labels. Photographs of what happens in each area assist children with hearing loss to function more independently in that area.

4-4d Traffic Management

Traffic should be minimized and must flow freely. **Traffic management** includes nearby storage of materials, space for adaptive equipment, absence of cross-traffic, and recommended routes for travel that can be identified with footsteps or colored lines, for example. Cross-traffic needs to be considered with the placement of activity areas. For example, it would not be a good idea to put the block building area near the classroom door as blocks take up a lot of space and can overflow into the traffic area where families are entering or exiting the room. When planning a center, efforts should be made to ensure that a child in a wheelchair can navigate in and out of the spaces provided. It is helpful to specify the number of children allowed in each center at any one time.

4-4e Noise Control

There are many detrimental effects of environmental noise on children's learning. It is crucial to control the noise level, especially when children who are easily distracted or children with hearing loss are included. Children who wear hearing aids and children who have information-processing problems often have difficulty discriminating sounds and blocking out background noise. Some quiet space should be available for children to work with minimal noise distraction. Obviously, the quiet, calm area should not be placed next to the large muscle or dramatic play areas. Sound-absorbing material, such as cork or carpeting, can be used in high noise areas. For a child with hearing loss, consultation with a Deaf and Hard of Hearing (DHH)

> **Helpful Hint**
>
> Some items should be visible but difficult to access. For instance, items of interest can be placed on a teacher shelf above the classroom bookcase. This will provide important motivation and an opportunity for children with language delay to use communication skills to request these items.

specialist and/or audiologist may be critical for enhancing her ability to accurately hear voices in this busy environment.

4-4f Lighting

Consider lighting when arranging an area that requires close, visually demanding activities. Even young children with normal vision are naturally somewhat far-sighted, and activities requiring attention to visual details can be tiring. Adding incandescent lighting and natural light from windows and skylights can counteract the stress sometimes caused by fluorescent lighting. For children with low vision, it is helpful to use lamps that can be attached to tables and moved from place to place as needed.

4-5 Designing Specific Activity Centers

Each activity center has factors that must be considered with optimally planning a learning environment. Many of these are discussed in the following sections.

4-5a Reading/Preliteracy Areas

A quiet, calm area should be created to provide opportunities for children to relax and be exposed to books and other materials designed to develop preliteracy skills.

Organizing the Reading Area

- To reduce distractibility and facilitate attention and concentration, this center should be located in a quieter area of the room.
- The area must be well lighted to assist children with low vision.
- Large-print books and books with textures to allow tactile exploration are important for children with low vision. Pictures with bold clear lines and "scratch-and-sniff" books are also recommended. Adapted books will help children with disabilities interact longer, as the adaptation can be specifically suited to support the child's developmental needs. Children who can independently turn pages with the support of page turns are more likely to be motivated to "read" books. (An example of page turns can be seen in Photo 13-2 in Chapter 13 on page 212).
- Furnishings should be inviting and encourage relaxation. Carpeting, beanbags, and comfortable chairs lend themselves to quiet involvement. Physical therapists can assist in the selection of appropriate furnishings to provide optimal positioning for children with physical disabilities.
- Books should be displayed on an open rack with covers clearly visible in the line of children's sight.
- Other materials that might be available in this area include a flannelboard with story pictures, magazines, puppets, felt or magnetic letters, lotto games or picture word cards, and writing materials.
- Adaptive equipment to hold a book, turn pages, or activate an iPad may be needed for children with physical disabilities.
- Accompanying storybooks with flannelboards or puppets may help maintain interest for developmentally young children who are not motivated by picture representations alone.

Helpful Hint

Be sure to include books that portray children with disabilities along with those depicting a wide variety of cultural groups.

4-5b Sensory Experiences, Art, and Water Play Centers

All young children and especially those with sensory impairments need a wide variety of multisensory experiences. Developmentally young children will enjoy the

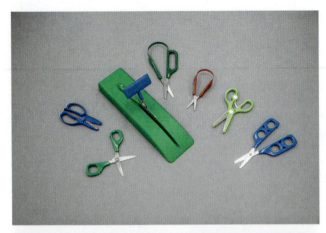

Photo 4-6 (A) Variety of Adapted Scissors; (B) Child using Adapted Scissors with a Peer for Support; (C) Variety of Adapted Writing Utensils

simple activities of sensory motor exploration. For children with low vision, art and water play provide important information through the alternate sensory channel of touch.

Art and water play centers are most appropriately placed outside or in a noncarpeted area near a sink to facilitate cleanup. Plastic aprons will help children with fine motor challenges avoid worrying about getting clothes wet or stained.

Materials to be included depend on the developmental levels of the children included. Some children with special needs do not know how to use materials such as crayons and scissors and may not learn through simply observing others. Choose activities that children can participate at varying developmental levels (for example, collage making, scribbling, painting, using clay or playdough).

Adaptive equipment such as those illustrated in Photo 4-6 allow children with special needs to function independently. Although some adaptations allow children to be better positioned to engage in fine motor activities, others directly modify the art utensils. Teachers can make simple adaptations. For example:

- Paintbrush handles can be enlarged with tape or other material to make them easier for children with motor impairments to hold.
- Crayons can be stuck through small balls to enlarge the gripping area.
- Children with visual impairments can enjoy the sweeping motions involved in moving paintbrushes, especially across large areas such as on wide pieces of paper or on real-life objects such as fences or big cardboard boxes. Children with physical impairments can be allowed to paint in other ways such as with their mouth as shown in Photo 4-7.
- Water play tubs can be moved outdoors in good weather so spilling isn't a concern. Or water can be replaced with other sensory materials such as leaves, Styrofoam packing materials, sand, noodles, or water with soapsuds. Some children with special needs may need to be carefully supervised to prevent them from putting the materials in their mouths.

4-5c Small Manipulative Activity Centers

Use of manipulatives can create special challenges for children with special needs:

- Children with special needs may need to be closely supervised to prevent choking on small items.
- Any centers featuring manipulative activities on a table must have child-sized tables sturdy enough to hold the weight of a minimally mobile child who may need support.
- Using a shelf liner on the table helps to stabilize manipulative materials so that they do not fall off onto the floor.
- Often it is easier for everyone if the manipulatives are placed on a carpeted floor.
- If working on the floor, it may be helpful to use tape, carpet squares, or placements to create borders to define work areas.

To assist children with physical disabilities, the following adaptations can be made:

- Consult with physical and occupational therapists to determine positioning and adaptive equipment needs.
- Use kidney-shaped tables or tables with cut semi-circles to allow children in wheelchairs or adapted seating to help them get closer to materials.
- Adapt battery-operated toys, radios, music devices, and other equipment using simple assistive technology devices such as pressure switches.
- Put a rim around the table edge to prevent small objects from being knocked off easily or use a shelf liner to stabilize small objects.
- Use larger versions of manipulative toys such as larger beads.
- Tape paper to table edges to stabilize the paper so it doesn't move around.
- Enlarge puzzle pieces by adding wood cubes or plastic knobs to make pieces easier to grasp.
- Enlarge the tips of shoelaces with tape or use pipe cleaners for bead stringing.
- Glue magnets to manipulatives and use on cookie sheets.

To assist children with visual impairments, consider the following:

- Consult a vision specialist to determine individual needs and appropriate adaptations.
- Give children wide markers so lines are easier to see.
- Put puzzles in a tray so children can keep track of the pieces.
- Provide knobbed puzzles and fit-in puzzles.
- Use glue to mark a line to be cut or traced.
- Use textured boundaries to define work areas. Placemats define work areas well for all children.
- Paste different textured fabrics on toys to help differentiate their parts and make them more interesting.

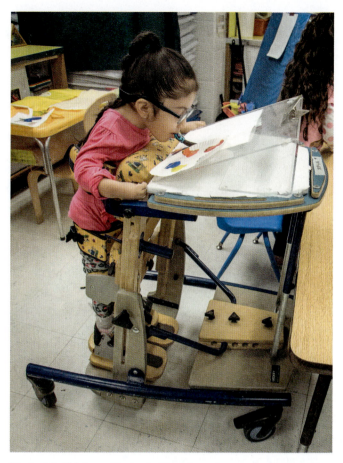

Photo 4-7 Children with physical impairments may need to use other parts of their body to participate in fine motor activities.

4-5d Outdoor Play Areas

Outside play is essential for children with special needs. Outdoor activities offer unique opportunities that may not be easily replicated indoors. It is important to maximize these opportunities through careful planning and use. The well-known Reggio Emilia approach to early education has long emphasized and advocated for the use of the natural physical environment as the ideal teaching and learning context for young children. Outdoor space enables children to develop relationships with the natural world around them. Similarly the NAEYC advocates for viewing outside spaces as important learning environments for young children (Spencer & Wright, 2014).

Planting and tending a garden is particularly valuable in supporting engagement and learning, as is exploring bugs and other creatures that inhabit the garden (Nimmo & Hallett, 2008). Educators may refer to this as a *project approach* to learning (Helm & Katz, 2010). When taking on gardening as a project, the enjoyment that young children experience when seeing, smelling, and picking flowers is universal. Flowers offer a multisensory experience that then can include picking a bouquet and displaying it proudly in the classroom.

In addition, Kuo and Faber Taylor (2004) found that the symptoms of children with attention deficit disorders (ADD) were significantly reduced when children played outside in green or natural outdoor settings in fresh air rather than indoors. An earlier study documented similar positive effects (Taylor, Kuo, & Sullivan, 2001). A garden "project" in this case might include the following:

- Reading a book about flowers and seeds
- Exploring different kinds of seeds
- Explaining that seeds turn into plants
- Planting the seeds in the garden
- Making signs identifying each type of seed
- Visiting the garden each day to see if there are "sprouts"
- Counting the plants, pulling out weeds, measuring the height of plants
- Being able to pick flowers for a bouquet, or vegetables for a salad

Although most children, with and without disabilities, enjoy outside environments, careful planning results in very positive benefits for children with autism and other disabilities. Nevertheless, there may be particular concerns to consider when designing outdoor experiences for individuals with a variety of disabilities. For example, Sachs and Vincenta (2011) offer the following guidelines when designing outdoor environments:

- Select a quiet location.
- Surround it with fencing that is at least 5 feet high.
- Use nonglare paving for wide pathways.
- Create clear edges along the pathways.
- Avoid toxic plants.
- Provide lots of shade.
- Include elements of consistency such a predictable plant patterns.
- Incorporate signs with simple, clear pictures.
- Include soothing areas where children can retreat when needed.
- Facilitate socialization through gardening activities.

These guidelines are based on an understanding of issues and challenges that a broad spectrum of children with disabilities face. Heightened sensory issues may make it difficult for children to filter the amount of information coming to them all at once. Such concerns were considered when developing these guidelines.

Thoughtfully creating an engaging outdoor play and learning environment encourages children to be connected with one another and with nature. A supportive environment is as essential outside as it is inside when it comes to promoting the quality of play that is so essential to all areas of development.

The outdoor environment provides a significant change in sensory-motor environment that is often very desirable:

1. Noise is less resonant and more diffuse so the outdoors may be less stressful for children who have auditory sensitivity.
2. Natural light is an advantage, though sunlight may pose problems for certain visual conditions.
3. Outdoor spaces offer access to certain gross motor and mobility activities that are not possible indoors, such as riding tricycles, pulling wagons, and swinging.

Helpful Hint

Be sure to check with families about special concerns or restrictions for children in outside environments and play structures. Sun sensitivity due to medication or medical condition, seizures, allergies (for example, to bees or pollen), and perceptual and balance difficulties are potential concerns.

Diversity Awareness

Gardening provides a wonderful opportunity for children and adults to celebrate diversity. Involving parents and grandparents will bring discussion of the difference in foods eaten or plants grown over time. Families can become involved in helping to plan an ethnic garden representing the various cultures within a classroom. Children can compare plants they eat at home and grow some of these in their garden. Gardening provides an interactive environment where children get to play in the mud and maybe even become willing to try new fruits and vegetables.

Certain considerations involving outdoor play environments may be particularly important for children with special needs:

- Swings need to be adapted with safety harnesses.
- The ground surface needs to be soft and resilient.
- To accommodate children with low vision, ground surfaces from one area to the next—such as the swing area to the sandbox to climbing structures and slides—need to be marked in some way, perhaps with bumps between areas or artificial turf in certain areas.
- Climbing structures need to be low, with easily grasped rails.
- Some pedal and wheel toys may need to be adapted with foot blocks and Velcro to accommodate smaller stature and poor motor control of legs.
- Bike tracks and "traffic" patterns need to be clearly marked and enforced. Sand tables, sandboxes, and water tables or small wading pools should be included and made easily accessible.

Summary

Careful planning and arrangement of the physical environment can make a significant difference in how young children with disabilities access, adapt, and enjoy inclusive environments. Particularly promising is the design of outdoor natural spaces. These modifications can benefit all children and help ensure that the physical environment supports rather than interferes with learning.

Read–Reflect–Discuss
Boundaries for Sung and Rafik

Mr. Ramirez is the teacher in a community preschool program. His classroom is in a small converted room in an old house. He has been frustrated about the fact that he really does not have enough room to design a good classroom environment. Two new children have joined the classroom, both of whom have some specific challenges. Sung has very limited vision, though her glasses enable her to be mobile and she can move around the room fairly safely. However, with the crowded space and clutter, she is unable to identify specific play areas or favorite toys. To solve the space problem, Mr. Ramirez has placed several bins of toys and materials on movable carts, which tend to be placed wherever is convenient at the moment to get them out of the way.

Rafik is a boisterous child in constant motion. According to his mother he is currently being evaluated for ADHD (attention deficit/hyperactivity disorder). He wanders around the classroom and is rarely able to focus on one activity. He may pick up an object, but then he throws it down and moves completely away from the area to another part of the room. Rafik particularly has trouble with circle time. It seems impossible for him to sit more than two minutes, after which he gets up and begins moving around the room as usual. Because there is not enough room for a separate area for circle time, Mr. Ramirez conducts his circle time in different areas: sometimes in the block area, sometimes outside, sometimes at the snack table. With the addition of the two new children, the classroom space now seems intolerably small.

Mr. Ramirez is very concerned about meeting the special needs of Sung and Rafik. He asks Ms. Thomas, the inclusion support provider, if she has any suggestions for supporting the two children. After observing the children on several occasions and talking at length with Mr. Ramirez and the assistant teacher, Ms. Thomas suggests several strategies. First, the movable carts need to be housed in one place until they are needed. Moving the carts into the appropriate area as they are needed has been incorporated into the daily schedule as a predictable, separate task with which children are assigned to help. Rafik especially enjoys pushing the cart from one place to another. This keeps the carts from just being part of the clutter.

Another strategy is to use colorful reflecting tape to mark off specific areas of the room—the block area, the library corner, and the dress-up area—each with a different color and one with a contrasting broken line pattern. Mr. Ramirez has also reduced the toys and materials available by a third, eliminating the less preferred or broken toys. This makes it easier to arrange materials on shelves, with more space between them, and to label the shelves so the materials can be consistently stored in the same place.

Finally, Mr. Ramirez decided that his class will have circle time each day in the library corner, because he often includes reading as a circle time activity. He has also noted that this is the area where Rafik seems to be the calmest, perhaps because it is a fairly enclosed space.

With some assistance Sung has learned to use her residual sight to move quite confidently around the room and to find her favorite toys, which are now stored in a consistent place. Rafik seems calmer and has begun to prefer the block area and the library corner, where he spends at least a few minutes focusing on a single activity.

Read–Reflect–Discuss Questions

1. Which accommodations were most helpful for Rafik? Why?
2. Which accommodations were most helpful for Sung? Why?
3. If Mr. Ramirez were given $5,000 to improve his classroom environment, how would you recommend he spend it?

Key Terms

activity area   manipulatives   traffic management

Helpful Resources

Organizations and Reports

American Society of Landscape Architects, 636 Eye Street NW, Washington, DC 20001-3736, (202) 898-2444, www.asla.org

Assistive Technology Educational Network (ATEN), 1207 Mellonville Avenue, Sanford, FL 32771, (407) 320-2379, www.icdri.org

International Play Equipment Manufacturers Association, 2207 Forest Hills Drive, Harrisburg, PA 17112, (717) 238-1744, (888) 944-7362, www.ipema.org/main.cfm

Public playground safety handbook, U.S. Consumer Product Safety Commission, 4330 East West Highway, Bethesda, MD 20814, (301) 504-7923, www.cpsc.gov

Standard consumer safety performance specification for playground equipment for public use (#F1487-98) and *Standard specification for determination of accessibility of surface systems under and around playground equipment* (#F1951-99), American Society for Testing and Materials, 100 Barr Harbor Drive, West Conshohocken, PA 19428, (610) 832-9500, www.astm.org

United States Access Board, 1331 F Street NW, Suite 1000, Washington, DC 20004-1111, (202) 272-0080 or (800) 872-2253, www.access-board.gov

Playground Equipment Companies

KOMPAN Playgrounds, 930 Broadway, Tacoma, WA 98402, (800) 426-9788, www.kompan.us

PlayDesigns, 6536 Oak Hollow Circle, Indianapolis, IN 46236, (800) 667-0097, www.playgroundequipment.com

Catalogs for Adaptive Equipment

AbleNet Inc., 2625 Patton Road, Roseville, MN 55113-1308, (800) 322-0956, www.ablenetinc.com

Guide to toys for children who are blind or visually impaired, FamilyConnect, American Foundation for the Blind, 2 Penn Plaza, Suite 1102, New York, NY 10121, familyconnect.org/info/toy-guide/2

Rifton, P.O. Box 260, Rifton, NY 12471-0260, (800) 571-8198, www.rifton.com

Tumble Form, for positioning, seating, and mobility (#3431), and Pediatrics: Special needs products for schools and clinics, Sammons Preston, P.O. Box 5071, Bolingbrook, IL 60440-9977, (800) 323-5547

Curricula

Dodge, D., Aghayan, C., Berke, K., Bichart, T., Burts, D., Colker, L., Copley, J., Dighe, J., Heroman, C., Jones, C., & Tabors, P. (2010). *The creative curriculum for preschool*. Washington, DC: Teaching Strategies Inc.

CHAPTER 5

Preventing and Managing Challenging Behaviors

LEARNING OBJECTIVES

After studying this chapter, you will be able to:

LO 5-1: Describe how challenging behavior is defined.

LO 5-2: Explain how specific disabilities might increase the likelihood for challenging behaviors.

LO 5-3: Identify the three causes/functions of inappropriate behavior.

LO 5-4: Recognize the impact language differences can have on behavior.

LO 5-5: Discuss teaching strategies to prevent or reduce challenging behaviors for children with disabilities.

LO 5-6: Describe how a multitiered system of support might help to enhance the development of ALL children.

LO 5-7: Explain behavior modification and the use of reinforcement techniques.

LO 5-8: Define the steps of a positive behavior support plan.

LO 5-9: Discuss the advantages and potential disadvantages of assigning a one-to-one aide.

The following NAEYC Standards and DEC Recommended Practices are addressed in this chapter:

naeyc

Standard 1: Promoting Child Development and Learning
Standard 4: Using Developmentally Effective Approaches
Standard 6: Becoming a Professional

DEC

Practice 2: Environment
Practice 4: Instruction
Practice 5: Interaction
Practice 6: Teaming and Collaboration

Many behavior challenges often displayed by children with special needs can be prevented using simple strategies:

A *behavior challenge* is not an absolute. Many may be considered to be challenging in one situation and not a challenge in another context or by other people. Behavior challenges are socially and culturally determined. Teachers must be able to specifically define the behavior and state why the behavior is unacceptable. They must also try to understand the *function* of the behavior:

- **Children who have special needs may be more likely to develop challenging behavior patterns.** This may be due to difficulties with impulse control, low frustration tolerance, hyperirritability, and lack of appropriate communication skills.

- **Inappropriate behaviors in young children with special needs often function as an attempt to communicate.** They may be signaling a need to escape an unpleasant situation or sensation, a desire to obtain a preferred object or activity, or a need for attention.

- **Prevention is the key.** Teachers can implement general strategies to prevent challenging behaviors from happening in the first place or to reduce the occurrence of challenging behaviors.

- **The assistance of a behavior specialist or inclusion consultant may be needed for persistent and severe behavior challenges.** Specialists conduct a careful functional assessment of the antecedents and consequences of persistent and severe behavior challenges, and design a behavioral intervention plan that will eventually modify children's behavior.

- **Positive behavior support techniques consider many challenging behaviors as attempts to communicate.** In these cases the goal is to provide acceptable replacement behaviors that allow children to communicate in more appropriate ways. This approach also focuses on identifying the trigger or antecedent of the behavior.

Introduction

One of the most common causes of failure of inclusive placements for children with special needs is the challenge of dealing with difficult behaviors. Young children with special needs often demonstrate behavior that is atypical or inappropriate. Sometimes this behavior is truly disruptive. Occasionally the behavior is dangerous. Early childhood educators must have some understanding of how such behaviors develop and which strategies and resources are available for preventing and managing them.

5-1 What Is a Challenging Behavior Anyway?

Although some behaviors—particularly those that cause pain or injury to others—are clearly unacceptable, many behavior challenges are defined by the individuals or community around the child. In these cases the behavior challenge often consists of breaking a rule. For example, when you visit two elementary school classrooms, you notice that Mrs. Quincy's classroom is very quiet, while Mr. Nelson's class is very noisy. This reflects the rules and expectations set by the two teachers. Mrs. Quincy believes that a quiet classroom is essential to learning. Mr. Nelson, on the other hand, believes that young children must be actively engaged in the learning process and that children cannot learn in silence. Thus, although children's noisy chatter in Mr. Nelson's classroom is considered evidence of active learning, the loud talkative child in Mrs. Quincy's room may be considered a behavior problem.

In another example, you visit two preschool classrooms. In the first classroom you notice a three-year-old boy aggressively push another child away who is trying to take his toy. His teacher says to him, "Don't push him. Say, 'No, I'm playing with this now.'" Later you are observing another preschool classroom. A similar episode occurs. But in this classroom the teacher swiftly intervenes saying, "That's too rough. You may not push him. You can go to the time-out corner until you are ready to play nicely and learn to share." The teacher in the first class sees the boy's behavior as age appropriate, and not a problem. She believes the child will eventually learn more appropriate behavior with proper modeling. The teacher in the second classroom strongly believes any kind of physically aggressive behavior is unacceptable and wants children to learn this quickly.

In the first preschool class the behavior is seen as normal; in the second it is considered a behavior challenge. Sometimes the easiest way to deal with such challenges is simply to change the rules (for example, allow everyone to take off their shoes), or to *extinguish* the behavior by ignoring it. The story of "Joey's Shoes" demonstrates this idea in practice.

Joey's Shoes

Joey had been in the center-based program for three months. On a hot day shortly after beginning the program, his teacher, Miss Puente, took all the children's shoes off so they could wade in the wading pool. Joey enjoyed this activity. Unfortunately, from that day on, Joey insisted on taking his shoes off every day as soon as he arrived at the center. Every day a major battle was waged over Joey's shoes. He was unhappy until his shoes were off. Then he seemed fine. The teacher spoke with his father about the problem. He insisted Joey should keep his shoes on. Joey's father bought him a new pair of shoes, just in case he had outgrown the old ones, which might make them uncomfortable. Joey still insisted on taking off his shoes at the center, and he would cry and kick when the teacher put them back on.

One day Miss Puente asked Joey's dad if he minded Joey taking his shoes off while in the center. Dad indicated that Joey did not do this at home, only at the center. But, he reluctantly agreed that it would be all right for Miss Puente to try ignoring the behavior.

Once this policy was implemented, Joey's tantrums subsided and he participated willingly in the daily activities. He continued to wear his shoes at home with no problem. Within three months Joey began to forget about taking his shoes off on some days at the center. By the end of the year this behavior had disappeared.

In Joey's case, the so-called challenging behavior was simply redefined to not be a problem. Teachers are often hesitant to change a rule or expectation because it may seem as if they are giving in. But sometimes, as happened with Joey, the behavior is eventually *extinguished* when it is no longer an issue. However, teachers really should realize the advantage of changing expectations if they learn the expectations are unreasonable or developmentally inappropriate.

5-2 Behavior Challenges in Children with Special Needs

Any child, regardless of whether or not he has special needs, can develop patterns of behavior that are disruptive or considered unacceptable. The characteristics of certain disability conditions, however, may increase the likelihood that a child will develop challenging behaviors.

5-2a Neurological Disorders

One common cause of behavior challenges in children with neurological disorders is difficulty with impulse control. These children often react quickly and aggressively to any situation that increases frustration. Young children who have suffered head trauma, for example, may be *emotionally labile,* resulting in frequent unexplained crying.

5-2b Autism

Children with autism can often engage in disruptive behaviors such as tantrums or running away. They frequently have extreme sensitivity to certain sounds and to being touched (**tactile defensiveness**). As a result they may engage in inappropriate behaviors to escape certain unpleasant or overwhelming situations. Some children may engage in **repetitive behavior**, such as twirling objects, hand flapping, and rocking, as a means of reducing anxiety and calming themselves. Such behavior may enable a child to block out something stressful in the environment. As is the case with many children with special needs, children who have autism may have difficulty coping with *unpredictable* environments. Thus, the less predictable and organized the environment is, the greater the likelihood that children will develop challenging behaviors.

5-2c Communication Disorders

Children who have limited communication skills may develop disruptive behavior patterns as a primitive means of controlling their environment and communicating wants and needs. Assisting these children in learning functional communication skills, which may include words, gestures, signs, or pictures, will often significantly reduce behavior challenges.

5-2d Seizure Disorders

Occasionally, unusual or explosive behaviors can be the result of seizures. Teachers must be aware of seizure disorders in children and be familiar with appropriate first aid and medication schedules.

5-3 Causes/Functions of Inappropriate Behavior

If you've determined that a behavior cannot simply be defined away or ignored and that it is truly disruptive (for example, screaming or throwing things) or potentially harmful (biting, hitting, or self-injurious behavior), the next step is to determine its cause and/or function. Behavior specialists are trained to conduct a detailed functional behavior assessment to help teachers and parents manage and support children with extremely challenging behaviors (Cipani & Schock, 2011). There are a limited number of possible reasons why a child might engage in unacceptable behavior, including the following:

- To escape something unpleasant
- To get attention
- To gain access to something the child wants

5-3a Escape

In some cases the child may be trying to alleviate an **internal state**. For example, the child may be in some kind of discomfort or may feel extremely stressed or anxious, related to physiological or biological factors rather than external conditions. Such internal states may be affected by medication, diet, illness, and emotional upset at home or in the classroom. Children who are extremely hyperactive due to attention deficit/hyperactivity disorder (ADHD) may experience a strong neurologically based drive to move and act in the environment. If this is not properly directed, this hyperactivity can easily translate into behavior challenges.

More often, the child is trying to escape environmental conditions that cause stress, anxiety, or discomfort. A child with sensitive hearing (often the case for a child with autism, for example) may experience discomfort in a noisy room. The most common environmental conditions that cause stress or discomfort include:

- Noisy and/or highly resonant acoustic environment
- Too many children
- Other children in close proximity
- Cluttered, disorganized classroom
- Visually overstimulating environment such as one with colorful materials on every bit of wall space and collages hanging from the ceiling
- Large open spaces with no boundaries

The child may be trying to escape a specific task or activity he dislikes or that is difficult for him to do. For example, a child may hate brushing his teeth, or he may not want to touch the cornstarch-and-water *goop*. Also, a child may try to leave the table during fine motor activities, such as writing and cutting, because it is hard to be motivated and stay on task when the activity is difficult. Teachers must ensure that activities are at each child's developmental level or provide appropriate adaptations by using the EESS acronym and levels of support discussed in Chapter 2. For example, during activities such as cutting three drawn circles for an art activity, teachers can:

Photo 5-1 A child's tantrum can sometimes be interpreted as an escape behavior.

- **E**nlarge the scissors by wrapping pipe cleaners around the finger holes to better fit tiny hands.
- **E**nhance the circles by outlining them in yellow so it's easier to see where to cut.
- **S**tabilize the paper by using heavier paper such as card stock as it is not so flimsy to hold while cutting.
- **S**implify the instructions to allow children to cut out half circles if they are not able to cut out a complete circle or ask them to cut fewer circles.

Examples of Escape Behaviors. Some escape behaviors are obvious, such as running away or refusing to stay seated. Just as often, however, the behaviors are less easily interpreted (see Photo 5-1). Consider the following list of behaviors that are frequently caused by a need to escape:

- Running away
- Refusing to stay seated
- Crawling into an enclosed space or under a table
- Having a tantrum
- Covering ears
- Screaming
- Throwing objects
- Hitting or biting
- Biting own hand or other self-injurious behavior
- Rocking, hand flapping, or other self-stimulatory behavior

5-3b Attention Seeking

Many children, with and without disabilities, need and enjoy adult attention. Frequently the primary motivation of unacceptable behavior is to gain attention and interaction from a caregiver or significant adult. An effective general strategy to significantly reduce behavior challenges is to make sure you are giving children adequate

Photo 5-2 Providing one-on-one attention to each child can help reduce the challenging behaviors associated with attention seeking.

individual attention while providing warmth and support. Make sure you connect with each child on an intimate, one-on-one basis, frequently throughout the day. This means being at children's eye level, patiently listening to both words and feelings, and validating them as individuals (see Photo 5-2). The following are common attention-getting behaviors:

- Running away
- Wandering in the classroom
- Leaving an activity
- Picking on peers
- Having a tantrum
- Removing clothing
- Destroying property
- Turning water/lights on or off
- Crawling under table

5-3c Gaining Access

In this case a child engages in unacceptable behavior to gain access to an object, sensation, or activity the child finds pleasurable. For example, a child may not be running away to escape or to gain attention, but because she loves being outside. The child may turn the lights on and off not because she wants the teacher's attention, but because she loves the visual effect of the flickering lights. A child might also try to gain access to another's toy by snatching it away. Frequently, children with disabilities lack the communication skills to ask for a turn or to enter into play.

5-4 The Impact of Language Differences on Behavior

We have become increasingly aware that children from homes where languages other than English are spoken find learning English to be a challenge. The extent of the challenge and the time it takes to function well in English vary from child to child. Learning is impacted by children's age, personality, motivation, knowledge of their native language, and exposure to English. While they are going through the stages of learning, they are likely to go through a nonverbal period. They may choose not to speak, primarily use gestures, or isolate themselves as they observe and listen to what is happening around them. They may also seek an isolated place to practice new words they have heard. They might pretend to understand, when they don't actually grasp what is going on. They could be inconsistent in responding as directions given are not totally clear (Santos & Ostrosky, 2002).

It is critical that teachers work with families to gather information about a child's skill development, in English, so they can readily distinguish between a challenging behavior and behaviors associated with second-language acquisition. Such behaviors may include not following directions, not responding when asked, showing difficulty expressing ideas and feelings, and inconsistently responding to questions.

5-5 General Strategies for Preventing and Reducing the Occurrence of Challenging Behaviors

Certain classroom organization strategies and ways of interacting with children can prevent or significantly reduce the frequency of unacceptable behaviors in a center-based setting. This section summarizes both of these strategies.

5-5a Keep the Number of Rules/Expectations Small

The more rules there are, the more likely children are to get into trouble. Keep rules to no more than three or four. Some children with special needs may not be able to handle more than one or two rules. Rules must be clearly defined by telling children what is expected and realistic for the range of developmental levels represented in the group. The concept of rules might be better stated as *expectations*. Expectations are usually stated in the positive and tell children *what to do* rather than *what not to do*.

5-5b Select Rules/Expectations Carefully

Important rules and expectations for very young children are intended to prevent behaviors that are harmful to themselves or to other children and to teach children what behaviors are expected. Thus, aggressive behavior—hitting, biting, throwing, or kicking—is always unacceptable, as is behavior that is dangerous to oneself, such as climbing up on a counter, head banging, or running inside. Teachers should clearly inform and remind children that such behavior will not be permitted. At the same time, it is just as important to remind children what to do. Rules and expectations need to be explained and written in the positive so that they tell students exactly what behavior is expected. For example, instead of saying, "No running!" say, "Please walk." The following examples tell children what to do and what is expected.

> Say: *Put your feet on the floor!*
> Instead of: *Don't climb on the table!*
> Say: *Use your quiet voice inside.*
> Instead of: *Don't scream!*

This is especially crucial for children who have issues with impulse control. Learning self-control can be a major challenge, and frequently reminding children about *what to do* is critical to children's success and the development of prosocial behavior.

5-5c Be Clear and Consistent about Enforcement

Children with special needs have difficulty learning rules and expectations if they are not clearly demonstrated and followed up with consistent consequences. Keep in mind that some children who have special needs cannot comprehend what you say through words alone. They will need clear demonstrations of what to do using gestures, signs, pictures, and modeling. Simply saying to the child "One of our rules is that you may not climb on the tables," may have no effect on some children. Through consistent consequences for climbing on the table, children will eventually learn that this is unacceptable. In addition, making sure to remind them about what to do will help them learn a more acceptable behavior, that is, saying "Place your feet on the floor." Your facial expression and intonation also help convey that the behavior is unacceptable. Saying "Get down from the table" with a pleasant facial expression will *not* help children understand that they are breaking a rule or not meeting an expectation. Because they may not understand your words, if the intonation in your voice is pleasant and you're smiling, they may be confused and think they're doing a good thing!

5-5d Avoid Overstimulating, Disorganized Environments

Environments that have unclear traffic patterns and are noisy, visually *busy*, cluttered, and messy are more likely to produce behavior challenges (see Chapter 4).

5-5e Maintain a Predictable Daily Schedule with Regular Routines

ECSE teachers insist this is one of the most effective strategies for reducing behavior challenges. When children are confident about what happens next and activities are scheduled in ways that maximize participation and minimize fatigue, they are less likely to engage in unacceptable behavior. However some children might need a more specific strategy. For example, Hayden needed to get his diaper changed before he was able to line up to go outside. He screamed, cried, and had a lot of anxiety about going into the bathroom. He kept trying to line up instead. He was given a *first-then* schedule where staff pointed to a picture of a diaper and then a picture of the playground. After many repetitions of seeing and hearing, "first diaper, then outside," Hayden was able to predict and trust that after getting his diaper changed he was going to get to go outside. His unpleasant behavior decreased and, eventually, he no longer needed to misbehave. A more detailed discussion of the daily schedule is found in Chapter 2.

5-5f Carefully Plan Transitions

Transitions from one activity to another can present challenges for children with special needs. Carefully planned transitions take into account signals, sequences, and consistency. Children are less likely to engage in challenging behavior when they are aware of and can anticipate changes. Avoid unproductive waiting time.

Provide Clear Signals. Develop a series of signals to signify the end of an activity and the beginning of a transition, such as playing or singing a certain song, or ringing a bell. Many children with special needs may respond well to objects or pictures as signals rather than to auditory signals. Such signals can be especially important for learners of a second language. Equally important is to make sure we give children a warning signal that the transition is coming up. Teachers frequently give a five-minute warning through specific strategies such as using a visual timer, telling children they have five more minutes to play, or showing a picture such as a hand with the number 5 on it. Some teachers then give a one-minute warning to help students prepare for the transition. A few children may benefit from being given a specific task such as putting the bowls in the sink rather than just being asked to "clean up."

A Specific Sequence. Follow a regular sequence of events within the transition, such as this example of progressing from an outside activity to snack:

1. Give a five-minute warning.
2. Bell rings, signaling end of outside activity.
3. Teacher says, "Okay, time to clean up and then go in for snack."
4. Children put away trikes, cover sand and water tables, and collect other toys.
5. Children line up at the door.
6. Teacher says, "Okay, everyone is ready to go in for a snack!"
7. Teacher leads children inside.

Consistency. Use the same cues and sequence each time the transition occurs.

5-5g Give Attention *Before* Inappropriate Behavior Occurs

For children whose disruptive behavior seems to be motivated by the need for adult attention, paying extra attention to them before they demand attention can significantly reduce inappropriate behaviors. The way to do this is to give positive attention and encouragement when a child is doing what he is expected to do or when he is engaging in an appropriate activity.

5-5h Use Touch to De-Escalate Behavior

Sometimes touching a child can help the child gain control of herself. This may be particularly true for a child who has issues with attention and hyperactivity or for a child with poor **receptive language**, meaning poor understanding of language, who cannot rely on verbal cues alone. Even using proximity (standing near a child) might be all the support a student needs to gain control. It's a reminder to the child that the teacher is near to add support if needed.

> **Helpful Hint**
>
> For children who engage in dangerous and/or difficult-to-manage disruptive behavior, it may be helpful for teachers and staff to receive certified training in safe and effective de-escalation techniques.

5-6 Multitiered Systems of Support

The **Teaching Pyramid Model**, advocated by Fox and colleagues (2003), is an example of a **multitiered system of support** within the classroom learning environment that is increasingly being used to promote social, emotional, and behavioral development of young children. Even a well-planned learning environment cannot prevent all challenging behaviors. The first tier as shown in Figure 5-1 emphasizes the development of positive relationships with children, families, and colleagues as the foundation of effective inclusion for ALL children. The second tier, as one climbs the pyramid, is also for ALL children. It includes previously mentioned preventative classroom interventions that support high-quality environments.

Social-emotional teaching strategies, such as helping children learn vocabulary that they can use to express their feelings, are a part of the third tier. When working

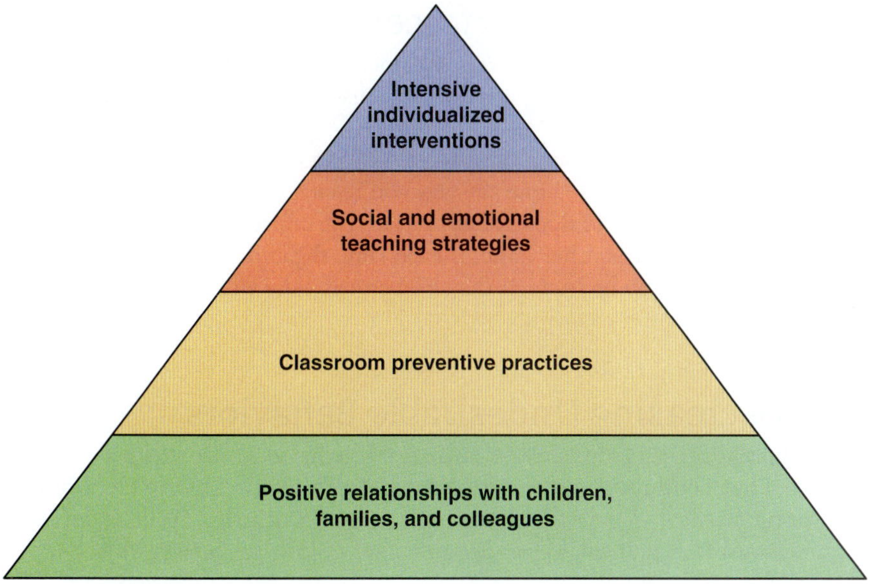
Intensive individualized interventions
Social and emotional teaching strategies
Classroom preventive practices
Positive relationships with children, families, and colleagues

Figure 5-1 The Teaching Pyramid

at this level, teachers will find that some children will need more targeted social and emotional supports such as specific strategies for identifying emotions, problem solving, and making friends. Finally, tier four provides the intensive, individualized assessment and support that might be needed to enhance the development of a few children. This more targeted support is usually outlined in a specific behavior plan as discussed in the following sections. (For additional information on the multitiered approach, see the resources at the end of the chapter.)

WEBLINK

For more information and a wealth of teacher resources, see the Center on the Social and Emotional Foundations for Early Learning (CSEFEL) at http://csefel.vanderbilt.edu/.

5-7 Behavior Modification and the Use of Functional Behavior Assessment and Positive Behavior Support

One of the most commonly used strategies for understanding why children engage in challenging behavior is referred to as *functional behavior analysis.* This is the fourth and final level of the Teaching Pyramid Model discussed earlier. It is intensive, individualized support usually developed and implemented with a team of professionals, including a behavior or inclusion specialist. Space does not allow for a detailed description of this procedure here. However, the basic elements include the principles of **behavior modification**, that is, what happens immediately *following* a child's behavior may strengthen or weaken that behavior, depending upon whether the child enjoys it or dislikes it:

- What happens immediately *following* a behavior is called a **consequence**.
- If the child finds the consequence pleasant and the behavior increases or is strengthened, the consequence is called a **reinforcer**.
- If the consequence is unpleasant, it is called an **aversive stimulus**.
- If the behavior is weakened or decreases in frequency, the consequence may be considered to be a **punishment**.

For example, if a dog growls and walks away every time a child tries to pet it, the child will soon quit trying to pet the dog (assuming that he finds the dog's growling unpleasant). On the other hand, if the dog comes closer and licks him, he will probably pet the dog even more (assuming that the child enjoys being licked!).

5-7a Identifying a Reinforcer

Of course the key to using positive reinforcement is figuring out what is positively reinforcing. If a child does not experience the consequence as *pleasurable,* it will have no effect.

For example, a teacher may intend to reinforce a child for sitting during circle time by using praise such as "I like the way you're sitting. You are sitting quietly at circle." However, if the child does not appreciate the praise, it will have no effect on increasing sitting. On the other hand, if each time the child sits down, her favorite friend sits down next to her (which the child enjoys), she will continue to sit down willingly at circle time.

5-7b Decreasing Undesirable Behaviors

Several approaches can help decrease undesirable behaviors once they are already established. First, conduct a *functional behavior analysis* by observing and describing the inappropriate behavior in detail (for example, carefully describe the behavior—when it occurs, how often, and what precedes and what follows the behavior):

1. Determine whether the behavior is being inadvertently reinforced and remove the reinforcing consequence (see example of Elena).
2. Provide positive behavior support (PBS) by teaching a new *replacement* behavior that is more acceptable. For example, teach a child who kicks when a peer takes away his toy to say "no" instead of kicking.
3. Provide positive behavior support by reinforcing the replacement behavior. This can be especially effective if the replacement behavior is incompatible with the problem behavior, such as when a child signs *Stop* rather than hitting.
4. Provide natural consequences that are unpleasant. For example, a child's playmate may get up and leave the offending child alone in the play area.

Elena's Favorite Adult

Elena had difficulty focusing on any appropriate activity during free play. She tended to simply wander around the room, occasionally stopping to kick or push another child. Because the behavior seemed to be escalating and causing other children to be fearful of Elena, the teacher requested that the behavior specialist conduct an assessment.

The itinerant behavior specialist agreed to carefully observe Elena in the classroom to conduct a functional behavior analysis and recommend and develop a positive behavior support plan.

The first step of a functional behavior assessment is to conduct an A-B-C analysis by carefully observing the behavior over several days:

1. Observe what happens before the behavior occurs (the *antecedent*).
2. Describe the disruptive *behavior* in detail.
3. Describe what happens after the behavior occurs (the *consequence*).

The behavior specialist observed that Elena's disruptive behavior usually resulted in her favorite teacher, Miss Long, taking Elena by the hand and pulling her away from another child. Miss Long would spend a few moments engaging Elena in playing with a toy and then walk away. Elena would then abandon her play, walk around the room, and grab a toy away from another peer. Thus, Elena was being *reinforced* for kicking and pushing because it resulted in an interaction with her favorite adult. And she was being *punished* for engaging with the toy because as soon as she became interested in it, her favorite adult walked away! Elena was only able to obtain Miss Long's attention again by repeating her disruptive behavior. In this case, the *function* of Elena's disruptive behavior was to obtain attention from her favorite person.

Using the results of this functional behavior assessment, Miss Long decided to try another approach. Each time she noticed Elena engaged with other children in any appropriate activity, she approached her and played with her. If Elena behaved aggressively toward another child, Miss Long would walk away from her, and have a classroom volunteer or other less familiar adult approach Elena and sternly say, "Elena, you may not kick!" Then the adult would swiftly move her to another part of the room. By using this new approach, Elena was being reinforced by the presence of Miss Long for appropriate positive behavior, and her aggressive behavior was not being reinforced.

5-7c Use of Extinction

When the purpose of a behavior is primarily to gain attention, another effective way to decrease the behavior is through **extinction**. The behavior disappears when it is ignored. Obviously, some behaviors are too serious to be ignored. However, for behaviors that are not extremely disruptive or dangerous, extinction can be an effective strategy. With this procedure children learn that the behavior produces no effect. Eventually the rate of the behavior will diminish significantly. (The behavior may *intensify* initially for a period of time. It is important for all staff to not be surprised by this result, or they will become discouraged with the procedure.)

Extinction Procedure for Jill

Jill dumped out all the Legos, scattering them on the floor, almost every day. Mr. Clay began to suspect that this was a way of getting his attention. His typical response was to express his frustration by saying, "Oh there she goes again!" He would promptly sit down beside her while he helped her put the Legos back in the box.

Mr. Clay implemented an extinction procedure by paying no attention to Jill at all when she dumped the Legos. He also had to ignore the children who were compelled to tattle on Jill when he failed to notice her. For about a week, Jill dumped the Legos two or three times a day. But no adult responded to her behavior. By the end of the fourth week, Jill no longer dumped the Legos.

A note on attention seeking: It is important that attention seeking not be viewed negatively. All children—indeed all humans—seek attention. It is part of our DNA to be social. Children who do not seek or enjoy attention are atypical. The caution here is that adults should avoid *unintentionally reinforcing* disruptive or aggressive behaviors in children. Adults should be mindful of paying *positive* attention to the child's appropriate bids for attention, and ignore inappropriate attention-seeking behaviors (that is, if those behaviors pose no threat to themselves or others).

5-7d Problems with the Use of Punishment/ Negative Consequences

Even though it is possible to decrease the rate of a challenging behavior through punishment (providing negative consequences), in most cases, use of punishment should be avoided.

A common negative consequence used in early childhood programs is the familiar time-out. A preferred term is **time away**. This procedure should be used cautiously and infrequently and never with children under the developmental age of two. A carefully implemented time-away procedure can provide an opportunity for some children to *reorganize* themselves after losing self-control. Some children actually learn to use a self-imposed time away, which can increase their confidence in their ability to manage themselves (Cook, Klein, & Chen, 2016). If you choose to use time away, the following considerations are important:

- Make sure the child understands exactly what behavior will result in time away.
- Warn the child, calmly, only once.

- Be sure the child is within the teacher's view at all times.
- Keep the time away very short.
- Be positive at the end of the time away; praise the child for being in control of himself or herself. Help the child choose and engage in another activity.
- Monitor the behavior of other children to be certain they are not giving the child either positive or negative attention.

In reality, time away can sometimes inadvertently reinforce negative behaviors. Being away can become a positive experience for young children. In fact, if certain children are repeatedly in time away, then it may be possible that time away is serving as a positive experience for that child. It may help the child avoid an aversive experience. It may provide attention and access to a favorite adult. And it may provide the child with a much-needed break from an overstimulating or very demanding situation. In such situations, time away is not an effective approach to the management of behavior. The child is likely to repeat the behavior that earlier led to the consequence of being sent away. Most of all, time away should never be the only approach to dealing with challenging behaviors.

Another commonly used negative consequence is taking something away or not rewarding the child, such as not giving the child a sticker. For developmentally young children this is an ineffective and inappropriate practice. Young children, especially those with cognitive disabilities, will have a difficult time understanding the meaning of **delayed reinforcement**, when responses are not given at the time of the behavior. They will not grasp the connection between the behavior and the consequence.

One common use of negative consequences, which is somewhat controversial, is a color-coded card system in which a red, yellow, or green card is placed next to the child's name on a display in front of the classroom. There are numerous variations of this approach. For example, children start the day with their name on the neutral yellow card. When a child does something that the teacher deems as negative, she announces that the child now is on the red card; when the child improves or does something positive, the child's name is moved to yellow or green, and so on.

Although this system may work well for some children, it is essentially a system of *shame and praise*. For some children, public shaming may be experienced as severe and degrading. Also, for many children with cognitive delays, the system is not understandable.

Teachers of preschool children with special needs sometimes use a modified version of this system. It focuses more on acknowledging "good" behavior by placing the child's name on a particular card to acknowledge a positive behavior (for example, "Samuel has been sitting so nicely and listening to the story this morning. So he's on green.") Although this is a more positive approach, some children may still be sensitive to *not* being on the *good* card.

Finally, even if punishment can sometimes help control an undesirable behavior, it may produce unwanted and unnecessary emotional side effects. Thus, the authors of this text believe that punishment (or *negative consequences*) should be used very cautiously and reserved for the most severe behavior disorders. If used, it should be used in careful collaboration with a behavior specialist.

Now that we have addressed some of the common approaches to the management of challenging behavior, it is time to consider the additional assessment and support services that might be needed if challenging behaviors persist beyond what can be considered developmentally appropriate.

One Five-Year-Old's Perception of Classroom Management

Many young children are extremely aware of their peers' *good and bad* behaviors, and how teachers respond to them. The following describes an interview with a five-year-old when asked what happened when children misbehaved in his classroom.

WEBLINK

For a discussion of the downsides of the color-coded card system, see the following site: www.progressivepreceptors.com/blog/rip-those-behavior-charts-off-of-the-wall-and-burn-them.

Alex is a well-behaved—and very *observant*—kindergartner! Here are some highlights of his lengthy response:

> Oh, it works really well. Sometimes my teacher will tell Brandon to look at how nicely Alex is sitting. So, it makes me want to stay like that. One boy is really good. He never ever says *anything!*
>
> If someone does something bad, like Eric, she says, "If you do it again there will be consequences." And, then if it doesn't stop, you get something bad on your report card.
>
> If they do something really, really bad, and then do it again, they get benched in the principal's office!

It is abundantly clear that Alex is very aware of good behavior and bad behavior, which may be a plus. Unfortunately, he is also beginning to identify certain peers (and himself) as *good* or *bad,* depending on their behavior.

5-8 Designing Positive Behavior Support Plans

Positive behavior support is an approach to managing behavior that focuses on understanding the function of the behavior and attempts to prevent the behavior rather than following through on consequences for the behavior after it occurs (Dunlap et al., 2013). This approach also determines what factors can be put in place that will support positive behavior rather than triggering or reinforcing negative behavior.

5-8a Understanding Challenging Behaviors as Communication

Often problem behaviors occur in children who cannot express themselves verbally. Many children with special needs have limited language skills. They frequently express strongly felt needs in nonverbal ways. All too often these nonverbal communications are inappropriate and consequently identified as behavior challenges (see Figure 5-2).

Understanding Frederika's Behavior as Communication

Frederika was a child who was very tactilely defensive. She hated being touched and crowded by the other children. When another child got too close to her, especially if the child was noisy and moving fast, she would immediately throw whatever object was within her reach. Throwing things was the only way (and a very effective way) she knew to communicate that children were getting too close to her. Her teacher selected a more acceptable communication behavior as a replacement. Frederika was taught to hold up the palm of her hand to signal "Stop!" The other children in the class were taught to respect this communication and to back away slightly. This gave Frederika a great feeling of control. Once she had generalized this communicative response to several play situations, she rarely threw things. She also gradually became more tolerant of children in close proximity.

Figure 5-2 Disruptive behavior may be a child's only or most effective way of communicating. A replacement behavior must be taught.

Traditional applications of behavior modification have concentrated on eliminating the unacceptable behavior by applying consequences such as time away. However, in recent years there has been an increasing emphasis on preventing challenging behaviors by analyzing the cause and/or purpose (function) of the unacceptable behavior. This approach, which is an important step to reducing challenging behaviors, involves determination of the **communicative function** of the behavior. One effective way to determine the communicative function of a behavior is to do an **A-B-C analysis**. In this analysis, one carefully observes the *antecedent,* the *behavior,* and the *consequence* of the behavior over several days. By determining the antecedent and consequence of an undesirable behavior, teachers and others can speculate about the purpose of the behavior. Once the purpose is determined, a more appropriate communicative behavior can be taught. This is referred to as a **replacement behavior**. The implementation of a functional behavior assessment may require the assistance of an extra person. The elements of this technique follow in Figure 5-3.

Understanding what happens immediately after behavior can lead to an understanding of what the child is trying to gain from acting as he or she has acted. Figure 5-4 illustrates the functional behavior assessment of Frederika's challenging behavior.

Step 1: Carefully describe the unacceptable **behavior**.
- What does the child actually do? Describe the sequence. For example:
- Child looks at the teacher.
- Child begins to scream.
- As teacher approaches, child runs toward door. Notice:
  - When does he do it?
  - Where does the behavior occur?
  - Who is usually present when the behavior occurs?

Step 2: Identify the **antecedents** (behavior triggers).
- What happened immediately *before* the behavior?
  - Does it happen at the same time every day?
  - Does it happen with the same child or adult?
  - Does it happen in the same area or with the same materials?
  - Do the adults always react in the same way?
- What sets off the child's behavior?
  - Someone else grabbing the toy
  - Someone else getting too close
  - A teacher saying something or giving directions

Step 3: Watch closely to see the **consequences** of the child's behavior.
- What happened immediately after the behavior?
- What do the other children around him or her do?
- What does the teacher do?
- Is she somehow reinforcing the behavior?
- What does the child with the inappropriate behavior do?
- Does he get to keep the object or continue to play?

Understanding what happens immediately after behavior can lead to an understanding of what the child is trying to gain from acting as he or she has acted.

Step 4: Hypothesize about why this behavior occurs.
- Is the cause internal (for example, medication, illness, fatigue, low threshold)?
- Is the child trying to escape?
- Is the child trying to get attention?
- Is the child trying to obtain a desirable object or activity?

Step 5: Determine a possible communicative value of the behavior.
- Is the child using this behavior noted in Step 2 to try to tell us something? Like:
  - "I'm in pain."
  - "Let me out of here!"
  - "Please touch me (look at me, talk to me, come close to me)."
  - "I would rather play with the Legos or be outside on the swing."

Figure 5-3 Functional Behavior Support Analysis Procedure

⌄⌄ **Professional Resource Download**

Behavior Observation Chart
A-B-C Analysis

Student Name: **Frederika**   Observer Name: **Teacher Gloria**

Date	Activity (Where, when, who, what?)	Antecedents (What happened immediately before behavior?)	Behavior (What actually happened?)	Consequences (What happened immediately after behavior?)	Comments
2/15	9:32, at tabletop activities when playing interlocking blocks. Another boy is playing at the table three chairs away from Frederika. The tub of blocks is in front of Frederika.	Shaikh stands next to where Frederika is sitting. She reaches across Frederika to get some blocks out of the tub.	Frederika shifts her body away from Shaikh and throws the block she has in her hand. She picks up three more and throws them in the same direction.	Ms. Julia goes over and puts her hand on top of Frederika's so she cannot throw. Frederika uses her other hand and throws the blocks again. Julia holds both hands and tells her, "I can't let you throw blocks." Frederika squirms her body to try to get away from being held. The teacher lets her go, she leaves the area, and goes to the library corner where she is alone.	The teachers notice that Frederika tries to squirm away every time they touch her.
2/16	9:05. Dramatic play area while playing alone, sitting at the table playing with teapot and cups.	Three other girls come into the area laughing. Two sit down at the same table while the other one says, "I will cook you pizza."	Frederika throws the teapot at the girl cooking the pizza. "Stop that," yells the girl. Frederika then throws two teacups across the room.	Ms. Camille goes over to her, puts an arm around her, and talks to her about sharing the toys. Frederika moves away from the teacher, looks around, then goes to the science area where there are no other children.	Two times Frederika has gone to an area where there are no other children.

Figure 5-4 Frederika's Functional Behavior Assessment Analysis (See Appendix E for a blank version of this form.)

» Professional Resource Download

Based on the previous "Functional Behavior Assessment Steps," create a plan to positively support the child.

A. Begin by making changes in the **antecedent** to reduce triggering the behavior.

For example:

- Place certain items out of reach.
- Keep other children a certain distance away.
- Change acoustic characteristics of the room to dampen sound.
- Schedule a favorite activity *after* a nonpreferred activity, not before.

B. Identify replacement **behavior**, if needed.

For example:

- Child will make sign for *Stop* rather than hitting.
- Child will point to card that says *Quiet Zone* when he needs to escape to a less stimulating area.
- Child will sign *all done* when he or she is full rather than dumping food.

C. Change the **consequence** or what happens after the behavior occurs.

- Do not give attention when he or she uses inappropriate behavior. Instead, give attention when he or she behaves.

Figure 5-5 Create a Positive Behavior Support Plan

≫ **Professional Resource Download**

Once the communicative function of a behavior has been determined through careful analysis, a positive behavior support plan can be developed. Such plans are usually developed through a collaborative team including a behavior and/or inclusion specialist. The steps for such a plan are included in Figure 5-5.

Plan with staff how the adults will respond to whatever behavior occurs. Remember, if you choose to try an extinction procedure (ignoring the behavior), the frequency of the behavior will probably increase for a while.

Monitor frequency and intensity of behavior to make sure it is decreasing. Teachers must realize the behavior is not going to just suddenly disappear using this procedure. Thus, it is important to periodically *measure* the behavior (in terms of how many times per day the behavior occurs or how long the behavior episode lasts) to determine if it is gradually decreasing. Often, teachers think the procedure is not working and abandon it too quickly. Figure 5-6 includes a positive behavior support plan for Frederika. A blank copy of a Positive Support Plan can be found in Appendix E.

5-9 Assigning a One-to-One Aide

If the behavior is extremely difficult to bring under control, it may be necessary to assign a **one-to-one aide** (assistant) to shadow the child for a period of time. In most cases the role of this individual is to provide another pair of eyes and hands to intervene to prevent such behaviors as running away, hitting or biting other children, destroying property, or endangering self. The assistant must learn to identify the behavioral cues and environmental factors that indicate that a child is about to engage in the behavior.

For example, when the noise level in the room increases, one child may briefly cover his face with his hands, then suddenly bolt for the door. The assistant would learn to recognize these cues and either use a prevention procedure, such as moving the child to a quieter area, or a control procedure, such as simply holding him so

Name: Frederika	**Date:** 2/22	
Team Members: Teacher Gloria, Marcia (parent), and Michael (the inclusion specialist)		

Antecedents/Triggers	Behavior(s)	Consequences
Behavior happens when a child gets too close to Frederika or touches her whether accidentally or on purpose. Happens with all different children in all different areas.	She throws whatever toy she has near her or is holding. She squirms whenever an adult touches her, leaves the area when they let go of her, and goes to an area with no other children.	The adults come over to her and give her attention by putting an arm around her or holding her hands.

Function of Behavior (hypothesis and possible communication)

When a child gets close to Frederika, she throws her toys as a possible way to communicate that she is too crowded or that she doesn't want to be touched. When an adult comes over to intervene, they usually touch her and she tries to escape by squirming. When they do let go of her, she escapes to a new center where there are no other children. It appears that she gets very overwhelmed when someone touches her, which makes her want to flee and be alone. She appears to have some tactile defensiveness.

Prevention	Replacement Behavior(s)	New Consequences
1. Monitor when other children are getting close to Frederika and remind her to hold up her hand.	Frederika will hold up the palm of her hand to signal "Stop!"	**To old behavior:** Adults will not touch her when they approach. They will say, "Is ___ getting too close to your body? Let's put our hand up to say, 'Stop.'"
2. Teach other children that when Frederika puts up her palm, they should move back a little bit. However, encourage them to stay in the area and continue to play.		**To replacement behavior:** Teachers will say, "Wow you asked for more space by holding up your palm. You did it!" (Smile and show her a thumbs-up gesture.)
3. Play with Frederika and one other child by gradually increasing their proximity to each other to build up her tolerance of having someone near her space.		
4. Speak to an occupational therapist to help with desensitizing her to touch.		

Figure 5-6 Frederika's Positive Behavior Support Plan

Professional Resource Download

he cannot run. Obviously, this is not a permanent solution to managing the child's behavior. A carefully planned behavioral program with the assistance of a behavior or inclusion specialist should be implemented with a goal of eliminating the need for a one-on-one assistant.

5-9a A Word of Caution on the Use of One-to-One Aides

Some potential problems associated with the use of a one-to-one aide may cause additional behavior challenges:

- The child may become extremely attached and refuse to interact with any other staff or peers.
- The assistant may do too much for the child, making the child too dependent on her.
- The teacher may come to expect the assistant to do nearly all of the interacting with the child, thus isolating the child from the rest of the staff and from other children.

It is important to clarify precisely the role of a one-to-one aide and to use the assistant only to the degree necessary to manage the behavior. The early childhood educator should not assume that the one-to-one aide has received any training. It is very important to determine how (or whether) the assistant has been trained. Parents or the inclusion specialist should be aware of the aide's training and can assist in arranging for any additional training that might be helpful. Such assistants, given sufficient training and realistic expectations, make valuable contributions to a smoothly functioning classroom.

Summary

Behavior challenges present some of the greatest obstacles to successful inclusion of children with disabilities. It is critical that teachers form nurturing and positive relationships with children and design classrooms in ways that decrease the likelihood that difficult behaviors will emerge. Clearly, there are also effective strategies for preventing behavior challenges before they occur. Despite use of these best practices, however, some children need carefully planned interventions. Early childhood educators must be realistic and understand that in these cases they may not have the time, resources, or staff necessary to adequately manage and accommodate for such children. Only with the teamwork of parents, specialists, and inclusion support personnel can an optimal solution be implemented. This is a standard worth pursuing!

Read–Reflect–Discuss

Julian's Towel

Julian is a four-year-old with Down syndrome who was recently placed in a Head Start program. Julian is an only child with older parents, and this was his first experience in group care. His teachers complained that whenever he was in the manipulatives area (a U-shaped configuration of shelves with containers of Legos, small blocks, dominoes, and other toys), Julian would frequently throw manipulatives around and would sometimes bite other children. The teachers reported that he did not play appropriately with any of the toys there, though occasionally when the area was less crowded, he would entertain himself by dumping the Legos back and forth from one container to another.

Working together with the inclusion support specialist using the A-B-C analysis, the teachers quickly identified that Julian was most likely to be aggressive when other children got too close to him. Several simple interventions eliminated this behavior challenge:

1. The teacher limited the number of children who could play in the small manipulative area at any one time.
2. The teacher bought a beach towel with Disney characters on it (Julian's favorites) for Julian to sit on when he played in this area. The other children were taught that this was Julian's space; if they wished to share the towel space with Julian, they needed to ask permission.
3. Julian was taught a replacement behavior to use instead of biting when a child did bump or crowd him. He learned to extend his arm to convey "you're too close!"
4. If Julian did bite someone or have an outburst of throwing things, he was immediately removed from the area and placed in a less preferred play center.

Within a month of consistently using these procedures:

- Several children requested their own towels to sit on!
- Julian learned to use the arm signal fairly quickly, though the other children did not always comply.
- By the end of the month the biting behavior had been extinguished and the frequency of throwing things had diminished.
- A peer was able to engage Julian in dumping and filling a toy dump truck with Legos.
- Julian's tolerance for other children crowding and touching him had decreased significantly.

Read–Reflect–Discuss Questions

1. What elements of positive behavior support can you identify? That is, what strategies were used to reduce Julian's throwing and biting behaviors?
2. What was Julian trying to communicate by throwing toys and biting?
3. What are possible reasons why Julian was more interested in "dumping and filling" the containers of Legos, than in playing "appropriately" with the Legos?
4. Do you think the typical characteristics of Down syndrome may have contributed to Julian's play behavior?

Key Terms

A-B-C analysis
aversive stimulus
behavior modification
communicative
   function88
consequence
delayed reinforcement

extinction
internal state
multitiered system of
   support
one-to-one aide
positive behavior support
punishment

receptive language
reinforcer
repetitive behavior
replacement behavior
tactile defensiveness
Teaching Pyramid Model
time away

Helpful Resources

Books and Articles

Cook, R., Klein, M. D., & Chen, D. (2016). Promoting social and emotional development. In *Adapting early childhood curricula for children with special needs* (pp. 162–203). Columbus, OH: Pearson.

Dunlap, G., Wilson, K., Strain, P., & Lee, J. K. (2013). *Prevent-teach-reinforce for young children: The early childhood model of individualized positive behavior support.* Baltimore, MD: Paul H. Brookes.

Essa, E. (2008). *What to do when: Practical guidance strategies for challenging behaviors in the preschool.* Boston, MA: Cengage Learning.

Hemmeter, M. L., Ostrosky, M. M., & Corso, R. M. (2012). Preventing and addressing challenging behavior: Common questions and practical strategies. *Young Exceptional Children, 15*(2), 32–46.

Kaiser, B., & Rasminsky, J. S. (2012). *Challenging behavior in young children: Understanding, preventing and responding effectively.* Upper Saddle River, NJ: Pearson.

Shea, T. M., & Bauer, A. M. (2011). *Behavior management: A practical approach for educators.* Upper Saddle River, NJ: Pearson.

Organizations and Centers

Council for Children with Behavior Disorders, www.ccbd.net

The University of North Carolina TEACCH Autism Program, CB# 7180 UNC-Chapel Hill, NC 27599, (919) 966-2174, www.teacch.com

Empowering People: Positive Discipline, www.positivediscipline.com

National Association for School Psychologists, 4340 East West Highway, Suite 402, Bethesda, MD 20814, (866) 331-NASP, www.nasponline.org

Technical Assistance Center on Social Emotional Intervention for Young Children (TACSEI), challengingbehavior.fmhi.usf.edu/index.htm

Center on the Social and Emotional Foundations for Early Learning (CSEFEL), Vanderbilt University, Box 228/Peabody, Nashville, TN 327203, (866) 433-1966, http://csefel.vanderbilt.edu/resources/training_modules.html

The Pyramid Model Consortium, www.pyramidmodel.org

CHAPTER 6

Monitoring Individual Child Progress

LEARNING OBJECTIVES

After studying this chapter, you should be able to:

LO 6-1: Describe the Individualized Family Service Plan (IFSP) process and content.

LO 6-2: Explain the Individualized Education Program (IEP), including the components of instructional objectives.

LO 6-3: Discuss the rationale for and techniques to monitor progress.

LO 6-4: Elaborate on techniques for planning that result in effective inclusion support.

The following NAEYC Standards and DEC Recommended Practices are addressed in this chapter:

naeyc

Standard 1: Promoting Child Development and Learning
Standard 3: Observing, Documenting, and Assessing to Support Young Children and Families
Standard 6: Becoming a Professional

DEC

Practice 1: Assessment
Practice 2: Environment
Practice 3: Family
Practice 4: Instruction
Practice 5: Interaction

A key to successful inclusion of children with special needs is ongoing monitoring of their progress.

Specific documents and procedures are used to outline educational goals and monitor the progress of children with special needs:

- **The Individualized Family Service Plan (IFSP) and Individualized Education Program (IEP) are legal documents.** Each child with special needs placed in an inclusive setting will have either an IFSP or an IEP that spells out the specific goals, outcomes, and priorities for that child.

- **The teacher must have those documents.** If the parents and/or service coordinator don't provide a copy, the teacher should request one.

- **The child's progress must be monitored and documented.** ECE teachers must work with an inclusion specialist to determine who is responsible for each aspect of progress monitoring.

- **Progress must be monitored on a regular basis.** The progress monitoring system must be designed so that it is easy to use and functional.

- **The teacher, families, and specialists must plan how children's goals will be addressed in the ECE program.** Children's specific goals are included in an IEP or IFSP and are embedded in naturally occurring daily opportunities in the classroom and home environment.

Introduction

Early educators need to realize that an Individualized Family Service Plan (IFSP) or an Individualized Education Program (IEP) has been developed for each child who is eligible for special education support or services. These are legal documents that result from a process involving individual child and family assessment and multidisciplinary planning.

If a child is under three years old, then the document is referred to as an **Individualized Family Service Plan (IFSP)**. It contains a list of services that must be provided to the family to meet the child's needs. It also contains current developmental levels and specific outcome statements that teachers should use as guides when they plan adaptations or activities for the child. For children over three years of age, an **Individualized Education Program (IEP)** is used. It also contains developmental levels as well as specific goals and objectives that also guide program planning.

Teachers should request and carefully review these documents. They can be obtained from the family. Once family permission has been obtained, teachers may also request these documents from the service coordinator or from a special educator who provides inclusion support.

Early childhood programs that include young children with special needs must assist children in achieving the specific goals, objectives, or outcomes that are contained in these documents. This chapter will briefly discuss these individual plans and programs and will present ways of monitoring children's progress toward reaching the stated goals, objectives, or outcomes. Finally, it focuses on strategies designed to offer the supports necessary to facilitate fulfillment of the goals and objectives outlined in individualized plans and programs.

6-1 The Individualized Family Service Plan (IFSP)

The IFSP is the written document specified in the law to guide the implementation of services for infants and toddlers from birth to age three. Formats for the IFSP document vary from state to state, but in all cases the **outcomes** described in the IFSP should be the result of a collaborative process between families and professionals involved in assessing and serving the child and family. Therefore, it is desirable for any agency serving the child to be a part of the IFSP process. Other participants include the parent(s) or guardian(s) of the child, other family members as desired by the parent(s), an advocate if requested by the family, the child's service coordinator, a person or people involved in the assessment process, and others who may be providing direct services to the child and family, such as a physical therapist or speech-language pathologist. The two parts of the IFSP that relate most closely to the goals for the child and family are the "Family Concerns" section and the "Outcome Statements."

6-1a Family Concerns

These are often stated in the family's words and reflect what concerns them in regard to their child's developmental progress or their ability to parent the child effectively. Families are encouraged to prioritize their concerns related to both family issues and concerns about the child.

Examples follow:

> We are concerned about our ability to help our child learn. Cerebral palsy seems like such a serious disability.

> Our greatest priority is that he has friends someday.

6-1b Outcome Statements

Each IFSP must include outcome statements that clearly state changes family members want to occur for their child or themselves. In other words, what do they hope will happen over the next six months? These outcome statements are expected to directly reflect the family concerns and are used to guide the choice of services to be delivered. These statements should refer to practical activities that fit into a family's daily life and represent skills that enhance the child's ability to cope with daily environmental demands.

Phrasing outcome statements as *"in order to"* and identifying the context for the behavior clarify the functional purpose of the action to be encouraged. For example, when parents are eager for a child to learn to walk, they may not be satisfied with an outcome statement that states "Mikey will pull to stand." However, they will be pleased when the outcome statement states "Mikey will pull to stand and cruise along the couch *in order to* begin walking." Inclusion of these three key words, "in order to," makes it clear that the process (pulling to stand and cruising) contributes to the product (walking). The daily routine in which the process is embedded is also readily identified (Cook, Klein, & Chen, 2016).

Early childhood educators should plan adaptations and involve children in activities clearly designed to help promote the changes listed in the outcome statements. Examples of such outcome statements follow:

> Mr. and Mrs. Gomez will attend the support group at Centro de Ninos y Padres in order to learn more about parenting a child with cerebral palsy.

> Jose will make more attempts to communicate in order to let people know what he wants and to positively interact with others.

Early childhood educators can use the outcome statements as guides in assisting families to obtain services, planning activities appropriate for all children, selecting strategies, adapting environments, and recording progress. In addressing the outcome statements for the Gomez family, information is provided to parents about how to become involved in an appropriate support group. Perhaps Mr. and Mrs. Gomez might be introduced to other parents who are available to answer questions and provide support and encouragement. Jose will be included in activities that encourage communication, and specific strategies will be planned to foster positive interaction with others. His attempts to communicate will be charted to note progress before his IFSP is reviewed after six months.

An IFSP must be developed for each child within 45 days of initial referral for special education services, and it must be reviewed and updated every six months. Early educators must be certain that the contents of the most recent version of each child's IFSP is available to be used in activity planning. Each family is assigned a **service coordinator** who is the designated person responsible for integrating services and keeping the family involved. However, teachers must obtain the family's permission before they can receive information from the IFSP.

6-2 The Individualized Education Program (IEP)

The IEP is the legal document that directs services for children over the age of three. It is the result of a multidisciplinary assessment and planning process conducted by the local public school district in which the children live. Again, early educators who serve children with special needs should seek to be involved in this process if at all possible. Others who may be involved include:

- The child's parents or guardians
- At least one general education teacher if the child is involved in a general education program
- A member of the school staff who is qualified to provide supervision of any specially designed instruction
- An individual who can explain assessment results
- An interpreter, if appropriate
- A school administrator who can make commitments for the school district
- Other individuals whose expertise may be desired by the family

The IEP often differs from the IFSP in that it contains more specific statements related to goals and objectives, rather than the sometimes broadly stated outcomes found in IFSPs. IEPs are also more focused on a child's *educational* goals and services rather than on the *family/home* like the IFSPs. Early educators should pay particular attention to the goals and objectives listed on IEPs.

6-2a Identifying Individuals Responsible for Achievement of Goals

At the time of this publication, policies at both the state and federal levels vary in identification of individuals responsible for monitoring a child's progress toward annual goals and for ensuring that these goals are met. ECE teachers should attempt to determine what individual or individuals are responsible for meeting the IEP or IFSP goals. Without this accountability, the effectiveness of the document is undermined. ECE teachers can begin with the school district or state agency responsible for generating the IFSP or IEP. Parents or guardians must also be part of the process of determining who will take responsibility for monitoring and achieving goals.

6-2b Goals and Objectives

IEPs are required to include yearlong goals. Short-term objectives or benchmarks that represent achievements on the way toward reaching the annual goal can be included at a state's discretion. With parent permission, early educators should review the IEP goals and objectives that are recorded for each child. These should be systematically incorporated into the child's naturally occurring daily activities instead of pulling the child away from peers and working on objectives on a one-to-one basis. Because daily activities happen frequently and naturally in the classroom, children will have many opportunities to practice and make steady progress toward each objective. For example, note the following goal and objectives that can be implemented in the naturally occurring activities of playing in the dramatic play area:

Long-term goal: *Marti will cooperatively play with her peers.*

Short-term objectives: *While in the dramatic play area with one or two other children,*

Marti will share the dress-up clothes.

Marti will show some response to the verbal initiations of others.

6-2c Daily Instructional Objectives

When writing daily instructional objectives, educators should include behaviors and teaching activities that typically occur or can be easily incorporated into routine activities. (Chapter 2 includes examples of how to break down daily activities into small, teachable steps.) These objectives should contain three components:

1. Under what *conditions* will the child be expected to demonstrate the behavior? What will the adult do? In what activity? Where? For example:

   > "When playing in the block area with no more than three children . . ."

   > "When given no more than two verbal prompts . . ." (see "Helpful Hint" for more information on prompts.)

2. What will the child do? (Describe the desired *behavior* in detail so all adults know exactly what to look for.) For example:

   > "Jeremy will play comfortably alongside other children without hitting or running away."

   > "Sarah will sign 'Eat cookie' to request a snack."

3. How well or how often do you expect the child to perform the behavior? How do you know the child has achieved the objective? What are the *criteria* for success? When can you move on to the next step or the next level of performance? For example:

   > ". . . for at least five minutes on four out of five days over a two-week period."

   > ". . . on three of five occasions over a three-week period."

The following objectives might guide daily activities designed to accomplish the long-range goal stated earlier for Marti:

a. Marti will tolerate two other children being in the dramatic play space and will allow another child to put on a clothing article in three out of four different occasions over a two-week period.
b. With no more than a single verbal prompt from an adult, Marti will initiate at least one interaction and will verbally respond to another child's initiation at least once in each dramatic play episode over a one-month period.

Once teachers have obtained the IEP document, it is essential to review the document and become familiar with its complete contents. However, IEP documents can be quite lengthy, making it difficult to remember important information. Consequently, teachers can use the IEP Summary in Figure 6-1 to help keep track of pertinent information for each student. A sample copy of an IEP is included in Appendix D.

WEBLINK

To learn more about IEPs, see Wrightslaw at: wrightslaw.com /info/iep.index.htm

6-3 Monitoring Progress

Developing an IEP requires careful consideration of the strategies likely to be most effective in supporting inclusion and monitoring progress. Before progress can be monitored, each child must become involved in activities that will result in fulfillment of their individualized goals, objectives, or outcomes. This next section briefly discusses effective techniques for implementing goals and objectives; Part II of this text will offer numerous specific examples.

6-3a Implementation of the IEP and IFSP Goals and Objectives

Implementing goals and objectives may seem like a daunting task for early childhood educators. It does not have to be. Goals and objectives can be embedded into naturally occurring opportunities throughout the day. An inclusion specialist can help to embed an objective in the daily routine. Or, just ask yourself where and when

IEP SUMMARY

Student:		Strengths/Preferences/Interests:
Birthday:		
Age:		
Disability:		

Summary of Present Developmental Levels and Abilities:

Summary of Goals/Objectives:

Summary of Adaptations/Modification/Needs:	Important to Know/Other Information:

Questions or Items to Follow-Up On:

Figure 6-1 IEP Summary

children would typically be practicing this skill in the classroom. For instance, there are several natural opportunities for working on an objective of identifying shapes and naming them. Children can do the following:

- Learn the names of various shapes while building in the block area.
- Name different shapes during a collage art activity.
- Recognize and name the different shapes in a puzzle.
- Name color and shape of a carpet piece upon which they are sitting.

Of course, children with special needs will more than likely need prompts and adaptations to successfully work on their objectives. They might need different levels of support by adapting the environment, activity or routine, materials, or the requirements of instruction and by using the EESS acronym.

Children might also need frequent reminders to help stay on task and/or complete any task. These reminders are called **prompts**. Prompts can be done in many ways:

- Gesture prompts are nonverbal such as pointing or facial expressions.
- Verbal prompts are short phrases to remind students what to do.
- Picture prompts are drawings, photographs, clipart, or icons.
- Object prompts hold up or show a real object.
- Physical prompts partially or fully physically help children do an activity (use sparingly only after you have tried the other prompts).

Prompts are typically described in the objective as conditions, that is, with no more than a single verbal prompt from an adult. The object is to fade out the prompts so that children can become as independent as possible. The amount of prompts given to a child will become important when we start to monitor the progress a child is making on his/her objectives so we know what level of support has been provided.

6-3b Rationale for Progress Monitoring

Some state-funded early childhood programs are becoming accustomed to systematically recording the developmental progress of children due to a standard-based assessment system for early learning in many states. However, non–state-funded early childhood programs may not be accustomed to systematically recording progress of children. Nevertheless, the IEP or IFSP process requires that certain information must be recorded, updated regularly, and made available to families and other members of the child's intervention team. To gather this information, progress must be monitored on a regular basis. Progress monitoring is critical for children with special needs for several reasons:

1. The IDEA law requires that efforts to achieve outcomes and goals stated in the IFSP or IEP be planned and carried out. Thus, there must be some documentation that the plan is being implemented.
2. Progress for a child with special needs may occur slowly and in very small steps. Without careful data recording, it may be difficult to know for sure if a child is learning the desired skills and behaviors.
3. It is important to determine whether or not a particular intervention or teaching strategy is effective and whether steady progress is being made toward achieving a child's outcomes and goals. If not, a change must be made in the instructional plan and methods.

Ideally, early childhood teachers would rely on the inclusion support provider to design and implement data-recording systems. Realistically, however, this level of support may not be available for every child.

Obviously, for children included in large group settings, the monitoring system must be simple or it will not be used. In addition, the system must be designed to be functional. Notes and records must be immediately usable to make adjustments in program adaptations, whenever necessary. In short, records of each child's progress must be kept, and the system must be simple enough to be used on a regular basis (see Photo 6-1).

Photo 6-1 Children's progress should be monitored on a regular basis.

6-3c Types of Data Recording

The kinds of **data recording** addressed here are informal records that will assist with evaluation and documentation of child progress on an ongoing basis. Special educators and therapists will also carry out more formal evaluations at annual intervals to determine whether new goals need to be identified and to recommend appropriate program modifications or placement changes. The following discussion of data recording considers the purposes as well as the formats. Three purposes are described: (1) assessment, (2) planning, and (3) progress monitoring.

Informal Assessment. Some informal assessment is usually necessary to plan effectively for inclusion support. Two examples of informal assessment are an activity/standards inventory and systematic observation of child behaviors (Beukelman & Mirenda, 2012). Careful observations of children in various activities can be made to determine their greatest needs for support. Here are examples of the kinds of systematic observations that may be helpful. Observe *each* of the following for at least three minutes:

- Observe the child playing alone and list what the child does.
- Observe the child playing with toys or objects and describe how the child uses the toys. Also describe the child's pace of activity.
- Observe how long the child plays with one toy. How often does the child switch activities?
- Observe the child playing with other children. What does the child do during that time? Does the child initiate interactions with others, or respond to initiations of other children?
- Observe the child with an adult. How does the child interact with the adult?

An **activity/standards inventory** (see Figure 6-2) carefully observes how children *without* disabilities participate in an activity (hence, the *standard*) and compares this with the participation of a child who has special needs. The differences, or discrepancies, between the two are noted. Then the barriers that are responsible for the discrepancies are analyzed, and the necessary adaptations to enable all children to participate are identified and planned. The adaptation in Figure 6-2 could be to change the level of requirements or instruction. In other words, instead of requiring the children to call out the name of the song, the child with special needs can point to a picture of the song.

Finally, the IEP goals and objectives for each child should be obtained and summarized. They should be readily available for frequent review, and they should be incorporated into the planning documents described later.

Data Recording to Monitor Progress. When keeping track of progress toward the accomplishment of IFSP outcomes or IEP goals or objectives, **anecdotal record keeping** can be a simple yet effective record-keeping strategy. Anecdotal records, diaries, or logs

Child's Name: Frankie			Date: Sept. 15	
Situation/Activity	**Peer Behavior** How do peers participate?	**Target Child Behavior**	**Barriers to Participation**	**Adaptations**
Requesting song during circle time	Call out name of song	Waves hands; vocalizes	No way to make song selection audible and intelligible to teacher	Create pictures of circle time songs so student chooses a song

Figure 6-2 Activity Standards Inventory

⌄ Professional Resource Download

ANECDOTAL RECORD OF DEVELOPMENTAL PROGRESS	
Name: Marti	**Date: Oct. 20**
SUMMARY OF OBJECTIVES	**COMMENTS**
Social Skills 1. Increase number of children Marti will tolerate. 2. Increase appropriate social initiations.	1. She has played with Sharon and Fabio several times this week. 2. She offered Sun Yee one of her dolls.
Communication 1. Use signs to request play materials. 2. Use sign to request choice of snack.	1. She still only does this if prompted. 2. She will use either "juice" or "milk" sign at snack.
Motor Skills 1. Make continuous snips across paper. 2. Copy horizontal, vertical, and circular strokes.	1. She makes individual snips on paper provided. 2. She consistently copies the horizontal and vertical stroke, and imitated a circular stroke two times.
Self-Help 1. Clean up after lunch without prompts. 2. Put jacket on and get backpack at the end of the day.	1. She has met this goal for the last two weeks. 2. She begins putting jacket on and getting backpack at the end of the day.

Figure 6-3 Anecdotal Recording Form for Monitoring Student Progress

⌄ Professional Resource Download

may be kept on a daily, weekly, or biweekly basis. One simple strategy for recording observations is to make a single page for each child, listing the outcomes or objectives in each domain along one side of the page and leaving ample space to write comments next to each outcome or objective. Each week the progress for each outcome or objective is summarized, providing a running narrative of progress across all targeted outcomes or objectives. This information is then readily available to review during parent conferences and team planning meetings. Figure 6-3 shows a sample of such a record sheet.

More precise data-recording procedures may sometimes be necessary to monitor progress toward specific goals where change has been slow or inconsistent. For example, it may be important to determine whether a specific behavior plan is working or whether progress is being made in toilet training. When change occurs slowly, it may be impossible to objectively determine whether there is improvement through informal observation and anecdotal records alone. In these situations it may be necessary to keep more precise records. Figures 6-4 and 6-5 are examples of data recording to monitor two different objectives: toileting and self-feeding.

It can also be helpful to simply monitor the child's participation in each activity of the day. It is useful to record whether the child performed the task independently or with assistance, as shown in Figure 6-6. Make sure to use a simple key so that the level of support can quickly be written down. If the system is too complicated, the data won't get collected.

Another example of the need for precise data recording is to monitor changes in disruptive behavior, such as the use of an ABC analysis. Refer to Chapter 5 for a review of this topic.

Blank forms and additional examples of planning and data-recording forms are included in Appendix E.

PROGRESS DATA					

NAME: <u>Jon</u>

OBJECTIVE: <u>Jon will urinate when placed on potty</u>

KEY: D = dry   W = wet
      P = placed on potty   V = vocalized
      + = urinated in potty   — did not urinate in potty

Time	MONDAY	TUESDAY	WEDNESDAY	THURSDAY	FRIDAY
8:00	D	D	D	D	D
8:30	W	W	P—	VP+	P+
9:00	D	D	W	D	D
9:30	D	D	D	D	D
10:00	D	VP—	D	D	D
10:30	VP—	D	D	VW	VP+
11:00	W	W	VP+	D	D
11:30	D	W	D	D	D

Figure 6-4 Monitoring Progress in Toilet Training

⌄⌄ **Professional Resource Download**

PROGRESS SUMMARY					

Name: <u>Sung Lee</u>   **Week:** <u>Jan. 12–16</u>

OBJECTIVE: <u>Drink from cup independently at lunch</u>

KEY: + = bring cup to mouth independently, holding cup with both hands
      ⊕ = support at elbow only
      A = total assistance required

Trials	MONDAY	TUESDAY	WEDNESDAY	THURSDAY	FRIDAY
1.	A	A	⊕	A	A
2.	A	A	A	A	⊕
3.	A	⊕	A	⊕	+
4.	A	⊕	⊕	+	+
5.	A	A	+	+	+
6.	A	A	A	⊕	⊕
7.	A	A	A	⊕	+

Figure 6-5 Monitoring Progress in Self-Feeding

⌄⌄ **Professional Resource Download**

6-3d Issues Related to Resources for Progress Monitoring

Careful progress monitoring can be time consuming and sometimes labor intensive. This can be a challenge in inclusive early childhood settings. The following strategies may be helpful:

- Assign a portion of the progress-monitoring responsibility to the inclusion support provider.

ACTIVITY	Monday	Tuesday	Wednesday	Thursday	Friday
Free play	W	A	A	W	I
Circle	A	A	I	I	I
Outside play	W	W	A	A	W
Snack	I	I	I	I	D
Toileting	D	A	A	A	A
Centers	W	W	A	W	W
Computers	I	I	I	I	I
Good-bye circle	A	A	I	W	A

Child's Name <u>Sheree</u> **Week of** <u>Oct. 17–21</u>

LEVEL OF PARTICIPATION IN DAILY ACTIVITIES

Key: A = Participated with assistance
   I = Participated independently
   W = Wandered around
   D = Did not participate

Figure 6-6 Level of Participation in Daily Activities

⌄⌄ Professional Resource Download

- Use both teachers and assistants as data recorders.
- Keep Post-Its handy and collect them at the end of the day and simply paste them into a record book.
- Keep duplicates of forms on clipboards around the room in each activity center. Be sure to place a sheet on top of the form that says "confidential."

6-4 Planning Inclusion Support

When it becomes clear from progress monitoring just what goals and objectives require additional support for any child to be successful, careful planning is required. Adaptations and teaching strategies to be used to support the children's successful participation in each activity of the day must be planned and written on an easily understood form. In addition, specific strategies that are necessary to help children learn certain skills related to IEP objectives must also be written on a planning form. This should be done both for routine activities in the daily schedule and for special activities. Figure 6-7 describes the support that will be used for a specific child in a daily activity.

An **objectives-by-activity matrix** (see Figure 6-8) is a commonly used planning form that depicts where IEP objectives will be addressed across the activities of the daily schedule. Each activity in the daily schedule is placed on a grid. At the top, each IEP goal is listed. Within the matrix, notes can be made related to whether and how that goal will be addressed during each of the daily activities. (This could also be used as a weekly recording form to comment on how the child performed during each of the daily activities.)

It is also important to plan specifically for a special, nonroutine event. Novel, unfamiliar, or unexpected activities can be stressful for many children who have special needs. For this reason, it is important to plan ahead and try to anticipate extra supports that may be necessary to enable the child to access and enjoy the activity (see Figure 6-9).

CHILD'S NAME: JT	DATE: Sept. 15
TEACHER NAME(S): Martha	CENTER: Kid's Place
INCLUSION CONSULTANT'S NAME: Anne	

SCHEDULE	SPECIFIC SUPPORTS/ADAPTATIONS (What staff will do for child that will help child be part of activities)
ARRIVAL	Assign favorite adult to greet JT Help him find cubby; prompt him only if necessary Use consistent phrase: "Find your cubby"
MORNING ACTIVITIES (FREE PLAY)	Encourage JT to play next to a peer while using the same materials. Draw attention to what the peer is doing and what JT is doing. If he starts to wander the classroom, then get a choice board and put three to four of his favorite toys on the front and ask him to choose one. If he begins self-stimulatory behavior, try to reengage him with a toy or peer.
CLEANUP	Give JT one simple direction at a time: "Put the block in the box" (Point to the picture on the box.) Now, put the box on the shelf. (Point to the picture on the shelf.) Dismiss early, while others finish cleaning up, so that he has time to start the next activity.
TOILET/HAND WASH	Point to each picture of the hand washing poster, one at a time, and encourage him to do each step. Provide modeling and assistance as needed.
SNACK	Provide adapted spoon and fork, if needed. Provide snack pictures so he can point to his choice.
CIRCLE TIME	Provide a cube chair that has soft Velcro on the arm rests so he can touch it with his fingers while sitting. Offer pictures of song choices. Give him a fidget toy if he gets distracted or is inattentive.
SMALL GROUP (WORK TIME)	Simplify art activities to a two-step process. Use a glue stick instead of a squeeze bottle. Use adapted (loop) scissors. Simplify activity to his level of two to three continuous snips. Use broken crayons or short markers to encourage pincer grasp.
OUTSIDE PLAY	Encourage JT to wait his turn for his favorite bike by using a three-minute sand timer.

Figure 6-7 Individual Support Schedule

❯❯ Professional Resource Download

Child's Name Rafik			Date: Oct. 30		
OBJECTIVE					
ACTIVITY	Self-feeding	Taking off/on jacket	Requesting	Using marker	Attending to story
9:00 Arrival		X			
9:15 Free play			X	X	
9:30 Circle			X		X
9:45 Centers			X	X	X
10:15 Outside		X			
10:45 Potty					
11:15 Snack	X		X		
11:30 Story/music					X
11:45 Departure		X			

Figure 6-8 Objectives-By-Activity Matrix

❯❯ Professional Resource Download

Child's Name: JT	Date: Sept. 30
ACTIVITY	**STRATEGIES**
Description: Trip to library for preschool story time	**Read:** Read the library field trip social story to the whole class over two to three days before the day of the trip. **Peers**: Assign "best friend" to walk with JT, holding his hand.
Purpose and Objective(s): For Group: To learn about the library: Goal for JT: To handle unfamiliar situation without trying to escape	
Materials: None	**Adults: 1.** Begin to prepare JT the day before by individually reading the social story to him. Discuss each step and what is going to happen. Read the story one more time the day of the trip. **2.** Keep close proximity to JT, and keep him away from street. Take his other hand if he becomes upset.
• EVALUATION •	
Outcomes: **Suggestions for Future Activities:**	

Figure 6-9 Special Activity Plan

Summary

Although the importance and social advantages of inclusion in a high-quality early childhood program cannot be overstated, it is equally important to ensure that the specific goals identified for children with special needs are met. To help children achieve their potential, educators must take care to address these goals during naturally occurring daily activities while carefully monitoring progress toward specific outcomes. Just as important, when this monitoring indicates that progress is not being made, make changes in curriculum in the form of adaptations and teaching strategies in a timely fashion.

Read–Reflect–Discuss
Lazaro's Potty Learning Experience

Lazaro's mother shared with his teachers that Lazaro was becoming fairly consistent at going to the potty at home. Most of the time he did not need to wear diapers. The teachers commented that they had tried putting him in training pants a few times before, but he still had accidents so they stopped. As Lazaro is nearly five years old and will be transitioning into a general education kindergarten, both his mom and the teachers thought they should revisit toilet training at school, especially because he was having success at home. Maybe now he was ready. Everyone knew that if he was not successful in underwear, he would present a major challenge to the kindergarten teacher.

Lazaro's teacher, Sarah, agreed to work with the early childhood special educator to prioritize this important goal. The first step was to take careful data to determine whether Lazaro's bowel habits were regular and also to determine if Lazaro was currently using any communicative cues at school to indicate that he needed to go to the bathroom.

A simple recording system was devised. Lazaro's favorite teacher, an assistant in the classroom, volunteered to take data. Every hour the assistant checked Lazaro to see if he had had a bowel movement. The teacher also recorded what Lazaro's activity had been during the time period prior to the bowel movement. After three weeks, they could detect no regular pattern related to time. However, they noted that he was most likely to go following vigorous exercise of some kind. They also noted that he frequently stopped in the middle of whatever he was doing and put his hand briefly on his stomach.

After evaluating this data, a plan was devised in which they would watch him carefully following any energetic activity. As soon as he touched his stomach, the teacher would say in a very positive way, "Lazaro, let's go to the bathroom!" Fairly quickly, Lazaro started looking for the teacher and trying to make eye contact when he felt the need to void. All the staff was particularly vigilant and sensitive to his cues, until he was consistently indicating his need to go and he could delay voiding until he went into the bathroom.

Read–Reflect–Discuss Questions

1. Careful data collection and record keeping are often labor intensive. What are some creative ways of collecting data, especially when programs are already short-staffed?
2. How might better communication between the school and the parents have been helpful in Lazaro's toilet training at school?
3. Can you think of ways of structuring the daily schedule of a child care program that would build in support for toilet training for all the children who need it?

Key Terms

activity/standards inventory

anecdotal record keeping

data recording

Individualized Education Program (IEP)

Individualized Family Services Plan (IFSP)

objectives-by-activity matrix

outcomes

prompts

service coordinator

Helpful Resources

Allen, K. E., & Marotz, L. (2013). *Developmental profiles: Pre-birth through adolescence.* Belmont, CA: Wadsworth, Cengage Learning.

Beaty, J. J. (2014). *Observing development of the young child.* Boston, MA: Pearson.

Bricker, D., & Macy, M. (2013). *Developmental screening in your community: An integrated approach for connecting children with services.* Baltimore, MD: Paul H. Brookes.

Cohen, D. H., Stern, V., Balaban, N., & Gropper, N. (2016). *Observing and recording the behavior of young children* (6th ed.). New York: Teachers College, Columbia University.

Cook, R. E., Klein, M. D., & Chen, D. (2016). *Adapting early childhood curricula for children with special needs* (9th ed.). Boston, MA: Pearson.

Fawcett, M. (2009). *Learning through child observation.* Philadelphia, PA: Jessica Kingsley Publishers.

Gronlund, G. (2013). *Planning for play, observation and learning.* St. Paul, MN: Redleaf Press.

Marotz, L. R., & Allen, K. E. (2016). *Developmental profiles: Pre-birth through adolescence.* Boston, MA: Cengage Learning.

McAfee, O., Leong, D. J., & Bodrova, E. (2015). *Assessing and guiding young children's development and learning* (6th ed.). Boston, MA: Pearson.

Zabar, L., & Lerner, C. *Learning through observation,* DVD. Retrieved from www.zerotothree.org/bookstore

CHAPTER 7

Managing Arrival, Departure, and Other Transitions

LEARNING OBJECTIVES

After studying this chapter, you will be able to:

LO 7-1: Describe potential challenges and techniques for supporting smooth transitions when children arrive at an early childhood center or program.

LO 7-2: Discuss the importance of establishing a consistent departure routine to smooth transitions at the end of the daily program.

LO 7-3: Explain successful strategies for supporting smooth transitions during the day from one activity to another.

The following NAEYC Standards and DEC Recommended Practices are addressed in this chapter:

naeyc

Standard 1: Promoting Child Development and Learning
Standard 2: Building Family and Community Relationships

DEC

Practice 2: Environment
Practice 3: Family
Practice 4: Instruction
Practice 5: Interaction
Practice 6: Teaming and Collaboration

Well-managed transitions can create important teaching and learning opportunities.

Arrival and departure mark important transitions of a child's day. Children with special needs often require assistance with transitions. However, transitions, if planned carefully, can provide important learning opportunities:

- **Arrival may continue to feel like a new experience for some children, even though it is a routine event.** It may take children with special needs longer to adjust to the separation from a parent or guardian to the hustle and bustle of an early childhood center. This "settling in" period each day may continue for a longer time than it would for children without disabilities.

- **Arrival provides an opportunity to touch base with a parent or guardian each day.** Some kind of consistent contact with families is extremely important to successful inclusion of children with special needs. A teacher who says, "Good morning! How is Joseph doing today?" provides an important opportunity for the family to briefly share important recent concerns or accomplishments that might not otherwise be shared.

- **Arrival provides an important opportunity to help children work on separation.** As separation can be particularly challenging for children with special needs, it should be viewed as an important goal, to be addressed over time. Sometimes parents and guardians as well as the child have difficulty separating.

- **Arrival and departure can provide occasions to work on many functional skills.** These include taking off and putting on jackets, recognizing one's own name, and mastering the independence of placing and identifying one's belongings in the proper cubby.

- **All transitions need to be carefully planned and viewed as important learning opportunities.** In addition to the major transitions of arrival and departure, numerous transitions occur throughout the day and are to be considered in the planning process so appropriate learning will take place.

Introduction

Arrival and departure mark the beginning and the end of the center-based day. Thus, they represent major **transitions** of the day. For children with special needs these two transitions may pose significant challenges. In addition, transitions from one activity to another that occur within the daily routine of the center-based program can also present difficulties for ALL young children. Some children may find transitions physically or emotionally overwhelming. They may be unsure of what is happening; the increased noise and activity level may feel threatening; and ending a comfortable, familiar activity may be difficult. It is estimated that a third of the time in preschools is spent going from one activity to another (Murphy, 2011). This chapter suggests strategies for supporting children with challenges related to transitions and ideas for maximizing the learning potential of these daily events.

7-1 Arrival

A child's arrival at an early childhood education center presents both challenges and learning opportunities. In this section we will consider strategies to deal with both.

7-1a Arrival: The Challenge of a New Experience

For many children the early childhood center is a new experience. Even those children who have been attending center-based early intervention programs may find the hustle and bustle—the rapid pace, the noise level, and the large numbers of children—of a child care center or preschool program very different, at times even overwhelming.

They might need extra time to *warm up,* both in the long run and in the immediate situation. In other words, the transition into the center may be difficult for several weeks or longer. In addition, children may take an unusually long time each morning to settle in to the routine. It can also be difficult when a child who is dropped off in the middle of a large group activity such as circle time instead of at the beginning of the day when children gradually come into the classroom.

Change in Environment. Even when a child is familiar with the center-based environment, traveling to the center and entering a room containing a number of active children can create a challenging transition, even though it occurs every day.

Separation from Family, Parent, or Primary Caregiver. Separation can be a major hurdle for young children with special needs. This may be their first experience with separation in a strange environment. Perhaps, more often than is the case for many children, a child with special needs may have had very little or no experience with babysitters and unfamiliar adults. Depending upon the nature of the disability, parents may have difficulty finding competent care providers for their child. Many parents are simply reluctant to leave their children with anyone other than a familiar family member.

Developmentally young children may not be ready for separation. A four-year-old who is functioning at the two-year level may have the same difficulty as a two-year-old separating from his primary caregiver.

Caregivers may send ambivalent messages. The parent may be somewhat fearful about how the child will manage in an environment with peers of different functional levels. Young children with special needs may be particularly sensitive to the emotional state of their primary caregivers, and their behavior may reflect this anxiety.

7-1b Learning Opportunities during Arrival

Depending on how arrival time is managed, educators are presented with many important opportunities for supporting the development of ALL children, especially children with special needs (see Photo 7-1). Arrival offers the following:

- Regular opportunities to touch base with a child's family
- Opportunities to make one-on-one contact in welcoming the child
- Support for transition from home to center
- Opportunities for development of self-help skills and emergent literacy
- Consistent opportunities to create confidence and security in children

7-1c Useful Strategies during Arrival Time

Although we cannot rush the developmental milestone of acceptance of separation, we will address some strategies that will support smooth transitions.

Keep Arrival Routine Fairly Consistent. Try to maintain a regular pattern for arrival. For example:

- Parent or caregiver brings the child to the center.
- Teacher greets the family member.
- Teacher greets the child.
- Teacher guides the child to find the cubby with his name, and provides whatever assistance is necessary to help the child remove his jacket and place things in the cubby. Teacher helps the child transition to the free play area and select a toy or activity. (Keep in mind that if a child arrives during a large group activity, extra "settling in" time might be needed.)

Photo 7-1 Teachers can use arrival time to welcome children and parents.

Photo 7-2 It is important to greet children with an eye-level welcome, especially those with disabilities.

Welcome Children at Eye Level. Whenever possible, it is best to speak to young children at eye level. This approach is even more crucial when communicating with children with special needs. It is easier for children to focus on your face and process what you are saying. For children with vision or hearing loss, eye-level communication increases the intensity of the signal by being closer.

Speak with Parents or Primary Caregiver. Taking this natural opportunity to communicate and build rapport with parents can enhance your understanding of a child's special needs.

Touching base with the family is important. Children with special needs may have health-related concerns, financial issues, and requirements for multiple services that significantly impact the family's daily life. In addition, children may have sleep and feeding disorders and behavior challenges that further complicate family and child functioning. Parents may find it helpful to explain some of these issues, though they may not necessarily bring up concerns and questions unless they are asked. Also, this information can be helpful to teachers in that it increases their overall understanding of the children.

Ask specific questions to elicit information. Simply asking "How are you?" or "How are things going?" may not be sufficient. You may want to pose questions that invite more detailed information: "How is Andrew doing this morning?" "Did he have a good night?" "Have there been any difficulties?"

Accentuate the positive. Be sure to routinely mention positive things about the child ("He ate a really good lunch yesterday," "Those are great looking new shoes!").

Photo 7-3 Children may need assistance with various self-help skills, like putting on jackets.

Also, reinforce the parents: "Thanks so much for your note yesterday; I like that you keep me informed."

Work on establishing true rapport. This type of communication helps establish a rapport with families that will eventually make it easier for parents and caregivers to share more difficult information and feelings. Keep in mind:

- The more you know about the child, the easier it will be to support him.
- No one has more information about the child than the family.
- The better your communication is with the family, the easier your job will be!

Support Self-Help Skills. Arrival is an easy time to work on independence. Taking off one's jacket, finding the correct cubby, hanging the jacket, and placing a backpack in the proper place are self-help skills that children can usually learn readily with consistent practice and support. This is a wonderful opportunity to work on fine motor skills such as buttoning/unbuttoning or zipping/unzipping jackets and backpacks. Some children might need an adaptation such as a key ring attached to a zipper to make it simpler to pull.

Support Emergent Literacy. Arrival is an easy time to reinforce name recognition. Cubbies should be clearly marked with the children's names. Photos may also be attached. Each day, encourage children to find their own cubby. Point out their printed name. It is also helpful to point out other children's names and to notice the differences: "Oh look, here's Robert's name. His name starts with R just like yours. And here is Ann's. Her name starts with A. Her name is very short."

Arrival and departure time provide opportunities for connections with families. By developing an environment reflective of the languages and cultures of the children, families will feel welcome as they enter the classroom. Having a designated area with a bulletin board, especially for families, with pictures of the children participating in daily activities and announcements in both English and other home languages helps to create a sense of belonging (see Photo 7-4). Families can be greeted by posting a welcome sign saying hello in the languages represented in the classroom. Laminated menus from ethnic restaurants in different languages along with multiethnic dolls will enrich the dramatic play area. A book with pictures of the children and their families will bring smiles in the library corner.

Children's belongings should also have names on them in clear large print so these names can be compared to the name on the cubby. These simple strategies do not represent a major investment of time, but they can make a significant contribution to children's awareness of print.

Help Children Enter the Free Play Area. Without brief assistance, it may be difficult for children with special needs to direct their attention to this activity and successfully engage with a peer or focus on a specific play activity. Linking children with a peer or interacting briefly with children with a favorite toy will make this transition easier.

Assist Children with Separation. When parents or caregivers leave, include a good-bye ritual such as, "Daddy's leaving now. Give Daddy a kiss. He'll be back after lunch. Tell Daddy good-bye." Parents of children who cry when they leave are often tempted to sneak away to avoid having to deal with a scene. Teachers should encourage parents not to do this. This practice leads children to believe that their parents may disappear at any time without warning, and that fear can increase children's insecurity. Children can learn to be confident that they know when their parents are leaving and returning. A clear good-bye routine helps the children anticipate the separation. Despite the emotional protests, this ritual actually increases children's ability to cope. Some children benefit from bringing a beloved object (transition object) from home to help ease separation. They might also benefit from reviewing a visual schedule of the day's activities so they can actually see when their daddy will come back to pick them up.

Photo 7-4 Classrooms can use a bulletin board to say good morning in Spanish and English.

7-2 Planning Effective Departures

Departure marks another significant transition in the center-based day. For most children, departure is not as stressful as arrival, because it usually involves reunification rather than separation. However, it is still a good idea to plan the departure routine carefully.

7-2a Establish a Consistent Departure Routine

Obviously a child care setting does not necessarily have a consistent end of the day because families pick children up at different times. As a result, there may not be a group routine related to departure such as a good-bye circle. However, it is still possible to have a brief individual routine as shown in the following examples.

Example of an Individual Departure Routine.

1. Alert the child that it is almost time for the parents to arrive.
2. When their parent arrives, help the child gather artwork and other projects to take home.
3. Communicate with the parent, and draw attention to any written communication, such as teacher notes and newsletters.
4. Say good-bye to the center's pet rabbit.
5. Encourage the child to find his own cubby.
6. Assist with putting on the child's jacket as necessary. (Use "backward chaining" as described in Chapter 2 to assist children with gradually learning the steps of putting on and taking off a jacket.)
7. Make specific reference to the next day:
   "Tomorrow is Thursday. I'll see you then. Remember it's pudding day." Or, "Tomorrow is Saturday, then Sunday. I'll see you again on Monday."

Example of Group Departure Routine.

1. If your center day ends at the same time for all children, you may want to include a short good-bye circle.
2. Finish snack; "toilet" children as needed.
3. Clean up; signal circle time by playing or singing the good-bye song.
4. When children are convened in the circle, sing the good-bye song again.
5. Briefly recall events of the day.
6. Discuss events that will occur the next day.
7. Call children's names to line up at the bus, or, if most children are picked up by parents, have the children stay in circle until their parents arrive. (In the latter case, have the assistant lead the circle so the teacher can touch base with parents.)
8. Help children gather any artwork to take home, paying particular attention to children's names as you look at their creations and accomplishments; then go to their cubby. Provide assistance as necessary, helping children recognize names on belongings, put on boots, and button jackets.

Don't Rush. One of the most difficult situations for children with special needs is being rushed to leave. Because departure is the final event of the center's day, if the teacher is behind schedule, the departure may feel harried and disorganized. It is important for teachers to be aware of time so that the departure routine need not be rushed.

Remember, the best learning opportunities are embedded within the child's daily routines. For example, all of the learning opportunities that occur during arrival also occur during departure. This is another opportunity to touch base and build rapport with families, especially about children's participation in the day's activities. And, it is a time to continue work on self-help, developing fine motor and emergent literacy skills. Families, like teachers, can be in a rush.

> **Helpful Hint**
>
> Teachers can create a *What Did We Do Today?* sheet to support the school-to-home connection. This sheet can be a short checklist (with words accompanied by simple pictures) of the classroom's daily activities and learning centers. Teachers can check off what the child did on that day, and it can be used as a starting point for a conversation with the family when they get home. Many children with special needs might not be able to answer the question, "What did you do today?" but they might be able to point to the pictures to show what they did.

It can be helpful to ask families to give you a heads-up with a phone call or text so you can have their child ready to avoid the stress of rushing if they need to leave immediately.

7-2b Support Development of Time Concepts

Departure is an ideal opportunity to support the development of time concepts and memory skills. For example, you can:

- Help children anticipate that it is almost time to go home.
- Emphasize the concepts of today and tomorrow. In circle time, ask children, "What did we do today?" "What day is tomorrow?"
- Teach past and future tense: "Who can remember what we did today?" "What will we do tomorrow?"

7-2c When Children Arrive and Depart via Bus Transportation

Sometimes building rapport with a family can be difficult if the child with special needs arrives and departs on a school bus. It is especially important that the teacher makes an extra effort to stay in contact with the family in this instance. Teachers can use communication books that go back and forth from home to school and are kept in the child's backpack. Messages from both home and school can frequently be written in the book to keep communications open. Frequent phone calls, texting, and e-mailing are also ways to build rapport and communication with families that you don't see on a regular basis.

7-3 Planning Other Transitions

As we have noted, arrival and departure present major transition challenges for many children with special needs. Though smaller in magnitude, but not in quantity, other transition challenges continue to occur throughout the day. Simply moving from one activity to another can be difficult and stressful for some children. The following sections offer some of the reasons.

7-3a Challenges Posed by Transitions

Even moving from one minor routine to another can upset some children and result in challenging behaviors:

- Transitions require ending an activity in which the children may have just settled in and become fully engaged.
- Transitions require refocusing, which may be difficult for some children.
- Transitions introduce ambiguity and often reduce predictability.

- During transition events children's behaviors are less predictable. Some children may become fearful if they are not sure exactly what is going to happen.
- Transitions are often characterized by an increase in noise level with many children bustling about, going in different directions. Children who are hypersensitive to noise and touch may feel out of control.

7-3b Learning Opportunities during Transitions

Learning happens all day long, including during transitions. But, are children learning what we want them to learn at this time? As mentioned at the beginning of this chapter, children spend a third of their time transitioning. This time needs to be intentional and well planned, especially because it comes with many challenges that can lead to difficult behavior. It is extremely important to make sure that young children know exactly what to expect during this time. Remember, when some children do not know what to expect, challenging behavior may result. Let's look at some of the learning opportunities that can occur during transition times so we know what skills to teach. During transitions, children are learning to:

- Follow one- to two-step directions.
- Follow more complex directions such as a sequence (like hand washing).
- Match, sort, and classify toys and materials.
- Understand prepositional phrases such as on top, under, behind, and so on.
- Take responsibility and care for the classroom.
- Move their body in relationship to others, toys, and furnishings.
- Wait, take turns, and cooperate.

7-3c Successful Transition Strategies

Careful planning for transitions can significantly reduce challenges that may arise for any children. The following are suggestions for successful transition strategies.

Give a Five-Minute Warning. Some children with special needs might not attend to a general statement given by the teacher to the whole class. Teachers might have to go to children with special needs, get their attention, and give them their own five-minute warning. The warning might need to be accompanied by a visual support such as a picture, holding up five fingers, or a visual timer. Some children might also need a reminder at one or two minutes before the transition.

Use a Clear Signal. Initiate the end of one activity and the beginning of a transition with a recognizable sound, gesture, or routine. Ideally, a different signal would be used for each major transition. The most effective signal varies with the special needs of the children. For example:

- For children who have limited vision, auditory cues such as a bell with a verbal announcement may be most effective.
- For children who have auditory-processing difficulties or hearing loss, visual cues such as a bright colored sign and signing may be helpful.
- For children with multiple disabilities, some kind of touch cue may be necessary, like allowing the child to feel an object representing the next activity, such as a spoon, if it is time for the transition to lunch.

Use a Specific Sequence of Events. Figure 7-1 presents an example of a specific sequence within the transition from a free play activity to snack.

Use Multiple Cues and Redundancy. A single verbal announcement, such as "Okay, it's time to clean up," may be the least effective signal for children with special needs. However, consistently pairing attention-getting visual or auditory cues (for example, holding up a "stop" sign or ringing a bell) with verbal instructions can help children

1. Teacher gives child with special needs a two-minute warning of end of play time.
2. Teacher begins singing cleanup song.
3. Children pick up and put away toys with teacher help.
4. Teacher sends children to sink to wash hands as each area is cleaned up.
5. Teacher puts snack on table and waits for children to sit down.
6. Teacher shows children snack ingredients, labeling each, and distributes snack.

Figure 7-1 Example of Transition Sequence: Transition from Free Play to Snack

Professional Resource Download

begin to understand the spoken instructions. For example, sound a chime before announcing "It's time to go outside." Move to the area where you want the children to gather and talk quietly. They will notice and will follow to see what you are doing.

Be Consistent. Using the same cues and sequence each time will increase the ease of the transition. If possible, try to use a different cue for each major transition so that the cue itself conveys to the child what is coming next.

7-3d Examples of Effective Transition Cues

The following are just a few examples of transition cues that have been effective in programs including children with a wide range of disabilities:

- Playing the song "Hi ho, hi ho. It's off to work we go!" to signal a transition to activity centers
- Directing children's attention to the visual schedule of the classroom day at the front of the room
- Using a chime or bell to signal the start or end of an activity
- Chanting, such as "Clean up, clean up, let's all clean up" to signal the end of free play
- Pointing to a visual schedule of large pictures posted on the wall that represent the sequence of the day's major activities to announce what comes next (for example, "Let's check our schedule. Look, after we clean up, we line up to go outside.")

These are examples of *whole class* transition cues. However, some children in certain situations will need their own unique transition cue. For example, a child who avoids circle time may be more successful if he is given his favorite book to take to circle. Placing a spoon in the hand of a child who has low vision can signal the transition to lunch.

A Note about the Importance of Visual Cues

For most children who have learning challenges, visual cues such as picture schedules to support transitions in daily routines are extremely helpful—except for children who have visual disabilities. (For those children, auditory and touch cues will obviously be more useful.) Auditory information, especially spoken language, is extremely complex, *and very fleeting.* Unlike pictures, which have greater permanence, spoken words disappear immediately! Words are made of rapid sequences of speech sounds (phonemes). Remembering and making sense of this complex auditory input without visual support can be a very difficult task. Pictures are static, and do not instantly disappear the way speech sounds do. (For detailed ideas related to the use of visual supports, see Cohen and Gerhardt [2016].)

Summary

In preschool settings, there are many transitions from one activity to another, which can occur seamlessly with essential planning. However, for children with special needs, these transitions can present challenges, as well as opportunities for learning. Although transitions can be challenging, they also present important, repeated contexts in which children can take advantage of repetition to learn and practice new skills. The key is careful and intentional planning, as more thoroughly discussed in Cook, Klein, and Chen (2016).

Arrival may require consideration of the difficulty many young children have separating from a parent or caregiver, and the need for some transition support as they enter the classroom and join the group setting. Throughout the day, any transition from one activity to another has the potential to be stressful. Departure, though generally less stressful, should also be carefully planned as a daily routine to maximize its value as an opportunity for learning. For a list and summary of adaptations discussed in this chapter as well as other possible adaptations, see Figure 7-2.

Adapted from CARA's Kit

Goal: To use adaptations (least amount of support) instead of physical assistance (most amount of support) whenever possible in order to increase independence and confidence skills

Adapt the environment:
- Provide a visual support such as a taped line on the floor for lining up.
- Provide a visual support (footprints) on the floor to the sink, indicated where to stand while waiting.
- Place colored paper inside a child's cubby to make it stand out and easier to find.

Adapt activity or routine:
- Squat down to greet children at their level.
- Have a child's favorite activity ready upon arrival to help with separation anxiety.
- Use auditory supports, such as a bell, song, or chant, to signal transitions.
- Use visual supports, such as pictures or objects, to signal transitions.
- Use gestural supports, such as holding up five fingers, to signal transitions.
- Use a touch cue such as a tap on the shoulder to gain a child's attention.
- Transition a child a bit earlier than others to give more time to get to the next activity.
- Ask family to drop their child off at the beginning of the day, not in the middle of group activities.
- Use backward chaining to assist a child who is gradually learning steps of a transition sequence.
- Use verbal cues, gestures, and sign language to emphasize prepositions such as *under, behind,* and *on/off.*

Adapt materials:
- Place a key ring on zippers of jackets, lunch boxes, and backpacks.
- Place name, picture, and color on cubbies.
- Place picture labels on toy cupboards and toy containers for cleanup.

Adapt requirements or instruction:
- Allow children time to warm up before joining an activity upon arrival.
- Allow a transition toy or stuffed animal from home.
- Provide a classroom visual schedule for the day's activities.
- Provide an individual visual schedule.
- Give a child an individual five-minute warning.
- Allow a child to only pick up a specific number of toys for cleanup.

Physical assistance: *Use only as last resort once you've tried the previous adaptations.*

Source: Adapted from Milbourne, S. A., & Campbell, P. H. (2007). *CARA's Kit: Creating adaptations for routines and activities.* Philadelphia, PA: Child and Family Studies Research Programs, Thomas Jefferson University.

Figure 7-2 Summary of Transition Adaptations

⌄ Professional Resource Download

Read–Reflect–Discuss

Marta's Dessert

Marta is a shy, quiet four-year-old. She is blind. With the help of her orientation and mobility specialist, she is learning to move around the room independently. One of her favorite activities is eating. She especially likes desserts! The staff notices, however, that almost every day as Marta eats her dessert, she appears upset and sometimes starts to cry. She remains upset as the other children clear the table and throw away their trash, and she often does not calm down until she is safely settled in the good-bye circle before departure for home. The teacher, Mr. Jamal, carefully observes lunchtime to try to discover why Marta gets upset. At first Mr. Jamal theorizes that something might be wrong with the taste of the dessert or with Marta's utensil. As he observes more carefully, however, Mr. Jamal realizes that the end of lunch is quite chaotic. As the children finish, they leave the table in a haphazard, noisy way and crowd around the trash can to throw away their trash.

Marta has not yet learned to accomplish this task. She remains seated until an adult notices that she is finished. Then she is led by the hand to circle time. Mr. Jamal wonders if perhaps Marta finds this time confusing, maybe even scary. There is a great deal of activity, but she seems to be left alone. Maybe as soon as she receives her dessert, she realizes chaos will immediately follow. Mr. Jamal believes Marta reacts negatively in anticipation of this time of the day when she feels vulnerable.

As a solution, Mr. Jamal and the assistant teacher design a transition plan in which he clearly announces, "It's time to clean up and throw away our trash. Who's already finished? Jason, would you like to clear your table and throw away your trash?" Rather than having a free-for-all after lunch, children take care of their trash one at a time, with the teacher describing who is doing what (for example, "OK, now it's Frederico's turn. He puts his trash in the trash can, and his dishes in the sink. Thank you, Frederico!"). These narrative cues help Marta understand what is happening. Also, Mr. Jamal asks the orientation and mobility specialist to begin working with Marta so she can participate independently in clearing her own dishes. Within a few days, Marta becomes much more comfortable with this transition.

Read–Reflect–Discuss Questions

1. This strategy worked well for Marta. Can you explain why it seemed to work well for Marta?
2. Think about a child who is just learning to move about with leg braces. How might the challenges for that child be different from Marta's?
3. What kinds of adaptations might be helpful for a child just learning to use leg braces during the transition described in this scenario?

Key Terms

separation

transitions

Helpful Resources

Feldman, J. (2009). *Transition tips and tricks for teachers*. Beltsville, MD: Gryphon House.

Heroman, C., Dodge, D. T., Berke, K., Vickart, T., Colker, L., Jones, C., Copley, J., & Dighe, J. (2010). *The creative curriculum for preschool* (5th ed.). Bethesda, MD: Teaching Strategies.

Mathews, S. E. (2012). Singing smooths classroom transitions. *Dimensions of Early Childhood*, 40 (1). Retrieved from www.southernearlychildhood.org/upload/pdf /Singing_Smoothes_Classroom_Transitions_Sarah_E_Mathews.pdf.

CHAPTER 8

Engaging Children with Special Needs in Free Play

LEARNING OBJECTIVES

After studying this chapter, you will be able to:

LO 8-1: Explain the reasons why some children with special needs might need support during free play time.

LO 8-2: Describe a variety of support techniques that will assist children's learning when they are participating in free play.

LO 8-3: Identify toys and materials that are likely to appeal to children representing a wide range of developmental levels.

The following NAEYC Standards and DEC Recommended Practices are addressed in this chapter:

naeyc

Standard 1: Promoting Child Development and Learning
Standard 2: Building Family and Community Relationships
Standard 4: Using Developmentally Effective Approaches
Standard 5: Using Content Knowledge to Build Meaningful Curriculum

DEC

Practice 2: Environment
Practice 3: Family
Practice 4: Instruction
Practice 5: Interaction

Unstructured play presents significant challenges for many children with disabilities.

Some children who have disabilities may need special assistance in free play activities. Although free play provides important opportunities for child initiation, choice, and exploration, it can be challenging because of its lack of structure and its unpredictability:

- **Free play provides many opportunities to assist the development of young children with special needs.** These include opportunities for one-on-one scaffolding and following the child's lead, teaching language through labeling and repetition, and supporting peer interaction.

- **Many strategies are designed to support children's engagement during free play.** Examples include teaching children to engage in trial-and-error exploration, arranging the physical environment in certain ways, teaching children how to activate a toy or play a game with peers, training peers, and requesting help from the disability specialist to adapt toys.

- **Careful consideration of the types of toys available can increase children's participation in free play.** Some toys are more easily adapted to a wide range of abilities and interests than other toys. Teachers may need to include toys appropriate for developmentally younger children, and some toys may need to be specially adapted.

Introduction

Free play or *unstructured* play is a major component of all early childhood programs, though the proportion of time devoted to unstructured play varies considerably among early childhood programs. This can be a difficult time for young children with special needs. Some children may find free play chaotic and react with increased behavior challenges. Other children may find the lack of structure disorganizing and may simply withdraw or wander the classroom. Still others may need assistance engaging in meaningful play with materials and others. A variety of strategies may be helpful in engaging children with special needs in free play.

8-1 Possible Challenges of Free Play for Children with Special Needs

Some children with special needs have particular difficulty with unstructured child-directed play. Children with special needs often require support during free play, at least initially, for the following reasons:

- They may be unfamiliar with the toys and materials and have no idea what to do with them.
- They may be overwhelmed with the number of choices.
- They may have difficulty selecting and getting started with a toy or activity.
- They may have poor task persistence.
- They may be easily distracted and have difficulty focusing.
- Increased noise levels during free play may be stressful.
- They may not find the available materials interesting because they are not appropriate for their specific developmental level.
- They may not have achieved the ability to engage in trial-and-error exploration.
- They may feel threatened by the number and proximity (nearness) of other children in the room, all doing different, unpredictable things.

The nature of their special condition may interfere with their ability to play. Given the challenges noted, it is not surprising that children with special needs might not initiate play and may have a unique way of playing. As Sluss points out, "Teachers must know the child well enough to understand her unique play" (2015, p. 250).

8-2 Special Opportunities to Assist Learning in Free Play

Free play provides several important opportunities for adults and peers to assist children's learning, particularly by incorporating many of the facilitating techniques described in Chapter 2.

8-2a An Opportunity for Self-Initiated Exploration

It is critical that children realize that they can discover interesting things and solve problems by themselves. The children, who have learned self-initiated **trial-and-error exploration** and have developed some *task persistence* (see Chapter 3), will be greatly rewarded. Many children with special needs, however, need to be assisted in these important cognitive processes. Sometimes children with special needs require lots of repetition in play before they feel comfortable enough to persist with a task that has been difficult to master. You may need to actually teach a child to use trial-and-error exploration and task persistence, as in Jason's example.

Teaching Trial-and-Error Exploration

Jason often appeared to be in a daze during free play. He would briefly examine a toy, but then throw it down and stare off into space. Miss Monson sat down next to him and showed him a small radio. She said, "I wonder how this works." She shook it and encouraged him to do the same. Then she started pushing anything that looked like a button and again encouraged Jason to do it. Then she turned the on/off knob until the radio came on. She said, "Oh, that's how it works!" She turned it off and handed it to Jason, who promptly turned it on and then off. She then left Jason alone. He spent several minutes turning the radio on and off and eventually learned how to turn the volume way up. Not everyone was pleased with his discovery!

8-2b Teaching Children How to Play with Toys

Often children are limited in their ability to play successfully with others because they don't know how to play with certain toys. During free play the teacher can directly teach certain play skills, thus increasing the likelihood that a child can play on his own or join in the play of others. It is especially helpful to use this opportunity to directly teach children how to play with typical classroom toys and materials, such as blocks and manipulatives. It should be noted that typically, children without disabilities don't need to be taught how to play with most toys and materials, because they are usually curious and naturally initiate trial-and-error strategies to try to figure out how to make toys and materials work. However, children with a disability might not persist with this curiosity or might not have the repertoire of ideas to explore materials. Teachers need to carefully

---

Helpful Hint

The following behaviors might be indicators that a child with special needs does not know how to play with toys and needs direct facilitation to learn:

- Wandering the classroom by frequently walking around and not necessarily engaging with the toys and materials
- Moving quickly from toy to toy, but not doing any actions that lead to meaningful play
- Doing the same thing over and over with a toy such as lining up the cars instead of driving up and down the car ramps of a toy garage

observe how children actually use materials to determine how much support will be needed. They might find that children will need to be specifically taught how to play appropriately with toys and materials, which, as we said, is a departure from what we know about children without a disability.

8-2c Opportunities for One-on-One Interaction

Free play allows teachers to use strategies such as following a child's lead, which takes advantage of the child's existing motivation and interest, and scaffolding (see Chapter 2) to support children to the next skill level. Children with special needs sometimes are not easily motivated. Thus, when a child is engaged in an activity and you want to assist the child's processing and learning from the activity, it is important to follow the child's lead and build on this interest, rather than attempting to redirect the child's attention.

As you observe children, you can determine what kind of support they need to perform tasks at a slightly higher level. This is called *scaffolding*. The following example demonstrates these one-on-one strategies.

Following the Child's Lead and Scaffolding

Miriam's teacher notices her trying to pull off a doll's dress. She is repeatedly just pulling at the hem of the dress. She is beginning to get frustrated. The teacher joins Miriam and says, "You're trying to take her dress off, aren't you? Can I help you?" She then points to the doll's arms and says, "We have to take the arms out first." She demonstrates by pulling the doll's arm out of the sleeve. She then pulls the other arm halfway out and encourages Miriam to pull it the rest of the way. The teacher then pulls the dress halfway over the doll's head and shows Miriam how to pull it the rest of the way.

The next time she notices Miriam trying to get the dress off, she points to the doll's arm and says, "Remember? Arms first." Miriam pulls each arm out, but still cannot get the dress over the doll's head. The teacher again pulls the dress halfway and lets Miriam pull it the rest of the way off.

Within the next couple of days, Miriam has learned how to take off the doll's dress. She now busies herself taking off all the dolls' clothes. Her teacher makes a mental note to use the same technique to show Miriam how to put the clothes back on!

8-2d Building Language Skills during Free Play

Specific language input strategies to teach vocabulary, concepts, and sentence structure can greatly enhance children's development of communication. One-on-one or small group interaction during free play provides an ideal opportunity to offer careful language input. Using key words and phrases that match what children are focusing on, repeating those key words, and expanding on children's own words are important strategies.

Language Mediation with Roger

Roger is stacking blocks, then knocking them down. Mrs. Chen joins him, saying, "I see you're stacking the blocks, Roger." She starts counting as he places each block: "One block, two blocks, three blocks." Roger enjoys her participation and starts to wait for her to count before placing the next block. Soon he starts to imitate her counting, repeating the number. When the stack gets quite high, Roger knocks it over. Each time he knocks over the stack, Mrs. Chen says, "Oh, oh. The blocks fell down!" Roger does not imitate her. However, later in the day a stack of empty boxes fell over. Roger noticed this, looked at Mrs. Chen, and said "Oh, oh. Fell down!"

> **Helpful Hint**
>
> For children who have *visual disabilities,* remember to add tactile and auditory—even olfactory—cues to language input. In Roger's example, the teacher could help the child by placing his hand on the top block, then helping him feel as they add a block together. The teacher could scaffold to help Roger take his turn until he learns to judge how to place the next block. The noisier the blocks are as they stack them, the better. For a child who is blind, it is better to do this activity on a hard surface rather than a rug so there is more sound when the blocks crash. After the blocks crash, help the child feel that they are now scattered all over the floor.

> **Helpful Hint**
>
> For a child who has a *hearing loss* and who uses manual sign, be sure to sign the key words. Also emphasize speech by speaking close to the child. (This is an advantage of a one-on-one situation over a group activity.) You can provide a more optimal acoustic signal by speaking close to the child's hearing aid while facing the child so she may see the movement of your mouth. Also, be sure to direct the child's attention to the noise the blocks make when they fall; otherwise, she might not be aware of this sound.

8-2e Demonstrating Interaction and Teaching Strategies to Families

If parents or caregivers are visiting the center or stay with their child, free play can be an opportunity to not only demonstrate, but also to discuss how to use scaffolding, how to follow the child's lead, and how to use language in ways that enhance a child's opportunity to learn. It can also be a time to point out the child's strengths and abilities. Given that the play materials and expectations should match the child's developmental level, teachers might be able to point out strengths and abilities that might otherwise go unnoticed.

8-2f Encouraging Children to Play with Peers

Often children who have special needs prefer interacting with adults instead of with other children. One of the challenges for children with special needs in a typical child care center is that they may feel overwhelmed and threatened by the number and proximity of other children. Because they have difficulty processing the many children and activities going on around them, free play may be a particularly stressful situation for children with special needs. It may be helpful to find ways to enable the child to feel *safe* from these other children.

Psychological safety is as important as physical safety, which tends to be more obvious. **Relational bullying**, or bullying that occurs when one child becomes isolated by a group of children, may occur and is often unnoticed. In fact, it sometimes occurs without intention by peers. Young children can get so enthusiastic that they just don't notice when they are leaving another child out who cannot keep up for whatever reason.

The following strategies will help avoid such instances.

Strategies for Encouraging Peer Interaction

1. **Begin with one peer rather than several.** If a child has expressed some preference for a particular peer, encourage that peer to be a play partner. Keep the same partner until a successful pattern has been established, then gradually introduce new playmates. Also, gradually increase the number of children.

2. **Begin with parallel play.** If a child with special needs resists the proximity of a peer, begin by having the peer engage in **parallel play,** rather than interactive play, and keep the peer out of reach of the child. When there is no contact between children, children can gradually get used to having others close by. When a child with special needs does become more comfortable, then the teacher can help the children to start noticing each other. She can do this by verbally drawing attention to what each child is doing to help them make a connection and possibly interact on small levels. It would be as if she were interpreting what each child is doing to help them pay attention to one another, because children with disabilities might have difficulty attending to what others are doing. If children are playing next to each other while stringing beads, the teacher might say, "Look at Johnny! He is looking for a red bead in the bin to add to his string. Can you help him find one?"

3. **Have a peer participate in something in which the child is already engaged.** Rather than trying to engage a child with special needs in a peer's activity, invite an interested peer to join in something in which the child is already involved. This may need to be done very carefully at first. A simple way to encourage peer interaction is to create a turn-taking game out of the child's activity. Let's say, for example, that the child is engaged in pounding a drum. The peer might interrupt the pounding by taking her own turn. The child with special needs often finds this type of interaction fun because:
   - He is obviously interested in it because he was already doing it.
   - He understands the activity.
   - The activity is predictable; he knows what to expect.
   - He can make sense of it, and the activity is nonthreatening.

4. **Select simple activities that *require* interaction or cooperation.** The best example is playing catch or batting the ball. Also good are activities that require cooperation to be successful, carrying something very heavy, or riding in a wagon.

> ### Helpful Hint
>
> This turn-taking strategy is particularly useful with children who have *low cognitive ability.* Finding activities that appeal to children who are functioning at a significantly younger developmental level can be frustrating for both teachers and peers. Making a turn-taking game of a simple activity in which a child is already engaged can help establish an interaction.

Photo 8-1 Book reading can be more fun with a friend.

For a child who has a *motor disability*, ask a therapist or disability specialist for assistance in adapting activities. Try to figure out what kind of simple adaptation might enable the child to participate in some way. For example, a child who is unable to use her hands and arms may be able to use her leg or head to bat a small beach ball. A basket could be attached to the front of the wheelchair tray, making it possible for the child to "catch" the ball.

Another adaptation would be to simplify the batting activity by placing the ball on top of an orange construction cone. A carpet square placed by the side of the cone will act as a visual support to remind the child where to stand. This is a fun, cooperative activity because it encourages social interaction by having one child bat the ball while another child runs to retrieve it and brings it back to the batter.

8-2g Helping to Develop Crowd Tolerance

Children with special needs may have more difficulty tolerating large numbers of other children than do most children without disabilities. As noted earlier, they may feel threatened by the proximity of other children. Teachers may have difficulty recognizing when a child is having difficulty with crowding. Children might use subtle cues to let you know that they're interested in an activity, but are having difficulty with crowding. For instance, a child with a disability might look at a tabletop activity as if interested, but then walk away. A child also might, upon invitation, sit down but then get right back up and leave the table. The interest appears to be there, but there is a barrier with the number of children. One strategy could be to invite the child back to the table when fewer children are involved in the activity. The following strategies may be helpful with development of increased tolerance for larger numbers of children:

- **Provide a quiet zone.** This should be a somewhat enclosed space, such as a library corner, which is relatively quiet and where there are only two or three children at a time. Children should be allowed to *retreat* here whenever the environment becomes overwhelming because of noise level, too many children, or too many different activities. It provides a calm environment whenever the child feels stressed, even if there is no external reason.
- **Introduce number and proximity of play partners gradually.** It may be helpful to allow only one play partner at a time to be within the child's physical space. By gradually increasing the number of children playing in this space, the child with special needs can gradually increase his tolerance.
- **Avoid large open spaces.** Some children with special needs have difficulty in large open spaces and feel particularly threatened by numbers of peers roaming around in such a space. During free play, these children may be more comfortable playing within an area that has at least a partial boundary or enclosure of some kind, such as shelves placed at right angles (see Chapter 4).
- **Create a space buffer.** For example, a child can sit on a favorite towel or blanket (see Photo 8-2). Other children learn that they may not cross the boundary of the blanket edge unless the child invites them to do so.

Photo 8-2 A child with low crowd tolerance may feel more comfortable playing on a space buffer.

Whether play is seen as something that children do on their own or whether adult participation is valuable may differ given the influence of culture. If solitary play is highly valued, involvement with others may be discouraged. However, if play is thought of as an opportunity for socialization, then the interaction with others will be encouraged. Also, whether or not adults regard play as a valuable learning experience and how they plan for and facilitate it is influenced by culture (Gonzalez-Mena, 2007). Although Western thinking sees a connection between children's play, learning, and development, some cultures do not recognize its value, and play is viewed as a superfluous activity. For example, in some cultures, children's participation in work and work-related activities is thought to be far more important than is their participation in play activities (Roopnarine et al., 2003). Therefore, it is important to be sensitive when learning to understand the perspective of families when they observe their child in play.

8-3 Selecting Toys and Materials for Free Play

As with all children, it is impossible to predict exactly what toys will be the most interesting and engaging for children who have special needs. Experienced teachers in the field of early childhood education, however, find certain types of toys to be more captivating and accessible. It is important to identify those toys that appeal to a wide range of developmental levels. Examples of appealing and accessible toys are listed later in this chapter.

Early childhood programs often rotate toys to maintain children's interest. For children who have special needs, some toys should stay constant and always in the same location. Children with special needs often need many more repetitions—more practice and exposure—to master a toy, activity, or skill. In addition, once they are very familiar with the toy (or book or song), they do not usually get bored with it. Rather, they often love the sense of mastery and competence that comes with something highly practiced. Indeed, don't most of us prefer doing things we're really good at rather than struggling to master new things?

We absolutely do not wish to suggest that children with special needs should never be encouraged to experience new things! Rather, the point is that it is important that certain things be predictable, familiar, and comfortable. Only within the context of a secure base will children feel confident enough to try the difficult and unfamiliar.

8-3a Toys That Appeal to Different Developmental Levels

Some toys are easier than others to support children at any skill level. For example, even the simplest computer game requires certain minimal motor, perceptual, and cognitive skills. However, a whiteboard or easel with large markers can be challenging to both a child who is just beginning to get the hang of making marks on a surface and to a precocious artist whose drawings are complex.

Materials such as whiteboards and easels are also **open-ended** in the sense that there is no one right way to play with them. In contrast, a jack-in-the-box is a **close-ended** material. To experience the toy successfully, children have to do it the right way by turning the crank a certain number of revolutions in a particular direction. It's important to have many open-ended materials in the classroom so that children with a variety of developmental levels can be supported in the same classroom. Open-ended materials provide opportunities for children to interact with the same materials as everyone else, but at a different developmental level. A toy like Legos allows for an infinite number of creations, while being simple enough to provide enjoyment to children who just want to stack them, pull them apart, or match the colors. Playdough also has wide appeal to all ages and allows engagement with the material regardless of the disability, because it can be explored on a variety of levels, from simple to complex.

Beanbags offer multiple possibilities for all children. They are easy to grasp and hold. They provide a low-risk opportunity for aggressive throwing and mock injuries when someone is hit. They enhance gross motor abilities of throwing and catching that can support development of valuable ball-playing skills. They provide an easily accessible opportunity for competitive games of throwing the bags into a large basket or through a small hole.

An example of a common commercial toy that has wide appeal is a garage play set. Children with and without disabilities will make up pretend scenarios and sequences related to pumping gas, parking, and auto repairs, and they may increase complexity by incorporating toy people. At the same time, children with limited cognitive ability can enjoy the cause-and-effect feature of cranking the car up the lift, watching it roll down the ramp, and stopping at the traffic arm if it is down. Children who understand the cognitive achievement of object permanence will enjoy putting the car inside the garage and closing the doors, then being delighted to discover it is still there when the doors are opened again!

8-3b Considerations for Children who are Developmentally Young

Often what is fun for children are those activities and tasks that activate the specific cognitive skills they have just mastered. Thus, children who are developmentally young (for example, a child who has a cognitive delay associated with Down syndrome) and are just mastering object permanence find looking for hidden objects particularly intriguing. A child at an even lower level might prefer the simple sensations offered by sensory experiences such as water and sand play.

On the other hand, a child at a slightly higher level may just be beginning to enjoy the symbolic representation of **auto symbolic play**, such as pretending to have a tea party, wash the dishes, take a nap, or be the mommy putting a baby doll to bed. When a child with special needs seems unable to engage in a particular activity, try to adapt the activity for the child by using the EESS acronym and thinking how to make the activity easier for a child to access and participate at his own developmental level. Teachers can:

- Enlarge toys and materials by using a variety of sizes of materials, such as having larger beads to string.
- Enhance activities by adding texture to toys to make them more interesting.
- Stabilize toys and materials with shelf liners so they don't move around and slide off the tables.
- Simplify the activity by:
  - Reducing the amount of the materials so children are not overwhelmed with too many choices.
  - Reducing the number of steps a child has to do.

Most early childhood centers have a variety of puzzles that appeal to the age level of the classroom. It will also be important to make sure to have puzzles that are appropriate for those who are a bit developmentally younger than the average age of the classroom. The following are some examples of types of puzzles as well as adaptations:

- **Nonconnecting puzzles with separate pieces.** Some children might need a simple puzzle with no more than four separate pieces. Increasing the number of pieces will increase the difficulty level. Teachers can simplify some of the existing puzzles in their class by taping a piece of construction paper to hide half of the puzzle pieces. The shape of the pieces is also important. A piece in the shape of a circle is easier to put in than a rectangle or an object like a car that has many curves and angles.

Photo 8-3 This puzzle has been adapted with handles and colored construction paper.

- **Connecting puzzles that form a picture.** These puzzles can be more difficult but do come in a variety of sizes with as few as four pieces. Teachers can have some of these simpler puzzles available for children who are developmentally younger.
- **Puzzles with handles.** These puzzles can simplify a child's ability to grasp the puzzle piece (see Photo 8-3). Many puzzles can be purchased with handles, or teachers can adapt existing puzzles by hot gluing a cork or a small block onto the puzzle piece.
- **Puzzles with a picture background.** This simplifies and enhances the puzzle and turns it into a matching activity by giving the child a visual cue. These puzzles can also be purchased, or a teacher can copy or photograph the puzzle piece and glue it into the puzzle. Note how in Photo 8-3 a matching colored construction paper was glued into the puzzle to make it simpler.
- **Interlocking or jigsaw puzzles**. These can be extremely challenging for some children who are developmentally younger. Interlocking puzzles are frequently sold in boxed sets that require children to match and connect two pieces that go together while continuing to do this for all the pieces in this set. For instance, the set might consist of *things that go together* such as matching objects like a sock with a shoe. A teacher can simplify this activity by drastically decreasing the number of sets children have to connect by starting with just one matching set.

8-3c Common Toy and Activity Categories

This section considers the most common types of early childhood toys and activities and makes suggestions regarding their use for children with special needs.

Dramatic Play Materials. Children who have special needs often have difficulty engaging in pretend play. This is particularly true for children with low cognitive ability, limited vision, and difficulties with self-regulation. Children with motor difficulties who do not have cognitive delays can enjoy pretend play as long as appropriate adaptations are made for their physical limitations. Photo 8-4 shows how an adapted toy shopping cart allows children to access the dramatic play area without physical support from an adult. A child who needs support when walking can get around independently with the shopping cart that has a homemade weight added to it. The weight stabilizes the cart so she can use it almost as a walker. Without the weight, the cart would not be able to support her and would tip over very easily. The weight consists of a large coffee can filled with sand and duct taped to the bottom shelf of the shopping cart.

These pretend play materials often have high interest value for children with special needs because of their familiarity and opportunities for repeated exposure in daily life:

Telephone
Dishes (tea set)
Plastic utensils
Pots and pans
Broom and mop
Sink and stove
Doll

Doll bed and bedding
Baby bottles
High chair
Purse
Hats
Shoes

Shirts and jackets (good for self-dressing practice)
Shopping cart
Food cartons with recognizable brand logos

Children may need initial assistance in participating in dramatic play activities. With a little bit of coaching from a teacher, peers can effectively involve children in ways that are appropriate to their developmental level. Some dress-up clothes for dolls and children can be adapted with larger buttons, key rings to enlarge the zipper handles, and Velcro instead of zippers or buttons.

Also helpful can be the development of **mini-scripts.** This involves creating routines, such as putting the doll to bed or having a tea party, which the teacher models in pretty much the same way each time until the child learns the sequence. Once the child has mastered such a script, he has a way of participating with peers, even if the peers don't *stick to the script* exactly. (See Read–Reflect–Discuss at the end of this chapter.)

Blocks. Children with special needs may have difficulty creating three-dimensional structures and including additional objects like cars, trucks, and animal and people figures in their block play. When attempting to involve children with special needs in block play, it is helpful to be aware of what younger children do with blocks. Figure 8-1 reviews the developmental stages of block play.

Even though children may not be able to play at the same conceptual level as peers, blocks can still be very motivating. The following are examples of the kinds of block play activities that may be appealing:

- Stacking blocks and knocking them down.
- Lining them up. (You can help children elaborate this activity by incorporating cars and trucks and making *block streets.*)
- Using blocks to make fenced-in enclosures. (Help children elaborate by placing animals in the enclosures.)
- Assisting children in setting blocks up like dominoes, then knocking them down.

Photo 8-4 Adapting a shopping cart using a homemade weight will stabilize it for a child with a physical disability.

1 to 1½ years	Child mouths, bangs, bangs together, drops, and watches blocks fall.
1½ to 2 years	Child carries blocks around or puts/drops into container.
2 to 2½ years	Child stacks blocks or lines them up on floor (single line).
2½ to 3 years	Child uses blocks to make "road" and pushes a car along it.
3 to 3½ years	Child makes an enclosure (fence) and places animals inside.
3½ to 4 years	Child makes three-dimensional structures, such as a bridge, garage, or abstract design.
4 to 6 years	Child makes increasingly complex structures and groups of structures; incorporates play themes into structures; and often provides setting for dramatic play.

Figure 8-1 Developmental Stages of Block Play

- Building a ramp and letting cars race down the ramp.
- Sorting blocks by color or shape; placing in proper bin or shelf at cleanup time.

The type of blocks selected may be a consideration for some children. For example:

- *Traditional wooden blocks* can be dangerous for children who throw them or enjoy knocking down stacked blocks.
- *Soft foam blocks* have many advantages: They are lighter and easier to manipulate, they're not dangerous, and they can be used in water because they float. One disadvantage is that younger children may bite or chew them.
- *Oversized cardboard blocks* are cheap and easy to stack. Larger structures and taller stacks can be made, and they are safe. Larger blocks also encourage coordination of whole-body movement. You can make your own cardboard blocks by placing milk cartons inside one another (see Figure 8-2).

Playdough. With some adult or peer help and repetition, playdough can be a motivating medium for young children with special needs. If your class includes children with cerebral palsy or children who have low muscle tone, it is important that the

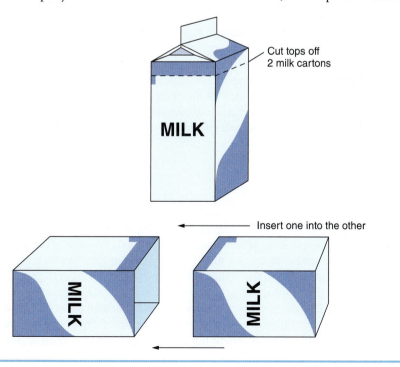

Cut tops off
2 milk cartons

MILK

Insert one into the other

MILK   MILK

Figure 8-2 Make your own cardboard blocks.

modeling clay not be too stiff. Children may have difficulty manipulating the dough with just their hands, so a variety of *utensils* are helpful.

At first children with special needs might not know what to do with playdough. They might actually need to be taught the different things that most children without disabilities naturally do with playdough. Teachers can teach children simple activities with playdough by encouraging children to touch the playdough, pull it apart, squeeze and squish it in their hands, poke at it with their fingers, flatten it, and make snakes and balls. Having these skills can then lead up to more complex sequences such as using cookie cutters with playdough.

Rolling pins. Children may need help at first rolling the rolling pin. Once they get the hang of this, however, it will be easier for them to roll snakes, which is often difficult for children with low tone or muscle control problems.

Cookie cutters. Cookie cutters can be used to help children learn sequences:

1. Roll the dough flat.
2. Push the cookie cutter down and pick it up.
3. Examine the resulting imprint.
4. Pick up the playdough cookie.

Helpful Hint

The following is a playdough recipe that, once cooked, becomes very soft and easily manageable for most children with disabilities. It is easily stored in a closed ziplock bag.

Ingredients:
- 2 cups flour
- 2 cups water
- 1 cup salt
- 3 tablespoons oil
- 4 teaspoons cream of tartar
- Food coloring of your choice

Directions: Add all the dry ingredients together and then add the water and food coloring. Blend well with a spoon. Pour into a large pan and cook over low heat. Just when you think, "*This is taking too long and it's never going to solidify!*" it will suddenly start to take shape and become rubbery. Knead the dough until it becomes warm (not hot), and then let the children have a great time exploring. Of course, this can become a participatory cooking activity as children discuss the different ingredients, measure and stir ingredients, and watch the transformation.

Helpful Hint

For a child with severe motor disability, rolling the dough and picking up the cookie may be impossible without help from an adult. However, a disability or inclusion specialist should be able to help you adapt the cookie cutter so that it can be attached to the child's hand (so she doesn't have to grip it). For example, it might be attached by wrapping a piece of Velcro around the child's hand or wrist. This way the child only has to press her arm down and lift it up to see the imprint of the cutter. If the child has some ability to grip, another *prosthetic* adaptation might include hot gluing a large wooden knob or a small block to the cookie cutter.

Plastic knives and scissors. Children love cutting sections from snakes. This provides an opportunity to practice using scissors and knives on something easier to cut than paper or food. Foam curlers can be used to build up the handles of plastic knives to make it simpler to grasp.

Mini-muffin or cupcake tins. Children may enjoy pushing the playdough into small muffin tins or other small containers.

Candles. Making birthday playdough cupcakes and putting in the candles is a fun *pretend* activity. Be sure to sing the "Happy Birthday" song!

Cause-and-Effect Toys. Many cause-and-effect toys are uninteresting or lose their appeal quickly. However, the following cause-and-effect toys tend to maintain some degree of interest:

- Baby pop-up toys, busy boxes, and toys with buttons to push may be engaging for children with significant cognitive delay.
- Hammer the ball mazes, drop the ball mazes, or marble toy mazes are extremely fun, and with much practice can eventually turn into a simple turn-taking game. Mazes can be good cause-and-effect toys because the *effect* is slow and allows children some additional processing time. Ball mazes were included here because some children place objects in their mouth, which would make marbles unsafe and not appropriate to use.
- Specially adapted or commercially available switch-activated toys interest many children. Examples are a car, cash register, or music player that can be turned on by pressing a large button, as well as toy computers, and music boxes.

Photo 8-5 Pushing buttons to activate toys helps teach cause and effect.

Water Play. Many children with and without special needs love water play. They also may often enjoy washing things like tabletops and dirty bicycles. The trick is to help them *explore* different ways of playing with water. Otherwise, for some children, the activity can become highly repetitive and somewhat mesmerizing, as when a child constantly pours water out of a container, fills it, and pours again. The below list provides suggestions for water play activities that may engage a child's interest.

Suggestions for High-Interest Water Play Activities

- Squeezing water in and out of sponges (adding soap bubbles can be extra fun)
- Pouring water down a water wheel (great for social interaction and cooperation)
- Counting the number of cups of water required to fill a large container
- Making paper boats and sinking boats when you make waves
- Adding food coloring to make water easier to see for children with visual impairments
- Filling squeeze bottles and then squeezing all the water out
- Filling spray bottles and making designs on dry concrete or wall
- Painting a wall, concrete floor, or fence with water
- Filling a bucket with soap and water, making suds, and then washing dirty things like outside play equipment (bikes, and so on) tables, windows, and the slide
- Giving the doll a bath, including undressing and dressing the doll
- Washing doll clothes and hanging them out to dry in the sun
- Wiping off tables following snack time or an art activity
- Playing in a plastic wading pool

Other Sensory Activities. Several other sensory activities may be available during free play, such as a sand or rice table or a wading pool filled with lightweight plastic multicolored balls. These materials often provide pleasurable sensations. For some children, these activities may be very calming.

For developmentally young children, hiding objects in sand or rice or under plastic balls may have substantial appeal. Helping children sustain a search for a hidden object can assist them with grasping the concepts of object permanence, trial-and-error exploration, and task persistence.

Photo 8-6 This wading pool filled with balls is an example of a sensory activity.

Books. Children with special needs have specific challenges related to enjoying books. Developmentally young children may not relate to pictures. Children with impulse control problems and high activity levels may have great difficulty concentrating on the auditory and visual properties of a book or story. Children with visual impairment and perceptual difficulties may not be able to make sense of the pictures in many books.

Books likely to appeal to young children with special needs have the following properties:

- Repetitive phrases and pictures
- Sturdy design and pages that are easy to turn
- Interactive components, inviting action through opening doors and pulling tabs
- Simple and clearly drawn pictures, with maximum contrast between foreground and background
- Illustrations that represent common objects and activities of daily life
- Depictions of appealing absurdities, such as someone wearing a shoe on her head (*Wacky Wednesday* by Theodore Lesieg is an excellent example of such absurdities.)
- Duplicates of a book read frequently by the teacher during circle time
- Rhyme and rhythm
- Story structure that invites *call-and-response* participation

Bubbles. Bubbles are universally appealing, particularly to children with disabilities:

- They are visually interesting.
- They move slowly so they are easy to track and to reach out to touch.
- Bubbles demonstrate cause and effect as they appear and disappear.
- Bubbles lend themselves to teaching communicative requests ("more bubbles!") and to describing events by saying "Pop!"
- Blowing bubbles can be used to develop fine motor skills of opening the container, dipping the wand, and blowing.
- They have the added benefit of helping to support oral motor development.

Manipulatives. Manipulatives present many challenges. Most manipulatives, like small Legos, can be a significant challenge for children who have special needs because they are physically difficult to manipulate and because they may be too complex to hold interest.

> ### Helpful Hint
>
> For children with *visual impairments,* books can be adapted by enhancing the pictures with meaningful added textures or small representative objects to the pictures. For children who are blind and who have good cognitive skills, a visual impairment specialist may want to start working on Braille versions of favorite books.

> ### Helpful Hint
>
> The following are examples of books that often appeal to children who have special needs;
>
> ***Brown Bear, Brown Bear, What Do You See?* (Bill Martin)**
> Rhythmic, repetitive text with clear simple drawings lends itself to other activities, such as finger puppets.
>
> ***Where's Spot?* (Eric Hill)**
> This book supports memory object permanence (the hiding theme is appealing), and hands-on participation with opening doors, lifting flaps, and simple labels of familiar animals.
>
> ***The Very Hungry Caterpillar* (Eric Carle)**
> This book has bright pictures, a simple concept (eating), and repetition. (This book is a little too long for some children. However, the lesson found in Appendix C offers more possibilities for including this book.
>
> ***Five Little Monkeys* (Eileen Christelow)**
> This book has chanted rhyme and rhythm, simple number concepts, familiar interesting animals, and simple pictures.
> (See list at the end of the Chapter 13 for more ideas.)

Large bins of small manipulatives may be overwhelming and often entice children to dump and throw. In addition, choking is a potential hazard for developmentally young children who mouth objects.

Generally, manipulatives tend to be difficult for children with significant challenges, especially those with fine motor delays. The following suggestions may increase children's success with this type of toy:

- Manipulatives that are larger, easier to grasp and stick together easily will be more engaging such as Lego Duplos.
- Sometimes more appealing are less abstract manipulatives, such as separate containers with such items as small cars, small wind-up toys, Fisher-Price people, or commercial movie characters. Such a combination of small items may offer more familiarity and interest than more abstract manipulatives.
- One strategy for storing manipulatives is to place picture labels that can be clearly understood on difficult-to-open containers. For example, keeping several toy cars in a large lunch box or tackle box offers the extra challenge of figuring out how to open the box.
- Collections of visually and tactually interesting items in such boxes may also be appealing. An example might be a collection of shells or rocks of varying colors, some that are prickly and rough and others that are shiny and smooth.

Balls. Balls offer a number of challenges for children with special needs:

- Children with special needs often require a great deal of help learning to throw (including both grasp and release) and catch.
- Catching is much more difficult to learn than throwing.
- Children may not be able to hold on to balls of stiffer material.
- They may have difficulty controlling the intensity and direction of their throw.
- When they first learn to throw, they may enjoy throwing the ball wildly and aggressively.

The following recommendations may enable children to play successfully with balls:

- Maintain a supply of several different types of balls.
- Keep beach balls on hand. They may be easier to hang on to and because these large, light balls move slowly, they are easier to catch.
- Offer Nerf balls or beanbags. They are easier to grasp and cause less damage if thrown wildly!
- Practice rolling, throwing, and catching by sitting down first. Once a child is successful, you can increase the amount of space between the two of you. Later, the harder movement component of standing up can be added.

Summary

Free play can provide many opportunities for supporting the learning of young children with special needs that other activities cannot. If free play is to achieve its potential as a great learning activity, teachers must develop some skills in how to engage children with various disabilities in different types of play. They must learn how to adapt typical early childhood materials and activities. For a list and summary of adaptations discussed in this chapter as well as other possible adaptations, see Figure 8-3.

Read–Reflect–Discuss
Shopping Mini-Script for Raul

Raul has diplegia. He has learned to use a walker. He has fairly good use of his arms and hands, though fine motor movements are slow and inaccurate. He is good at recognizing logos, like the golden arches of McDonald's, and he loves going to the grocery store with his mom. He enjoys being with other children and gravitates to

Adapted from CARA's Kit

Goal: Use adaptations (least amount of support) instead of physical assistance (most amount of support) whenever possible to increase independence and confidence skills.

Adapt the environment:
- Have toys and materials available that are appropriate for children who are developmentally younger such as cause-and-effect toys and simpler puzzles.
- Use toys and materials that are open-ended for a wide range of abilities.
- Provide toys and materials in a variety of sizes for all abilities.
- Create a quiet zone in the classroom for children who get overwhelmed.
- Weigh down a toy shopping cart so a child with a physical impairment can use it to get around the classroom.
- Place picture labels on toy bins and shelves.

Adapt activity or routine:
- Use a blanket or towel for a space buffer.
- Begin social interaction with one peer using parallel play and gradually add more play partners.
- Draw verbal attention to what children are doing to encourage social interaction.
- Encourage a peer to join a child with special needs who is already engaged in play.
- Create a simple turn-taking game to encourage socialization.
- Encourage cooperative activities such as throwing, kicking, or batting a ball.

Adapt materials:
- Place larger buttons, a key ring on zippers, or Velcro on doll and dress-up clothes.
- Simplify puzzles with handles, covering some of the pieces, and gluing matching pictures in puzzle inset.
- Use a construction cone to stabilize the ball for batting.
- Stabilize toys and materials with shelf liners so they don't move around or slide off tables.
- Simplify by reducing the number of materials so children are not overwhelmed with too many choices.
- Provide a variety of blocks such as wooden blocks, foam blocks, and different-sized blocks.
- Build up handles of cookie cutters and utensils for playdough.
- Use books with texture, repetition, and hands-on features (lifts and flaps).

Adapt requirements or instruction:
- Repeat key words and phrases and expand on child's own words.
- Allow child to join activity when there are fewer children.
- Break down the play task into smaller steps and teach each step.
- Use mini-scripts to teach routine play activities such as a birthday party.
- Add tactile and auditory cues for children with visual disabilities.
- Use gestures and manual signs for children who have a hearing loss.

Physical assistance: *Use only as last resort once you've tried the previous adaptations.*

Source: Adapted from Milbourne, S. A., & Campbell, P. H. (2007). *CARA's kit: Creating adaptations for routines and activities.* Philadelphia, PA: Child and Family Studies Research Programs, Thomas Jefferson University.

Figure 8-3 Summary of Free Play Adaptations

⌄ **Professional Resource Download**

the dramatic play corner, even though there is little he can do there. He cannot put on dress-up clothes or dress and feed the dolls, and the little plastic teacups are too small for him to manipulate.

Miss Julia, his teacher, decides that Raul might enjoy a pretend game of shopping. With the assistance of the physical therapist, weights are placed in the toy shopping cart so Raul can use the shopping cart like a walker in the dramatic play area. The children help design a store that is stocked with empty containers of familiar grocery items: a counter, a cash register, and oversized play money. Miss Julia asks the physical therapist to show her how to help Raul grasp the bills and coins and place them in a small waist pack. This is excellent fine motor practice for Raul, and he seems to love practicing putting in and taking out the play money. He pushes his shopping cart a short distance, requests items, place them in his cart, takes out his money and gives it to the cashier, and pushes his cart away. Sometimes he gets stuck turning the cart, but one of the other children is there to help him. He thoroughly enjoys mastering this play routine.

Miss Julia decides to write a mini-script and tells the children they are writing a play. The script goes like this:

> Cashier: *Good morning. Can I help you?*
> Shopper: *Good morning. I'd like some orange juice, Cheerios, and a box of soap.*
> Cashier (places items on counter): *That will be 5 dollars and 50 cents.*
> Shopper: *Okay.* (He takes out some bills and coins and places them on the counter.) *There you are.*
> Cashier (places money in cash register): *Thank you. Have a nice day!*
> Shopper: *Thanks. You have a nice day, too. Bye.*

The children enjoy learning the script and repeat it for several days. By the time the children begin to tire of the script and start making up their own, Raul has learned the lines as a result of the many repetitions. He uses many key words appropriately and continues to participate even after the children start changing the routine. In the process Raul also greatly improves his fine motor skills, starts counting bills to five, and becomes much more mobile.

Read–Reflect–Discuss Questions

1. Make a list of all the adaptations made for Raul. What skills did each of the adaptations support?
2. What might be another play scenario that would be motivating for Raul given his interests and his challenges?
3. Do you think the mini-script described in the scenario would be fun for Raul's peers? Why or why not?

Key Terms

auto symbolic play

close-ended

mini-scripts

open-ended

parallel play

relational bullying

trial-and-error exploration

Helpful Resources

American Journal of Play: www.journalofplay.org

Activities for the Classroom and Home: www.gryphonhouse.com/activities

Barbour, A. (2016). *Play today: Building the young brain through creative expression.* Beltsville, MD: Gryphon House.

Dodge, D., Aghayan, C., Berke, K., Bichart, T., Burts, D., Colker, L., Copley, J., Dighe, J., Heroman, C., Jones, C., & Tabors, P. (2010). *The creative curriculum for preschool.* Washington, DC: Teaching Strategies Inc.

Linder, T., & Anthony, T. (2008). *Transdisciplinary play-based intervention.* Baltimore, MD: Paul H. Brookes.

Macintyre, C. (2010). *Play for children with special needs: Supporting children with learning differences.* New York, NY: Routledge.

Phillips, N., & Beavan, L. (2012). *Teaching play to children with autism: Practical interventions using Identiplay.* Thousand Oaks, CA: SAGE Publications, Inc.

Saracho, O. N. (2012). *An integrated play-based curriculum for young children.* New York: Routledge.

Sluss, D. (2015). *Supporting play in early childhood: Environment, curriculum, assessment.* Stamford, CT: Cengage Learning.

CHAPTER 9

Circle Time, Including Music and Rhythm Activities

The following NAEYC Standards and DEC Recommended Practices are addressed in this chapter:

naeyc

Standard 1: Promoting Child Development and Learning
Standard 4: Using Developmentally Effective Approaches
Standard 5: Using Content Knowledge to Build Meaningful Curriculum

DEC

Practice 2: Environment
Practice 4: Instruction
Practice 5: Interaction

Careful planning of circle time will ensure successful inclusion of children with disabilities.

Circle time can provide important learning opportunities for children who have special needs. It provides structure to the day, helps children learn to focus in group activities, and can assist children in learning names of other children. Music and rhythm activities are not only fun and energizing, but for many children with special needs they provide opportunity for total participation:

- **There are many learning opportunities for children with disabilities during circle time activities.** Circle time can create a sense of community and a sense of self as well as encourage speech and language development, physical awareness, emergent literacy, and cognitive development.

- **Teachers use many different types of circle time activities as well as adaptations for children with special needs.** Activities include songs and finger plays, books, classroom schedule and calendars, music, dance, movement, and social games. Adaptations can be made in various ways to meet a variety of special needs.

- **Certain key dimensions of circle time need to be in balance on a regular basis to increase the success of circle time.** For example, using a consistent format, planning seating carefully, designating teacher roles, frequently explaining expectations, and signaling transitions clearly can help circle time run smoothly and prevent challenging behaviors.

- **Supporting children who wander away from circle time can be a challenge.** Specific strategies may be helpful, such as allowing a child to sit on the periphery of the circle, gradually increasing the length of time the child sits in circle, and allowing the child to bring a *security object* or fidget toy to circle time.

- **Detailed activity plans can be created for circle time.** Examples include Follow the Leader and What's in the Box? (discussed later in this chapter).

Introduction

Circle time is an opportunity for the classroom to come together as a community and participate in a large group activity. Many different types of activities can be planned during circle time to enhance and support children's learning. Yet at the same time, there is potential for development of some challenging behaviors. For children with special needs, predictability, structure, routine, and adaptations during circle time can significantly enhance their ability to be participating members during circle time activities. We will discuss here how to make the most of learning opportunities and prevent behavioral challenges at circle time.

9-1 Learning Opportunities During Circle Time

Circle time, a period when children gather as a group with their teachers to listen, actively participate, and share with each other, provides important opportunities for developmental learning in many areas. Rituals included in circle time offer excellent opportunities for concept development, especially the concepts of time during calendar time (for example, *yesterday* and *today*). Social development including self-identification and identification of others ("Who is here today?") along with speech and language development are stimulated as children listen to and discuss concepts and ask/answer questions. For preschool-age children, circle time is also an ideal opportunity for development of number concepts ("How many children are here today?") and emergent literacy (recognition of name cards).

9-1a Opportunities for Creating a Sense of Community and a Sense of Self

A group circle time that includes music and social routines of welcome and belonging can help create a positive sense of both self and group identity for a child with special needs. Learning other children's and adults' names, as well as the process

Photo 9-1 Music and rhythm activities can build community in the classroom.

of coming together on a daily basis, can create a great sense of membership and belonging to a community. Being a member and part of a group helps children with disabilities make sense of the world and learn concepts and specific patterns of behavior. Equally important, this structure creates feelings of mastery and security, which support the child's social emotional development.

Something for Everyone. Through music and rhythm activities at circle time, everyone can experience a feeling of belonging, regardless of abilities. All children can feel a sense of community when music and songs are used regularly to bring the whole group together. The large group setting offers a variety of opportunities for reacting to music and rhythm. Children often respond in different ways to music. Some get up and dance, while others sit, listen, and observe their peers. For a child with special needs, any positive reaction to music is acceptable in the large group setting. When it comes to dancing and rhythmic movements, there are no rules, no *right way* to do it. The activity provides the chance for all children to feel successful whether they are sitting and listening, moving their head, shaking a maraca, clapping hands, or jumping up and down.

9-1b Opportunities to Encourage Speech and Language Skills

All types of different activities done at circle time encourage speech and language development from children with disabilities. Children listen to rich language models

---

Disability Awareness

Circle activities can naturally involve music, rhythm, and social games from families, allowing their cultures to be represented in the classroom. Families can be invited to teach the children and staff their child's favorite song in their home language. They might share a favorite childhood social game or their native type of dancing music. Imagine how wonderful children, and especially a child with disabilities, would feel if everyone is learning their favorite song in the same language they speak at home. This can help children feel they are contributing members of the group as their culture has importance and is represented in the classroom.

as they hear stories being discussed through books, songs, puppet shows, and flannel board stories. Children can also communicate in narrated stories by singing along, asking questions, answering questions, reciting parts and repetitive phrases of the story, and making choices. Various adaptations to facilitate communication will be described throughout this and other chapters.

9-1c Opportunities to Enhance Physical Awareness

Circle time activities, especially activities with music and movement, offer an opportunity for children to become more aware of their bodies in space as they move to various tempos and rhythm. Dancing, marching, shaking, stomping, and clapping are only some of the actions the body can do when music is played. As young children move their bodies to different types of rhythms, they become aware of what they can and cannot do as they move. Most children can move some part of their body to music. Children with severe motor disabilities can be held and danced with or moved in their wheelchairs. Moving to different tempos helps young children to become aware of how to organize their body to keep the beat. The tempo may actually help some children pay more attention to what is happening around them.

9-1d Opportunities to Support and Reinforce Emergent Literacy

Children with special needs often require many repetitions to master the prerequisites necessary for development of literacy. Circle time can offer specific opportunities for emergent literacy support and practice, such as:

- Choosing picture cards representing songs.
- Name/photo recognition (of self and others).
- Reading the daily schedule or calendar.
- Short story/flannel board stories told at circle time. These must be repeated frequently for this age range, include props and audience participation, and have multiple copies of the same book available in the book area.

9-1e Opportunities to Support Cognitive Development

Books, flannel board stories, songs, and movement games can all teach a variety of concepts that support cognitive development. For example, concepts such as *stop* and *go* can be taught using the following strategy:

1. Play music and have all children move to the music—or play instruments; shake flags, scarves, a small parachute; or march in place.
2. Abruptly turn off the music. Say and sign STOP.
3. Wait quietly until everyone has stopped and it is quiet.
4. Build children's anticipation, then turn on the music again and resume movement.

Helpful Hint

The stop-and-go activity provides a chance for a child with motor disabilities who has difficulty holding and shaking instruments to be in charge of the activity by using a switch to start and stop music. Also, rhythm instruments or materials such as maracas can be attached to the child's hand with Velcro, or ribbons can be tied around the child's wrist. A simple movement of the child's hand can allow the child to experience the control of restarting the music and making the maraca or ribbon move.

In addition to teaching *stop* and *go,* music and rhythm can be used to teach *fast* and *slow:*

- Teach *fast* and *slow* by using rhythm instruments or marching.
- Play music that is fast or slow and shake to that beat. Be dramatically fast or slow and exaggerate each concept while labeling the movement speed.
- Chant or sing songs that can be sung either fast or slow.
- Select specific children's songs that teach these types of concepts.

9-2 Types of Circle Time Activities and Adaptations for Children with Special Needs

Teachers can do many different types of activities to enhance learning and development during circle time. Teachers typically choose between two and five of these activities to create successful circle times depending on the children's ages and developmental levels. We will discuss the different types of activities as well as adaptations for children with disabilities.

9-2a Attendance: Who Is Here Today?

A simple form of attendance can be taken in a variety of ways:

- A greeting song names and acknowledges each child.
- The teacher shakes hands with each child or says "Give me five" while all children count to five (variation: "Give me two" or "Give me four.")
- The teacher selects a name card and each child responds. For variation, other children can identify the owner of the name card. Children with intellectual delays may need their picture along with their name.
- Each child comes up and selects his own name card, which is then placed on the "Who is here at school or home" board.
- Instead of a group choral response, each child can practice a formal greeting. The teacher says to each child, "Good morning, ___, and how are you today?" The child responds "Fine, thank you."

9-2b Classroom Schedules and Calendars

Circle time for preschool children often includes a calendar ritual. For toddlers, however, calendar time is usually not appropriate. Calendars can be particularly problematic for most children with special needs because of their difficulty with time concepts, as calendars are usually for the week or month. Cook, Klein, and Chen (2016) describe a useful procedure of the calendar activity for children with cognitive disabilities. Figure 9-1 presents an adaptation of this procedure.

A classroom schedule depicting the activities for the day might be more understandable for young children with disabilities than a calendar of the week or month. The schedule can consist of pictures, drawings, or icons of the day's activities and

---

Helpful Hint

For a child with blindness, write his name in large Braille on the card, help the child feel his name, and let him feel other cards without Braille. For a child with low vision, use large, black, block letters on contrasting white or yellow background. Children who have a hearing loss can sign their greeting. Children with severe motor disabilities can activate an augmentative communication device with recorded speech output saying their name or "Fine, thank you."

The calendar time procedure described here can assist many children with special needs in handling the relatively abstract concepts of time that are inherent in this activity. Features of the adaptation include:

- Reducing the time frame to one week
- Associating each day of the week with a special activity and a particular color
- Using visual devices to help represent the passage of days and to depict *yesterday, today,* and *tomorrow*

To begin:

1. Create a large board with each day of the week represented by a different color.

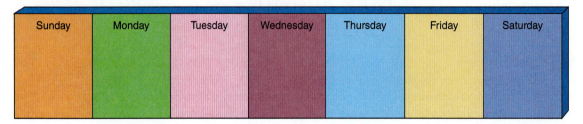

2. Make Velcro-attachable laminated pictures (either photos or drawings) of different activities done only on a certain day of the week. In the following example, Monday is *Library Day;* Tuesday is *Discovery Walk Day;* Wednesday is *Popcorn Day;* and so on.

3. At the beginning of the week, ask children if they know what special activity is on that day. Select a child to place the picture on the board. Reinforce with the phrase "Today is Monday." (For children with severe cognitive disabilities, present the picture during the actual activity until they associates the picture with its reference.)

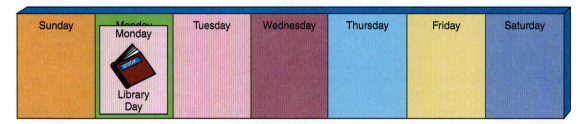

4. Toward the end of the day, refer again to the calendar and ask, "Who knows what day it will be *tomorrow*? Tomorrow is Tuesday. What do we do on Tuesday?" The teacher shows the Tuesday card but does not place it on the calendar until the actual day.

5. On Tuesday, repeat the routine described previously. Have a child select the Tuesday card and place it on the calendar. Now ask the children, "What day was *yesterday*? Yesterday was Monday. What did we do yesterday? We went to the library."

Figure 9-1 Adapting Calendar Time

6. Proceed each day in this way, always reviewing the concepts *yesterday, today,* and *tomorrow,* as well as the days of the week. Eventually children will begin to master the temporal concepts required, along with the vocabulary. (As appropriate, the teacher can begin to place the weeks into a monthlong calendar.)

Figure 9-1 (Continued)

can help children with disabilities anticipate what is going to happen throughout the day. The schedule can also be used for individual children to help them anticipate what is going to happen next, alleviating anxiety or challenging behaviors.

9-2c Songs and Finger Plays

Songs with words and actions can support children with limited language skills. Songs can be valuable teaching tools for children with communication delays, limited language skills, or disabilities. Using songs and finger plays to encourage language development is not a new curriculum activity for early childhood teachers. Children learn how to count, use their fingers, and follow tunes while engaged in circle time music activities. The following suggestions may help children with language delays participate in songs and music.

Pair Songs with Body Movements. Songs with clear, simple motions that reinforce key words can be an excellent support for early development of speech and language. Take "Eensy Weensy Spider," for example. The movements of the arms up as the

Photo 9-2 Using movements while singing "Eensy Weensy Spider" helps children understand the concepts in the song.

WEBLINK

Many sign language dictionaries are available on the World Wide Web. For further information on specific manual signs for simple concepts such as *spider,* go to American Sign Language Dictionary at www.handspeak .com/word.

spider crawls "up the water spout" and then down for "down came the rain" not only reinforces children's understanding of the concepts, but may eventually enable children to *say* the words. A variation of this movement would be to actually use the correct manual sign for the word *spider.* You could cross your wrists in front of your body, bend your fingers to simulate the legs of the spider, and wiggle the legs as you move your arms slightly away from your body.

Choose Simple Songs. Stick with familiar, favorite songs and chants, and repeat them often. Then leave out key words and ask children to fill in the blank as you sing. Often, you don't need to give any directions to the children. Simply sing the song and stop at the word you want them to say. If it is familiar enough, they will keep singing using all words. Slowing the song down will make it easier by providing enough time for children with special needs to respond. Children without disabilities may find the slower beat an interesting twist on a familiar song:

> "The eensy weensy (___) went up the water spout.
>
> Down came the (___) and washed the (___) out."

Children with intellectual or motor disabilities can also learn through this approach as long as they have ample opportunities for repetition, the songs are relatively simple, and they are sung at a slower pace. They might also say the words by signing them or pointing to a picture.

Music, Dance, and Movement. One of the best ways to make circle time motivating and fun is to include music and rhythm, such as the Freeze game, rhythm or marching band, musical instruments, and rock-and-roll or salsa dancing. Beanbags, scarf dancing, and rhythmic sticks are also fun to do with music. An activity that is virtually ageless in its appeal is the Freeze game. Participants keep time to a good beat, but must stop when the music stops and wait for it to resume. Freezing awkward postures during wild, uninhibited dancing can meet the needs of even the most active children. It can help children get their wiggles out before they are expected to sit down to a more quiet activity such as attending to the teacher reading a book.

9-2d Books and Stories

Reading books and telling stories are great ways to help children with disabilities learn the concepts in the book, the sequence of the story, and how to anticipate what

Helpful Hint

For children with hearing loss, vibrations are important. Select music that has a heavy identifiable beat and a strong bass pitch. Giving a child with physical disabilities the responsibility of starting and stopping the music can allow the child a feeling of control and participation.

Photo 9-3 Playing musical instruments and dancing with scarves are fun activities to do at circle time.

is going to happen next. Here are some adaptations that can help assist children with their learning opportunities:

- Repeat key phrases, terms, and concepts, and demonstrate the manual signs.
- Frequently read the same book as children with disabilities need many repetitions.
- Use big books so that all can see the pages.
- Place a child with a hearing loss close to the teacher or sit next to the side with his or her best hearing.
- Intentionally skip an important page of a familiar story to create an opportunity for the children to show you that you missed something important in the sequence of the story.
- Add props such as puppets, stuffed animals, and flannel board patterns to enhance learning.
- Vary the tone of your voice (speak softly, speak louder, exaggerate, or elongate words) to keep the attention of the children.
- Provide another copy of the book to a child who has difficulty attending so he may follow along as you read.
- Use books that have been adapted with pictures, drawings, or icons. Teachers can hand out the pictures to the children before reading. They can then anticipate showing the matching picture when the teacher gets to the correct page. This technique actually helps children attend much better to the story. Or teachers can have children come up to the front to find the matching picture.

Social Imitation and Movement Games. Imitation and movement games, like partner activities such as holding hands with another child while singing "Row, Row Your Boat" and Follow the Leader can motivate learning. Imitation games can teach attention and observation skills while providing practice of certain motor movements, vocal production skills, and social interaction. Games such as Ring around the Rosie might need to be taught with a smaller number of children first before a child with disabilities is ready to coordinate his movements with the larger group. And it would help to slow down the song to give children with disabilities time to move their body as well as time to get back up.

9-2e Introduce New Activities or Concepts

Circle time may or may not include a section on new activities or concepts. Novel activities during circle time can present particular challenges for many children with special needs. Preschool concept learning, such as reviewing the life cycle of a butterfly, can be difficult for children with disabilities. Concepts needs to be developmentally appropriate, highly interactive, and taught with many props such as puppets, visuals, pictures, and photos. Attending to unfamiliar activities while in a large group can be difficult for children who have difficulties focusing attention or who cannot sit for more than a few minutes.

An advantage of including a new activity or concept during circle time is that it adds variety and interest. It also provides an opportunity to help build children's tolerance for novelty and unfamiliar experiences. In some cases, keeping the beginning and ending of circle time the same may help children with special needs recognize and discriminate the new and interesting activity from the predictable and familiar routine.

Examples of circle time activities for both preschool and toddler age children are included at the end of this chapter: What's in the Box? and Follow the Leader. These examples demonstrate the detail with which activities must be planned to ensure successful inclusion. These activities have been well tested and have a high probability of success for children with a wide range of special needs. They can be easily enhanced to challenge children without disabilities.

Helpful Hint

For children with expressive language delays or hearing loss, who are learning to use sign language, this is a good opportunity to practice simple signs for key words with all children in a natural type of setting.

WEBLINK

The Center on the Social and Emotional Foundations for Early Learning (CSEFEL) has a wonderful Book Nook section that consists of easy-to-use lesson plans using popular children's books for social emotional learning. Because circle time can frequently result in challenging behaviors, these plans extend the book to prosocial activities. These activities are useful not only during circle time, but also throughout the classroom daily activity and routines. For more information, see http://csefel.vanderbilt.edu/resources/strategies.html.

Children with autism often may have a characteristic called **insistence on sameness,** which renders them quite agitated or frustrated when routines are unpredictable and different. For some children with autism, even slight changes in routine or physical arrangement of their environment can cause them stress, resulting in challenging behavior.

Children with autism generally attend better and are calmer in a highly structured environment and can certainly benefit from a classroom schedule of the day's events. At the same time, it is important for children with autism to develop strategies for coping with changes and unexpected or unfamiliar events and settings. Varying the activity within the structured framework of circle time can be a way of gradually increasing their tolerance for change.

9-2f Transitions to Next Activity

The close of circle time should include a transition to the next activity. The next task may be a center or art activity. It is helpful to demonstrate what children will be doing at the centers or art table. This provides an opportunity for children with special needs to establish an expectation or mental set for what will be happening next. It also provides an opportunity for the teacher to introduce and repeat key vocabulary and concepts. In an integrated setting, *helping partners* can be assigned to children who can benefit from peer modeling and assistance.

Following is an example of how to introduce an art activity during circle time.

Introducing Contact Paper Autumn Collage Activity at Circle Time

1. Children will have gone on a discovery walk the day before to collect leaves, sticks, and flowers. These have been placed in bags with their names on them.
2. During calendar time the teacher reminds the children they went for a walk the day before and collected many wonderful things.
3. At the end of circle time, the teacher presents a tray with the bags of collected samples (with names prominently written on each bag) and a square of contact paper. The teacher opens the bag with his name on it.
4. The teacher labels and repeats the names of all the materials.

    "Here is my bag from our walk yesterday. See, here is my name written on my bag,"Mr. Gibbs. "I have some sticks, some leaves, and one blue flower in my bag. This is a type of paper. This is called contact paper. Can you say 'contact paper?' It's very sticky!"

    Children can be encouraged to participate in feeling the sticky paper and naming items or describing items to whatever extent is developmentally appropriate for the children in the group.

5. The teacher then briefly demonstrates placing some of the items from the bag onto the contact paper.

Ending Circle Time. For children who have special needs, it is helpful to have a regular song, chant, or phrase that always marks the end of circle time. For example, if centers are the next activity, the teacher and children can all sign and say, "And now it's time for work." Because this is a short phrase, it can also be easily translated into another language that everyone can learn. Or music (preferably the same song) can signal the end of group time by having children march to their next activity.

9-2g Final Considerations

Although circle time can be an important activity for children with special needs, it can also be particularly challenging especially for children with autism and sensory integration disorders. Many children with behavior difficulties will find participating in large group activities particularly challenging. (See Chapter 5 for suggestions.) Children might not be able to handle the large group or the amount of noise and movement and may need to be given extra time to gradually increase their tolerance for staying and attending in a large group.

Suggestions for Children Who Wander Off or Resist Circle Time

- Allow the child to sit on the periphery or in an adapted chair.
- Encourage participation for only a brief time, initially, especially for activities of high interest, then gradually increase time.
- Provide a break card so the child has the ability to tell the teacher when he needs a break from the group activity.
- Allow the child to have a **security object** (a familiar attachment object such as a piece of material, a favorite toy, or stuffed animal).
- Allow the child to have a fidget toy such as a squeeze or Koosh ball, textured fabric cloth, or Silly Putty.
- Provide a weighted vest, lap pillow, or blanket if recommended by the inclusion specialist, or physical or occupational therapist.

9-3 Key Dimensions of Circle Time

A balance of the following key dimensions can help prevent challenging behaviors during circle time.

9-3a Length

The length of circle time will depend on the age and developmental level of the children. For instance, toddlers have a shorter attention span than preschoolers. Therefore, they should have a shorter circle time. Toddlers are still learning to move their body and need lots of opportunities to practice movement skills:

- Avoid the tendency to make circle time too long. Instead, have two short circle times throughout the day.
- If you have a large class, think about dividing the group in half. Half the children can be in circle time while the other half go outside.

9-3b Physical Setting

Considerations noted in Chapter 4 should be kept in mind when determining where to hold circle time activities.

Arrangement of Seating. Configuration of the circle is critical for children with special needs. Some children need to be close to the teacher, such as a child with hearing loss. The traditional semicircle works well for small groups. However, if groups are large, some children end up being too far away from the focal point. A *cluster* or two semicircle rows may work better in those cases.

Closing in the circle may reduce distractibility. However, sitting close may be difficult for children who resist the proximity of other children. Teachers must strategically assign positions of staff and other adults in the classroom to maximize the participation of each child and to support all children during circle time. See Figure 9-2 for examples. Children can also be distracted by sitting too close to toy shelves and the amount of wall decorations near circle time. Try to limit materials hanging on the wall where children are directly looking at the class schedule and calendars.

Types of Seating. Having a visual of where to sit can help most children find a space quicker and in a more orderly fashion (that is, carpet squares, shapes on the floor or rugs, or colored tape on the carpet as shown in Photo 9-4). Using visuals, with staff arranging them, helps circle time organization and controls the spacing

Closed-in small group circle
(T= teacher, A= assistant)

Large group circle
(T= teacher, A= assistant)

Not recommended

Random seating with nonstrategic placement of adults

Figure 9-2 Examples of Circle Time Seating Arrangements

Photo 9-4 Blue tape on the carpet helps children know where to sit for circle time

between children. However, some programs allow children to get their own carpet square and find their own spot. For children with low cognitive ability or difficulty with motor skills, the task of getting a carpet square and bringing it to the circle may need to be task analyzed. Gradually increase independence skills by teaching each of the following steps:

- Go to the carpet square pile.
- Pick up one carpet square with two hands.
- Look around for an empty space.
- Walk to the space.
- Put your carpet square down on the space.
- Sit down on the carpet square.

Some children with special needs might need a more defined space than sitting on the floor. The floor might be too much of a temptation to lie down, touch your neighbor, or move around. Furthermore, children with physical disabilities might not have the trunk stability to sit comfortably on the floor. Instead of using the most amount of support by having a child sit in an adult's lap, think of different types of chairs that could be used so the child can sit independently. There are many options such as specialized chairs, adapted chairs, cube chairs, benches, or stools (see Photo 9-5). A physical therapist or inclusion specialist can help determine the most appropriate seating arrangements for children with disabilities.

Helpful Hint

To assist children with visual impairments, mark carpet squares with a contrasting black-and-white design or put the name in large, contrasting colored letters. Place an easily identifiable texture on the back of the square, such as fur or rubber.

Photo 9-5 Seating can be adapted in many different ways.

Photo 9-6 Teachers work together at circle time to support everyone.

9-3c Teacher Roles

As circle time is typically a large group activity, intentional planning will need to take place so the maximum number of adults can be present to support the selected activity. Two roles are important to mention.

Circle Time Leader. The leader's role is to plan and implement all circle time activities. This teacher's job is to keep the pace of circle time flowing while being aware of the whole group, taking cues from the group, and adjusting the activities as needed.

Circle Time Supporter(s). The supporter's role is to walk around and help individual children maintain interest and prevent challenging behaviors. The supporter prevents challenging behaviors by frequently scanning the group, intervening before challenging behaviors happen, and assisting individual children as needed. This will require the supporter to get up and move around quite frequently. Photo 9-6 shows how the circle time leader and supporter can work together to create a successful circle time.

9-3d Circle Time Expectations

All children and especially children with disabilities need to understand exactly what the circle time expectations or rules are. Teachers need to frequently explain and demonstrate their expectations. As shown in Photo 9-7, this can be done by using visuals and asking children to give examples of the expectations.

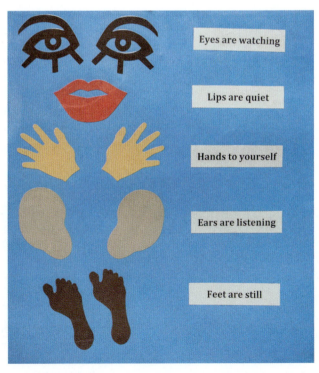

Eyes are watching

Lips are quiet

Hands to yourself

Ears are listening

Feet are still

Photo 9-7 Circle time expectations can be explained and reinforced using visuals in the classroom.

9-3e Balance of Circle Time Activities

There needs to be a good balance of activities to help children with disabilities attend and be successful at circle time. Actually having a balance of activities will help all children. For instance, all children will probably have difficulty if circle time consists of sitting down while the teacher reads three books in a row, or if she reads one book, sings a song, then reads another book while children continue to sit. Children need a balance between sitting/movement, listening/participating, quiet/noisy, alone/together, and slow/fast activities. Here are some strategies to keep in mind:

- Decrease the amount of sitting and increase movement activities. For example, instead of sitting down while singing the song "Wheels on the Bus," stand up and have children do large motor movements to the song.
- Do a stand-up movement activity to get children's wiggles out before a sit-down listening activity such as reading a book or reviewing new concepts.
- Create activities in which children get to pair up with a partner to develop social interaction skills, that is, dancing with a partner and mirror games in which children have to imitate each other's actions.
- Make activities more interactive so children are participating and not just being passive learners. Have children come up to the front to show what we mean by the expectation of "hands to self." Then the other students can imitate the action instead of just having children sit down and listen while teachers talk about the expectations.
- Pace activities so that you have a good variety of slower and faster activities as well as quiet and louder activities. Children with disabilities might not have the stamina to do three busy movement activities in a row. Break that up with a sit-down quiet activity.

9-3f Consistency with Flexibility at Circle Time

Consistency helps children with disabilities be able to predict the sequence of activities and the flow of circle time. Typically, they anticipate the beginning of circle time with a consistent cue such as turning on the same opening music to signal that circle time is beginning. They can also anticipate that circle time is ending by singing the same song or consistently marching with the same marching music to the next activity. Activities in between will frequently change. Teachers need to be flexible and take their cues from the children. If there are many wiggly bodies during a sit-down, quiet activity, the children might be telling you that they need to get up and move. Have the flexibility to follow the children's lead, even if it means altering lesson plans.

9-4 Examples of Detailed Activity Plans

As we have noted, detailed planning is necessary to ensure that activities are designed to accommodate participants' special needs. The following examples offer appropriate activities for circle time, and demonstrate the necessary level of planning.

9-4a Toddler Circle Time Activity: What's in the Box?

Any activity where things are *found* is appealing to children who are either just mastering object permanence or who like the challenge of discovery, but need practice learning how to search systematically for something. Toddlers without disabilities and older children who are developmentally young enjoy the simple activity of finding something inside a box or sack. Although problem-solving and discovery strategies may be difficult for a child with a visual impairment or a severe attention deficit, it can be rewarding to master the art of systematic search.

One item that can be used over and over is a large box with something inside. Toddlers know something is in the box. They can remember what was in the box on a previous day and are constantly surprised when something new is inside the same box. The following plan can be used to introduce all types of circle time activities. When the box is used dramatically, it can increase toddlers' interest and attention to large group activities.

Detailed Activity Plan. Suggestions for objects that can be placed in the box follow.

Step 1: Introduce the box:

1. Seat toddlers in a circle with the teacher. Children should be seated so that the teacher can reach each child with as little movement as possible.
2. Bring the box into the circle in front of the teacher. The box should contain props (objects) for a game or activity. The box can also be hidden in some part of the room after children become familiar with it. You can say, "Where's my box? Where is that box?" Let children tell where it is or *find* it. Then exclaim, *"Oh! Here* it is! *Here's* my *box!"*
3. Begin to pat on the top of the box to get toddlers' attention. Keep patting until all attention is on you and the box. (You can also begin by shaking the box above the children's heads while saying, *"Listen,* what do you *hear?"*).
4. Say (very slowly), "Knock, knock, knock, *what's* in the *box?"*
5. Repeat the rhyme two or three times.
6. Stop patting and saying the rhyme, and ask the children, *"What's* in the *box?"*:
   - Wait for children to give some type of response.
   - Toddlers may approach the box. Let them pat the top or push the box toward them so that they can stay in their assigned places, but still touch it.
   - Hold the box lid down so that no one can lift it up until you are ready.
7. Lift up one corner of the lid and look inside, "I *see* it!" Be dramatic and build suspense.
8. Choose one child to open the box or do so yourself. Hold the box so that all children can see inside.
9. Take hidden object(s) out (with a flourish) and continue with related activity.

Step 2: Begin activity related to contents of the box (for example, pull parachute out of box and demonstrate its use).

Step 3: End the activity:

1. Bring box out again.
2. Place in center of circle.
3. Return object(s) to box or have children return objects.
4. Close the lid saying, "We're *all done* with this activity (describe specifically)."
5. Foreshadow or introduce the next activity or lesson.

Examples of Objects That Can Be Used with the Box

- **Parachute**—Children can feel the parachute inside the box, and then all can help to pull it out.
- **Musical instruments**—Have children shake the box and identify the instruments by sound. Continue with a music activity after opening the box and distributing the instruments.
- **Beanbags or balls**—Use for a variety of circle time activities.
- **Puppets**—Use a special puppet for a specific song or several puppets for all children.
- **Wrapped presents**—Wrap one item for each child in tissue paper or place in individual small bags so that children get a second hidden *something*, such as sunglasses if the class plan includes going for a walk that day, or cookies or another treat.

- **Small containers**—Choose those that require different types of fine motor hand movement: screw-top containers, such as plastic spice or cake decoration jars, different-sized small boxes with lids to match, or small toys that can be hidden in containers and boxes as a reward for opening them.
- **Song props**—Include items such as plastic animals to accompany "Old MacDonald Had a Farm."

Specific Suggestions for Children with Special Needs. To make the box activity a success for children with specific disabilities, incorporate the following strategies into your activity planning.

For children with visual impairments:

- Keep the child seated close to the circle leader.
- Use lots of specific verbal descriptions such as color, shape, size, and prepositions (open/close, in/out, on/off, and so on).
- Allow children to touch all objects as they are presented to the group.
- Give the children a smaller replica of the large box with one object inside so he can take his time to explore the box and become aware of the *boxiness* of the object and then open the box to explore what's inside.
- Keep in mind that objects inside the box may be a bit scary because the only way a child will know what the objects are is to *touch* them, whereas the other children have all been able to *see* the objects and can then choose to touch!
- Use a hand-under-hand approach to help the child explore a new object by reaching his fingers through the safety of an adult hand first, then gradually feel more of the object when ready.

For children with behavior challenges or inability to focus attention:

- Seat the child in an adapted chair and next to a favorite peer or adult for support.
- Allow the child to be that teacher's helper to pass out objects, giving them opportunities to positively interact with others.
- Place the child off to one side of the lead teacher so the child is close enough to see objects.
- For some children, offering them the choice of a chair or sitting next to the leader of the group (or another preferred adult) will help them decide where they want to sit. If they cannot maintain control, then the consequence is sitting in a less desirable place.
- Allow the child to tap on the box or peek first so he does not have to wait for what might seem an excruciatingly long period. (Do not allow child to do this if he is misbehaving right at the moment—catch the child being "good.")
- Allow the child to leave circle time early if he requests appropriately by saying "all done" or "go," for example. Gradually help the child increase the amount of time spent in the circle.
- Give the child a concrete action that will signal the end of circle time, such as, "When we sing the 'Wheels on the Bus' song, you can leave the circle."

For children with physical disabilities:

- Provide adapted chairs or seating so the child can be as independent as possible. If the child needs to be in a wheelchair, consider having peers sit in chairs for circle time rather than on the floor.
- Assign a peer buddy to help the child manipulate objects from the box if he needs assistance. Peers can share musical instruments and puppets, for example.
- Encourage peers to help the child unwrap *gifts* by asking the child if he needs help and waiting for an answer. If the child answers "yes," provide assistance; if the child indicates "no," return after a few minutes to ask again. (The child may want to watch other children first.)

- If containers are too difficult for the child to open, such as screw tops, then provide adapted objects that are simpler such as a small box with a lid that has a cube glued to it for easier gripping.
- Place musical instruments in the box and play a Freeze game. Provide a switch for a music player so the child can start and stop the music when children are dancing or marching with instruments. Peers must freeze when music stops and wait for the child to reactivate the switch to turn the music on.

For children with intellectual delays:

- Use this activity frequently and follow a similar sequence and script each time.
- Include familiar and favorite objects, toys, and snacks in the box.
- For unfamiliar items, provide later opportunities for the child to explore the box and objects from the circle time, such as during a free play or outside time, so he becomes familiar with the various objects and has opportunities to use them successfully.

What's in the Box? For Ben

Tom is a toddler teacher at a child development center. There are 12 two- to three-year-olds in his room and he has one aide. One of the children, Ben, has severe visual impairments. He can perceive bright light and with his left eye can perceive dark objects against a light background, but otherwise he relies on his other senses to tell him about the world. Ben wears glasses to help him focus more on the objects and to remind him not to poke at his eyes (a common self-stimulating activity), but he does not really like to wear them and will often toss the glasses if not reminded to wear them.

Today, Tom is going to introduce hats and sunglasses to the children by using the What's in the Box? lesson plan. After the children have found their glasses and hats, they'll go on a discovery walk together. Tom brings the children into the large group and sits Ben next to him. He introduces the box, which contains 12 paper bags, each one with a pair of children's plastic sunglasses and a little baseball cap inside. He has used the box before in circle time, and Ben has had many opportunities to feel and climb around and into the box (during times other than circle time). However, this is the first time that bags with something inside are being introduced.

Tom proceeds through the lesson, using many descriptive words as well as describing his own actions out loud, and helps guide Ben's hand onto the box as he lifts up the lid. As Tom takes out the bags (per the lesson format), he passes one to Ben so he can touch it. He places it between Ben and himself, tells Ben where the bag is, and helps guide his hand to it. Ben touches the bag carefully while Tom distributes the rest of the bags and the children begin to open them. He has rolled the bags tightly closed so the children spend some time opening them, with help as needed from peers and adults.

Meanwhile, Tom turns back to Ben and asks Ben to help him open the bag. He places Ben's hand on top of his and lets Ben feel as much as he wants to through Tom's fingers. When the bag is open, Tom asks Ben to feel what's in the bag. Ben slowly inches his hand in and feels a pair of glasses just like his! Ben smiles and pulls them out of the bag. Tom draws attention to Ben, telling the toddlers that "they have glasses just like Ben." Ben smiles again. Later, Tom asks some of Ben's friends to let Ben feel the glasses on their faces. Tom pulls Ben's hat out of his bag, lets Ben feel it, then asks him if he wants it on his head. Ben taps his head and says "hat on head." Circle time ends with the children putting on their glasses and hats and going for the walk.

9-4b Preschool Circle Time Activity: Follow the Leader

Preschoolers enjoy playing Follow the Leader in many situations. They will follow other children's leads during outside play, in the housekeeping area, and during block play. During large group or circle time, this activity can be used to attract and maintain children's attention. The game should end before losing preschoolers' attention—no more than 5 to 10 minutes. Use the game (with variations as needed) over several days. Children will become familiar with the idea and may begin to initiate their own suggestions during circle time.

Detailed Activity Plan. The following is an example of one way to use Follow the Leader. Suggestions for variations will follow:

Step 1: Introduce Follow the Leader:

1. Get students' attention by putting your hands on your head.
2. Say, "Look at me. Can you do the same thing?" Begin very slowly and give children verbal and visual cues such as, "Put your *hands* on your *head.*"
3. Wait for all or most children to follow your lead:
   - Use teacher aides, parents, or other helpers to assist those children needing physical cues.
   - Tell classroom helpers to limit verbal cues. Have only one person (the teacher) tell children what to do; too much noise may result if everyone repeats the teacher's words.
   - Reinforce children's actions: "You did it, Luis! You put your hands on your head!"
4. Move hands slowly to another place, such as your legs or stomach or a chair, and say, "Can you put your *hands* on your *feet?*" Exaggerate motions and words to maintain children's attention. Always wait for most of the group to follow your lead and give verbal praise/acknowledgment to individual children.

Step 2: Continue the activity.

1. Repeat as described previously:
   - Stress key words for objects and actions.
   - Pace movements to group response.
   - Physically model the verbal direction if children are not following through with verbal command only; gradually fade physical cues (that is, begin but don't finish movement) as children become more familiar with the game.
   - Be sure that classroom assistants are helping children who need extra support to stay with the activity.

2. Introduce variety as children become more used to the activity:
   - Use other body parts instead of hands: "Stomp your feet," "Put your nose on your chair."
   - Use directions that require more movement: "Put your hand on the door," "Put your stomach on the floor," "Shhh, follow me quietly."
   - Use *humorous* commands to maintain attention and interest: "Put your head on your nose!"

3. Continue the activity for as long as most children are engaged (no more than 7 to 10 minutes).

Step 3: End the activity:

1. Give warning of the end of the game: "This is the last time—one more, then we're all done."
2. Finish the game with a final direction.
3. Say and sign, "We're all done."
4. Comment/summarize: "You guys did a great job. You really paid attention! We did some silly things, didn't we?!"
5. Foreshadow or introduce the next activity or lesson.

Variations on Follow the Leader. The following section suggests some variations on this popular activity:

1. Use verbalizations and facial expressions rather than body movement. Emphasize consonant/vowel combinations and *silly* sounds. This group activity is excellent for development of phoneme awareness for all children and for

speech production practice for children with speech and language difficulties. Use only visual cues with no verbal directions. Reinforce silence by putting finger on lips if children begin to make noise. Use exaggerated movements to maintain interest.

2. Play different types of music and do a silent *Follow the Leader* to various tempos.

3. Encourage children to take turns being the leader after you have modeled the activity several times:
   - Ask for a volunteer: "Who wants to be the leader?"
   - Model any action (verbal or physical) the leader makes to reinforce the idea of following that child.
   - Reinforce the child's silent actions verbally to provide labels: "James is shaking his foot."

4. Use props (puppets, bells, streamers, scarves, and so on) to maintain interest:
   - A puppet can "lead" the activity.
   - Props, such as draping scarves and waving flags, can be used for a quiet Follow the Leader.
   - Noisy props, such as bells and maracas, can be used with music.
   - Provide pictures, photos, or drawings of the actual actions and movements.

Suggestions for Children with Special Needs. Use these strategies to get children with specific disabilities involved in Follow the Leader.

Children with visual impairments:

- This activity needs to be verbally directed for a child with a visual impairment. Have an assistant whisper directions to the child if doing the activity silently.
- Some children might also need physical cues from an adult or friend. For "Put your hands on your head," for example, a friend taps child's head.
- Allow time after each verbal direction for the child to think about what to do. Pause before giving physical cues as well.
- Use silly sounds and syllables rather than motor movements.

For children with hearing loss:

- This is a wonderful opportunity for children with hearing loss because they can easily be successful since Follow the Leader often does not require auditory processing.
- To reinforce learning key words, use signs or have an assistant sign to the child.
- Don't avoid the *silly sound* version described earlier. This will encourage the child to really listen.

For children with behavior challenges who cannot focus on the activity:

- Seat the child next to the leader or favorite friend or adult.
- Provide touch cues to get the child's attention.
- Help the child respond, then reinforce him for imitating the leader.
- Use the silent variation described earlier. The reduced noise may help the child focus.
- Allow the child to ask to leave circle before he escalates inappropriate behavior.

For children with physical disabilities:

- Position the child so he is seated at the same height as peers (in a teacher's lap or ground-level adapted seat, for example) as much as possible. If the child needs to be in a wheelchair, consider having peers sit in chairs for circle time rather than on the floor, so children are all at same level.
- Let this child be the leader after children understand the rules of the game. The child will model those movements he is capable of making, such as eye blinking, moving head, and making sounds. (See Read–Reflect–Discuss at the end of this chapter.) Teach the child to use an AAC device to activate a music or voice output device giving verbal directions. For example, the child could use a head switch to activate the device to say, "Put your hand on your tummy" or "Jump up and down and turn around."

Summary

Circle time can offer important opportunities for children with special needs. It provides a pleasurable, salient contribution to the structure of the daily schedule. It offers opportunities for self and group identity. It provides an enjoyable context in which children can develop attention and self-regulation. If the types of activities are selected carefully and have a balance of key dimensions, circle time can be designed to enhance many skills. For a list and summary of adaptations discussed in this chapter, along with other possible adaptations, see Figure 9-3.

Adapted from CARA's Kit

Goal: To use adaptations (least amount of support) instead of physical assistance (most amount of support) whenever possible to increase independence and confidence skills

Adapt the environment:

- Use visuals such as a circle time carpet, carpet squares, or shapes taped on the carpet so children know where to sit and for spacing.
- Use tape to outline the circle time area for organization and so children know where to sit.
- Use one or two semicircle(s) so all children can see and participate comfortably in activities.
- Minimize the wall displays near the circle time area so children will be less distracted.
- Place a child with a visual impairment, attention difficulties, or hearing loss up at the front or next to the circle time leader.
- Have a circle time leader and supporter keep the circle organized and support individual children.

Adapt activity or routine:

- Provide a daily schedule instead of a calendar or use a calendar with pictures of activities for the week.
- Sing songs and do finger plays while standing up instead of sitting down.
- Decrease sitting activities and increase movement activities—have a balance.
- Allow children to take breaks, stand back and observe, or do a different quiet activity as needed.
- Allow children to gradually increase the time they stay in circle time.
- Shorten circle time or do two short circles at different times instead of one long one.
- Split the group up in half—half the children go to the circle while the other half go outside.
- Sing songs a bit slower to give children time to do the movements.

Adapt materials:

- Use adapted seating such as cube chairs, stools, and Rifton chairs.
- Provide visual supports such as gestures, sign language, pictures, icons, drawings, puppets, and real objects for circle time activities.
- Use big books, adapted books, or Braille books.
- Allow children to use a security object, stuffed animal, or a fidget toy during circle time.
- Give children story and book props to hold or maintain attention.
- Use the correct manual signs instead of gestures for finger plays and songs.

Adapt requirements or instruction:

- Allow child to communicate in different ways such as using gestures, sign language, and pointing to pictures or objects.
- Give an extra copy of the book that is being read to an individual student to maintain attention.
- Give opportunities for children with disabilities to be the circle time helper by giving out and collecting materials.
- Provide a visual for classroom expectations and frequently review and teach the expectations.

Figure 9-3 Summary of Circle Time Adaptations

⌄ **Professional Resource Download**

Read–Reflect–Discuss

Amy and Bartholomew

Ms. Diaz turns on the dancing song that signals the start of circle time. As the children come to the rug, Ms. Diaz brings out a corner chair for Amy, who has a diagnosis of cerebral palsy. The corner chair is designed to provide support for Amy's back but the seat is on the ground. Amy sits independently in the corner chair.

After welcoming the children and singing their regular morning song, Ms. Diaz tells the children they are going to play a new game today called Follow the Leader. She explains the lesson briefly and begins. The children are noisy at first but Ms. Diaz continues with simple directions and calls attention to children who are following. She notices that Amy is smiling as she watches her peers but is lagging behind on some of the commands. For instance, it is difficult for Amy to quickly move her hands up to touch her head. Ms. Diaz knows that Amy can move her feet back and forth on the rug while supported in the corner chair so she introduces that movement and is then able to compliment Amy. Ms. Diaz inserts directions throughout the lesson that she knows would be easier for Amy. Occasionally, she reaches over and helps Amy with a physical movement that is more difficult.

The class participates in this lesson for several days in a row as Ms. Diaz introduces variations to keep it interesting. By the third day, she asks for a volunteer to lead the group. Bartholomew, who frequently has behavioral challenges, volunteers. At first Bartholomew acts silly when he realizes everyone is looking at him but Ms. Diaz reminds him of the "expectations and rules," and he begins to lead the class. As the children practice taking turns being the leader, they begin to introduce variations of their own. Ms. Diaz asks Amy to choose a friend each day to help her with parts of the game that she cannot do alone. Amy's favorite helper is Bartholomew, who loves this special status! Ms. Diaz coaches peers when and when not to help Amy so that she has opportunities to move on her own.

Amy volunteers on the fifth day of the lesson and the children imitate the movements she makes. Amy has difficulty saying words but this game doesn't need verbal directions so Amy can be the leader with no help from anyone. This makes her feel really good because she usually needs help for just about everything!

This activity has many positive outcomes:

- Amy takes her turn as a participating member of the group.
- She can be truly independent during part of the activity and "call the shots."
- The group begins to understand and accept Amy.
- Amy and Bartholomew develop a special friendship.
- Bartholomew feels *in charge* when he is the leader, and it provides an appropriate outlet for his activity level.
- The activity itself encourages children to pay close attention and develop their observations skills.

A very successful circle time indeed!

Read–Reflect–Discuss Questions

1. Identify the adaptations that Ms. Diaz implemented to help support both Amy and Bartholomew.
2. If you were the teacher and had only one assistant in your center, how would you use the procedures described in the scenario? Who would do what? What would you change?
3. What other ideas and adaptations come to mind from this scenario that might be helpful when supporting a child with a physical disability?
4. What other ideas come to mind from this scenario that might be helpful when supporting a child with challenging behaviors?

Key Terms

insistence on sameness   security object

Helpful Resources

Books

Connors, A. F. (2004). *101 rhythm instrument activities for young children*. Beltsville, MD: Gryphon House.

Herr, J. (2013). *Creative resources for the early childhood classroom* (6th ed.). Belmont, CA: Wadsworth, Cengage Learning.

Herr, J., & Swim, T. (2001). *Creative resources for infants and toddlers*. Belmont, CA: Wadsworth, Cengage Learning.

Mosley, J. (2015). *Circle time for young children*. New York: Routledge.

Oliphant, J. (Ed.) (2011). *Circle time activities*. Greensboro, NC: Carson-Dellosa Publishing Company.

Websites

Booth, C. "Circle Time Lesson Plans." Retrieved April 2016 from www.tes.com /teaching-resource/circle-time-lesson-plans-3000887

Tomlin, C. R. "10 Circle Time Games." Retrieved April 2016 from www.earlychildhoodnews.com/earlychildhood/article_view.aspx?ArticleID=444

CHAPTER 10

Tabletop Activities

LEARNING OBJECTIVES

After studying this chapter, you will be able to:

LO 10-1: Discuss different types of developmental skills that children with disabilities learn through tabletop activities.

LO 10-2: Clarify why careful preparation for tabletop activities is essential.

LO 10-3: Design effective strategies to support learning objectives through tabletop activities.

LO 10-4: Develop a variety of adaptations for tabletop activities to support children with different types of disabilities, including those with tactile defensiveness.

The following NAEYC Standards and DEC Recommended Practices are addressed in this chapter:

naeyc

Standard 1: Promoting Child Development and Learning
Standard 4: Using Developmentally Effective Approaches
Standard 5: Using Content Knowledge to Build Meaningful Curriculum

DEC

Practice 2: Environment
Practice 4: Instruction
Practice 5: Interaction

Often children with disabilities involving the development of fine motor skills will need special support or adaptations to participate in tabletop activities.

Tabletop activities can support the development of many skills for children with special needs. For example, fine motor skills, task sequencing, understanding cause and effect, language skills, problem solving, carrying out plans, and sharing with others are just some of the skills that can be addressed. Although working together near one another, children have the opportunity to work alone or cooperatively with others:

- **Specific strategies can be used to adapt tabletop activities to make them meaningful and accessible to children with disabilities.** For instance, adjust the activity so it interests children, use physical adaptations of materials and equipment where necessary, analyze the task sequence, and plan concepts and vocabulary.

- **Certain types of activities will be more appealing than others.** Most likely to engage children with special needs are activities in which they can see cause and effect. Projects should provide interesting sensory experiences and be easy to repeat.

- **Tabletop activities can be important contexts for achieving IEP objectives.** Children with special needs can accomplish educational goals across developmental domains. In addition to fine motor and school readiness skills, communication, cognitive, self-help, and social skills are also being addressed.

Introduction

Tabletop activities can offer wonderful opportunities for children with special needs to not only develop important fine motor and school readiness skills, but also to engage in activities that are creative, expressive, and enjoyable. However, these activities present certain challenges and may be complicated and difficult for some children. This chapter suggests specific adaptations of these activities to maximize enjoyment and educational value for children with special needs.

10-1 Value of Tabletop Activities

In addition to being fun and creative, tabletop activities have many potential benefits for children with special needs. Very often, all developmental domains are being addressed during these activities. In addition, the following briefly lists some of the other important benefits. More detailed examples will follow.

10-1a Fine Motor Skills for School Readiness

Children with special needs may require extra assistance learning fine motor skills that will be necessary for success in school. These include using paintbrushes and writing utensils, crayons, puzzles, gluing, folding, and cutting with scissors. Sometimes, the motion and control necessary can be particularly challenging for children with physical disabilities, such as cerebral palsy, and for children with low muscle tone, a common characteristic of children who have Down syndrome. The ECE teacher must observe how children currently manage these activities and assist them in gradually mastering these tasks.

10-1b Task Sequencing

Children with cognitive and information-processing disabilities often have difficulty learning and understanding **task sequencing,** the sequence of behaviors and events that make up an activity. Explaining, demonstrating, and reviewing the steps of an activity can provide important support for the development of cognitive processes in these children. Providing a visual support for each step of the sequence can be extremely helpful in supporting cognitive processes.

10-1c Demonstrating Cause and Effect

Activities that dramatically demonstrate **transformations** or alterations are particularly helpful for assisting children with cognitive delays in understanding cause and effect.

10-1d Learning Key Vocabulary and Concepts

For a child who has special needs this is an important opportunity to develop vocabulary and concepts. If a child is truly engaged in the activity, hearing the teacher use key words several times as she observes the matching events provides a major boost to vocabulary and concept development.

10-2 Planning Tabletop Activities for Children with Special Needs

Tabletop activities may require more careful preparation than other activities. Particularly when children with special needs are included in the classroom, teachers must think through not just all the materials that need to be prepared, but also the adaptations that may be necessary as well as the level of support needed so children can be as independent as possible. Chapter 2 discussed strategies to help determine the level of support needed and offered specific suggestions for adaptations to enlarge, enhance, stabilize, and simplify (EESS) classroom activities.

10-2a Providing a Clear Transition

Providing a clear transition into the table activity is extremely helpful. Showing the materials to be used, major steps in the sequence of the activity, and possible outcomes of the activity can help children understand what is coming up and focus more easily.

Keeping the procedural logistics consistent will keep the stress level low and assist children in moving easily to the activity table or center. The following is an example:

Step 1: An assistant has completed preparation by placing all materials near the tables.

Step 2: The teacher gives a clear cue that it is time for centers (which includes a tabletop activity as one choice) in which all children will participate. In this case the teacher puts on the song, "Hi ho, Hi ho, it's off to work we go," and the children automatically move to find their chairs at the tables.

Step 3: Children put on smocks or shirts that are hung nearby, to protect clothing if the activity is messy.

Step 4: Teacher shows children the materials that will be used in the activity and labels them. She demonstrates examples of how the materials can be used and shows examples of possible outcomes.

10-3 Supporting Learning Objectives Through Tabletop Activities

Carefully planned tabletop activities can help children with special needs accomplish IEP and developmental objectives. This section offers strategies to support their learning.

10-3a Fine and Gross Motor Skills

Difficulty with fine motor skills is often the greatest challenge to full participation in tabletop activities. ECE teachers need to systematically encourage and support the movements and coordination for such skills as cutting, painting, folding, gluing, stirring, and pouring. These skills involve both fine motor movement (manipulation of arms and hands, and eye-hand coordination) and gross motor skills (sitting, balance, and control of trunk, head, and neck.) The following simple steps should enable ECE teachers to provide important assistance to many children with these challenges.

Helpful Hint

Children who have difficulty focusing and sustaining attention and children with behavior disorders may have extreme difficulty sitting and waiting for materials to be placed on the table. Teachers should either set up materials on the work table prior to having the child sit down or should have prepared materials an arm's reach away.

Helpful Hint

If circle time directly precedes the art activity, the teacher can demonstrate while the children are still in the circle.

Obtain Pertinent Information from Fellow Professionals. An occupational therapist (OT) or physical therapist (PT) can discuss the nature of the child's motor difficulty and suggest specific strategies to enhance her experiences with tabletop activities. Keep in mind that for children with severe physical disabilities such as cerebral palsy, *positioning* will be critical, as discussed in Chapter 3. If children are not properly seated:

- They may not be able to concentrate on the difficult fine motor tasks presented because their energies will be directed toward maintaining balance.
- They may be uncomfortable when placed in an inappropriate position, thus decreasing motivation to participate.
- The position may interfere with head control, making it difficult for them to maintain visual focus on the materials.

The following general rules can be used as guidelines for placing children in a seated position. First, be sure feet are placed flat on the floor. The chair must be the right height and hips must be squarely positioned at the back of the chair. A pillow or ream of paper can be taped to the back of the chair, as shown in Photo 10-1, to support children so their feet do not dangle. It is usually recommended that the angle of alignment at the elbows, hips, and knees should approximate 90 degrees. However, this positioning is sometimes not the most appropriate for every child. Therefore, the advice of a physical or an occupational therapist should always be sought for any specific child. If the chair is too high, a thick book, ream of paper, or other flat object can be placed under the child's feet. The child's forearms and hands must rest comfortably on the table's surface.

Photo 10-1 Adaptations can be made to make sure a child is seated comfortably and properly for tabletop activities.

Perform a Task Analysis. Watch children who do not have special needs performing the skill and analyze the sequence of their actions. For example, what sequence of movements is required to use a paintbrush?

- The child grips the handle (certain grips work better than others).
- She dips the end of her brush into paint.
- She wipes off extra paint on the side of the paint container.
- She swipes or dabs paint onto paper until there is little paint left on the brush.
- She repeats the sequence.

Determine the activity/standards discrepancy as described in Chapter 6.

Carefully Observe How a Child with Special Needs Performs the Task. What parts of this task can she approximate? Which steps are most difficult? For example:

- JT can grip the brush handle.
- JT dips the end of the brush into paint.
- JT cannot wipe off excess paint; paint drips all over as she moves the brush to paper.
- JT has difficulty keeping the brush within the boundaries of the paper.

Provide Just Enough Assistance to Allow the Child to Do the Task. In JT's example, two types of assistance were needed. First, she needed direct instruction on how to wipe off the excess paint. The teacher first demonstrated the movements for wiping off the excess and then used hand-over-hand techniques to help JT do it. An adaptation was also necessary to help JT keep the paint on the paper. The easiest solution was to place the paper inside a food tray to bring visual attention to the boundaries. To the extent possible, gradually reduce the amount of assistance provided until the child can perform the task independently.

Figure 10-1 Paper is placed in shallow tray to stabilize the paper and create a boundary.

Helpful Hint

For some children it will be necessary to provide adapted equipment, such as specially designed scissors and paintbrushes with extra large handles that can be attached to the child's hands. Also helpful is securing the paper to the table with tape so that it cannot move around, or placing the paper in a shallow tray (see Figure 10-1).

For children with severe motor disabilities, several adaptations might be necessary to enhance their independence. Photo 10-2 and Figure 10-2 demonstrate how common materials can be used to create the adaptations necessary to provide the least amount of support to promote independence. The benefit of these adaptations is that one-to-one support from a staff member is not necessary.

Common Materials	Purpose of the Adaptation (EESS)	
Binder: 3 inch	**E**	Use *the 3-inch binder to* **e**nlarge and **e**nhance the workspace by raising the angle of the surface to make it easier for the student to access the
	E	paper.
Tape	**S**	Use tape to **s**tabilize the paper onto the binder so that it does not slide around.
Shelf liner		Use the shelf liner to **s**tabilize the binder so it does not slide on the table.
Marker	**S**	Use *the marker to* **s**implify the writing process because it requires less hand pressure than a pencil.

Figure 10-2 Chart of Adapted Materials and Their Purpose

Diversity Awareness

To promote diversity awareness, it is critical that toys and equipment within the classroom reflect cultural diversity. For example, care must be taken to include multicultural crayons, marking pens, and construction paper that represent the diversity of skin tones. These are available through a variety of sources including www.HatchEarlyLearning.com.

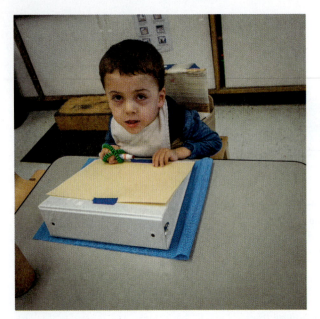

Photo 10-2 Adaptations make it possible for this student to work independently.

10-3b Developing Cognitive Skills

Children with special needs often require assistance developing certain cognitive skills. Two examples are understanding cause and effect and task sequencing for children who have difficulty sustaining attention and processing information.

Cause and Effect. Activities that dramatically demonstrate transformations or changes are particularly helpful for assisting children with cognitive delays in understanding cause and effect, especially when the teacher carefully uses language to map these events onto the child's experience.

For example, combining vinegar and baking soda results in a dramatic bubbling effect. If the teacher repeatedly says things like, "Now watch, when we pour in the vinegar, it will cause the baking powder to bubble." The teacher pours the vinegar, and says, "See. We poured the vinegar, *then* it bubbled." The child with cognitive delay has the opportunity to observe the effect of a specific event and can see the alteration taking place by observing the task sequence.

For children who do not have a language delay, this type of exchange can be an opportunity for development of more complex sentence structure. The teacher can model and repeat complex sentence structures that reflect the cause-and-effect relationships being demonstrated in the activity. For example, encourage children to say:

"When we pour the vinegar in, the baking powder will bubble."

Emphasizing *cause and effect* can create an opportunity for hypothesis testing and experimentation. For example, the teacher can ask, "What do you think will happen if we pour water on the baking soda?" Several different substances can be mixed and the results observed and described.

Task Sequencing. Task sequencing is often a challenge for children with special needs. Children who otherwise seem quite capable may not be able to carry out a task that has multiple steps.

Explaining the steps of an activity before beginning a task can serve as an important opportunity for children with cognitive challenges and information processing difficulties to learn and understand the sequence of behaviors and events that make up the activity. For example, a teacher can help children anticipate an event by explaining the steps in the activity and demonstrating using a **picture sequence board,** shown in Figure 10-3. For example:

1. First, we will lay out all the leaves we collected on our walk.
2. Next, we will put a little spot of glue on our sheet of paper.
3. Then we will put one of our leaves on the glue.
4. Next, we put another spot of glue on the paper and put on another leaf.
5. We will do this until our paper is covered with leaves.

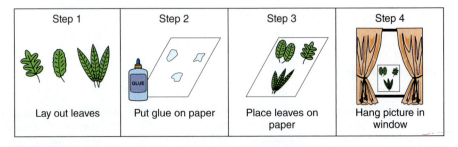

Figure 10-3 Picture Sequence Board for Leaf Collage

6. Finally, when the glue dries, we can hang it up on the window.
7. Pictures or symbols can also be put on shelves or containers to turn cleaning up into a matching game.

Within the task sequence, adaptations can be used to provide the level of support needed for each step. For example, the teacher can:

- **Adapt the materials** by using different types of glue in step #2. Glue sticks are easier to use because they don't require squeezing. Furthermore, smaller bottles of glue are easier to squeeze than larger bottles. Some children might find it even easier to use a brush that is dipped into the glue.
- **Adapt the requirements** of instruction by reducing the requirements for step #5. Instead of requiring the students to cover the whole paper with leaves, they could cover half of the paper or glue a specific number of leaves on the paper.

10-3c Learning Key Vocabulary and Concepts

For children with special needs, tabletop activities are an important opportunity to develop vocabulary and concepts. If children are truly engaged in the activity, hearing the teacher use key words several times as the event occurs provides a major boost to vocabulary and concept development.

In the earlier example involving vinegar and baking soda, depending on the child's level, the key vocabulary might be *pour* and *bubbles,* or it might be *vinegar* and *baking soda.* Key concepts might be the fairly abstract words *cause* and *effect.*

To ensure that these activities are effective in supporting vocabulary development for children with a language delay or disability, keep the following points in mind:

1. *Plan* the vocabulary ahead of time. If necessary, write out key words as a reminder to assistants so everyone is consistent in what things are called.
2. *Repeat* the key words several times. Encourage children to say the words.
3. *Repeat* the activity several times. Often, children with special needs will have difficulty learning from a single event, unless the event is spectacular in some way. Thus, once you have identified an engaging and interesting activity, it is important to repeat that activity often.

10-3d Development of Representational Skills

Art activities provide focused opportunities to assist children with special needs in the development of **representational skills**. Unlike children without disabilities, a child with special needs may not have already developed an appreciation for two-dimensional representation of the world via pictures or have experience drawing simple figures. Problems with visual attention, cognitive delays, and reduced visual acuity may interfere with the child's understanding that pictures can represent objects and activities.

This understanding is clearly a critical prerequisite for the development of symbolic skills and literacy. It is also a potential source of shared enjoyment between child and caregiver and provides opportunity to enhance language development. ECE teachers can play a critical role in helping children with special needs develop representational skills.

Helpful Hint

For children who do not speak or have a significant hearing loss, be sure to introduce a sign for the key words and assist children in making the sign. Or allow children to point to pictures representing the key vocabulary.

For children who are blind, use a touch cue of some kind as you say the word. Children with blindness will not immediately understand the act of pouring. They will need to:

1. Feel the container.
2. Feel the liquid in the container.
3. Feel the movement of tipping the container to pour.
4. Feel the edge of the container.
5. Feel the liquid coming out of the container.
6. Feel the transformation of the mixture as the vinegar mixes with the baking soda.

Once this has been demonstrated and practiced many times, a potential touch cue can be introduced to accompany the word *pour*. The touch cue might be moving a child's hand in a pouring motion or simply letting her touch the container as the teacher says, "Okay, now we're going to pour the vinegar."

Helpful Hint

A potential conflict may arise from the ECE teacher's concern about keeping all children engaged. A simple solution here is to vary the activity in some way, starting with a basic, familiar activity and expanding on it in interesting ways. Thus, repetition is maintained for children with special needs while adding interest and challenge for other children.

Obviously storybook reading is the most significant activity related to the understanding of pictures as representation. However, some children with special needs will not be ready to understand the meaning of pictures and storybooks. ECE teachers can support the development of representational skills for these children within tabletop activities, such as:

- Learning to draw simple shapes and objects (circles, faces, houses, flowers).
- Outlining body parts (hand, foot, whole body).
- Looking for pictures in magazines to cut out, and making collages or booklets around certain themes or categories of pictures.
- Taking snapshots and making photo albums.

10-3e Enhancing Early Math Skills

What might be referred to as math readiness skills are often encouraged through tabletop activities involving a hands-on/sensory motor approach to learning. Manipulated objects readily lend themselves to developing number sense and numeration. Concepts such as bigger/smaller, more than, less than, sets, equals, one-to-one correspondence come about naturally. Number concept games such as counting, naming numbers when shown the number, and matching numbers to groups of objects are easy to direct. Mathematical reasoning is facilitated when children make comparisons by noting similarities and differences, are asked to estimate the number of blocks in the jar, and measure the distance between objects. One could go on

Number Sense: *"How many cars do you have in your garage? Let's count! You have five cars. Three are red and two are yellow. Oh look! Here's an orange car. Now you have more. Let's count again. One, two, three, four, five, six. Six cars altogether!"*

(One-to-one correspondence) *"Timmy, please set the table. Remember, each place gets one napkin and one cup. The table will seat four of you. How many cups will you need to get from the cupboard? Yes, four cups. Please get them and set one at each place. And then get the napkins and set them around the table."*

(Quantity*) "I have one cookie. You have two cookies. Who has* more?*"*

Rote counting (Starting a car across the table): *"One, two, three, GO!"*

Patterning: *"Let's make a pattern with these blocks: yellow block, red block, blue block, yellow block, red block.—What comes next? Right, a blue block!"*

Geometry (Teacher holds up a round disc-shaped block and a square block, saying): *"These are different aren't they? They're different* shapes*. How are they different? Yes, this one is* round, *but this one has corners. It is* square.*"*

Measurement (Teacher places several different-colored straws of different lengths on the table. She asks the children to figure out): *"Which one is the* shortest *and which one is the* longest?*"*

Estimation (Teacher shows children a glass jar with several marbles inside and asks): *"How many marbles do you think are in the jar?"* (Teacher writes down their guesses on a whiteboard. Then, she takes them out one at a time while the children count.)

Figure 10-4 Embedding Early Math Skills in Tabletop Activities

and on offering suggestions illustrating how young children learn early mathematical concepts by exploring their natural environment.

Recognizing the vital foundation for future mathematics learning, National Association for the Education of Young Children (NAEYC) and the National Council of Teachers of Mathematics (NCTM) issued a joint statement outlining recommendations for teachers of young children (2002). Figure 10-4 includes just a few of the activities that readily enhance math readiness.

WEBLINK

To see the "Position Statement on Early Childhood Mathematics: Promoting Good Beginnings," go to www.naeyc.org/positionstatements /mathematics.

10-4 Strategies for Children with Tactile Defensiveness

Any fine motor task that requires coming into contact with a variety of unfamiliar textures and materials can be stressful for some children with special needs. Avoiding tactile contact, or *tactile defensiveness,* is particularly common in children who have autism. Also, children with severe visual impairments often appear to be tactile defensive. However, sometimes the issue for children who are blind is simply a lack of careful cueing to help them anticipate what is happening next. Thus, avoidance may be based more on fear and insecurity than on increased tactile sensitivity.

The following strategies can be helpful with children who demonstrate tactile defensiveness.

10-4a Use Hand-Under-Hand Guidance

Rather than trying to use a hand-over-hand method where you guide the child's hands through the required movements, place the child's hands on top of your hands while you engage in the activity. Hand-under-hand guidance allows a child to experience the activity initially through you, which allows him to feel more in control. Once he has become familiar with the activity, you may try to guide his hands. (These techniques were discussed in more detail in Chapter 3. See Figure 3-6.)

10-4b Use the Premack Principle

The **Premack principle** simply states that an unpleasant task or activity should be followed by a pleasant or highly desired one (Premack, 1965). You can encourage partial participation in an unpleasant activity, then allow the child to engage in a preferred activity. For example, encourage the child to finger paint briefly even though she resists somewhat, and then allow her to go to the sink to wash her hands (an activity she loves). Or, after you help a child to glue two or three flowers on a collage, then allow her to return to the block area.

10-4c Incorporate the Child's Security Object

Particularly in the case of children who have autism, you may be able to use a favorite object within the activity. For example, one child loves a set of tiny plastic bears that she carries around obsessively. She consistently refuses to play with playdough or any such substance. One day her teacher buries the bears in the playdough. Though briefly upset, the child becomes intrigued with finding the bears in the playdough, and her tactile defensiveness is significantly reduced. As long as she can have her bears in the vicinity of the art activity, she is fairly willing to participate.

10-4d Provide Physical Boundaries

When children are very close to one another or are tempted to grab another child's things, working on a plastic tray, shelf liner, or on a placemat that provides visual/physical boundaries will discourage disruption.

Helpful Hint

A *first/then* visual support (see Figure 10-5) can be useful in helping implement the Premack principle. This visual reminder helps children see and understand that after they participate in their less preferred activity, they will be able to participate in their preferred activity. This visual support can help to calm and reduce children's resistance of the less preferred activity and help build trust that they can anticipate becoming involved in their preferred activity.

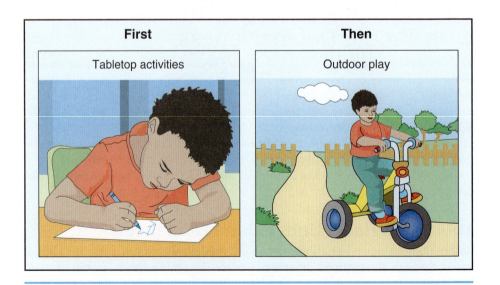

First — Tabletop activities

Then — Outdoor play

Figure 10-5 First/Then Support

10-4e Provide Role Models

One of the advantages of inclusive classrooms is the possibility of placing a child who is reluctant to participate near a child who is enthusiastic and familiar with the materials.

Summary

Tabletop activities can be motivating for young children with special needs, particularly if they are carefully selected and planned and if they are repeated often enough to give children a sense of mastery. These activities also provide important opportunities to work on specific skills that are part of children's IEPs. Again, planning is the key.

Tabletop activities can also present significant challenges to many children, particularly if they do not understand the activity or if the activity presents too many physical challenges. Several strategies can be used to increase children's successful participation in these activities. For a list and summary of adaptations discussed in this chapter as well as other possible adaptations, see Figure 10-6.

Adapted from CARA's Kit

Goal: To use adaptations instead of physical assistance whenever possible to increase independence and confidence

Adapt the environment:
- Use placemats with children's names on them so they know where to sit.
- Define individual space/boundaries at the table with placemats, trays, tape, or shelf liners.
- Provide footrests under chairs using books, reams of paper, or large blocks for support.
- Use adaptive chairs for correct posture.
- Use sturdy three-inch binders for slant boards.

Adapt activity or routine:
- Allow students to stand up at the table instead of having to sit.
- Do activities standing up at the wall or at the easel.
- Place sensory activities on the floor for better access.
- Provide a visual support using pictures, icons, or real objects for each step of the activity.
- Pair two children together to do one activity to encourage peer interaction, sharing, and imitation.

Adapt materials:
- Allow children to have a security toy near the activity.
- Use different-size glue sticks and glue bottles.
- Incorporate children's favorite materials into the activity.
- Provide larger/thicker materials or objects that are easier to pick up.
- Use adapted scissors and heavier paper such as card stock or paint swatches for cutting activities.
- Use broken crayons to encourage pincer grasp.
- Use markers instead of pencils as they do not require so much hand pressure.
- Enlarge writing utensils by building up the handles with curlers, tape, pencil grips, and so on.

Adapt requirements or instruction:
- Ask a child who quickly gets overwhelmed to join the activity when there are less children at the table.
- Ask a child who is fidgety to help pass out materials to the other students.
- Do half the steps on one day and half the steps the next day for activities with many steps.
- Reduce the number of steps in the activity.
- Reduce the number of materials provided.

Source: Adapted from Milbourne, S. A., & Campbell, P. H. (2007). *CARA's Kit: Creating adaptations for routines and activities*. Philadelphia, PA: Child and Family Studies Research Programs, Thomas Jefferson University.

Figure 10-6 Summary of Tabletop Adaptations

⌄ Professional Resource Download

Read–Reflect–Discuss

Marciana's Resistance

Marciana joined Mr. Podvosky's classroom two months ago. Initially she was extremely agitated at the beginning of the morning and engaged in rocking and hand flapping. She was also obsessed with the plastic letters M and A, which she insisted on carrying with her at all times. By making sure that her arrival routine is consistent, she finally seems to be settling into the classroom routine. However, the one activity Marciana will have nothing to do with is any kind of tabletop activity.

After consulting with the early childhood special educator who observed Marciana carefully for several days, Mr. Podvosky determines that she is extremely uncomfortable and resistant to touching unfamiliar substances, though she enjoys water play. She has apparently come to associate all tabletop activities with materials like finger paint, glue, and glitter. The consultant describes her reaction as *tactile defensiveness*. She explains this is not something the child will simply grow out of, and it will be helpful to Marciana to increase her tolerance for tactile stimulation. The consultant also notes that Marciana does not enjoy situations where she feels crowded by other children.

The consultant and Mr. Podvosky work out a plan for Marciana. Initially, Mr. Podvosky has some misgivings about the plan because it seems overly directive. His classroom allows choice in all activities, and he is uncomfortable trying to coerce Marciana into doing anything she does not want to do. The inclusion consultant expresses her concern that this might result in Marciana becoming even more isolated and disconnected from the class over time, because her preference is to be alone and engage in comfortable, highly repetitive activities. They agree to implement the plan for one month and then reassess at that time.

According to the plan, Marciana's favorite aide, Miss Chu, sits with her near the table, at a smaller table. Here they play with tubs of water. She is encouraged to put her plastic letters in the water to watch them float. Gradually, Miss Chu begins to experiment with adding materials to the water. She starts with small amounts of cornstarch. She places Marciana's letters in the water and encourages her to retrieve them. As she changes the consistency of the water more dramatically by adding more cornstarch, she has Marciana place her hand on top of Miss Chu's hand, while Miss Chu stirs the mixture.

Miss Chu also experiments with food coloring, dramatically changing the color of the water. Marciana became fascinated with this interesting transformation. She then demonstrates similar color alterations by mixing finger paints. Miss Chu models using just the tip of her index finger to dip in the finger paint and make a letter on the paper. Marciana loves making letters, so watching this new way of writing sustains her attention. Using a gentle hand-over-hand technique, Miss Chu then begins to dip Marciana's index finger into the paint and make an *M* on the page (Marciana's favorite letter!). Initially Marciana resists touching the paint and becomes agitated. Miss Chu then places a bowl of warm water at the table, and as soon as Marciana makes her letter on the page, Miss Chu immediately places her hand in the warm water, saying "Okay, let's wash off the paint." Over time Marciana becomes so interested in making letters with different materials such as glue and glitter that her tactile defensiveness and her anxiety level significantly decrease.

Read–Reflect–Discuss Questions

1. How do you feel about the potential conflict between the importance of child-centered environments and free choice, and the more directive strategy used in Marciana's scenario?
2. What are some of the keys to success in the strategy described in this scenario?
3. Can you think of other strategies that might have been useful in helping Marciana deal with her resistance to engaging in tabletop activities?

Key Terms

picture sequence board   representational skills   transformations
Premack principle   task sequencing

Helpful Resources

Adaptive Equipment, Special Needs Products and Activities

eSpecial Needs: Source for adaptive equipment enabling fine motor development, sensory motor integration, body awareness, balance, self-calming, and participation in generally all daily activities: www.especialneeds.com

Learning 4 Kids: Fun and simple ideas that promote creative play and learning. Choose by age or categories such as shapes, fine motor, numbers, alphabet, and so on:
www.learning4kids.net

Catalogs

Tumble Forms: For positioning, seating and mobility (#3431), and *Pediatrics: Special needs products for schools and clinics,* Sammons Preston, P.O. Box 5071, Bolingbrook, IL 60440-9977, (800) 323-5547.

Books

Eckenrode, L., Fennell, P., & Hearsey, K. (2013). *Tasks galore.* Raleigh, NC: Tasks Galoe Publishing, Inc.

Houts, A. (2012). *Kids cooking and learning through food activities.* Maryville, MO: Images Unlimited Publishing.

Isenberg, J. P., & Jalongo, M. R. (2014). *Creative thinking and arts-based learning: Preschool through fourth grade.* Columbus, OH: Pearson.

CHAPTER 11

Outside Play

LEARNING OBJECTIVES

After studying this chapter, you will be able to:

LO 11-1: Enumerate the learning opportunities promoted in the outdoor environment.

LO 11-2: Describe techniques to encourage peers to play and interact with children with special needs.

LO 11-3: Discuss important considerations to keep in mind when planning an outdoor environment.

LO 11-4: Create a simple outside lesson plan including adaptations for children with disabilities.

The following NAEYC Standards and DEC Recommended Practices are addressed in this chapter:

naeyc

Standard 1: Promoting Child Development and Learning
Standard 2: Building Family and Community Relationships
Standard 4: Using Developmentally Effective Approaches
Standard 5: Using Content Knowledge to Build Meaningful
          Curriculum

DEC

Practice 2: Environment
Practice 4: Instruction
Practice 5: Interaction

All children, including children with disabilities, often love the change in environment from indoor to outdoor play.

A daily change from inside to outside environment is essential. Many children with disabilities need opportunities for learning and practicing large motor activities, which are often much easier to do outside:

- **Children with special needs often need to learn how to play with outside equipment.** Children may not learn how to ride a bike, catch a ball, run, or slide down the slide without specific help and repeated opportunities for practice.

- **Outside activities can provide opportunities for developing social skills.** These include negotiating turns, pretend play, and watching out for others' safety.

- **Sand and water activities may work better outside for children who have certain disabilities.** Certain classroom themes and activities can be extended to the outdoor environment to reinforce and repeat concepts, such as putting toy fish in the water table.

- **Special concerns and adaptations may need to be addressed for safety and access.** Children who cannot participate in large muscle activities still need activities that are appropriate for outdoors, such as being pulled in a wagon or pushed in a specially adapted swing. Use of textures and contrasting surfaces can help children with limited vision move around the playground independently.

- **A regularly scheduled discovery walk can be an excellent outdoor activity.** Careful planning for children with special needs will make this a rich opportunity for meeting children's goals.

Introduction

The importance of outside play as part of the daily curriculum cannot be underestimated. Young children (and their teachers!) need a change of environment. Opportunities for using large muscles while running, climbing, or riding bikes are usually not available inside the classroom. This kind of play may also be more limited at home for some children.

Because of limited opportunities to practice, the development of these large muscle play skills may be a particular challenge for children with special needs. This is obviously true for children who have motor disabilities. But it is also true for children who have special needs related to cognitive delay, autism, and visual impairment because they need close supervision in the outside environment.

11-1 Opportunities for Learning in the Outdoor Environment

Going outside provides not only a welcome change from the classroom but also opportunities to develop large motor skills and enhance play and social skills. Several strategies and adaptations can turn the playground and surrounding neighborhood into an extension of your classroom.

11-1a Change of Environment

If you've ever been inside a classroom for three hours with a group of 8 to 12 toddlers or preschoolers, you probably understand the need to change environments! For many people, being outside has a calming effect. The natural lighting, fresh air, different acoustic characteristics, and opportunity to run and shout offer a welcome change from the classroom environment. Also, moving from the classroom to outside during the course of the day provides an opportunity for children to practice motor and play skills often quite different from the classroom. In fact, Kuo and Faber Taylor (2004) found that children who have attention deficit disorder (ADD) exhibit a greater ability to focus immediately after spending time outside with nature.

Some children with disabilities might actually need adaptations just to get to the playground, as some classrooms are not located right near the playground. Children might need more time to walk to the playground. Children who are nonambulatory or who tire easily might need to use a wheelchair or be pulled in a wagon. Furthermore, access to the playground and its corresponding areas might be difficult as there could be environmental barriers such as cement or wood curbs, or lack of ramps and clear pathways to enter the areas.

Sometimes, access to the playground is actually dictated by the weather. If rain or extreme weather conditions make it impossible to go outside, teachers should still try to move out of the classroom to a different environment during the regularly scheduled outside time:

- **If the center is in a large building, take a walk through parts of the building rarely visited.** This will provide children with the opportunity to exercise large muscles while maintaining interest because of the novelty.
- **Switch classrooms with another teacher.** This will at least provide a change of environment although not necessarily meet the needs of the children to use large muscles.
- **Use a hallway or an unused room.** A space where small groups of children can throw beanbags or negotiate an obstacle course can occasionally substitute for going outdoors.

Specific planning of areas and activities will be discussed later in this chapter.

11-1b Opportunities for Using Large Muscles

Outside environments can provide the opportunity for a variety of activities for children with a range of developmental ages and abilities. These activities should be different from activities found inside the classroom. Typically, outside areas focus on large muscle or gross motor development as well as perceptual motor learning. Through **perceptual motor development**, children integrate motor behaviors and perception (visual, auditory, tactile, and kinesthetic perception).

Due to severe motor disabilities or medically fragile conditions, a few children may not be able to engage in large motor activities. Special accommodations will be needed to provide appropriate outside activities for these children. Their participation may need to be more passive, such as being pushed in a swing, pulled in a wagon, or simply walked around the playground in a wheelchair.

The following gross motor equipment should be available for children in outside areas:

- Padded rubber ground covering under climbing structures and slides
- Climbing structures (some with lower height)
- Swings (some with adapted seats, seat belts, and so on; see Figure 11-1)
- Toys that rock, such as a rocking horse or boat
- Slides of different sizes, with high rails at top
- Tricycles of various sizes, including tricycles that have been adapted for children with special needs
- Wheeled scooter-type toys
- Balls (many sizes, some soft) and beanbags
- Low basketball net or other containers to throw into
- Wagons to push or pull
- Pedal or foot-powered cars

Space for riding wheeled toys and throwing balls must be planned carefully to ensure safety and freedom of movement for children who are using the equipment and for those who are not.

Information about safety requirements for typical playground equipment can be obtained from the manufacturer and/or licensing agencies. For children with unsteady walking

Figure 11-1 Adapted Swing

abilities, seizure disorders, or limited vision, additional safety measures are desirable. For example:

- Ground covering should be made of resilient material and should be level.
- Equipment should be positioned with care to avoid protrusions that may be difficult to see or that extend into otherwise clear pathways. Protrusions that cannot be avoided should be painted a bright color so all can see them.
- A variety of adapted swings can be installed such as those shown in Figure 11-1. Or bucket swings can be substituted for regular swings.
- Blocks and Velcro straps can be placed on pedals of some of the wheeled toys with the assistance of a physical therapist or inclusion specialist.
- Texture/tactile cues can be designed for children with limited vision to provide contrast both visually and the way it feels underfoot. For example, a boundary between the swing area and the sandbox could be created by black and white stripes painted on rubber matting under swings, with grass or sand around the sandbox.
- Paths for wheeled toys should be clearly marked with colored lines. Stop signs, arrows, or other road signs should be placed on bike paths for safety and development of literacy.

11-1c Developing Play Skills

Some children with special needs may require assistance in learning how to play in an outside environment. For example, learning to climb up and slide down a slide can be a daunting but exciting challenge for many children with special needs. Sliding done on one's tummy, feet first, may be the beginning of learning to enjoy the slide. This position can be safer, easier, and less frightening than a sitting position. Furthermore, children with disabilities might need specific help with planning how to move their body to go down the slide. They might need to be told and shown exactly what to do with their body using task analysis. When teaching gross motor activities, it's important to verbally discuss and physically show where to place hands, feet, and other body parts throughout the task. Here are the steps for children who have climbed up the climbing structure and are now about to go down the slide on their bottom:

- Hold on to the rail with your hand.
- Sit down on your bottom.
- Put your feet in front of you.
- Use your hands on the floor to push your bottom forward to go down the slide.
- Place your hands on the sides of the slide while you go down.

In addition to the obvious need to learn how to go down a slide, ride a bike, swing, climb, and play in the sand, opportunities also exist for turn-taking, playing simple games, and joining in pretend play with cars and bikes. For a few children, outside time may be an opportunity for children to have some *alone* time and recover from the often more intense enclosed classroom environment. Teachers must carefully observe young children during outside play periods to determine how much socialization and what levels of assistance they need and can tolerate.

Outside time may also create opportunities for learning how to negotiate conflicts among children. It is important to allow children to attempt to solve their own conflicts by carefully monitoring situations and intervening only when necessary. However, some children's immature perceptual motor development may create inadvertent conflicts. For example, when riding a tricycle, children need to coordinate their muscle movement of the tricycle with the visual obstacles in their path to avoid crashing into other children who are riding bicycles or walking. Children with special disabilities might need to be specifically taught how to pay attention (using eyes and ears) to others as well as the environment and to plan accordingly.

Photo 11-1 Racing can be done in different ways so all children can participate.

To involve all abilities during gross motor activities, allow children to participate in the same activity but in a different way, depending on their developmental level. Noncompetitive racing games, for example, are a fun and exciting way to get kids moving and practicing their motor skills. Keep the games open ended in a way that allows children to race any way that is comfortable for them. Photo 11-1 shows all the different ways this inclusive classroom allows children to "run" the race. For example, children can "run" the race by using:

- an adapted bike with an adult pushing the bike;
- two different-sized tricycles (large and small);
- wheeled carts for pushing; and
- feet for running.

Planning varying activities to supplement outside equipment can provide wonderful opportunities to develop play skills. Often, a classroom theme can be expanded during outside play. Also, art activities may be repeated outside for children who need more time to experience the process.

The following list offers specific outside play suggestions that typically appeal to children with special needs.

Appealing Outside Play Activities for Children with Special Needs

- Bring dolls outside to feed, bathe, push in the swing, and accompany down the slide.
- Expand on a fish or animal theme and bring plastic models outside to play with in the sandbox or water table.
- Build a playhouse out of a large cardboard box (cut out windows and doors); include paints and brushes for children to decorate their house. Children at younger cognitive levels often love playing peekaboo through the windows.
- Provide different-sized cardboard boxes for children to play in. Attaching a string to the box can turn the activity into a social game by pulling a friend around in the box. Children with perceptual motor delays can work on motor planning by getting in and out of the boxes safely and comfortably.
- Create a garden center where children can request help with selecting and planting seeds. They can water and pull weeds in already established gardens.
- Set up obstacle courses using tunnels, balance beams, stairs, and carpet squares for children to crawl through, walk on, climb, and jump off.
- Provide buckets of water and sponges for washing the outside equipment: bikes, toy cars, and climbing structures. The children have fun and learn while the playground gets a good cleaning!
- Create an art area where children can paint with a variety of tools, including brushes, sponges, flyswatters, even their hands. They can draw with large pieces of chalk on the cement or paper, experiment with drawing using shaving cream,

and create *goop* from cornstarch and water. Provide aprons, water, and towels for easy cleanup.

- Teach children with special needs to play hide-and-seek. Have a peer buddy assist them initially. Create interesting places to hide on the playground, such as tents or cardboard boxes.

11-1d Developing Social Skills

Outside environments offer some of the best opportunities for children with special needs to develop social skills. Examples of specific outside play opportunities that can help develop social skills include:

- taking turns going down the slide;
- pulling a friend in a wagon, or being pulled in a wagon;
- negotiating around one another on trikes;
- playing Follow the Leader with trikes or big wheels;
- playing catch and baseball with foam balls;
- sharing toys at sand and water tables; or
- engaging in simple cooperative activities like filling a large bucket with a cup or digging a big hole.

11-1e Opportunities for Sand and Water Play

Outside time provides an opportunity for children to experience activities not easily managed inside the classroom. Sand and water play are two experiences that can also be expanded into a variety of activities and combinations.

Outdoors can be a much better setting than inside for sand and water play, especially for children with special needs. Unlike playing in the classroom with sand and water where there is always some concern for containment of the materials, playing with these materials outside allows the focus to be on exploring and expanding play schemes.

Sandboxes. Sandboxes can be built or purchased quite easily. Adding enough sand to provide a quality experience can be difficult: it is heavy and you need lots! Depending on the ages of the children, you may want to purchase sand that has been sterilized and free of toxic materials. Sandboxes need to be covered when not in use. If water has been added, it is important to allow the sand to dry out before covering.

Children can play with dry sand or add water to change the texture. A variety of toys should be available for children to use during sand play. The following lists several of the most popular sand toys.

Sand Toys

Containers of different sizes and shapes
Bowls in a variety of sizes
Shovels and spoons
Flour sifters
Watering cans
Funnels
Cars, trucks, dumptrucks, bulldozers, and so on
Small plastic animals and people

Children with disabilities might actually need to be taught how to play appropriately with sand. They might not have a large repertoire of ideas and might get stuck in a repetitive motion with sand, such as sifting it through their hands or

Photo 11-2 Sand play provides important sensory motor experiences for all children.

WEBLINK

For more information on national health and safety performance standards regarding sandboxes, see Standard 6.2.4.1: Sandboxes at the National Resource Center for Health and Safety in Child Care and Early Education: http://cfoc.nrckids.org/StandardView/6.2.4.1.

throwing it. Children can be taught using the typical scripts that most children do with sand. They can be taught to:

- scoop with a shovel to fill a pail;
- scoop with a shovel to fill a dump truck and then lift the truck bed to dump the sand;
- fill a pail with wet sand, quickly turn it over, and lift the pail up to make a sand castle;
- use a large bowl and large spoon to stir and cook something;
- dig a hole in the sand, pile up the sand to make a mountain, and then have fun climbing the mountain; and/or
- dig a hole in the sand to make a lake or river.

Water Tables. Water tables are versatile pieces of equipment that can be used with any number of materials. These tables are also excellent for encouraging social play with young children, who gather around the table to play and must stand next to each other to participate. Children with physical disabilities who may need practice standing can play naturally at the water table with peers. If children have difficulty standing, water can be placed in tubs on a lower table so children can sit in chairs for stability to participate. The water tubs can also be placed directly on the ground with children sitting on the ground around the tub. Water tables can be used to introduce new materials to children as well as used to introduce small amounts of a new substance to a child with tactile defensiveness. The following lists some ingredients that are often found in water tables.

Suggested Water Table Ingredients

- Water with a variety of containers, funnels, scoops, and strainers
- Water with food color added
- Sand with a variety of containers, funnels, scoops, and strainers
- Sand with water added (provide containers for children to add water and observe the changes in consistency)
- Sand (with or without water) and various groups of objects, such as plastic animals, plastic fish, and shells
- Cornstarch, flour, or cornmeal with containers and/or other objects
- Cornstarch and water to make "goop" (food coloring may be added)
- Styrofoam pieces, especially the recyclable kind that dissolve when water is added
- Cups of food color when dyeing eggs (if the cup of dye spills, it's contained within the water table—no big mess to clean up!)
- Dirt/garden soil (add small cups and seeds plus watering cans for planting activity)
- Bubble mixture (dish soap plus water) and bubble-making tools (commercial bubble wands in various sizes, six-pack soda plastic rings, and any other tool that can hold soap to make a bubble)
- Soapy water and dolls with washcloths, sponges, and towels

Helpful Hint

Monitor the number of objects in a water or sand table—too many containers, shovels, plastic animals, and so on, interfere with children being able to organize their play if they are bombarded with too many choices.

11-2 Encouraging Peers to Play with Children with Special Needs

Some children with disabilities, especially with neurological differences, may need support in developing essential social and play skills. Instead of watching and showing interest in the play of others, they may appear to be uninterested or avoid social interactions by disengaging quickly. Some may wait for others to initiate interaction or focus all of their attention on toys or other objects. Still others may play in repetitive ways that seem developmentally younger. The following are some strategies that provide support in helping children learn to appropriately respond, initiate interaction, imitate, approach, share, and stay in the play situation:

1. Set up activities that are repetitive and predictable where all children are involved in the same activity, such as sliding down a slide or riding a bicycle around a track.
2. Carefully observe children to see what activities they actually watch or seem drawn to.
3. Draw a child's attention to a peer and the peer's attention to the child by commenting on what the other is doing with enthusiasm and excitement.
4. Be certain children have whatever is needed to participate in the activity, drawing their attention, for example, by using a ball to roll toward the bowling pins.
5. Assign roles to the children (for example, "You're the train engineer. Marty gets to take the tickets.").
6. If you notice that a child is paying special attention to a peer, ask that peer to be a peer buddy. Asking the buddy to do something specific like pulling the child in a wagon can help promote interaction. Encourage peers to figure out other ways to interact with the child.
7. Remind peers that all children want to interact and have friends. It is just harder for some.
8. Coach peers to notice a child's attempt to communicate and interact. Encourage peers to persist in their efforts to play with children who are less responsive.
9. Provide adaptations so that a child with a disability can participate in the same activity, but maybe in a different way. Use the EESS acronym. To play "red light green light," where children are supposed to stop their body when you say "red light" and move their body when you say "green light," teachers can:
   - **E**nlarge the area by making sure all children have enough space to move and are not crowded.
   - **E**nhance the game by using a visual support of a picture of a red circle that says *stop* and a picture of a green circle that says *go*.
   - **S**tabilize children who have difficulty moving by allowing them to push a weighted cart, use a walker, or move in a different way such as crawling.
   - **S**implify the activity by slowing down the directions and giving children extra time to stop their body and extra time to get moving or by using sign language for the directions.

Diversity Awareness

As mentioned earlier, perspectives that vary by culture influence the value of play and its learning potential. Even within Western societies, where play may be more highly valued, there is a tendency to push children rather than just letting them be children. Some cultures may see outdoor activities as more strongly related to recreation and leisure while indoor activities are more connected to learning. Even if outdoor play is highly valued, it is often in the form of organized sports rather than more creative play. Unfortunately, children's opportunities to participate in outside play also vary by socioeconomic status and, thus, neighborhoods. If families do not feel it is safe for their children to play outside without adult supervision, the opportunity to engage with others in creative, spontaneous play is limited and very unlike bygone years. This is all the more reason why early educators need to provide the environment and encouragement that facilitates creative and constructive outdoor as well as indoor play. For further information on the varied perspectives on play and learning present throughout the world, see Lillemyr, Dockett, and Perry (2013).

11-3 Planning the Outdoor Environment

Planning an outdoor environment that will meet the needs of all children by providing a variety of fun activities while contributing to the achievement of child-specific objectives can be a challenge. The following suggestions may help make the process easier.

11-3a Start with a Survey

Survey the outdoor space that is available while keeping in mind the need for several key areas:

- Safe areas for climbing, swinging, rocking, and sliding
- Tricycle paths for wheeled toys away from areas where children may be standing or playing
- Open space for ball play and running
- Shaded area for children who cannot tolerate exposure to the sun for long periods
- Variety of surfaces such as grass, concrete, and soft padding
- A **movable soft area** for children who may not be able to move independently (assembled using various padded mats and wedges; see Photo 11-3)
- Shaded, comfortable seating areas for families (a lawn table with an umbrella offers a welcoming place for families and visitors)
- Art area for easels and large paintbrushes
- Large block play area
- Sandbox
- Water table area
- Space for obstacle course

Photo 11-3 Moveable soft areas make it possible for all to enjoy being outside.

Keep the outside area as clean and dust-free as possible. Provide drinking water for the children either through an accessible water fountain or a conveniently placed cooler. Many families provide a water bottle for their children labeled with their names. Remember to keep tissues, a first aid kit, and rubber gloves available. This can be accomplished by placing everything in a backpack or waist fanny pack.

11-3b Selecting Materials for Outside Areas

Don't change toys and materials too often. Children with special needs require time to get used to materials, and repetition is the key to mastery!

Choose appropriate wheeled toys that meet the needs of different children. Try to have at least two of the more popular items, because young children have a difficult time with the concept of sharing.

Variety is essential in other play areas so that all children may participate at their own developmental level. Include an assortment of balls in the ball area: small balls, large balls, beach balls, beanbags, sponges, and ping pong balls. Change soft area toys and materials only after children achieve mastery or appear bored. This area requires careful observation as children here may not be able to initiate or communicate their choices easily.

The art area materials should not be changed too frequently. If an art area is included outside, adding different tools or materials to a basic plan can extend children's interest. It may take some children several days to choose to explore this area, so changing materials often may be more confusing than exciting. Of course, materials might need to be adapted based on children's individual needs by using larger brushes, building up the handles on markers, and using adapted scissors. The same adaptations that are used inside the classroom need to be used outside the classroom for these activities.

Be sure that sandbox toys are working, in good condition, and well organized. Sand tends to clog wheels and joints in some toys. After regular inspections, line up the toys next to the sandbox for easy selection, and make sure enough containers and shovels are on hand for all children. Be especially vigilant about throwing out plastic toys that have rips or cracks in them as they are unsafe and can cut children's hands.

Photo 11-4 A portable inclusion cart facilitates intentional teaching of IEP objectives.

The water table toys need the same kind of attention. If possible, separate sand toys from water toys or have duplicates available. Water toys seem to last longer than sand toys! Check that the water table is not cluttered with too many small toys; an overabundance may affect the ability of some children to organize their play.

Leave an obstacle course assembled in the same sequence for several days. Children with special needs will enjoy mastering the course and can experience it with increasing levels of confidence. For variety, they can try it from either end or from somewhere in the middle!

Intentional Planning for Outside Activities for Children with Disabilities

Kathy Lewis, an early childhood special educator, has created a unique portable inclusion cart to support children with disabilities while they play outside (see Photo 11-4). There are several features that she has placed all on one portable cart that is rolled out to the playground each and every day. The cart consists of the following:

- Materials that support children's IEP goals in the areas of gross motor development and social emotional development
- A soft mat in which children who are nonambulatory can play with inside toys with other children
- A paper packet (located in a plastic sleeve attached to the cart by a clip ring) with descriptions of specific activities teachers or assistants can do with the materials
- Laminated sheets (attached by a clip ring) with individual children's IEP goals and specific examples of materials or activities that can facilitate practice of their goals
- Solution kit consisting of laminated pictures (trade, wait and take turns, ask adults for help, and so on) for positive behavior support
- Specific materials that encourage peer interaction and social skills such as beanbag toss and bowling

Photo 11-5 Outside activities encourage peer interaction and development of social skills.

11-4 Sample Outside Lesson Plan: Discovery Walk

In addition to typical adventures on outside play equipment, another activity that appeals to young children with special needs is the **discovery walk**. A discovery walk need not be a walk around the neighborhood if for some reason this is difficult to manage due to traffic and safety concerns. It can be as simple as a walk around the building and out to the parking lot. To make the discovery walk a learning experience for children with special needs, consider the following suggestions.

- The walk should be a frequent event, preferably once a week. (Children with special needs often require repetition of an experience several times before they begin to learn from it.)
- The route should be carefully planned and repeated until children are familiar with it.
- Once children are familiar with the route, make interesting changes and draw their attention to the change in the route: "Today we're not going to see the cars. Instead we're going to look at some very beautiful flowers."
- Include regular stopping points along the way, and label them clearly. Plan key words and concepts. For example:

  "Gate. Open the gate."

  "Mailbox. We can mail our letters here."

  "Stop. Stop at the stop sign."

  "Barking dog. This is where the barking dog lives."

  "Rock. Here's that very big rock."

- Take bags along and collect things. You may wish to have children collect anything they find interesting. On some trips, collect specific things, such as stones, leaves, and sticks.
- Hide interesting treasures to be discovered along the route. Children will be thrilled to find a bag of play money or toy jewelry.
- Upon return, draw pictures representing events along the walk or make collages of items collected.
- Help children learn the route and develop a sense of direction:

  "Ok, tell me where to turn."

  "Which way do we turn?"

  "What will we see around that corner?"

  "Show me which direction we go to see the dog."

> **Helpful Hint**
>
> Children with limited vision or blindness may need the assistance of an orientation and mobility specialist to help the child become independent traveling this route. This assistance can help the staff learn specific strategies that are unique to helping children with visual impairments.

> **Helpful Hint**
>
> Encourage higher-functioning children to expand on these basic labels:
>
> "I wonder why that dog barks when we walk by?"
> "Why do we have stop signs?"
> "Where do you think that rock came from? What is it shaped like?"
> "Who knows what happens to the mail after it goes in this box?"
>
> For a child who has a hearing loss and who uses signing as the primary mode of communication, signs will need to be taught for labeling key objects.

Summary

Outside play can provide a wealth of opportunities to support the learning and participation of children who have special needs. The key is good planning of the outside experience and incorporating specific adaptations. Sometimes those adaptations require specially designed or modified equipment. A particularly enjoyable outside activity is a discovery walk. To make the walk an effective learning experience for children who have special needs, repeat it frequently so that children learn the route and develop expectations for what might be encountered along the way. For a list and summary of adaptations discussed in this chapter as well as other possible adaptations, see Figure 11-2.

Adapted from CARA's Kit

Goal: To use adaptations (least amount of support) instead of physical assistance (most amount of support) whenever possible to increase independence and confidence skills

Adapt the environment:

- Use a soft mat with inside toys for children who are nonambulatory.
- Minimize barriers to access equipment and provide handrails.
- Paint curbs or protrusions a bright color so all can see.
- Provide a quiet area for children who get overstimulated and who need to take a break.
- Provide different textures and contrasting surfaces for children with limited vision.
- Have a variety of play equipment such as different size tricycles, wheeled toys, and push toys.
- Have simple and complex climbing structures for all levels.
- Clearly mark bike paths with colored lines, stop signs, arrows, and other road signs.

Adapt activity or routine:

- Allow children to sit on the ground or in a chair instead of standing.
- Paint a straight line or place duct tape on the ground if children need to line up before going inside.
- Provide visual cues such as a carpet square showing where to stand when waiting for a turn.
- Repeat gross motor and movement activities frequently.
- Break down the task into small steps and teach each step.
- Teach simple play scripts making sand castles, throwing and catching balls, and chase games.
- Help children plan their body movements by demonstrating where to put their hands, feet, and other body parts (perceptual-motor development).
- Encourage children to pay attention to what others are doing in the environment.
- Alert children to pay attention to the objects in the environment. Be specific: Instead of saying "Be careful," say "Look down; there is a block in your way."

Adapt materials:

- Use adapted equipment such as adapted bikes, adapted swings, and bucket seat swings.
- Use adapted markers, pencils, paintbrushes, and scissors for any art activities.
- Use a variety of different types and sizes of balls.

Adapt requirements or instruction:

- Allow children to participate in a different way, such as pushing a cart instead of riding a bike during races.
- Label and repeat key concepts, phrases, and directions.
- Simplify the movement activity by giving children more time to complete the task.
- Simplify movement games and songs by slowing down the pace while singing.
- Use a peer buddy to demonstrate and modeled the activity or movement.
- Use pictures, photos, gestures, and sign language to help support different learning styles.
- Provide a wagon so children can be pulled instead of having to walk long distances.

Source: Adapted from Milbourne, S. A., & Campbell, P. H. (2007). *CARA's Kit: Creating adaptations for routines and activities*. Philadelphia, PA: Child and Family Studies Research Programs, Thomas Jefferson University.

Figure 11-2 Summary of Outside Play Adaptations

⌄ Professional Resource Download

Read–Reflect–Discuss

Creating Space for Leila

Leila is a three-and-a-half-year-old girl with Down syndrome. During the first two years of her life Leila had frequent hospitalizations and her development was significantly delayed. A major achievement for Leila was that she recently learned to walk independently, though she was still fairly unsteady and fell occasionally. Despite this vulnerability, Leila was adapting well to the classroom.

Outdoors was another matter. She was often reluctant to go outside. Once there, she would only play near the sandbox. Although she would not climb into the sandbox (and resisted being seated in the sand), she would sit on the outside of the sandbox and play fairly listlessly, scooping sand with a small shovel.

Leila's mother mentions to her teacher that one of Leila's favorite activities at home is swinging. However, Leila's swing is a secured baby swing. The child care center has no adapted swings. Leila cannot hang on consistently so the swings are not safe for her. Leila would occasionally look longingly at the swings across the play yard from her safe vantage point near the sandbox. Because her walking is unsteady and there is a great deal of unpredictable activity between her and the swings, she never ventures out toward the swings. Because swinging is unsafe for her, the staff does not help her or carry her over to the swings.

After two months, Leila shows no inclination to move away from her comfortable spot at the sandbox. Her teacher Mrs. Martinez decides to make some adaptations to enable Leila to be more of a participant during outside play. She creates a soft area with mats and wedges right next to the sandbox. Several of Leila's favorite toys from inside the classroom are placed in the soft area. Quickly, Leila begins walking back and forth between the sandbox and the soft area. This area creates a safe, demarcated zone for her. Other children frequently join Leila in her play.

Another adaptation Mrs. Martinez has implemented is to contact the physical therapist to request help in obtaining a specially designed swing seat that is safe for Leila. She encourages the staff to take Leila to the swing frequently. Leila begins to enjoy her treks across the play yard to the swing. Because Leila is still not ready to walk across the play yard independently, a simple picture request strategy is designed. Leila approaches an adult and gives him the picture of the swing to request that activity. Eventually, one child takes a special interest in Leila. She often takes Leila by the hand, walks with her over to the swings, and helps her give her picture request card to the nearest adult.

Gradually Leila has become much more comfortable on the playground. She is steadier and more confident in her mobility skills, and her overall energy level has increased. The picture request system is so successful that the speech and language specialist has taught the staff to use the PECS (picture exchange system) with Leila. By summer, Leila is a very different child!

Read–Reflect–Discuss Questions

1. What are some other ways pictures could be used to increase Leila's opportunities to participate?
2. How would you design the "perfect" outdoor play environment for preschoolers? How would you ensure that your design supports children with a wide range of needs and abilities?
3. How would the design of this outdoor space differ for toddlers?

Key Terms

discovery walk

movable soft areas

perceptual motor development

Helful Resources

Book

Kuh, L. P. (2014). *Thinking critically about environments for young children: Bridging theory and practice.* New York, NY: Teachers College Press.

Solomon, S. G. (2014). *The science of play: How to build playgrounds that enhance child development.* Lebanon, NH: University Press of New England.

Tai, L., Haque, M. T., McLellan, G. K., & Knight, E. J. (2006). *Designing outdoor environment for children: Landscaping school yards, gardens and playgrounds.* New York, NY: McGraw-Hill.

Websites

American Association for the Child's Right to Play: www.ipausa.org

National Clearinghouse for Educational Facilities: www.ncef.org/

National Learning Initiative, College of Design. North Carolina State University: www.naturalearning.org

National Wildlife Federation: www.nwf.org/Kids.aspx

Outdoor Play Ideas: www.letthechildrenplay.net/p/play-outside.html

CHAPTER 12

Mealtimes

LEARNING OBJECTIVES

After studying this chapter, you will be able to:

LO 12-1: Discuss strategies that will help children take advantage of the learning opportunities that can be promoted during mealtimes.

LO 12-2: Describe common challenges and nutritional needs characteristic of young children with disabilities.

LO 12-3: Explain why toileting can present significant challenges for many children with special needs.

The following NAEYC Standards and DEC Recommended Practices are addressed in this chapter:

naeyc

Standard 1: Promoting Child Development and Learning
Standard 2: Building Family and Community Relationships
Standard 4: Using Developmentally Effective Approaches

DEC

Practice 1: Assessment
Practice 2: Environment
Practice 4: Instruction
Practice 5: Interaction

Some children with disabilities have very specific needs related to feeding. For others, meal-time provides strong motivation for learning a variety of skills:

- **For children with certain dis-abilities, snack time provides important opportunities for learning.** Snack times or meal-times provide opportunities to learn social skills such as passing a dish and waiting to be excused. Also, specific teaching strategies can be used to increase commu-nication skills of requesting and making choices.

- **Children with motor difficul-ties need help learning how to feed themselves.** Learning opportunities include the self-help skills of using utensils and cups.

Adaptations might be needed to help facilitate independence. Proper positioning is key to help-ing children with eating.

- **Children with special needs can learn other self-help skills.** These include pouring from a pitcher or carton, opening drink cartons, using a straw, cutting food, cleaning the table, and tak-ing care of trash.

- **Some children will need to be fed by an adult.** They may have extreme difficulties learning to chew and swallow. ECE teachers must obtain assistance from a

specialist who has expertise in feeding challenges. Mealtimes also provide opportunities to model feeding techniques for families and staff.

- **Some disabilities raise specific nutritional concerns.** Consult with families regarding special dietary needs. Snacks can provide important nutrients for children who cannot consume large por-tions at a time.

- Even though toileting can present some significant challenges, the learning opportunities presented need to be recognized.

Introduction

Mealtime is an essential component of early childhood programs. Most early child-hood programs at least serve a snack during a specific time each day. Some serve breakfast and lunch, and others provide a mid-morning snack, then lunch. After-noon programs typically begin with a lunch and serve a mid-afternoon snack. Some programs require children to bring their meals, whereas other programs provide snacks or meals as part of the curriculum. Children with special needs often have specific dietary needs, allergies, or food phobias and may bring their own snacks.

12-1 Learning Opportunities at Snack Times and Mealtimes

Children with special needs can gain a great sense of accomplishment by learning self-help and social skills related to mealtime. We will discuss strategies to encourage and support such skill building.

12-1a Developing Self-Feeding Skills

Opportunities for learning how to eat with utensils, discriminating which foods need utensils, and drinking from a cup are available on a daily basis during meal-times. Always use child-sized plates and utensils. Some children with special needs may require adaptations or one-to-one assistance to learn how to feed themselves.

Attention should be given to *seating arrangements*. Children needing one-to-one assistance should have an adult sitting next to or behind them. Often seating a child near the corner of a square or rectangular table allows an adult to sit and assist com-fortably but still be available to help other children nearby.

Asking for input from a physical or occupational therapist or a nutritional consul-tant may be very important if a child has severe physical disabilities that interfere with typical eating patterns. Children with severe physical disabilities may be unable to eat until they have correct postural positioning; for example, their feet and trunk must be adequately supported and their head held in an upright position. Equipment such as specially designed or adapted chairs, spoons, or cups may also help children eat or drink more successfully. Photo 12-1 demonstrates how a specialized chair improves a child's position for self-feeding.

It is often necessary to task analyze skills required for self-feeding. This involves breaking the particular skill, such as eating with a spoon or drinking from a cup, into small teachable steps. The following is an example.

Steps in Learning to Use a Spoon

1. The child grasps the spoon handle firmly.
2. She rotates her wrist to place the spoon into food.
3. She scoops food onto the spoon.
4. She rotates wrist and arm to bring the spoon to her mouth without spilling.
5. She opens her mouth.
6. She places the spoon in her mouth.
7. She closes her lips around the spoon.
8. She transfers food to her mouth.
9. She removes the spoon.

Some Children Must Be Fed by an Adult. Some children have such severe medical or motor disabilities that they must be fed by an adult. These children are sometimes accompanied by a one-to-one aide who performs this function. If this is not the case, ECE teachers must work closely with the family and a specialist who will provide specific feeding techniques, including positioning, strategies to inhibit reflexes such as biting or gagging, and strategies to facilitate chewing and swallowing.

For children without severe motor delays who need assistance to feed themselves, it is vital that the children are active participants in the process. The adult needs to make sure that child's hand is actually on the utensil or cup. The adult can then place her own hand over the child's for assistance (hand-over-hand guidance). This sets the expectation that the child is an active participant and will eventually learn to feed himself. In contrast, having an adult hold the utensil and feed the child might not give children ample opportunities to learn to become independent eaters. Furthermore, when an adult uses hand-over-hand guidance to help the child get food into his mouth, it is equally important to wait for the child to close his mouth over the spoon. This allows the child to work on controlling the muscles in his mouth, which will not only help with developing feeding skills, but also speech and language skills.

For a child who needs assistance drinking from a cup, Photo 12-2 is an example of an adapted cup, called a **cutout cup**, that permits an adult to view the liquid and allows the child with severe head control or postural control difficulties to drink without tipping her head back out of alignment. This type of cup is also good for children with disabilities who are just learning to drink from a cup. An adult can assist the child by using hand-over-hand guidance where the child holds the cup and then the adult places her hand on top of the child's hand. Gradually the adult can fade out the assistance until the child can hold the cup and drink independently. The child can then transition to a regular cup.

Assure Proper Positioning. If a child has a motor impairment or if the child is small and chairs are too large, consult with a physical therapist to determine how to best position the child for feeding or eating. Keep in mind that the child's feet should always remain on the floor. If needed, place a ream of paper or a stool underneath the child's feet for stability.

Use of Adapted or Specially Designed Utensils and Dishes. The following photos show examples of adapted bowls, cups, and spoons that make self-feeding much

Photo 12-1 This child's position is supported with an adapted chair allowing feet to be placed firmly on the floor.

Helpful Hint

The procedure for teaching a child to eat with a spoon might be best taught using the backward chaining method, starting with the last step and moving backward as the child masters each step.

Photo 12-2 Cutout Cups

easier for children who have motor disabilities. Many different types of specialty utensils and ways to adapt utensils are shown in Photo 12-3:

- The yellow spoon has a loop, which simplifies the ability for a child to hold the spoon.
- The fork is already curved for children who are not able to turn their wrist to get the food in their mouth.
- The next two spoons have simple adaptations to enlarge the handle by using a curler and masking tape.

Photo 12-3 Adapted Utensils

Photo 12-4 Adapted Place Setting

Photo 12-4 demonstrates an adapted place setting. Notice how a plate and specialized fork are placed on a shelf liner for stability. A tray is used for a boundary, and contrasting colors of the objects stand out for children with visual impairments.

The child in Photo 12-5 is using a special scoop plate that has a high rim and is curved on one side. This helps the child scoop his food without having the food fall off the plate. Can you imagine how frustrating it would be for a child to chase his food around the plate and then have it fall off? This special plate helps the child be successful and independent with feeding. Furthermore, a shelf liner is used to stabilize the plate on the table.

A child with a disability might not understand that she needs to use her other hand to help stabilize a dish while she eats. The bowl in Photo 12-6 has a suction on the bottom to stabilize the bowl so it does not slide around or tip over. Eventually, an adult can help the child learn to use her other hand to stabilize her dishes.

Modify Food Textures and Size. For some children, food textures or bite sizes may need to be altered. Consult with families to determine these accommodations. (Note: Some early childhood programs may have nutrition consultants who can meet with parents and order modified food delivered from the main kitchen to meet doctors' orders.)

12-1b Teaching Other Self-Help Skills

In addition to self-feeding, snack times and mealtimes provide opportunities for children with special needs to learn other self-help skills such as the following:

- Setting the table
- Pouring from a pitcher or carton
- Opening drink cartons
- Using a straw
- Cutting food
- Wiping up spills
- Cleaning the table
- Taking care of trash

Finally, some children with special needs may need help transitioning into and out of mealtime. Following a set sequence of events and providing maximal assistance for these

> **Helpful Hint**
>
> Sources for obtaining the specialty equipment for feeding are included in the Resource list at the end of this chapter and at the end of Chapter 4. Suction and scoop dishes as well as curved and thicker utensils can also be found at most retail stores that have a section for babies and toddlers.

Photo 12-5 A scoop plate can help a child eat more independently.

Photo 12-6 A Suction Bowl

children at first and gradually reducing that assistance is probably the most effective strategy.

The following example describes the use of a song to assist children in transitioning to a snack or meal.

Meal Transition Strategies

- If possible, having a short, quiet activity before lunch will help relax children and prepare them to follow directions.
- Warn child of the impending transition: "It's time to eat in two minutes."
- Sing the same song or use the same sign to signal the beginning of the transition to the meal. One example is "Today is Monday," sung to the tune of "Are You Sleeping?"

> Today is Monday. Today is Monday.
>
> What shall we eat? What shall we eat?
>
> Today we're eating soup. Today we're eating soup.
>
> Yum, yum, yum. Yum yum yum.

- Follow a set routine: Come inside, sing the song, set the table, wash hands, and find a seat.
- At the end of the meal, follow another routine: Throw away dish and cup, brush teeth, and move to the quiet area to look at books.

12-1c Developing Social Skills

Practicing beginning social interactions during snack times or mealtimes can be important learning opportunities for children with special needs because eating is often highly motivating and engaging. Examples of social skills include the following:

- Passing food (if served family style)
- Helping oneself to a single serving
- Waiting one's turn
- Requesting food or a second helping
- Waiting to be excused from the table

Some children may have difficulty being satisfied with one serving of food and also have difficulty waiting. They may need more direct adult assistance as they become familiar with the routine. A visual support showing the number of helpings for each item as demonstrated in Photo 12-7 can be helpful for all children while also encouraging the development of literacy and math skills.

Over time children will begin to understand the social rules for mealtime if these rules are consistently enforced. The need for adult assistance will lessen dramatically. It is helpful to have the adult sitting with the children model expectations and appropriate behaviors. Consider peer role modeling when planning the seating arrangements for mealtimes. Seat children with more challenging behaviors next to children who are more likely to model the expectations. Some children may need help understanding the sequence of events surrounding mealtime. Having a daily snack time routine is helpful. Displaying all steps of the routine through photographs or line drawings may assist some children.

12-1d Encouraging Communication Skills

Throughout a typical day, children use some form of communication to indicate what they want or need. Some children with special needs may have difficulty initiating communication with others or may not attempt to communicate at all. However, mealtime may be a highly motivating period for some children to communicate with others because they enjoy food and are hungry. Mealtime periods, if well organized, may also allow staff to pay attention to communicative intent and cues that might

Photo 12-7 A visual support shows the number of servings for each item.

be missed during less routine periods such as outside or free play. The following list offers some strategies for building communication and social skills.

Strategies for Building Communication and Social Skills during Snack Time

- Use family-style servings, if the program allows, for at least part of one meal (crackers in a box, sliced fruit on a plate, yogurt in a large bowl, or juice or milk in a small pitcher), and encourage children to point, sign, or verbalize when they want more. Let children pass the containers to each other and serve themselves an appropriately sized serving with adult help as needed.
- Pretend to *not see* a child who is not yet speaking, pointing to a desired food item until the child makes some type of vocalization to get your attention. Continue using this type of behavior occasionally to encourage vocalizations that begin to approximate the word you want the child to say.
- Seat children who are nonverbal next to children who are verbal.
- Direct a child who tends to look to adults for assistance to ask the child seated next to her for help. Also, make sure the second child learns the first child's cues for help.
- Set out everything for a meal—food, dishes, napkins—except one necessary item such as spoons. Wait for the children to realize what they are missing and ask you for the utensils. This strategy creates a need to communicate when such a need would otherwise not be there.
- Offer children opportunities to make a choice between two different foods or beverages. Choices can be given using the real objects such as a carton of milk and orange juice or pictures or drawings as illustrated in Photo 12-8.

Photo 12-8 Pictures of Food Items

- Allow a variety of ways for children to communicate their choices. Children can use eye gaze, sign language, pointing, choosing a picture or drawing, or verbal approximations of their choice. They can also touch an AAC device, as shown in Photo 12-9, which says the name of the food item for them.

12-1e Demonstrating Mealtime Techniques

Mealtime for some children with severe physical disabilities may be an opportunity to demonstrate effective feeding techniques to parents or caregivers. It is important to seek input from a physical or occupational therapist or a feeding specialist on seating adaptations and feeding strategies.

12-2 Special Nutritional Considerations

Some children with special needs have specific nutritional needs or challenges. Some of the most common are discussed in this section.

Photo 12-9 An AAC device lets a child communicate their food choices.

12-2a Children with Cerebral Palsy

Ongoing communication with a child's caregiver, physician, and occupational or physical therapist is important. Food intake is often decreased due to **tongue thrust** (protruding the tongue forward), poor lip closure, **tonic bite reflex** (vigorously clamping the teeth down when the mouth is stimulated in a certain way), or **abnormal gag reflex** (either exaggerated or weak).

Frustration, fatigue, and inadequate nutrition may result from prolonged mealtimes. Be sure the child is positioned with proper postural control to reduce fatigue and encourage successful chewing and swallowing.

Foods should be selected to provide the greatest nutrient intake possible. Examples of nutritional foods that children with cerebral palsy might more easily eat include sweet potatoes, mashed beans, and spreads made with fruits. Provide a variety of textures to encourage tongue and chewing movements. Always check with the family or occupational therapist before offering any new food.

Be aware that abnormal muscle tone and limited physical activity increase constipation. Increasing intake of fluids and high-fiber foods may reduce this difficulty. Also, for some children who are not mobile, spending a short period of time each day in an upright position, such as in a **prone stander** shown in Figure 12-1, may facilitate regular bowel movements.

Water can be very difficult to control and swallow. If a child has extreme difficulty swallowing watery liquids, it may be helpful to thicken them with yogurt or instant baby cereal.

12-2b Children with Epilepsy (Seizure Disorders)

Ongoing consultation with a child's physician and a nutrition consultant is essential because children with **epilepsy** are often at risk for dental problems and poor weight gain. Be aware that the primary nutrition problems of children with seizure disorders are often related to the side effects of their **anticonvulsant medication** (Eicher, 2013) and the interaction of this medication with foods. Such interactions can cause poor appetite, and low levels of folic acid and calcium in the blood. Swollen or tender gums caused by the drug Dilantin may cause serious dental problems and interfere with eating.

Anticonvulsant drugs may also interfere with the absorption of certain vitamins and minerals (Haesler & Mills, 2013). Physicians may prescribe nutrient supplements to offset the side effects of medication.

12-2c Children with Low Muscle Tone

Development of the necessary skills for eating table foods and self-feeding may be delayed because of low muscle tone. Low muscle tone is a common characteristic of children who have Down syndrome. Some children with low muscle tone may have difficulty receiving adequate oral sensation or maintaining adequate muscle tension with their mouth, lips, and tongue. Often this difficulty is related to excessive drooling. Children may not realize where the food or liquid is in their mouth, or they may not realize their mouth is full. This results in an increased risk for choking.

Some children may overstuff their mouth, which makes chewing even more difficult and may cause a gag reflex. Children who have a reduced gag reflex are more likely to choke.

As children with Down syndrome get older, they may be at increased risk for obesity if they are not walking or have low activity levels and low muscle tone. ECE teachers should encourage development of the ability to engage in active motor activities, and they should help these children select foods with high nutritional value and low calories. In some cases it may be necessary to refer the family to a nutritional specialist.

12-2d Children with Autism

Some children with special needs, particularly children with autism, may show unusual preferences for certain types of food based on color, texture, or taste. They may refuse to eat certain foods and develop **food phobias**.

Sometimes children develop **food obsessions**, insisting that they will eat only one or two things. Work closely with the family to determine how best to manage these issues. In some cases where a snack provides a very small portion of the child's daily nutrition, the family may opt to allow the child to eat the preferred food each day. In other cases a behavioral plan may be needed to work with extreme or disruptive food obsessions.

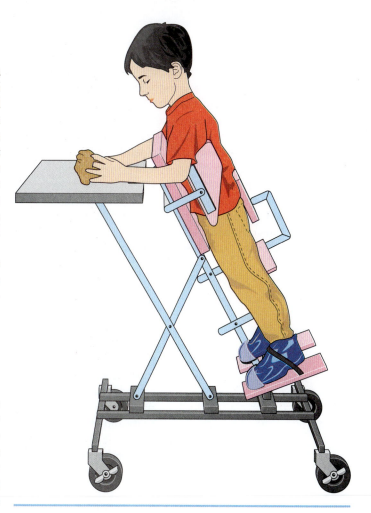

Figure 12-1 Upright position may facilitate bowel function in children who are not mobile.

Of course, culture affects the eating habits and preferences of children. It is expected that children share the food preferences of their families who have been making food choices for them since they were born. These food choices are also influenced by the availability and affordability of foods and ingredients. Culture also influences beliefs about the nutritional value and appeal of food. For example, some Hmong immigrants may tend to believe that only fresh food, nothing processed or frozen, is healthy. Some cultures prefer to eat hot and spicy foods, whereas others would prefer to taste the food itself. Also, the sensory properties of food, such as consistency, appearance, or taste, may affect the type of food consumed within an ethnic group.

Providers must not only become aware of the cultural preferences of the families when determining what to serve at mealtimes, but they also must become fully aware of health considerations for ALL children. Consider children who are lactose intolerant. They must avoid any product that has milk or daily products in it. Children with diabetes must have consideration given to the amount and types of carbohydrates they eat. Of course, families should be consulted to be certain that any recommendations from the child's pediatrician are followed.

12-2e Children with Prader-Willi Syndrome

Prader-Willi syndrome is a fairly rare condition. It is included here because of its association with a severe eating disorder. Prader-Willi is a chromosomal disorder. The most striking feature of Prader-Willi is obesity, which is related to insatiable overeating caused by an abnormality of the hypothalamic region of the brain. Typical behavior patterns include constant demand or stealing of food and general patterns of impulsivity and obstinacy. Although children may have cognitive skills in the near normal range, the behavior disorder related to overeating makes it very important to monitor children's food intake (Marotz, 2015). It is extremely important that ECE teachers work closely with specialists and parents to provide the best possible support.

12-2f Children with Pica

In rare cases, an eating disorder referred to as **pica** develops in which a child obsessively eats nonfood items such as paint or dirt. In some cases this may result from specific nutritional deficiencies. A danger in low-income neighborhoods or areas with older homes is that children with this disorder may ingest lead-based paint chips. Children who appear to crave nonfood substances should be referred to a nutritionist who is knowledgeable regarding children with special needs.

12-2g Children who Require Tube Feeding

For some children, oral feeding may be impossible or so insufficient that they cannot receive adequate nutrition. This may be the result of severe motor disability that interferes with basic suck and swallow functions or a tendency to aspirate food into the lungs. Children with complex medical needs are often tube-fed. The most common type of tube is a **gastrostomy tube (G-tube)**. This type of tube is placed through a small hole in the abdominal wall into the stomach. The child receives either a specialized formula or pureed feed through the tube several times a day. Parents or a pediatric nurse practitioner are the best sources of information regarding these procedures. Children who are tube-fed and who are in inclusive settings may have a one-on-one assistant.

12-3 A Word About Toileting

Bowel and bladder control and toilet training can be significant challenges for many children with special needs. Some children simply do not have adequate neuromuscular control or adequate sensation (due to such disorders as cerebral palsy or spina bifida). Low cognitive ability, limited communication skills, and the development of fear or conditioned reactions to toileting may be other factors. For example, children who have autism may become frightened of the sound of toilets flushing or loud hand dryers. One alternative could be to allow the children to use hand wipes instead of the dryer. Also, a child with a motor disability may not feel secure and in a stable position when placed on a potty, making it impossible to relax.

Specially designed adapted seats with rails can fit over the toilet to help stabilize children. However, for children who are not severely disabled, a more practical and simple solution could be to provide plastic or wooden toilet seat covers that accommodate toddlers and young children. Many such seat covers also have handles on the sides for more stability.

It is important to keep in mind that as children learn the process of toileting, there are other learning opportunities. Toileting accidents, for instance, present themselves as an unexpected opportunity to learn and practice dressing and undressing. If teachers can actually build time into their routine, they can encourage young children to practice the steps of undressing and dressing during a naturally occurring opportunity. Automatically changing the child's clothes, though it might not be able to be helped, can result in a missed opportunity for learning.

Space does not allow an adequate consideration of toileting in this book. However, successful toilet training, wherever it is a realistic expectation, is a critical goal for children who have special needs. Obviously the older a child becomes, the more the absence of this basic self-help skill becomes an increasing liability. Early childhood educators must work closely with specialists, possibly a behavior specialist or physical therapist, and families to plan an intervention strategy to achieve toilet training.

Summary

Children with certain disabilities may have special challenges related to eating. For example, children with severe motor disabilities may have difficulty even performing basic functions of chewing and swallowing; they need to be fed by an adult. If feeding difficulties are extreme, some children may be fed through a gastrostomy tube. Other children can have difficulty managing use of a spoon or drinking from a cup. Some children have food phobias or food obsessions. Mealtimes create opportunities to work directly on these challenges. In addition, mealtimes can also provide opportunities for development of additional self-help skills, such as pouring liquid and clearing a table, and social and communication skills. Toileting can present major challenges for children with special needs and may require a team approach to ensure success. For a list and summary of adaptations discussed in this chapter, as well as other possible adaptations, see Figure 12-2.

Read–Reflect–Discuss
Aaron's Fruity Os

Aaron was a four-year-old boy with a diagnosis of autism. He seemed bright in many ways. He could read many words; he could draw cars and trucks with incredible detail. Though he wasn't social, his language structure was fairly complex. He had adjusted well to Mr. Chinn's classroom, except for one difficult area: snack time. Aaron did not join the other children at snack time. He resisted nearly all foods, yet he was obsessed with Fruity Os. Mr. Chinn had made several attempts to *cure* Aaron of this Fruity Os obsession, but had been unsuccessful in his attempts to get Aaron to eat other foods. Mr. Chinn had given up trying to get Aaron to come to the snack table. He let him wander around the room with his container of Fruity Os while the other

Figure 12-2 Summary of Mealtime Adaptations

⌄ Professional Resource Download

children were at the snack table. (Mr. Chinn suspected that this might actually be a reinforcement for not coming to snack table, but it kept Aaron occupied.)

Mr. Chinn mentioned to Ms. Harris, the inclusion specialist for the center, that he was frustrated that he had had so little success in reducing Aaron's food obsession or in reducing his resistance of snack time. After observing Aaron at snack time, talking with his mother, and reviewing the information with Mr. Chinn and the teaching assistants, Ms. Harris and the classroom team came up with the following plan.

They would attempt to make snack time less stressful for Aaron by creating a more predictable snack routine. They decided to make laminated place mats with everyone's names on them, because Aaron loved reading words and could recognize everyone's names. Mr. Chinn assigned a specific seat for each child, placing their names on the back of their chair at the snack table. He created a mini-routine in which he signaled the transition to snack time by holding up the stack of place mats and saying, "Okay, let's get ready for snack." He handed the place mats to Aaron, who with very little prompting quickly became able to match all the place mats to the correct seats.

Aaron loved this activity. He also loved having his own place mat and quickly became comfortable sitting at the snack table. Rather than hassling him about trying new foods, Mr. Chinn would reinforce Aaron for helping and sitting down at his place mat by giving him his container of Fruity Os. Mr. Chinn was very pleased that Aaron was finally able to join the other children during this activity.

As Aaron became increasingly comfortable with this routine, Mr. Chinn noticed him looking at the other children's food. The teacher began placing new foods on the edge of Aaron's place mat. Usually Aaron would push away the food. Mr. Chinn would simply comment, "Oh, you don't like pretzels." Occasionally Aaron would actually try the novel food, and by the end of the year he had added two new foods to his repertoire of preferred foods: goldfish crackers and raisins. Although Mr. Chinn didn't exactly see this as great progress, Aaron's mother was thrilled!

Read–Reflect–Discuss Questions

1. Why do you think Aaron would only eat Fruity Os?
2. What adaptations were implemented to help Aaron during snack time?
3. How do you think the other children in the class responded to Aaron and to the strategies that were used to get him to participate at the table?
4. What do you think was the most important issue in the scenario: the lack of participation or the food obsession? Why?

Key Terms

abnormal gag reflex

anticonvulsant medication

cutout cup

epilepsy

food obsessions

food phobias

gastrostomy tube (G-tube)

pica

Prader-Willi syndrome

prone stander

tongue thrust

tonic bite reflex

Helpful Resources

Books

Endres, J. B., Rockwell, R. E., & Mense, C. G. (2003). *Food, nutrition, and the young child.* Upper Saddle River, NJ: Pearson.

Marotz, L. R. (2015). *Health, safety, and nutrition for the young child.* Stamford, CT: Cengage Learning.

Robertson, C. (2016). *Safety, nutrition and health in early education.* Boston, MA: Cengage Learning.

Sorte, J., Daeschel, I., & Amador, C. (2016). *Nutrition, health and safety for young children: Promoting wellness.* Boston, MA: Pearson.

Websites

Kids Health includes information and links on the food pyramid: kidshealth.org /en/kids/pyramid.html

Healthy Kids Snacks provides an easy and healthy recipe collection: www.healthy -kids-snacks.com/all/

Metro Child Resource and Referral offers a self-study guide aimed to further children's good health when preparing multiculturally inspired recipes:http:// metroccrr.org.

CHAPTER 13

Supporting Language and Emergent Literacy in Children with Special Needs

LEARNING OBJECTIVES

After studying this chapter, you will be able to:

LO 13-1: Describe various language strategies that can be used to support literacy in young children.

LO 13-2: Give examples of different ways to use pictures to support expression and comprehension of language.

LO 13-3: Explain how using pictures and symbols can provide a means of communication for children who have difficulty communicating verbally.

The following NAEYC Standards and DEC Recommended Practices are addressed in this chapter:

naeyc

Standard 1: Promoting Child Development and Learning
Standard 4: Using Developmentally Effective Approaches
Standard 5: Using Content Knowledge to Build Meaningful Curriculum

DEC

Practice 1: Assessment
Practice 2: Environment
Practice 4: Instruction
Practice 5: Interaction
Practice 6: Teaming and Collaboration

The use of pictures and print in the classroom can provide communication support for children with special needs while supporting emergent literacy for all children.

The development of early literacy skills can provide important advantages for children with special needs. ECE teachers should not assume that if children cannot talk, they cannot learn to read. For some children with special needs, literacy skills can provide support for communication:

- **Some children face specific challenges in the development of literacy.** Many highly motivating strategies can be used throughout each activity of the day to encourage emergent literacy skills.

- **Language and literacy are completely intertwined.** The language input strategies described in Chapter 2 can easily be applied to supporting children's development of literacy skills.

- **Pictures and print can be used to support expressive language in children who are nonverbal.** Communication boards and PECS are common ways of using pictures for communication.

- **Pictures and print can support children's language comprehension and memory.** Use of pictures can help children understand and anticipate events in the daily schedule and complex task sequences.

- **Use of pictures to help children's understanding of daily events may reduce behavior challenges.** Many children do not comprehend or cannot remember spoken language. For these children, pictures, schedules, and cues for transitions are helpful.

Introduction

It is important to realize that language and literacy are closely intertwined. "Literacy" is a form of language representation. "Speech" is typically children's first means of representing the words (that is, the "lexicon") of their language. However, some children with special needs may use sign language, pictures, or speech-generating technology (referred to as augmentative and alternative communication [AAC]) as their first means of expressing language.

Historically, educators have assumed that reading and writing are skills that develop *after* children learn to talk. Because many children with special needs have significant delays in language development, there is sometimes a reluctance to introduce literacy activities to these children during the preschool years. However, early exposure to literacy activities is important for *all* children, regardless of their speech and language ability. In fact, supporting a variety of means of communicative expression—including pictures and print—early in development may be even more important for children with speech and language challenges. As discussed in Chapter 2, how adults talk—and *respond*—to young children has enormous impact on language development. This is also the case for the development of children's literacy skills.

In recent years, ECE programs have put renewed emphasis on the importance of including phonemic awareness activities in preschool curricula. This activity can also support specific skills of listening, sound discrimination, and speech-sound production in children who have hearing loss, communication delays, and learning disabilities.

It is particularly important to realize that some children may *never* develop intelligible spoken language, so use of pictures and print may be a critical alternative.

13-1 The Relationship Between Language and Literacy

Chapter 2 summarized important communication strategies that adults can embed within daily routines that support children's language development. These same strategies can be used to support literacy. Language and literacy are completely intertwined. As a result, each of the language strategies described earlier can be used as a way of supporting literacy in children with significant disabilities and delays as well. For example:

- **Follow the child's lead.** As children develop awareness and interest in books, follow their lead by reading their cues of interest. For example, if a child is only interested in stacking books, rather than reading them, help him stack the books, pointing out the picture on the cover and naming each book. Then count them when you're done. If you're not in the child's zone of proximal development, your teaching attempts won't work.
- **Use semantic extension.** If a child vocalizes or comments in any way in reference to the book, extend her meaning. For example, if a child says "No" as you attempt to engage her with a book, say, "Okay, let's find another book!" as you actively examine other books.
- **Use labels and specific descriptors, repeating key words and phrases.** As a child turns pages, then turns the book upside down, say "Oops, the book is upside down. The ducky is upside down! Can you turn the page? Turn the page."
- **Use appropriate pacing and intonation.** Be careful not to speak too fast, and use slightly exaggerated intonation. Many children who have disabilities have difficulty processing rapid speech. Consider recording your own speech as you tell a story to make sure your rate and intonation are optimal.
- **Use progressive matching.** Model one step beyond the child's response. For example, Jonathan has shown little interest in books. He opens a book and looks at one page and throws it down. Say, "Oh, I love this book!"

13-2 Supporting Literacy within Daily Routines

In the typical ECE classroom, opportunities abound in which to encourage prereading skills within the daily activities of most ECE classrooms. Let's consider a variety of simple, but interesting, ways of exposing young children with special needs to literacy within daily classroom routines.

13-2a Environmental Print

Although recognition of environmental print may develop effortlessly in children without disabilities, children with special needs may require assistance learning to recognize everyday logos, trademarks, and symbols:

- Bring in items such as napkins, paper cups, bags, and wrappers with familiar commercial logos, such as McDonald's, Target, and Southwest.
- Use items with logos in pretend play activities, such as grocery stores and restaurants.
- Look for familiar logos in newspapers and magazines, and on TV.
- Look for familiar logos on walks in the community and on field trips.

13-2b Functional Print

Adults should demonstrate functional and interesting uses of print throughout the day:

- **Taking attendance.** Children recognize and count name cards.
- **Sharing the lunch menu.** Write the menu on the board or chart paper. Then return to it just before lunchtime to see who can *read* what will be served for lunch.
- **Assigning jobs.** Children look to see whose name is under "Setting the table," "Line leader," "Feeding the fish," and so on.
- **Writing notes.** Read a note from another teacher. Write a note to someone else, and ask a child to deliver it. Write a note as a reminder of something.

- **Ordering from a catalog.** Fill out the order form, address the envelope, and walk with the class to the mailbox or post office. When the item is received, read the address on the package.
- **Using labels.** Place certain play materials in similar cupboards or containers so the only way to know what is inside is to read the label.

13-2c Play Activities

The following discusses some playful activities that also foster critical skills.

Treasure Hunt. Even though children cannot yet read, a treasure hunt is a great demonstration of the function of print. Each note should be large so it can be easily shown to all the children before the teacher *deciphers* it. Children can also be given a card with a specific letter written on it so they can hunt around the room to find as many matching letters as possible. When children with special needs hold a card in their hand, they are more apt to remember which letter they are seeking.

Writing Letters in Pretend Play. Set up a writing table in the pretend play or library area of the classroom. Include pens and markers, envelopes, cards, and stationery. Somewhere else in the classroom or just outside the door, place a toy mailbox. Encourage children to *write* letters to each other and to family members, or help them spell and type words on the computer to be printed out as a letter to mom, or to a friend in the classroom, and so on.

For children with severe physical disabilities who can neither manage a writing tool nor dictate a letter, one possibility is to help them select pictures and words from magazines to be mailed. More advanced children who are learning to use computerized AAC devices may have the capacity to print hard copies of messages.

Multiple Copies of Familiar Books. Children with special needs may not begin to enjoy books until the books are extremely familiar. It is helpful to include multiple copies of those storybooks that are read most frequently during circle time. These books can also be sent home for parents to read to children.

Making Picture Albums. Making albums can be engaging for children with special needs. Looking at pictures of themselves and their families can be very motivating to children, especially if the pictures are of familiar activities in which they have participated:

- Take photos of the children with familiar people and activities. Field trips and special activities such as holiday events are wonderful examples of photo albums that children will enjoy.

- Let children find interesting pictures in magazines to cut out and place in the album.
- If photo albums are too expensive, children can make their own by using cardboard for the covers and clear plastic ziplock bags or construction paper for the pages.
- Be sure to identify each picture by writing names of people, key words, or a short sentence below it. Use a dark, thick marker and write in big letters.
- Keep all albums on a shelf with children's names or activities written on the spine.
- Read the albums with children frequently. Always emphasize the print. "Now what is this picture? Let me read what it says."
- Use iPhone and Android technologies to access photo albums and games.

13-2d Literacy Activities throughout the Daily Schedule

Each major component of the daily schedule can readily incorporate literacy activities that will appeal to children with special needs. The following suggestions are adapted from Cook, Klein, and Chen (2016).

Arrival. As they arrive, children locate their cubbies, which are clearly marked with their name and picture. If a child arrives without a parent but has some written communication for the teacher, such as a note or parent communication book, the teacher should briefly read what it says to demonstrate to the child that this is an important form of communication.

Posting the Daily Schedule. Be sure to have the daily schedule posted in large letters. Include a photo or drawing of each major daily activity (see Figure 13-1). At various times throughout the day, refer to the schedule by reading it. To help children better predict and read the sequence of the schedule, teachers could make the pictures removable by having Velcro on the picture. When the activity is finished, the teacher or child can turn over the picture to its blank side or remove and place it in an *all done* envelope attached to the bottom of the sequence board.

Support language and development of time concepts by asking questions like, "What activities are finished?" and "What comes after snack?" while referring back to the posted picture sequence representing the daily schedule

Circle Time. The following lists preparation tips for circle time, a major activity:

1. Identify carpet squares or chairs with children's names and/or pictures.
2. Take attendance using name cards.
3. Identify whose turn it is to perform certain daily tasks by looking for names under job headings.
4. Write the snack or lunch menu on chart paper. Refer to it later in the day.
5. Teachers can also turn calendar time into a literacy activity by reading the calendar with children. (See Chapter 9 for a more detailed description of how to make calendar time meaningful for children with mild cognitive abilities.)

Create a laminated card representing each favorite song or storybook. Include a drawing of a key element of the song and the written title. Attach the cards to a large board with Velcro so children can take turns selecting a song or storybook for the class.

Story Time. Obviously story time is an important opportunity to help children with special needs develop emergent literacy skills. However, this activity may

Figure 13-1 Daily Schedule Board

be challenging for children with certain disabilities, especially children with limited vision or cognitive delays:

- Pictures are often too small to see clearly or too cluttered to discriminate foreground from background. The examples in Figure 13-2 demonstrate this problem.

(A)

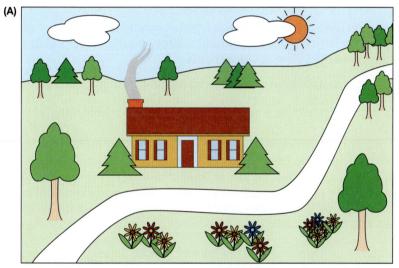

(B)

Figure 13-2 For many children with special needs, Picture A will be much more difficult to process than Picture B.

Photo 13-1 Shared Reading with a Teacher

- The language of many preschool storybooks may be too advanced, especially if the story is told without other props or visual aids.
- The concepts and experiences depicted in the story may be unfamiliar or too complex. The trick is to find stories and illustrations that are appealing and meaningful to children with special needs.

The following suggestions can make story time a good learning context.

Repeat stories frequently. The importance of repeated stories is being increasingly emphasized, even for older children. Repetition and familiarity are critically important for children who have special needs. As children become more and more familiar with the story, they can engage in shared *reading* with the teacher (see Photo 13-1). Children who are not yet reading can enjoy participating in the shared reading because they will have memorized the story via the frequent repetitions. Children with limited language may begin to participate in a simple repeated refrain, such as "You can't catch ME!"

Include stories with developmentally simple themes. Examples of conceptually simple themes that might appeal to children with low cognitive abilities include:

- Familiar daily activities
- Familiar animals
- Family members
- Body parts and clothing
- Food
- Big and little
- Hidden objects and surprises
- Some pop-up books
- Doors and flaps that open
- Books related to familiar TV shows and movies

Use effective story reading strategies. A literacy activity that is simple and effective is **dialogic reading** discussed by Zevenbergen and Whitehurst (2003) and shown in Figure 13-3.

Make photo albums. Use photos that reflect recent classroom activities, or children's families and pets. Or cut pictures out of old magazines to reflect favorite things and activities.

1. **Prompt child to say something about the book.**
   Examples of prompts:

   Completion prompt: "One, two, buckle my ___."

   Recall prompt: "Can you remember where the puppy is hiding?"

   Open-ended prompt: "What's happening on this page?" or "I wonder what's going to happen."

   Wh- question prompt: "Who is that? "Where did he go?" Why is he mad?" (NOTE: Don't overdo questions!)

   Distancing prompt: Adult makes reference to something <u>outside</u> the book: "Oh, we saw a spider yesterday, didn't we?" or "Does our kitty look like this one?" or "Sometimes *you* get scared too, right?"

2. **Comment on the child's response.** ("You're right! He only has one shoe!")

3. **Expand using topic extension/rephrasing.**

   Child: "Look dat kitty way up."

   Adult: "Oh my! That kitty is up on the roof!"

4. **Sometimes, repeat to check child's learning.**
   Adult: "Where's that kitty now?"

   Child: "Up roof!"

   Adult: "Oh! Maybe he's stuck way up on the roof!"

   Note: Try to stay in child's zone of proximal development (ZPD).
   Source: Zevenbergen & Whitehurst (2003).

Figure 13-3 Dialogic Reading Strategies

Add props to stories to help maintain children's attention. Use replicas of things in the story, flannel board figures, small stuffed animals, and puppets.

Select books with rhymes and predictable phrases. Use of poems and nursery rhymes not only increases appeal and participation for many children with special needs, but also increases phonological awareness for all children.

Include books with large print. This will be especially important for children with low vision.

Place extra copies of frequently read books in the library corner. Encourage children to read on their own.

Encourage active participation as story is read. For example, children can act out key elements of the story. Ask children what they think will happen next before turning the page.

An example would be using the monkey puppets to accompany *Five Little Monkeys Jumping in the Tree* or the motions to the familiar song with a book based on *The Eensy Weensy Spider*.

Help children act out the story. After the story becomes familiar, have children perform a play. Children with disabilities might need to use props such as a stuffed animal or a hat that represents the character they are playing. They could also hold a picture of their character.

Library Corner. Be sure the library corner is a literacy-rich center. In addition to books with the characteristics we have described, include the following:

- Pens, markers, and crayons
- Stationery and envelopes

Helpful Hint

Children with limited fine motor skills need adapted writing tools. One of the simplest adaptations is a rubber tube that fits over a pen or marker. This makes the writing tool larger and easier to grip.

- Ink stamps with letters and numbers
- Stickers to use as postage stamps
- Magazines and newspapers reflecting children's home culture
- Audio books
- Cookbooks
- Computer software for developing prereading skills
- Books with tactile and olfactory features, such as textures, flaps, pop-ups, and scratch-and-sniff

Many of the materials in this list can also be included in pretend play, housekeeping, and dress-up areas.

Use adapted books. Children with disabilities can benefit from having their books adapted to meet their individual needs. Books can be adapted in many ways by using common materials and by using EESS. Board books are very sturdy and lend themselves easily to being adapted. Paper books will need to be taken apart and laminated so that they will be sturdy enough to support adaptations.

Page turners. Page turners can be used for children with physical disabilities or children with low muscle tone in their hands. A book can be *enhanced* by adding materials that separate the pages to *simplify* the act of turning a page. This adaptation *stabilizes* the page and increases the likelihood that children can turn the pages without assistance. For example, placing a Velcro dot at the bottom of each page gives more space between the pages and makes it easy to turn (see Photo 13-2). Gluing half of a craft stick onto the page allows children to move the other half with their fist or thumb. Tabs of a variety of sizes and materials like felt and card stock can be taped or glued to books based on children's individual needs. Staggering the page turners makes it easier to turn the pages in order.

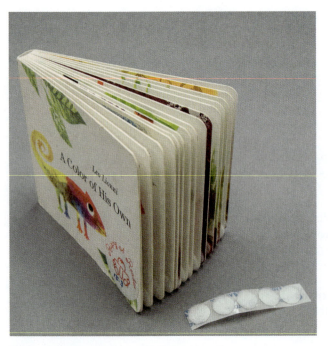

Photo 13-2 Adapted Book with Velcro Page Turners

Texture. Texture can help students with visual impairments, cognitive delays, or attention difficulties. Students can

Photo 13-3 Children can count the number of mice on each page and find the matching numeral.

attend longer to a book if it is *enhanced* with interesting materials to touch. You can enhance the book by covering numbers and letters in felt or by placing felt dots on pictures to be counted. This encourages the math readiness skill of one-to-one correspondence as children touch each dot while counting. Other materials can be used to add texture such as fur, sandpaper, bubble wrap, corduroy, and shiny paper.

Flip-out pages. Flip-out pages can assist with literacy concepts such as recognizing and matching pictures, letters, numerals, and key words. The flip-out page can be taped to the inside of the back cover while having matching pictures, numbers, or letters attached with Velcro. While the child reads the book, the flip-out stays open so that he or she can take off the picture and match it to the correct page (see Photo 13-3). The number of pictures on the flip-out page can be altered based on the child's needs. For example, a child with a cognitive delay might choose from only two to three pictures, where as a child with autism might have six to nine pictures on the page.

All of these book adaptations make books much more interactive and fun. They have the potential to increase children's motivation and attention span.

Snack Time. As suggested earlier in this chapter, share a written menu with children every day. Interesting snack foods include alphabet soup and crackers, cereal, and small cookies shaped like letters and other intriguing forms.

Diversity Awareness

Books provide an amazing opportunity to help children become aware of and be comfortable with the diversity surrounding them. The following are just a few of the most appropriate possibilities:

Hallinan, P. K. (2005). *A rainbow of friends*. Harlan, IA: Guideposts Books. Effectively reminds children to celebrate their differences.

Fox, M. (2006). *Whoever you are*. New York, NY: Harcourt Brace. A joyful picture book that celebrates the world's diverse cultures.

Parr, T. (2010). *The family book*. New York, NY: Little Brown & Company. Celebrates all kinds of families and shows how special each is in its own way.

Willis, J., & Ross, T. (2000). *Susan laughs*. New York, NY: Macmillan Kids. An inspiring story about a spunky little girl whose physical disability never gets in the way of living.

Woloson, E., & Gough, B. (2003). *My friend Isabelle*. Bethesda, MD: Woodbine House. A story about two friends, one of whom is a child with Down syndrome.

Read labels of food containers, and follow simple recipes as you prepare a snack for and with the children. Write recipe ingredients on large chart paper. Ask children if they can read what ingredient comes next.

To provide exposure to letters and numbers, laminate block letters and numbers along with children's names on the back of placemats.

Art Activities. Children with special needs may require direct assistance drawing representations of familiar things, such as a face, flower, or ball. By showing children the object and then helping them draw it, they will learn that pictures represent real objects and experiences. As children label and discuss their artwork, be sure to ask if they would like you to write the words down on paper. By doing this, the children start associating their picture with words. Furthermore, writing the words also gives families a starting point to discuss the artwork when it comes home. The student who drew the picture in Photo 13-4 represented each member of her family: her sister, Joan, and her mom. Imagine how wonderful it would be for the family to receive such a detailed picture.

Be sure to be fairly dramatic about writing a child's name on her artwork. Use a marking pen and write in fairly large letters. Say to the child, "Shall I write your name on your artwork? Let's see, how do you spell Jane?" Then say each letter clearly as you write the child's name. This will help draw her attention to print and individual letters. Once finished, give the child the writing utensil and ask her to write her name. Acknowledge any attempts at markings on the page. Because artwork is done frequently in the classroom, the child now has many opportunities to practice writing her name.

Later on in the day, have the child help you look for her artwork by looking for her name. Ask if the child would like you to write something about the picture on the bottom. (Note: Having easy access to dry-erase markers and whiteboards provides an easy way for teachers to write key words throughout the day. Children often enjoy watching adults write and draw, and will develop their interest in writing and reading letters and words, as well as ample opportunity to do it themselves.)

Draw attention to labels on art materials. Store some materials in containers that are not transparent so their contents can only be determined by the print label.

Photo 13-4 Writing down what children say about their artwork helps create associations between their pictures and words.

Outside Play. Post a chart with pictures and labels of each outside play area near the door. Ask the children where they are going to play before going out to the playground. Label major storage areas for bikes, balls, sand toys, and other outdoor equipment.

Play "Simon Says" using picture cards. The teacher or a student holds up a card that says "Run," "Jump," "Sit," and children follow those directions.

Departure. At the end of the day, encourage children to look for their names on artwork to take home. They can also locate their cubbies and possessions by identifying their name.

Give children notes to take home to parents. Read at least part of the note to the children. Or, better yet, if the note is an acknowledgment of something wonderful the child did, discuss the note with the parent in front of the child whenever possible. This type of acknowledgment tends to have a profound effect on the child's self-esteem and sets a positive tone for departure.

13-3 Assisting Children with Special Needs by Using Pictures and Print

Many children with special needs have difficulty processing, attending to, or understanding spoken language, and many also have difficulty communicating verbally. For these children, the use of pictures can be of great assistance in helping them make sense of the world around them. In addition, pictures and symbols can provide a means of communicating their wants and needs. Hodgdon (2011) offers detailed descriptions of these strategies.

13-3a Pictures and Print as Alternative Means of Expressive Language

Many children with special needs have delayed communication skills. Some will never be able to use spoken language. The use of pictures and print to communicate choices and basic wants and needs can be helpful for children who do not speak or whose speech is unintelligible. Also, as mentioned in Chapter 5, many behavior challenges are the result of a child's inability to communicate in more appropriate ways.

Examples of Ways to Use Pictures and Print to Support Expressive Language. Allow children to select a song or story during circle time by pointing to or removing a picture card from a large poster board.

Make cards with pictures and key words representing things that the child will most likely need to say. If the child is ambulatory, attach the cards to a large key ring. Attach the ring of picture cards to the child's belt. Teaching assistants can help the child learn to use each card at appropriate times. Examples of helpful pictures might be:

- I need to use the restroom.
- I'm unhappy.
- I have a tummy ache/headache.
- I'd like to play with (favorite toy).
- Someone hurt me.
- Someone took my toy.

Post pictures on the wall at eye level in various areas to depict important messages for that activity. For example, in the play yard, a poster could suggest possible play choices with pictures and word labels of the sand table, slide, and balls. This would be particularly helpful for children who have limited mobility as well as limited speech.

Helpful Hint

Some children with autism prefer communicating with printed words and pictures. Occasionally a child with autism can even read and spell. Unfortunately, without intervention, this interest often becomes repetitive and self-stimulatory. Thus, it is important to give these children every opportunity to use print in meaningful ways.

Elena

Elena has limited mobility due to cerebral palsy. She is in a wheelchair but has not learned to move it independently. Her speech efforts are not intelligible. She loves being outside and enjoys several outside activities. However, she is picky about which specific activity she wants at any particular time. She gets frustrated if the teacher misunderstands her preference. The special education consultant suggests placing a picture board on the tray of her wheelchair. The picture board has simple drawings and words for each outside activity. Elena can point to the one she wants by placing her fist on the picture and thus communicate her preference clearly.

Because of the success of this low-tech approach, Elena's teacher has requested that she be evaluated by the district's technology specialist to consider the use of a speech output device.

Helpful Hint

A child with severe physical disabilities who cannot speak or point can use **directed eye gaze** to select pictures on a clear acrylic board. The board is held between the child and the teacher or aide, and the child simply looks at the picture representing the item she wants. It is fairly easy to discern where the child is looking if the pictures are far enough apart.

Use of Communication Boards or Picture Exchange Systems. Two picture communication systems are commonly used for children who do not have expressive language ability: communication boards and the picture exchange communication system (PECS).

Communication board. A **communication board** can often serve as a precursor to development of a computerized AAC device for children with severe physical disabilities, or it can simply be used as a simple form of assistance for a child whose speech is unintelligible or a child who has no oral language and does not sign. A specialist may need to assist in the board's design.

The communication board involves placing photos, pictures, or simple line drawings on a board. The child points to a certain picture to indicate what she wants to say or do (see Figure 13-4). In some cases it may be more convenient to create several small topic boards and keep them in the area of the center where the child is most likely to need a particular vocabulary or set of expressions, such as in the bathroom, outside, or at circle time. For example, a small snack board can easily be made by cutting out pictures of snack items from the original containers or from grocery ads.

For children who are ambulatory, communication cards can be placed on a large key ring and attached to their belt.

PECS. The picture exchange communication system (Bondy & Frost, 2011) is very popular. It has been used with a wide range of children with special needs who

I'm happy

Bathroom

Computer

I'm angry!

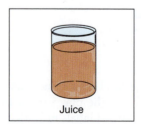
Juice

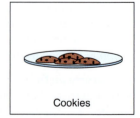
Cookies

Figure 13-4 Simple Communication Board

Figure 13-5 PECS Cards Placed on Velcro Sentence Strip

are nonverbal, particularly with children who have autism or who have little functional language. The system uses behavioral strategies to teach the child to select and exchange a picture for a desired object or activity or to make a comment. As children progress, they learn to create word combinations with the pictures as well (see Figure 13-5).

Pictures representing the high-preference interests of the child are attached with Velcro to a board or stored on the pages of a binder. Unlike the communication board, the child using PECS does not point at the picture but rather removes the picture and hands it to another person in exchange for the desired object or activity. Thus, PECS requires greater social interaction for the communication to be effective.

13-3b Using Pictures to Assist Comprehension and Memory

Pictures can also be used to support children with limited language comprehension and memory. Pictures can be helpful in assisting children with remembering the sequence of a task, such as hand washing, understanding and following the daily schedule, or understanding transitions from one activity to another. Behavior challenges can often be significantly reduced when pictures are used to help children anticipate the next activity or understand how to do a difficult task.

Strategies for Using Pictures throughout the Day to Assist Comprehension. Post pictures at eye level above the sink to help children remember the sequence of hand washing or brushing teeth. At each transition, show children a picture of the event that comes next or design a picture sequence board to represent the steps necessary in a particular transition, such as from arrival to free play (see Figure 13-6).

How to Make Pictures, Print, and Boards That Last. It's important to make sure that the visual supports you make are sturdy and will last for quite a while. The key is to use lamination and sturdy paper for both the pictures and the board. Contact paper can be an inexpensive alternative to lamination. Card stock and poster paper are good examples of sturdy paper.

Pictures can take on many forms: hand drawn; computer-generated art renderings or photos of real objects; cutouts from magazines, catalogs, weekly store ads, or product boxes; or symbols such as educational icons designed specifically for special education. They can range from simple black-and-white line drawings to symbols/

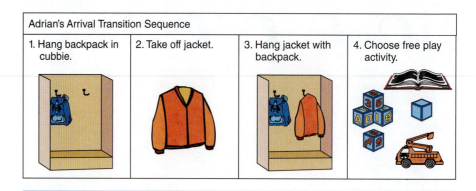

Adrian's Arrival Transition Sequence			
1. Hang backpack in cubbie.	2. Take off jacket.	3. Hang jacket with backpack.	4. Choose free play activity.

Figure 13-6 Example of a Transition Sequence Board

icons to color pictures/photos of real objects. The type of picture will depend on the abilities of the children.

Boards such as sequence, communication, and schedules can be made in a variety of sizes depending on the number of pictures you want to display. Use the following procedure.

Procedure for making visual supports

Pictures:

- Glue or print pictures onto sturdy paper and leave space between pictures.
- Cut out each picture and cover with contact paper, or cut out each picture, laminate, then cut out again.
- Add a Velcro dot to the back of each picture.

Board:

- Cut sturdy paper to correct size.
- Cover with contact paper or laminate.
- Add a strip(s) of Velcro or dots to match the number of pictures.
- Assemble with pictures.

13-3c Use of Technology Apps to Support Communication and Literacy

Increasingly, children with significant communication and literacy challenges can be supported via the technology of communication "apps," many of which are inexpensive and are widely available on iPhone, iPad, and Android devices. Use of apps must be truly interactive with an adult. All too often, the use of apps becomes a self-stimulatory obsession for children. Involvement with apps should not be a solitary activity. The goal is for children who are not able to produce speech to learn new vocabulary, initiate communicative interaction, answer questions, or obtain adult attention and practice labeling, and so on. Figure 13-7 offers some examples.

Jung Lee's Transitions

Jung Lee had a difficult time with transitions. After each activity she would wander aimlessly and become agitated if an adult tried to direct her to the next activity. Jung Lee often had difficulty engaging in typical daily activities of the center. Her greatest interest seemed to be with books and letters, which she would copy endlessly.

Her teacher decides to try to use this interest to help her make transitions from one activity to another. She makes a book with words and pictures representing each activity of the day. At the end of each activity, she opens the book to the picture of the next activity and shows it to Jung Lee. This seems to make it easier for Jung Lee to focus and anticipate the next activity.

Clicker Apps (www.cricksoft.com/us/products/clicker-apps/clicker-apps_home.aspx):

These clicker apps (Clicker Sentences, Clicker Connect, Clicker Docs, and Clicker Books) are specifically designed for the iPad, and represent different components of the Clicker 7 software. In addition, they provide Clicker Communicator, a child-friendly AAC app, and SuperKeys, an accessible keyboard app, to help facilitate learning for children with different needs.

I Spy with Lola (www.lolapanda.com/games/game1.html):

This game challenges students to a variety of literacy-based activities (vocabulary, word association, shape recognition) as Lola Panda travels around the world. There are easy-to-understand spoken instructions available in 12 languages to cater to diverse classroom needs.

Phonics Island (www.22learn.com/app/6/phonics-island.html):

This app uses a Montessori approach to help children learn initial word and letter sounds, while matching them to their orthographic forms. It has a child-friendly interface, and audio directions to encourage early literacy.

You can also find additional app recommendations using the following resources:

Apps for Children with Special Needs (a4cwsn.com)

10 Favorite Speech and Language Apps for Kids (http://nspt4kids.com /parenting/our-10-favorite-speech-and-language-apps-for-kids/)

Figure 13-7 Language Apps for Children with Special Needs

Helpful Hint

For a child who has limited vision—and especially if she also has a hearing loss—an **event sequence box** can be helpful. As in the drawing in Figure 13-8, actual objects representing each activity of the day are inserted in a row of boxes (like little mailboxes). For example, a small piece of carpet square is in the box representing circle time, a paint brush is in the box representing art activity, and a cup represents snack. The child goes to the boxes after each activity. She locates the next box with an object in it; the boxes to the left are all empty because these events have already occurred. This helps her understand what is coming next.

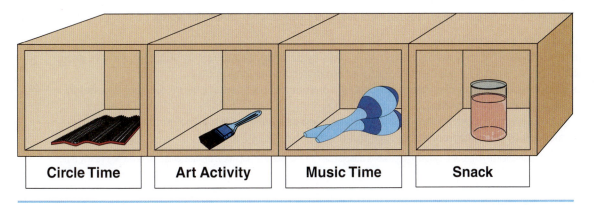

| Circle Time | Art Activity | Music Time | Snack |

Figure 13-8 An "Event Sequence Box" can be used to represent activity sequence for children with limited vision or both deafness and blindness.

At beginning of free play, show the children pictures of options and ask them to indicate the activity they prefer. At the end of the day during a recall activity, show picture cards representing major activities of the day. Ask the children to point to photos representing the things they enjoyed most.

Summary

This chapter has considered two important areas for children with special needs. The first concerns ways of supporting emergent literacy for children with various disabilities, including accommodations for children with visual impairment and children who have low cognitive abilities. Motivating uses of print throughout the day in predictable ways can help young children begin to understand written communication.

The second area considered in this chapter is how to use pictures and print to support both the expression and comprehension of language. This includes the use of picture communication systems such as PECS and communication boards for expression of communication as well as the use of pictures as an aid to children's understanding of daily schedules, task sequences, and transitions. For a list and summary of adaptations discussed in this chapter as well as other possible adaptations, see Figure 13-9.

Adapted from CARA's Kit

Goal: To use adaptations (least amount of support) instead of physical assistance (most amount of support) whenever possible to increase independence and confidence skills

Adapt the environment:
- Place children's names with pictures on chairs, placemats, and cubbies.
- Bring in commercial logos from restaurants and stores.
- Place original food boxes and containers from a variety of cultures in the dramatic play area.

Adapt activity or routine:
- Frequently refer to and ask questions about the classroom schedule to help children learn the sequence.
- Provide a first/then board to keep children motivated for difficult tasks.
- Label classroom shelves, toys, and materials with words and pictures.
- Use pictures, words, and menus for meals and cooking activities.
- Have multiple copies of familiar books for the library area and circle time.
- Write down children's ideas and verbalizations during art activities.

Adapt materials:
- Allow a child to have a security toy near the activity.
- Adapt books with page turners, texture, and flip-out pages.
- Choose books with simple themes and clear pictures that are not too cluttered.
- Enlarge writing utensils by building up the handles with curlers, tape, pencil grips, and so on.
- Use markers instead of pencils or crayons.
- Create classroom photo albums of field trips, families, and celebration—label with words.

Adapt requirements or instruction:
- Allow children to show what they know in alternative ways by pointing, gesturing/signing, directed eye gaze, giving a picture/object, or using augmentative and alternative communication (AAC).
- Provide visual supports such as classroom schedules, communication boards, picture exchange systems, sequence boards, and choice boards.
- When giving choices with pictures, start with two choices and gradually increase the number.
- Provide instructions by using appropriate pacing and progressive matching.

Source: Milbourne, S. A., & Campbell, P. H. (2007). *CARA's Kit: Creating adaptations for routines and activities.* Philadelphia, PA: Child and Family Studies Research Programs, Thomas Jefferson University.

Figure 13-9 Summary of Emergent Literacy Adaptations

⌄ Professional Resource Download

Read–Reflect–Discuss

Dahlia's Favorite Book

Dahlia was a shy four-year-old. She wore thick glasses, and Mrs. Wang, her teacher, had been told she had extremely poor vision. As a result, Dahlia never looked at books or pictures and did not seem to enjoy story time. Mrs. Wang tried to interest her in oversized books with simple pictures, but Dahlia still had no interest.

Mr. Smith, the vision specialist, suggested that Mrs. Wang encourage Dahlia to help her make a special storybook using textures and objects. Because Dahlia had usable vision, Mr. Smith did not think she would be a Braille user. He explained to Mrs. Wang that eventually Dahlia would learn to use a variety of print-enhancing technologies. But he agreed she needed some tactile cues and accommodations to help develop her interest in books and print.

Together, Dahlia and Mrs. Wang design a book about a treasure hunt where children search for a variety of objects. In addition to a picture of each object, they include a texture or object on the opposite page to represent each of the treasures. On the page opposite the picture of a green sock is a small green sock. On the page opposite the picture of a red flower, they paste a dried red flower. Opposite the picture of a sponge is a little piece of sponge, and so on. Mrs. Wang writes the name of each object below it.

Mr. Smith also provides a small magnifier of the appropriate power to match Dahlia's vision with her glasses on to encourage her to look at the pictures and objects in her treasure book as well as the print in smaller books. Mrs. Wang attaches the magnifying glass to the treasure book with a piece of string. Dahlia loves this book. She reads it to herself and to her friends, and she takes turns with other children looking at the words and pictures with the magnifying glass. Quickly she begins using a magnifying glass to look at the print in other books.

The book eventually becomes a favorite for many of the children. As a result Mrs. Wang develops a week of activities around a real treasure hunt, and all the children make their own special books. She also provides all the children with inexpensive magnifying glasses, which are quite a hit and lead to many science activities.

Upon reflection, Mrs. Wang realizes that something that initially seemed like a problem related to Dahlia's disability had been transformed into wonderfully engaging activities for all the children!

Read–Reflect–Discuss Questions

1. What strategies specifically address Dahlia's visual impairment?
2. Which elements of the adaptations would probably be effective with any children needing support in the area of literacy?
3. How might you simplify the strategies used?

Key Terms

communication board   directed eye gaze   event sequence box
dialogic reading

Helpful Resources

Articles and Books

Beukelman, D., & Mirenda, P. (2012). *Supporting participation and communication for beginning communicators.* In *Augmentative and alternative communication: Supporting children and adults with complex communication needs* (pp. 225–254). Baltimore, MD: Paul H. Brookes.

Fitzpatrick, Y., & Yuh, C. (2005). *Phonemic awareness: Playing with sounds to strengthen beginning reading skills.* Cypress, CA: Creative Teaching Press.

Register, D., Hughes, J., & Standley, J. M. (2012). *The sounds of emerging literacy: Music-based applications to facilitate prereading and writing skills in early intervention.* Silver Spring, MD: American Music Therapy Association, Inc.

Santos, R. M., Cheatham, G. A., & Duran, L. (2012). *Supporting young children who are dual language learners with or at risk for disabilities.* Monograph #14. Arlington, VA: Council for Exceptional Children.

Books That May Appeal to Young Children Who Have Disabilities or Difficulty Sustaining Attention

(NOTE: Although the concepts and language may be enjoyable and accessible to children with special needs, the illustrations in some of the books are problematic for many of the children, especially children with low vision or low cognitive ability.)

Animal Stories

Cookie's Week, Cindy Ward
Good Dog, Carl, Alexandra Day
Good Morning, Chick, Mirra Ginsburg
Harry the Dirty Dog, Gene Zion
Home for a Bunny, Margaret Wise Brown
Mary Had a Little Lamb, Sarah Josepha Hale
Moo Moo, Brown Cow, Jakki Wood
The Runaway Bunny, Margaret Wise Brown
Whose Mouse Are You?, Robert Kraus

Concepts (Colors, Letters, Numbers, Shapes, Sizes)

Big Bird's Color Game, Tom Cooke
Circles, Triangles and Squares, Tana Hoban
The Foot Book, Dr. Seuss
Five Little Monkeys Jumping on the Bed, Eileen Christelow
Five Little Monkeys Sitting in a Tree, Eileen Christelow
The Three Bears, A Golden Book
Is It Red? Is It Yellow? Is It Blue?, Tana Hoban
Little Gorilla, Ruth Bornstein
Mouse Paint, Ellen Stool Walsh
One Cow Moo Moo, David Bennett
1,2,3 to the Zoo, Eric Carle
Over, Under, and Through, Tana Hoban
Round and Round and Round, Tana Hoban
Ten, Nine, Eight, Molly Bang
The Very Hungry Caterpillar, Eric Carle

CHAPTER 14

Communicating and Collaborating with Families

LEARNING OBJECTIVES

After studying this chapter, you will be able to:

LO 14-1: Explain basic guidelines to be considered when collaborating with families.

LO 14-2: Describe the common stresses experienced by family members who have a child with a disability.

LO 14-3: Discuss a variety of strategies for effectively dealing with potential emotional reactions of family members.

LO 14-4: List and demonstrate communication skills thought to be essential to collaborating with family members.

The following NAEYC Standards and DEC Recommended Practices are addressed in this chapter:

Standard 6: Becoming a Professional

DEC

Practice 4: Instruction
Practice 6: Teaming and Collaboration

Successful inclusion of children with special needs depends upon strong partnerships between families and professionals:

- **Families are more knowledgeable than anyone else about their child.** Families also have a great deal of information about the disability and about effective intervention and accommodation strategies.
- **ECE personnel must establish partnerships with families.** It is impossible to provide optimal

support to children without this relationship with families. The key to successful partnerships with families is communication and respect.

- **Families of children with special needs experience a wide range of stresses and challenges in their daily lives.** These daily challenges can include frustration

and emotional reactions to the complex demands of obtaining and coordinating services for their children.

- **Most families experience strong emotional reactions to the diagnosis of their child's disability.** These reactions may be similar to the processes of grief and loss.

Introduction

In recent years, early childhood educators and special educators have increasingly prioritized the needs of families and have promoted family involvement in a variety of ways. Many programs for young children do an excellent job of inviting families to participate. They produce newsletters, establish active parent councils, and go to great lengths to support families on a daily basis. But for parents of young children with special needs, it is necessary to go beyond these connections and actually seek to include parents as full partners in their children's program. Early intervention programs that fully involve families through effective **parent-professional partnerships** produce better results. It is impossible to provide optimal, effective care and service to young children with special needs without establishing a collaborative relationship with their families.

14-1 Guidelines for Developing Parent-Professional Partnerships

The following basic guidelines should be considered when redefining the relationship between families and professionals into a partnership that will lead to successful inclusion of young children with special needs.

14-1a Development of Trust

Perhaps the most important ingredient in the process of creating a true partnership with families is the development of mutual trust. Trust will not develop unless families feel safe. Their right to privacy, to confidentiality, to ask questions, and to make choices for themselves and their children must be respected.

Parents of children with special needs—especially severe disabilities—might have often spent years engaging in difficult and adversarial relationships with professionals and agencies. Their lives may have been overwhelmed by the need to interact with and seek help from a wide range of individuals. Some parents will have had many painful experiences dealing with professionals; as they enter into yet another relationship, they may initially be cautious and wary. A trusting relationship may not develop quickly. Some families need more time and more support to develop the trust necessary to enter into a true partnership. However, other families have developed partnerships with prior service providers and will expect to be fully involved.

14-1b Recognizing Parents' Knowledge and Expertise

ECE educators must recognize the knowledge and expertise that families have about their children and their children's special needs. Generally, families are the primary

Photo 14-1 Including parents as critical team members is essential.

caregivers and have spent the most time with the children. They are the experts on their children's strengths, needs, desires, habits, and other relevant information. Therefore, early childhood educators must find comfortable ways to encourage families to share this information and to show that their opinions are respected. Families are, and should be, the *primary decision makers* regarding the services their children receive.

Early childhood educators must believe that most families, regardless of their background, care deeply about their children's progress and can contribute substantially if given opportunities and knowledge. Families look to professionals for affirmation of their efforts. Some families have experienced so many frustrations on the road to inclusion that their confidence in their own judgment and in the *system* may have been shaken. Families want and deserve to be valued as essential members of the team serving their children. Only then may they realize the importance of their role in furthering their children's development.

14-1c Families Are the Constant in Their Children's Lives

The family is the constant in a child's life while service systems and professionals within these systems fluctuate. Recognizing that the family is the most important and most stable element in the child's life, early childhood educators have an obligation to support and strengthen the family's resources, skills, and confidence in meeting a young child's needs. We should avoid approaching the family from a **deficit orientation**. Professionals have a tendency to believe that if the family has a child with special needs, the family is also disabled. It is important to realize that these families have the same strengths that all families possess, and that caring for their children with special needs and working with professionals can build on those strengths.

14-1d Making the Program Fit the Family's Priorities

ECE educators must negotiate a fit between the family's values, needs, and priorities and the program's approaches, goals, and services. The individual family service plans (IFSPs) required by law for infants and toddlers with special needs provide an opportunity to ensure a good match between the families' concerns and priorities for their children and the philosophy and services of the early childhood program. The process involved in developing these plans creates an opportunity for early childhood educators to ask parents or guardians what they want or expect from services to be provided to their children. In fact, the law clearly requires that the team developing these plans actively include families and that families be given the opportunity to express their concerns and priorities for services.

Viewing the Family as a Whole. The discrepancy between what families want and what they get often occurs because professionals may focus only on the needs of children rather than on the needs of families as a whole. Families function as systems in which whatever affects one family member automatically affects all other members in some way. As systems, healthy families seek to stay in balance where life may not be perfect for each member but at least is tolerable for all. When the team focuses only on the needs of one member or on only one family function, such as education, the system can get out of balance. The critical needs of families for food, shelter, employment, transportation, and child care may have to be addressed before families can focus on the unique needs of the child with a disability. This philosophy is referred to as a **family systems approach**, which Turnbull and colleagues (2015) have described in detail.

Honoring the Diversity of Families. Early childhood educators may think of themselves as knowing how to parent. This belief system is based on a combination of their own experiences, their own cultural upbringing and parenting styles, and the expectations and values found in textbooks reflecting the child-rearing attitudes of middle-class Euro-American culture. However, many children with special needs are being raised in a variety of family configurations that include single-parent families, foster placements, group homes, grandparents, and teenaged parents. In addition, increasing ethnic diversity within the U.S. population can be different from middle-class values and assumptions about child rearing.

Each family system functions according to its own values and experiences. These differences influence families' attitudes and practices related to child rearing in general and the purpose of early education. In addition, families' attitudes toward disability and their attitudes toward early intervention and special education are greatly influenced by culture. For example, some families may experience a great deal of guilt and shame related to having a child with a disability. Some families may have ambivalent feelings about seeking help. (For a thorough examination of these issues see Klein and Chen, 2001; Lynch and Hanson, 2011.)

Photo 14-2 Fathers bring a unique perspective.

14-2 Recognizing the Stresses Families Face

It is essential to recognize the extra stresses families of children with special needs have experienced and continue to experience in their daily lives.

14-2a Dealing with Multiple Needs and Multiple Agencies and Professionals

Families of young children with special needs have extra stresses created by their children's multiple needs and by the overall impact of those special needs on family life. These children require more frequent and more specialized medical services and therapy appointments. Families often must deal with significant behavioral challenges. Caretaking may be compounded by sleeping, toileting, or feeding challenges. The following comments sum up the views of one parent:

> There are constant stresses on our family. Since one child requires more help and attention than the others, resentments build up. I find myself doing a perennial balancing act with my husband and children trying to make sure that everyone gets their fair share of me. All this is aggravated by the fact that when you have a preschooler who is delayed, what you really have on your hands is a child who seems to be stuck in the *terrible twos*. She is destructive without meaning to be and is forever testing us. She frequently spills her drinks, and the other day she poured a whole box of cereal all over the floor. She still isn't toilet trained. I sometimes wonder if she'll ever be fully toilet trained or if she will ever sleep through the night.

As we note in the sections that follow, some of the extra stresses that parents experience make meaningful family involvement in early childhood programs more difficult.

14-2b Increased Time Demands and the Need to Set Priorities

Families of children with special needs do have greater demands made on their time. Families simply cannot do everything and are often forced to set priorities. Early childhood educators must ensure that all contacts with their program are positive so that families will want to make school/center involvement a priority. Above all, resist being critical of how families use their time. Families must often make difficult choices about how to spend their precious time. The last thing an educator should do is add stress to already stressful lives. Other suggestions for collaborating with families, even when time is limited, include:

- Call, e-mail, or text families regularly. Offer positive news. Often parents assume that communication must mean there is some new problem with their child. Establish a positive relationship early so that families look forward to hearing from you. Be sure to contact the family just to see how parents themselves are doing.
- Use communication notebooks, described in a later section of this chapter.
- Create social events that accommodate all family members at convenient family times.

The Easter Egg Hunt

Ms. Gonzalez is the director of a large urban child care center. After months of trying to involve several families of children with special needs in the program, she came up with an activity that broke the ice. The center held an Easter egg hunt and invited all family members. Student volunteers from the local college special education department supervised the children while parents met each other and interacted with staff. Eighty percent of the families participated, including several families of children with special needs. This was followed by an equally successful potluck dinner two months later.

14-3 Understanding Families' Emotional Reactions

Individual family members may react differently to the news that their child, brother or sister, or granddaughter or grandson has disabilities. The literature on disabilities has described the reactions of parents to the birth of a child with a disability as similar to the **grief reactions** experienced when someone loses a loved one through death. This theory suggests that, in a sense, the parent may be grieving for the loss of the *hoped-for* child. Although not all parents go through each stage of the grief cycle, most parents experience intense emotional reactions.

Reactions may be most intense when disabilities are first identified, though intense reactions may surface at any time as the family moves through its life cycle. Each time a transition arises, such as a move from a home-based program to a center program, long-forgotten feelings may resurface. The transition into an inclusive program may highlight how different a child is from his peers without disabilities. Families may then find themselves in need of extra emotional support as they, once again, confront the realities with which they live. The following reflections from a parent reveal one example of what can be normally expected:

> I decided to place my daughter in my neighborhood nursery school part-time where she was the only child with a disability. Although my daughter, who is very competent socially, adjusted fairly well, I felt lonely, isolated, depressed, and at times embarrassed. During my daughter's first few weeks there, when I stayed with her to ease her separation, I had to leave the room on a few occasions when I began to cry. Being around all those normal three-year-olds was a constant reminder of how verbal and adept little children are and how far behind my daughter was in her development.

It is important for early childhood educators to have some understanding of the typical feelings that families may experience. These reactions to the advent of a disability are described in much the same way the loss of a loved one is described in the literature on death and dying. Families may experience a strong sense of loss and grief for the child they had envisioned. They may also experience guilt, denial, anger, and depression as they work through the change in expectations that a child with special needs brings to a family. Sometimes, family members may not seem to be listening or following suggestions. When this happens, early childhood educators must be careful to avoid categorizing family members as being "in denial." It is critical to remember that feelings such as denial and anger are normal and should be thought of as internal coping mechanisms. Denial is positive when it allows families to pause and gather the strength necessary to cope with their daily demands.

Family members work through the process of accepting their child's disability at different rates. Just understanding possible parental reactions can help early childhood educators respond appropriately. Cook, Klein, and Chen (2016) offer suggestions for helpful responses. Some of these are listed in Figure 14-1. However, developing coping strategies often does not follow a linear progression or necessarily occur in predictable stages. A mother may have moved well along in developing coping strategies while a father pauses as he suddenly realizes that his son may not be able to play in Little League as he had planned. Just listening with compassion and patience may be the best approach at all times when in the presence of emotional expression.

14-3a Strategies for Supporting Families' Emotional Reactions

The following offer some general strategies for supporting the emotional reactions of family members.

Avoid Judgment. It is all too easy for educators to feel that families are in denial or being unrealistic if they are not ready to acknowledge the nature or extent of their child's special needs. An understanding of the grief cycle reveals that what appears

SHOCK AND DENIAL DISBELIEF	Listen with acceptance.
	Offer support and assistance.
	Connect emotionally with parents.
	Provide information.
	Refer to parent-to-parent support.
ANGER AND RESENTMENT	Employ active listening.
	Reflect parents' frustrations.
	Help parents accept feelings as normal.
DEPRESSION DICOURAGEMENT	Focus on child's accomplishments.
	Plan for short-term future.
	Try to encourage activity and engagement.
	Encourage parent-to-parent support.
	Make referrals for professional help if necessary.
ACCEPTANCE	Maintain ongoing relationship.
	Encourage parent to reach out to others.
	Help parents set new goals for themselves and their child.

Figure 14-1 Various Grief Reactions and Examples of Interventionist Responses

to be denial is often a healthy approach for families to take as they take time to work through their feelings. Early childhood educators should *never assume* they know what a family is going through unless they also have a young family member who has a disability. And, even then, their experiences may be very different.

Provide Both Emotional Support and Concrete Assistance.
In addition to being supportive and nonjudgmental, early childhood educators can take specific steps to provide concrete assistance to families. Here are a few actions to consider.

- Become knowledgeable about and refer families to community family resource centers and other parent support programs or groups. (It may be beneficial to collaborate with an inclusion support specialist or an early childhood special educator to secure this information.) These programs generally work with whole families and provide the training and support necessary to increase the ability of families to nurture their children. Most of all, they provide families with the opportunity to get to know other families who have been there. Families often find it comforting to know they are not alone in their experiences and their feelings.
- Get to know and develop collaborative relationships with the agencies in your community that serve children with special needs. Join an existing interagency coordinating council or help establish one in your community. You will not only become more knowledgeable about the system, but you will be able to assist families when they have frustrations dealing with the service delivery system. Knowing the right person to call can make a great difference when families are trying to access services.
- Become well acquainted with service coordinators or case managers from all the community agencies serving the children in your program. They are responsible for seeing that your families get the services they need. Building close relationships with these and other agency personnel will help ensure that all those working with the family have the same goals and objectives.
- Develop a notebook or file of community resources, such as community support groups, respite or child care providers, recreational programs, medical and dental services, adult education, and social service agencies that might assist with financial, housing, and transportation needs.

WEBLINK

Although siblings are highly influenced by their parents' attitudes, it is essential to remember that they have a lifetime relationship with the challenges and rewards of being the sibling of someone with a disability. They, too, need continuous support and understanding. Dedicated to the lifelong and constantly changing concerns of brothers and sisters is the Sibling Support Project, which has connections with sib shops around the world. Find more at www.siblingsupport.org.

- Develop or add specific materials to a parent lending library of particular interest to families of children with special needs.
- Invite people from community resources to assist in offering family education opportunities about such topics as the law, parents' rights and responsibilities, classroom methods and materials, IFSPs, IEPs, and transition to kindergarten.

Encourage Families' Participation in Support Groups or Parent-to-Parent Support. A number of parent organizations are often organized around a specific disability, such as the National Down Syndrome Society and Autism Speaks. These groups provide not only an opportunity to learn about the child's special needs, but to interact with many families with similar challenges and experiences.

Parent-to-parent support services provide the assistance of a parent who has been trained in peer support techniques and who has a child with special needs. This type of service is more personal and often can provide specific assistance with local services and bureaucracy. Families might not immediately welcome these support services or be ready for this type of interaction, especially when a disability has been recently diagnosed. Early childhood educators need to respect this reaction and perhaps suggest the support at a later time.

14-4 Communication: The Key to Building Partnerships

Early childhood educators must develop effective communications skills and methods to provide information to the families of children with special needs and to encourage their input into the program. Like education, communication is a two-way process.

14-4a Providing Information

Early childhood educators readily take responsibility for communicating by providing information about their programs and services to families through orientation meetings, handbooks, special events, and newsletters. This information is essential to families whose children have been included in typical programs. These families want and deserve to become a part of every aspect of their children's program even if their children cannot participate in every activity. Early childhood educators need to make every attempt to ensure that parents *understand* the information provided.

Provide Child-Specific Communication. Families of children with special needs are likely to expect and desire specific information about their child on a regular basis. They are used to or become used to their child being assessed and reassessed much more than having a child without a disability. Although many families might become tired of their child constantly being compared to others or to criteria found on some test form, they are still interested in hearing about their child's progress from those who work with him. Families are especially interested in their child's progress in the developmental areas they hold as priorities. In addition to keen observation and comprehensive record keeping, early childhood educators need highly developed skills in personal communication and problem solving.

Communicate on a Regular Basis. Parents of children with special needs often complain that whenever they receive a phone call, e-mail, text, or message from their child's teacher, they know it will be bad news. One effective communication strategy is to set up regular meetings or communications in which you *debrief* one another about the child's progress as well as difficulties. Make sure to include positive comments and amusing anecdotes, not just problems. If regular communications occur consistently, parents will eventually begin to look forward to hearing from the teacher and will use those opportunities to share information and feelings. Figure 14-2 gives two examples of how families and teachers can prepare for meetings. These

---

TEACHER PREPARATION FOR TEAM MEETING

Child's Name:

1. Describe the child's strengths and the things that he/she does well.

2. What improvements has the child made in school in his/her developmental skills and behaviors since we last spoke?

3. What concerns do you have about the child's development or behavior?

4. Based on question 3, what teaching strategies or adaptations have already been tried or are currently in place for these concerns?

5. Based on question 3, what goals would you like to see to help the child make progress and improvement in these areas?

Figure 14-2 Preparation for Team Meeting

FAMILY PREPARATION FOR TEAM MEETING
Directions: Please fill out this paper in preparation for our meeting.
Child's Name:
1. Describe your child's strengths and the things that he/she does well.
2. What improvements has your child made at home in his/her developmental skills and behaviors since we last spoke?
3. What concerns do you have about your child's development or behavior?
4. Based on these concerns, what goals would you like to see to help your child make progress and improvements in these areas?
5. How else can the staff help support you, your child, and your family?

Figure 14-2 (Continued)

⌄ **Professional Resource Download**

forms can also be a written record that can be used to monitor annual progress as they align with the contents in an IEP.

Use Daily Communication Notebooks. A simple, but effective strategy is to send a **communication notebook** back and forth each day with the child. Both the teacher and parents or guardians may write in the book whenever they wish. This is two-way communication in which professionals and parents not only give and receive information, but also work together in using that information to generate strategies to meet the many challenges disabilities may present.

14-4b Developing Effective Communication Skills

Let's review a few tips to increase the effectiveness of person-to-person communication between parents and professionals.

Perfect the Art of Listening. Create opportunities to give family members your full attention. Avoid trying to hold a detailed conversation with parents during arrival, departure, and other busy times. It is usually best to schedule a meeting or uninterrupted communication time. Let the family take the lead by asking open-ended questions if necessary to initiate the conversation, to clarify or gain more information. For example, you might say:

"Tell me more about . . ."

"Please give me an example so I can better understand."

Listen with Reflection. Only if they perceive that you are listening carefully will families continue to express themselves. After reflecting on their comments, you will be able to convey acceptance and concern. By responding with reflective comments based on facts and feelings offered by families, you can demonstrate understanding of what has been said. This approach helps to focus speakers and gives them a chance to acknowledge that the listener is on the right track. Here is an example:

Parent: I was wondering why Carrie still hasn't started walking after all of these months of physical therapy.

Teacher: You sound somewhat discouraged about Carrie's progress.

Such **reflective listening** and responding lets parents know you are interested in their concerns and feelings and that you want to be supportive. It gives parents a chance either to continue expressing their feelings or to seek answers more directly. This technique, also known as *active listening*, is a useful tool that all early educators should consider developing.

Avoid Jargon. Educators must be diligent to avoid using terms and acronyms that are unfamiliar to families. Many parents are reluctant to ask what such terms mean so the responsibility to offer clear communication belongs to the professional.

Phrase Negative Information Carefully. Always begin a conversation with something positive and keep the entire conversation as positive as possible. Even negative information can be phrased in a positive manner. For example, when a child continually seeks attention by blurting out and seeking to be the center of activities, the teacher might describe that challenge in this way:

When we are doing storytelling or another child is showing us something, George just can't wait to share what he is thinking. He is so interested in what is going on that he places himself right in front of the teacher. We checked to see that his hearing and vision are normal. So, we are wondering how we can work together to help George control himself a bit more. What do you do at home when George wants your attention?

Summary

Supporting young children with special needs demands that professionals establish close partnerships with families. Families know more about their children than anyone else. Early childhood educators need to understand thoroughly both the emotional impact of having a child with special needs and the complex day-to-day physical and time demands of coordinating the child's services. Developing support skills, the ability to connect emotionally with families, and effective communication techniques will enable early childhood educators to support children in the most optimal ways.

Read–Reflect–Discuss
Alfredo's Mother

Alfredo Sanchez has been attending Miss Lee's child care program for several months. All in all, he is doing fairly well. When he first entered the program, he cried for a good portion of each day, especially in the morning after his mother left. His mother insisted on staying with him for more than an hour. Miss Lee believed the reason Alfredo had such difficulty dealing with separation was because his mother had such a hard time leaving him. The situation had begun to improve, but recently Alfredo had been absent frequently and separation is again beginning to be a problem.

Alfredo is small for his age and appears to be developmentally young. At three-and-a-half he uses only a few words. But other than the crying, he does not present much of a problem at the center. From Miss Lee's perspective, the biggest problem has been Alfredo's mother! She seems extremely overprotective and prone to keep Alfredo out of school at the slightest sniffle. She is also fairly demanding. She asks a lot of questions about health and safety policies. Miss Lee also feels that Mrs. Sanchez gives the staff mixed messages about Alfredo's social interactions with other children. On the one hand she is constantly worried about bigger, more active children hurting Alfredo. But at the same time she wants the staff to help Alfredo make friends and be involved with other children.

The child care staff has started to avoid interacting with Mrs. Sanchez because they dread her complaints. They all increasingly believe that her son would do much better if she would make sure he attends the program on a consistent basis and if she could resist being so overprotective.

Miss Lee mentions her frustrations to the early childhood special education (ECSE) consultant. The consultant realizes she has not really given Miss Lee much background information about Alfredo. She explains that Alfredo was born prematurely, at only 27 weeks gestation. He weighed less than two pounds at birth! He was hospitalized for several months, and Alfredo's physicians weren't sure whether the infant would survive. Mrs. Sanchez came every day to the neonatal intensive care unit, taking three different buses to get there. A devout Catholic, she also stopped at her church every day to light candles for Alfredo. Mrs. Sanchez clearly saw her son's survival as a true miracle and a gift from God.

In many ways Alfredo's development has also been a miracle. Despite his developmental delay and possible mild intellectual delay, he has a sweet and even temperament, and he is making steady progress. The greatest challenge has been chronic upper respiratory problems, resulting in several hospitalizations. Alfredo seems to catch cold easily, and his colds frequently result in pneumonia. The ECSE consultant explains to Miss Lee that this is a common pattern in children who are born prematurely. The consultant also shares with Miss Lee that Mrs. Sanchez's husband was killed in a work accident, and most of her extended family lives in Guatemala. Despite the absence of family support, Mrs. Sanchez always keeps her doctor's appointments and stays with Alfredo during his hospitalizations. Her devotion and watchful care of Alfredo is nothing short of heroic and is probably a big factor in his developmental progress.

Miss Lee appreciates this information and tells the ECSE consultant that in the future she would like to receive this kind of information prior to her first meeting with the child and parent. Miss Lee then discusses this information with her staff at the center. She explains to them why Mrs. Sanchez seems overprotective and why Alfredo is frequently absent. The information gives the staff a different perspective and a new sense of respect and admiration for Alfredo's mother.

Read–Reflect–Discuss Questions

1. Can you think of an experience in your own work or personal life where learning more about an individual completely changed your perceptions and feelings about that person?
2. What do you think the mother might have done differently when she first brought Alfredo to the center that might have resulted in a different sort of relationship between her and the staff?
3. If you were the director of a center, what kinds of initial intake procedures would you design that might help avoid the misunderstandings and bad feelings that evolved in Alfredo's situation?

Key Terms

communication notebook

deficit orientation

family systems approach

grief reactions

parent-to-parent support

parent-professional partnerships

reflective listening

Helpful Resources

Books

Cook, R. E., & Sparks, S. (2008). *The art and practice of home visiting: Early intervention for children with special needs and their families*. Baltimore, MD: Paul H. Brookes Publishing Company.

Hanson, M. J., & Lynch, E. W. (2013). *Understanding families: Supportive approaches to diversity, disability, and risk*. Baltimore, MD: Paul H. Brookes Publishing Company.

Turnbull, A., Turnbull, R., Erwin, E., & Soodak, L. (2015). *Families, professionals and exceptionality: Positive outcomes through partnerships and trust* (7th ed.) Upper Saddle River, NJ: Pearson.

Organizations

Beach Center on Disability, www.beachcenter.org

National Parent to Parent Support & Information System, Inc. (NPPSIS), www.iser .com/NPPSIS-GA.html

PACER Center, www.pacer.org

Parents Helping Parents (PHP), www.php.com

Family Education Network (*Exceptional Parent*), www.eparent.com

CHAPTER 15

Collaborating with Disability Specialists and Paraprofessionals

LEARNING OBJECTIVES

After studying this chapter, you will be able to:

LO 15-1: Describe the roles and responsibilities of professionals who might be involved in a collaborative consultation team.

LO 15-2: Explain how to obtain and utilize available inclusion support.

LO 15-3: Discuss necessary considerations to perform effectively as a program manager.

LO 15-4: Outline the keys necessary to success in creating effective teams devoted to collaborative problem solving.

The following NAEYC Standards and DEC Recommended Practices are addressed in this chapter:

naeyc

Standard 6: Becoming a Professional

DEC

Practice 4: Instruction
Practice 6: Teaming and Collaboration

The shared expertise of several specialized educators, therapists, and paraprofessionals can enhance the classroom experience for children with special needs:

- **Early childhood special educators.** Early childhood special educators are trained specifically to provide developmental and educational services to infants and young children with special needs and their families.

- **Inclusion support specialists.** Inclusion support specialists consult as part of the support team to ensure appropriate supports are provided to all children based on their goals and specific needs.

- **Speech-language specialists.** Speech-language specialists address disorders of speech production, expressive and receptive language delays, and pragmatic disorders, along with less common disorders of fluency and voice quality.

- **Physical therapists.** Physical therapists provide therapeutic support for the development of mobility and postural control for children who have motor disabilities such as cerebral palsy or spina bifida.

- **Occupational therapists.** Occupational therapists are more concerned with the functional use of the upper body, including arms and hands. They also work to facilitate oral motor functioning for feeding.

- **Visual impairment specialists.** These specialists are trained to work with individuals who are blind or partially sighted. They can provide consultation related to optimal lighting, use of corrective lenses, strategies for increasing contrasts, and encouraging use of children's available vision.

- **Deaf and hard of hearing specialists.** Deaf and hard of hearing specialists usually are credentialed educators who specialize in working with children who have a hearing loss.

- **Behavior specialists.** Behavior specialists carefully observe children and assist in the development and execution of behavior support plans.

- **Paraeducators.** Paraeducators are playing an increasingly critical role in helping teachers support young children with special needs in inclusive settings.

- **The collaborative intervention team.** The most effective service to young children is provided when parents, professionals, and paraeducators work together as a collaborative team.

Introduction

Including children with special needs in the early childhood center often requires assistance from other professionals. The job of ECE teachers can be made much easier if they seek the help of the right specialists. A wide range of specialists may be of assistance in supporting children with disabilities. In this chapter we will describe the roles and potential contributions of each of these specialists.

15-1 The Collaborative Intervention Team

The most effective service to young children is provided when families, professionals, and paraeducators work together as a collaborative team. The following details the most involved specialists.

15-1a Early Childhood Special Educators (ECSEs)

Increasingly, early childhood special educators provide the primary support for young children with special needs in inclusive settings. In some areas this is a relatively new discipline; other professionals may not be familiar with their training backgrounds and roles.

ECSE professionals typically have credentials and/or a master's degree and are trained to provide developmental and educational services to infants and children to age five with special needs and high-risk conditions.

ECSE professionals are concerned with supporting the *whole child.* They are specifically trained to evaluate how the separate areas of development interact and influence one another. Early childhood special educators view children within the context of their family.

ECSE professionals work with *all disabilities* across all developmental domains including:

- Language and cognition
- Motor and adaptive skills
- Emotional and social development

For children who have unique or severe challenges in specific areas, ECSE specialists are trained to work collaboratively with specialists in those areas, such as physical or occupational therapists, speech-language specialists, and vision and hearing specialists. Many children with special needs receive one or more therapeutic services outside the center on a weekly basis. Other than families, early childhood special

INCLUSION OBSERVATION REPORTING FORM		
Date: 9-15 **Child: Joshua R.** **Center: Sunnydale Childcare**		
Teacher(s): Evelyn **Inclusion Support Specialist: A. Gibbs**		
Activity & Time	**Observations** **(what facilitator observes)**	**SUPPORTS/ADAPTATIONS** **(suggestions for teachers that may help child be part of activities)**
Arrival 8:00 AM	Mother leaves as soon as Josh is distracted by toys. When he notices she is gone he becomes upset. Assistant approaches him and tries to calm him. He becomes more agitated.	Establish consistent "Goodbye" routine, which includes same assistant each day.
Playing at water table 9:15 AM	Josh pushes anyone who comes near him. Children walk away, leaving him alone at the water table.	1. Teach peers to say "Stop!" when he pushes or engages in aggressive behavior. 2. Ask peers not to crowd Joshua until he is more comfortable with close proximity of others.

Figure 15-1 Inclusion Support Recommendations

⌄ **Professional Resource Download**

educators or **inclusion support specialists** are often most likely to be knowledgeable about these interventions.

ECSE professionals are trained to work closely with parents in a collaborative parent-professional partnership. Traditionally ECSE specialists have worked in either home-based programs or center-based programs. They often specialize in either the infant/toddler or the preschool age range. Increasingly, as more children are placed in inclusive settings, ECSE professionals work in a consulting role to assist ECE teachers to successfully include children with special needs in the general early childhood setting.

Role of Early Childhood Special Educators. ECSE specialists are likely to be people most familiar with children's educational goals. A young child with special needs will have an official document, either an IFSP or an IEP, listing the goals and services for the child and her family.

If ECSE specialists serve as consultants, they should have a wide range of teaching and intervention strategies to address specific challenges. In some cases they may work directly with the child as the child participates in the center. Other challenges are more effectively addressed by discussing with the ECE staff the possible adaptations that can be made. Figure 15-1 presents an observation reporting form for making recommendations for possible adaptations. Pullout or tutorial models (where the consultant works with the child away from the group) are less effective. Unlike other specialists, ECSE professionals are not therapists.

ECSE specialists may also be responsible for monitoring a child's progress. Individual goals for the child are based on specific assessments of the child's development and skills across the developmental domains of cognition, language, motor, adaptive, social, and emotional development. Other goals may be related to health, nutrition, and behavioral management. ECSE specialists can work with an ECE staff to determine the simplest ways to monitor a child's progress in each goal area.

In addition to or instead of ECSE specialists, inclusion support specialists are serving as support consultants. In some areas, inclusion support specialists serve the K–12 population as well as those in early education programs. The following reflections of an inclusion support specialist, who also happens to be a co-author of this text, offer insight into the responsibilities of one such specialist.

15-1b Inclusion Support Specialists

Reflections of an Inclusion Support Specialist

I am known in my district variously as the "inclusion teacher," the "inclusion specialist," the inclusion consultant," the "inclusion support specialist," and so on. Basically, I am an itinerant early childhood special education teacher. I have a caseload of 25 to 30 preschoolers with special needs. They attend Head Start programs throughout our school district, which encompasses 17 elementary schools and serves about 10,000 students.

As an inclusion specialist, I am assigned to IEP teams for children needing support in pre-academics, self-help skills, and social-emotional and behavioral needs. I work with team members to ensure appropriate supports are provided to all students based on their goals and specific needs. Most of the time, I serve as the case manager and coordinate with speech pathologists, occupational therapists, adaptive physical education teachers, and other specialists. I work closely with families, especially when their child is entering the school district for the first time at three years of age.

One of the most important parts of my job is collaborating with the early childhood teachers. I really enjoy this part of the job because the teachers I work with are so invested in the outcomes for their students. I've worked with many of these teachers for over ten years so we know each other quite well. When I first began my work, it took a whole first year to begin to establish relationships with teachers and other professionals. I work hard to let them know that I'm not coming into their classrooms to criticize them. I'm here to support them in meeting the needs of the students with disabilities.

There are times when an IEP team determines that a child would benefit from extra classroom assistance via a paraeducator. I am responsible for training and supervising this person. I often work to coordinate their schedules so that several children are served throughout the day, when there are specific needs (for example, helping one child with feeding skills at breakfast, providing support for another student during circle time, and so on)

One of my greatest challenges is time management and scheduling my consultation times. I try to observe my students during different parts of the school day or when teachers tell me that the child is struggling during a specific part of the routine. I see different children for varying amounts of time, depending on their needs. For some students, I may consult once or twice a week for an hour or more. Other students might be 30 minutes per week or less.

I also work closely with our district's special education personnel and the school psychologists to schedule IEP meetings and complete necessary assessments.

I used to have my own special education preschool class many years ago. The change to not having my "own" class was difficult at first. The amount of time I spent driving from school to school and working with so many different teams of people was challenging. After the first year or two, however, I found myself enjoying the novelty of each classroom and getting to know so many more families, children, and professionals. It can be tiring but is well worth it!

Anne Marie Richardson-Gibbs

15-1c Speech-Language Specialists

Many children with special needs typically have some delay or difficulty in the area of communication. Speech-language specialists are trained to address the communication development of both children and adults. They are certified by the American Speech-Language Hearing Association (ASHA). Speech-language specialists are trained to address a wide range of communication disorders.

Speech Production Disorders. Children who have **speech production (articulation) disorders** are difficult to understand. The underlying causes and characteristics of speech disorders are complex. Children often have both speech and language difficulties. In some cases there is no other disability. Sometimes the speech disorder is related to obvious motor delays or disabilities such as cerebral palsy or to more complex motor planning difficult. Sometimes the cause of the speech production difficulty is unclear.

Language Disorders. Although speech production involves the motor and sequencing ability to produce sounds and syllables, *language abilities* include vocabulary development and understanding the meaning of words, the rules for combining words, and the correct forms of words, that is, *grammar*. Thus, speech disorders and **language disorders** are not the same. Children who have difficulty using language in appropriate ways and have difficulty engaging in appropriate social communication, such as children with autism, are said to have challenges with pragmatics.

Many children with special needs have difficulty learning to talk. They may not talk at all, or they may use only single words or two- and three-word combinations. Language difficulties may be related to a variety of factors. Sometimes the child has a cognitive disability or delay. Occasionally the language disorder is related to severe emotional disturbance or to autism.

Some children with severe or multiple disabilities may have even more basic problems in that they have no communication system. In some instances children with multiple disabilities may not attempt to communicate, even with such nonverbal means as gestures, eye gaze, or vocalizations.

Fluency Disorders. Speech-language specialists are trained to provide therapy to children and adults with **fluency disorders** such as stuttering. They can differentially diagnose true stuttering behavior from typical early childhood language disfluency. Stuttering is a relatively uncommon disorder.

Voice Disorders. The most common type of **voice disorder** among children with special needs is hoarseness due to vocal abuse (for example, excessive screaming or yelling) or chronic upper respiratory infections. Occasionally children may also have disorders of pitch (for example, high-pitched voice) or loudness (a soft voice).

Role of Speech-Language Specialists. Because communication and language are very complex processes, it is often necessary to have an in-depth assessment to understand the specific nature of the child's communication problem. Following the assessment, a speech-language specialist can provide specific suggestions for intervention.

For some aspects of communication, a speech-language specialist may work primarily in the role of a consultant, collaborating with the child's teacher. This is particularly the case with children who are still in the prelinguistic stages of development or in the earliest stages of language development.

The best place to help children develop early language skills is in the context of the routine activities of everyday life, both in the classroom or child care center and at home. A variety of generic and specific strategies can support the development of language in young children. It is important that ECE teachers obtain clear descriptions of recommended interventions.

For other types of communication disorders, such as severe articulation disorders or stuttering, a more direct intervention approach may be necessary. However, ECE teachers should understand the goals and strategies involved and be able to support the speech-language specialist's efforts in the classroom.

Another area in which speech-language specialists may be able to offer support is in the development of augmentative and alternative communication (AAC) for those children whose motor disabilities are so severe they cannot develop intelligible speech or for whom speech development will proceed slowly. However, it is important to realize that many speech-language specialists may have *not* had training and experience in this area.

15-1d Physical Therapists (PTs)

For children who have motor disabilities such as cerebral palsy or spina bifida, therapy and consultation from a licensed physical therapist should be provided. Physical therapists are licensed and registered by state agencies. They have had intensive graduate-level training in anatomy and kinesiology, normal development of movement, and various therapy techniques for supporting the optimal development of movement and postural control. They may also have expertise in the evaluation and design of **adaptive equipment** such as hand splints, leg braces, and adapted seating. They can make practical adaptations in the child's daily environment that support the child's participation in activities. Physical therapists are concerned with:

- Development of postural control, including such skills as the ability to sit without support, to stabilize the head and neck, and to move from sitting to standing
- Development of **protective reflexes**, or movements that help children maintain balance and protect them in a fall
- Optimal development of movement of both upper and lower parts of the body. This includes the **fine motor skills** of reaching and grasping, and transferring objects from one hand to the other. It also includes the large or **gross motor skills** of crawling and walking.
- Evaluation and recommendations regarding adaptive equipment such as leg braces, hand splints, head and neck stabilizers, helmets, and special seating.

Photo 15-1 A physical therapist may suggest simple functional adaptations to support motor goals.

Role of Physical Therapists. Physical therapists can provide critical support for children with motor disabilities. These services do not simply support the development of motor skills; certain procedures and adaptations provided by a physical therapist can make a huge difference in a child's ability to participate in the child care center or preschool program. Photo 15-1 shows a simple, functional adaptation to support a child's mobility. The following are examples of services that might be provided by physical therapists:

- Suggestions for positioning children so they can use their hands during an art activity
- Practical suggestions for adapting chairs so that a child can maintain postural control and avoid excessive fatigue
- Designing hand splints so a child can grasp objects more easily
- Strategies to assist a child in learning to use a walker

15-1e Occupational Therapists (OTs)

Occupational therapists are not licensed, but are registered by the AOTA (American Occupational Therapy Association). Occupational therapy addresses the development of functional skills, including fine motor skills, eating, and movement of the body in space. In working with young children, the roles of the occupational therapist and physical therapist may sometimes overlap. Theoretically, a physical therapist is more concerned with the development of postural control and large muscle movements, such as sitting, standing, walking, reaching, balance, and head control.

The occupational therapist, while interested in many of the same aspects of development as the physical therapist, particularly focuses on the role of sensation in development. How the child discriminates, modulates, and integrates incoming sensory information is important to overall development.

Many occupational therapists are trained in the principles and intervention techniques of sensory integration. The theory and therapeutic techniques of sensory integration were developed by Dr. Jean Ayres (1973). Sensory integration therapy addresses the interrelationships of:

- The child's ability to manage and process incoming sensory stimulation
- The child's self-regulation efforts
- The development of motor skills

Sometimes children with special needs have difficulty processing or managing sensory information. An OT (or other therapists trained in sensory integration techniques) can offer therapeutic techniques and intervention activities that may be helpful for young children who have difficulty processing or integrating sensory input. Consider these sources of sensory information and examples of the kinds of sensations that some children with special needs may find difficult to manage:

- **Sights** (visual sensation)
  - Flashing lights
  - Visual clutter
  - Abruptly changing visual stimulation
- **Sounds** (auditory sensation)
  - Extremely noisy environments
  - Several people talking at once
  - Background music
  - Noisy fans or motors
  - Flushing toilet or running water
  - High-pitched sounds like sirens or whistles
- **Touch** (tactile sensation)
  - Feeling against the skin of clothing and other materials such as a washcloth
  - Reaction to being touched or grabbed by another person
  - Feeling of materials on the hands such as paint, glue, or foods
  - Sensation of various food textures in the mouth
- **Movement of body parts** called **kinesthetic sensation** or **proprioception**
  - Awareness of movement of various parts of the body, including the contracting and stretching of muscles and compression of the joints
  - Rotating the body or the head, bending over, squatting, leaning to one side, maintaining balance while seated without support
- **Sensation of the position of the parts of the body**
  - Knowing how close the body is to an object, including other children
  - Knowing how high to lift the foot to climb a step or step down off a curb
  - Knowing how hard to swing a bat
- **Movement of the body through space (vestibular sensation)**
  - Sensation of the movement and position of the body as it moves through space, such as swinging, being picked up, and moving against gravity
  - Sensation of where the body is in space, such as awareness of losing your balance
- **Smell** (olfactory sense) and **taste** (gustatory sense)
  - Strong odors like perfume or paint
  - Intense flavors such as spices or citrus

An OT tends to focus somewhat more on the functional movements of the *upper*-body rather than lower-body movements required for standing and walking. Examples include:

- Arm movements and wrist rotation involved in reaching and self-feeding
- Fine motor movements of the hands involved in grasping, manipulating, and transferring objects
- Movement and control of the oral motor musculature required in chewing and swallowing

Role of Occupational Therapists. OTs can be of assistance in a number of areas. Two common areas of assistance are feeding difficulties and challenges with sensory integration, especially with children who are extremely sensitive to sensory input, such as children who demonstrate tactile defensiveness.

Occupational therapy techniques are highly specialized and typically should be performed by trained therapists or under their direct supervision. However, OTs may be able, through careful assessment, to help ECE teachers understand a child's motor and sensory difficulties in a more detailed way and to make general suggestions for ways of modifying the child's sensory environment. For example, an OT may be able to provide these forms of assistance:

- How to reduce children's resistance to messy activities and materials
- How to help children learn to finger feed
- How to expand children's choices of foods and textures
- How to reduce drooling
- How to help children learn to dress themselves independently
- How to help children develop fine motor skills
- How to support children with excessively high or low muscle tone

15-1f Visual Impairment (VI) Specialists

Consultants in the area of visual impairment are usually special educators who have a credential in the area of visual impairment. They are knowledgeable about the nature of various eye conditions that cause blindness or limited vision. They are often trained to work as *itinerants* in school districts, traveling to several school sites. Thus they work well in a consulting mode.

Most children who have visual disabilities are not totally blind. VI specialists can assist ECE teachers in understanding the nature of a child's vision problem, including:

- The characteristics of the particular eye pathology
- The parameters of the residual vision. (Can the child see only light and shadows? Can she recognize objects at close range? What is the optimal distance at which the child can see?)
- A description of the child's **visual field**, or where the child can see best (such as upper left quadrant or right side only)
- The kind of lighting that is best for the child
- Colors that are most easily perceived

Role of Vision Specialists. The following are services that can be helpful in supporting a child with a visual disability.

Functional Vision Assessment. Through a functional vision assessment, VI specialists can provide ECE teachers with important information such as visual acuity, visual field preference, and color perception. In developing teaching strategies for young children, the information provided by a functional vision assessment is often more helpful than an ophthalmologist's or oculist's report.

Lighting. VI specialists can suggest the best sources and angles for lighting to optimize the child's use of residual vision.

Contrast. VI specialists can demonstrate simple ways to maximize contrast for children with visual impairments, such as placing a bowl on a contrasting place mat or covering a child's cubby with a black-and-white checkerboard pattern.

Use of Tactile Cues. VI specialists can provide information on how to use tactile cues, such as textures to identify personal belongings or textures and small objects added to children's books. Touch cues can also be used to help children anticipate transitions and different activities.

Strategies for Teaching Concepts. One of the greatest challenges for children with visual impairments is learning concepts that are visually based, such as concepts of space, size, and volume. VI specialists can provide specific teaching suggestions.

15-1g Orientation and Mobility Specialists (O & M)

An important subspecialty within the field of vision is that of **orientation and mobility (O&M) specialist**. Not all states provide O&M services to very young children. Orientation and mobility specialists are concerned primarily with helping children learn to move independently and safely from one place to another and also with the ability to orient oneself in space. They may assist children in learning to use a cane, in learning **trailing techniques** (such as trailing the hand along a strip on the wall that marks the route to the bathroom), and in using protective strategies.

O&M specialists can teach children how to move around safely in the ECE environment. They work closely with ECE teachers to ensure that mobility skills are developed through such strategies as maintaining a consistent physical environment and providing appropriate tactile and auditory cues.

15-1h Deaf and Hard of Hearing (DHH) Specialists

Deaf and hard of hearing (DHH) specialists are usually credentialed educators who specialize in working with children who have hearing loss. Some have a subspecialty in working with infants and young children. In some cases a speech-language specialist or an audiologist may provide services for young children with hearing loss.

DHH specialists have a broad knowledge of educational and developmental needs, the child's clinical needs for speech and language development, and use of hearing aids. DHH specialists do *not* conduct audiological assessments or hearing aid evaluations.

DHH specialists should be knowledgeable in both manual modes of communication (sign language) and oral approaches (speech and use of residual hearing).

Role of DHH Specialists. ECE teachers should be able to obtain the following kinds of information and services from a DHH specialist.

Interpretation of the Audiogram. The specialist should be able to provide a functional explanation of what a child can hear, both with and without the hearing aid, by examining the child's **audiogram**. This includes an explanation of the types of sounds (for example, high- versus low-pitch sounds) that are most easily heard and how the child hears various loudness levels. For example, a child may just barely be able to hear a high-pitched siren that is painful to the normal ear; another child may not be able to hear certain consonant sounds like *sh* and *f*.

Suggestions for Reducing Ambient Noise and Excessive Resonance. A specialist can analyze the acoustic characteristics of a classroom and make suggestions for simple modifications to cut down on extraneous or **ambient noise** that interferes with a child's ability to discriminate speech and important environmental sounds.

Strategies Related to the Family's Preferred Communication Mode. Children with hearing loss may be learning sign language, or families may prefer that a child concentrate more on learning speech and learning to use residual hearing; some families use both approaches. Many complex factors may determine the preferred mode of communication and the approach that is most successful for the child. A specialist can help ECE teachers understand these different approaches and can make practical suggestions regarding teaching and communicating with the child.

Information on and Demonstration of the Use of the Hearing Aid. A specialist (and a parent) can be very helpful in explaining the basic care, battery checks, insertion, and settings of the hearing aid. If there are problems with the aid, the DHH specialist can assist in referral to the audiologist. Today, such specialists are also called upon to support children with cochlear implants.

15-1i Behavior Specialists

As we have discussed often throughout this book, children who have behavior problems can present the most serious challenge to successful inclusion. When the strategies suggested here or recommended by an ECSE support facilitator are not sufficient, it may be helpful to bring in a behavior specialist.

Behavior specialists do not represent a clearly defined professional group. In many states they are unregulated. When they are licensed or certified, there is currently little consistency from region to region on the training and competencies required. However, the development of consistent credentials may occur in the years to come.

In most cases individuals who offer their services as behavior specialists are trained in traditional *behavior modification* approaches (see Chapter 5). Increasingly these individuals also incorporate functional behavior analysis and positive behavior support techniques. The following are typical services provided by a behavior specialist.

Careful Observation of the Child in Different Settings, Activities, and Times. As a result of careful observation and data collection, a behavior specialist can evaluate the frequency and intensity of challenging behavior, and conduct an analysis of antecedents and consequences of the behavior.

Designing a Behavior Intervention Plan. Using the data from the behavioral assessment and interviews with key individuals (ideally including a parent or caregiver), the specialist generates a functional analysis of the purpose and meaning of the behavior, including what triggers it and what reinforces or maintains the behavior. On this basis a specific behavior plan is drawn up. The plan may include certain changes in the child's environment, establishment of consistent ways of interacting with the child, and clear consequences for specific behavior. Behavior plans always require careful data collection and consistency as discussed in Chapter 5.

Assistance in Implementing the Plan. Ultimately, to be most effective, everyone who interacts with the child should implement the plan. One of the greatest barriers to effective use of behavior specialists is the impracticality of implementing elaborate behavior plans in programs with limited staff resources. Ideally, a behavior specialist will initially spend a significant amount of time demonstrating how the plan should be implemented and modifying aspects of the plan that are not feasible in a particular setting. Gradually the specialist should assist the staff in taking over responsibility for implementing the plan. The behavior specialist should also be responsible for determining if the plan is working and, in consultation with the child's intervention team, should make adjustments as needed.

15-2 Obtaining and Using Inclusion Support

ECE teachers should know how to contact specialists who can be of assistance in supporting young children with special needs. Often children's needs are complex, and no one individual has all the answers. This is why a *coordinated, team-based approach* is critical to successful inclusion.

This support team is not always readily available to an ECE teacher. It may be necessary to initiate requests for support and to make the assertion that the child has the *legal* right to these services. Unfortunately, in many areas of the United States there are significant shortages of many specialists. They often carry large caseloads and may work as itinerants covering a wide geographic area. Thus, ECE teachers may need to be persistent in their efforts to obtain services.

Once services have been obtained, however, another challenge often emerges. This is related to the intrusion and cumulative effect of specialists and consultants coming into the classroom. An ECE teacher must work with an ECSE specialist to coordinate and manage this team. Too many people going in and out the classroom will obviously become a very disruptive factor and in the end may not be effective. This list can serve as a simple guide for ECE professionals in obtaining and using inclusion support.

Suggestions for Obtaining and Using Inclusion Support

- **Identify sources of information and services:**

  Families
  Child's service coordinator (if child is under three)
  School district program specialist or teacher
  Social worker
  Therapist
  Speech-language specialist
  Occupational therapist
  Physical therapist
  Behavior specialist
  Disability specialist
  VI specialist
  DHH specialist
  Physical disabilities specialist
  Other professional or service provider
  Information about specific disabilities (from websites, the library, and various associations)

- **Be *assertive* about requesting information and services.** The child has a legal right to these services.
- **Establish *partnerships* with families and support personnel.** Your input is important!
- **Ask a specialist to *demonstrate*, not just talk and explain.**
- **Ask for *written* information and suggestions from the specialists.**
- **Use one-to-one assistants *appropriately*:**

  Clarify their expectations and role.
  Discourage one-to-one assistants from isolating and hovering over the child.
  Realize the assistant may have little or no training.

15-3 Working Effectively with Paraeducators

Effective inclusion of young children with special needs often necessitates working with a paraeducator (or paraprofessional) to assist the professional educator in making necessary accommodations and adaptations. The success of these instructional assistants depends not only on the skills and abilities of the paraeducators, but also on how well teachers and other licensed or certified professionals perform in the role of program managers.

It should be noted that IDEA 2004 uses, but does not define, the term *paraprofessional*. Nor does it define what paraprofessionals do. Given that the prefix *para* has been used to designate those who work with and assist licensed professionals in such fields as medicine and law (paramedics, paralegals), the National Resource Center for Paraprofessionals coined the term *paraeducator* to refer to someone who works alongside and under the supervision of a licensed or certified educator or other professional in an educational setting.

Paraeducators may be hired by school districts to provide support services in preschools or child development centers partnering with the district. In some cases, families at a private early childhood center may choose to hire an assistant to help their child. Other early childhood centers may hire their own paraeducators.

15-3a Early Educators as Program Managers

Licensed or credentialed early childhood educators who are provided with the services of a paraeducator will be expected, as the classroom leader, to perform the following managerial or supervisory functions.

Develop and Provide Specific Plans for Paraeducators to Follow. Paraeducators should not be expected to plan their own involvement in the daily routine of activities. They have not been trained to create or plan activity adaptations. Too often, teachers assume that paraeducators who have been assigned to assist certain children have sufficient training. The professionals who have been appropriately trained are responsible for providing activity plans with clear directions to paraeducators. These plans should be well described in writing. In short, supervision demands that job expectations be well defined and clearly communicated.

Devise and Manage Intervention (Instructional) Schedules. Although the daily program plan addresses the *what* and *how,* the schedule addresses the questions *when* and *where.* Successful use of paraeducators requires a detailed plan of their activities, including time and location.

Delegate Tasks Appropriately. The purpose of assigning paraeducators to inclusive programs is to free educators to do work that cannot be delegated such as planning activities, monitoring children's progress, and creating activity adaptations. No matter how many tasks a paraeducator can handle well, the ultimate responsibility for all children lies with the early childhood educator. The professional educator is accountable for the outcomes of the instructional activities.

Cook, Klein, and Chen (2016) offer the following list of some responsibilities that may be appropriately delegated.

- Preparing the room, including setting up centers, organizing materials needed for special projects, and locating daily supplies
- Greeting children and assisting with all routines
- Nurturing appropriate behavior, including working with misbehaviors acceptably and effectively
- Directing specific activities planned by the teacher
- Assisting children with eating and toileting
- Following specialists' instructions in helping to position and transport children
- Providing appropriate prompts to help ensure positive social integration
- Preparing, cataloging, and filing educational games and materials
- Preparing materials for art activities or snack
- Helping with end-of-the-day routines, including cleanup
- Cleaning and maintaining adaptive equipment
- Recording observations of children's performance

Take Care in Assigning a Paraeducator as a One-to-One Assistant. The assignment of a one-to-one assistant exclusively to a specific child, though often necessary, can have definite drawbacks. ECE teachers should not assume that an assistant has been

---

Helpful Hint

There is a tendency when paraeducators are assigned to help specific children in inclusive settings—as one-to-one assistants, for example—for an ECE teacher to avoid assuming responsibility for the development of the children with special needs. ECE teachers should continue to interact with these children individually and in group activities.

well trained to work with a child. Frequently, this is not the case. Another disadvantage is that the child often becomes very attached to the assistant because of the intensity and exclusivity of the relationship and may avoid interacting with the children and other adults.

In some cases, as with a child who runs away, who is extremely aggressive or self-injurious, or who is medically fragile and technology dependent, it is necessary to assign a one-to-one assistant—especially if the alternative is removing the child from the program.

Assess the Strengths and Needs of the Paraeducator. Once tasks are delegated by an ECE teacher and performed by the paraeducator, the teacher must observe carefully to determine the paraeducator's knowledge and skills, and the areas in which additional training may be needed. Although some specific training has been developed, many paraeducators have had no formal training. Even when such formal training has been obtained, it may not have included content related to children with special needs.

On the other hand, some paraeducators, though perhaps not formally trained, may have as much experience as the teacher. These can be challenging situations. In such cases the teacher must value and use the assistant's expertise while at the same time maintaining a leadership role in the classroom. Use of a highly collaborative model will be extremely important.

In some cases paraeducators are hired because of their cultural and linguistic backgrounds. They can play a critical role in connecting to children and families who share their culture.

Early educators can match their supervisory style with the qualities of paraeducators. For example, less mature or inexperienced paraeducators may need direct supervision whereas those with more experience might benefit from increased opportunities at self-reflection and the chance to direct their own learning.

Monitoring performance does not mean "hovering over" paraeducators as they work. Instead, the early educator can encourage independence and initiative by focusing on the outcomes of intervention rather than on perfect execution of intervention techniques and by valuing the ideas and observations of the assistant.

Create a System for Timely and Constructive Feedback. It takes time to develop skills. Paraeducators cannot learn everything at once. Early educators must have sufficient patience to allow paraeducators to practice. Feedback must focus on specific task behaviors and not on personalities. It should be descriptive, not evaluative or judgmental, and it should describe observable events or behaviors rather than being based on opinion.

Effective coaches provide specific feedback offering essential information so that changes can be made. For example, it is not helpful to tell paraeducators that they must become better organized. Instead, be specific and make such statements as, "It helps to place the crayons and scissors in buckets between the children rather than placing them in the middle of the table." Coaching and modeling appropriate behavior may be needed to assist paraeducators in developing their potential.

Recognize and Reward Quality Performance. Daily recognition of quality performance is essential. Like feedback, words of recognition should be specific so the paraeducator knows exactly what actions you are reinforcing. Consider the following two statements:

1. "Mrs. Garcia, I really appreciated how you jumped in to help out today."
2. "You jumped in just in time to help the children clean up the spilled grape juice. What a mess that would have been if the children had walked in it."

Of course, both comments are positive, but the second one tells the paraeducator exactly what type of action to repeat in the future. It also lets the paraeducator know that the early educator is observant and takes responsibility for the total situation.

Words of praise not only must be specific, but they must be sincere. If they just become rote words spoken at the end of the day, their learning and rewarding value will diminish. Feedback that could be taken as negative must always be given in private away from the eager ears of children or other adults.

15-3b Early Educators as Coaches

Most paraeducators are trained on the job. Even when paraeducators have had training, they must learn much about the situation in which they are placed. Therefore, early educators should learn to provide coaching on a daily basis. The challenge in the case of children with special needs, especially when they have unique or intense needs, is that often early childhood educators are also just learning strategies that are effective with these children. Nevertheless, ECE teachers should do their best to pass along this information to paraeducators, especially if it is essential information from the family or a specialist.

To do so, early educators must be skilled in the ability to evaluate the unique needs of their children and of their particular program. They must also be able to recognize the skills paraeducators bring to the job and the skills they will need to succeed.

Finally, coaching is only successful in an atmosphere of trust and experimentation. The goal of coaching is to assist paraeducators to make optimal use of their strengths and resources.

15-3c Early Educators as Communicators

Effective communication between early educators and the paraeducators working under their supervision is critical to success. Both paraeducators and early educators must learn to communicate their expectations and experiences.

An early educator's expectations must be consistent, clear, and realistic. Paraeducators must understand the outcomes or goals desired for each child. They should be involved in individual planning meetings. They must be instructed in which behavior management techniques are used for each student and why they are different for different children. A system can be developed so that paraeducators regularly inform the supervising teacher of unique observations they have made of children while working with them.

Meetings Must Be Conducted on a Regular Basis. As early educators and paraeducators are expected to function as a team, regular meetings are needed to communicate effectively and provide for sufficient planning time. Such meetings provide the opportunity to discuss progress toward the outcomes or goals for children, plot instructional strategies, solve problems, or resolve any existing conflicts. Programs must be creative in fitting in time for regular meetings. Use of practicum students, volunteers, and parents may be helpful in providing coverage during staff meetings. Whole-day programs are sometimes able to use naptime one day a week. Occasionally well-funded programs have a half day each week devoted to meeting time. Unfortunately, many programs rely on personnel giving up personal time at the beginning or end of the day to facilitate this critical communication. Despite the difficulty, the value of regular staff meetings cannot be overestimated.

Paraeducators Should Be Evaluated on a Regular Basis. Building in regular evaluation and feedback on a formal basis makes providing constructive feedback and dealing with problems a much easier task. It also provides an additional opportunity to discuss the implementation of programs and strategies for specific children. Another helpful strategy is to encourage paraeducators to evaluate themselves. See Figure 15-2 for an example of a self-evaluation form.

SELF-EVALUATION CHECKLIST FOR PARAEDUCATORS			
How consistently do I do the following?	*Rarely*	*Sometimes*	*Usually*
1. Ask questions when I am unsure of my responsibility.	1	2	3
2. Observe and understand the strategies used by the teacher with specific children.	1	2	3
3. Make sure I understand the plan for the day and the details for implementing specific activities and lessons.	1	2	3
4. Offer my assistance when there is an apparent need for help, even if it is not technically my assigned role.	1	2	3
5. Observe children closely and note their likes, dislikes, strengths, and limitations.	1	2	3
6. Provide children with choices.	1	2	3
7. Praise children for their efforts and appropriate behavior.	1	2	3
8. Listen carefully to what children say, and respond appropriately.	1	2	3
9. Make sure I understand how to use children's adaptive equipment.	1	2	3
10. Use effective behavior management strategies without being negative or punitive.	1	2	3
11. Allow children ample time to respond or perform a task on their own.	1	2	3
12. Accept constructive criticism and feedback without becoming upset.	1	2	3

Things I would like to work on or learn more about:

_____

_____

Figure 15-2 Self-Evaluation Checklist for Paraeducators

⌄ Professional Resource Download

15-4 Early Educators, Paraeducators, and Disability Specialists as a Collaborative Team

One of the keys to success in working with children with special needs is the creation of effective teams. It is nearly impossible for a single individual, no matter how skilled, to meet all the complex needs of a child who has a disability. Ideally, early educators, paraeducators, and disability specialists work together as a team to provide optimum support for the child. Parents must also be part of the team. To function as a successful team, these educators and specialists must foster an atmosphere of respect built on trust and good communication. The following characteristics are necessary for the team to function optimally:

- Team members must view themselves as part of a team.
- Team members must view their own involvement as essential to the team's success.
- Team members must be willing to work together.
- Team members must be focused on clearly defined goals.
- Team members must understand their individual role in the team effort.

Photo 15-2 A teacher meets with paraeducators and an inclusion support specialist.

- Team members must be given the opportunity to express themselves within an environment perceived to be psychologically safe.

15-4a Collaborative Problem Solving

A critical part of working as a team is engaging in problem solving. This can often be an emotional and stressful experience. Problem solving is a *skill* that requires a specific step-by-step process if it is to be successful (Heron & Harris, 2000). The following is an example of a step-by-step problem-solving process:

1. Clarify the issues and define the problem. Define the problem clearly. Often different members of the team see the problem differently. Understand each other's perspectives. All participants *must* define the problem as they see it. Don't assume everyone agrees with your perception of the problem. No single team member should consistently lead these discussions and share a perception first. Although it may be tempting to do so, do *not* try to generate solutions to the problem at this early stage!

Photo 15-3 An early childhood special educator discusses the inclusion support plan with a parent.

2. Describe the steps to be followed so that everyone knows what to expect during the problem-solving process.
3. Write down the problem. Obtain consensus from the group. Write the problem on chart paper so everyone can see it and edit it. Identify conflicts and differences of opinion.
4. Brainstorm possible solutions. Everyone must contribute. All ideas are acceptable during this activity. Write ideas down on chart paper or the board so the group can review and edit. It is extremely important that a consultant or facilitator *not* become invested in a particular solution, even if she is convinced that it is the best one.
5. Allow a practitioner to select a solution to try. For example, to prevent or manage a behavior challenge, the teacher may decide to begin with a careful A-B-C analysis (see Chapter 5). Whoever has the responsibility for implementing the plan must have the opportunity to choose which approach will be tried first.
6. Produce an action plan. What must be done to implement the solution? Who, what, where, by when? The action plan must supply this information. Figure 15-3 presents a simple action plan form.

Action Plan for Inclusion Support Team

Date: _____ **Name of Student:** _____

Team members present:

Name: _____ Role: _____

Name: _____ Role: _____

Name: _____ Role: _____

Name: _____ Role: _____

Purpose of action plan / desired outcome:

Procedure / intervention to be implemented:

What?

1.

2.

3.

4.

Who is responsible? _____

By what date? _____

Follow-up plan:

Date and time of follow-up meeting with team if necessary

Date: _____ Time: _____ Persons:

      1.   3.

      2.   4.

EVALUATION: Were strategies useful? Explain below:

Figure 15-3 Simple Action Plan Form

❯ **Professional Resource Download**

7. Evaluate success. Meet together to evaluate the outcome of implementing the action plan. Try to maintain a neutral position rather than investing in a particular outcome. If the action wasn't effective, select another solution from the original brainstorming session, or come up with new suggestions. An approach that is not successful must not be seen as someone's failure.

   If a solution *was* effective, determine if other challenges need to be addressed.

8. Recycle the problem-solving process, if necessary. Follow the same steps to address new or different problems.

Summary

Oftentimes, early educators and other licensed professionals have not been well prepared to take on their role as managers of a program team. Early educators who find themselves uncomfortable in this new role should realize that program management and team coordination are challenging areas of expertise. They will be provided with opportunities to enhance their skills in the various areas mentioned in this brief chapter.

Read–Reflect–Discuss
Mark's Story

Mark's mother Amy is anxious to enroll her son Mark, a toddler, at the local child care center. However, Amy is concerned about how Mark will adjust to the classroom because he is not walking and he often chokes on table foods during mealtime. Mark has been diagnosed with Down syndrome. The physical therapist has assured Amy that he will be walking within the next year, but is developmentally not ready at the present time.

Amy calls the center's director and after discussing her concerns, they agree that Mark will need extra help in the classroom. An assistant will help him as he learns to pull to stand, cruise, and walk. The assistant will also observe him carefully during snack time and mealtimes so that he does not choke on large pieces of food.

These concerns are shared with Mark's service coordinator at the agency responsible for overseeing his educational services. The team agrees that a one-to-one aide will be hired to assist Mark during his hours at the child care center.

Finding an assistant is difficult, and Mark needs to start child care right away because his mother is returning to work. A temporary nursing assistant is hired because of Mark's difficulties with choking. The assistant is a good caregiver, but she knows little about the education of young children. She often spends long periods of time cleaning Mark after he plays with paint. She does not encourage him to play with other children, and she takes such good care of Mark that his teachers see no reason to interfere. Thus, the assistant's level and type of care result in segregating Mark from his peers and teachers. On a positive note, he has no choking episodes while she is present.

Before long, an assistant with a background in child development is hired. At this time the team agrees that an inclusion specialist should be brought in to provide support to Mark's teachers and to supervise the training of the new assistant. The goal is to meet Mark's specific needs in ways that will allow him to become an active participant of the class, while avoiding isolating or overprotecting him.

Prior to the assistant's first day with Mark, the inclusion specialist asks for a meeting with the center teachers, director, Amy, the new assistant, and Mark's mother. The meeting agenda includes a review of how Mark has adjusted to the classroom, how the teachers feel about having Mark in their room, what the nursing assistant's role had been, and what the teacher sees as her needs to include Mark in her classroom.

The general consensus is that Mark is adjusting well to the classroom routine, moving around independently by crawling, and enjoying the large group activities. At the same time everyone agrees that Mark had been isolated by the first assistant and not allowed to explore as much as he was indicating that he wanted to. The teachers say they felt uncomfortable approaching him because the first assistant had "always been there first." They felt they had little opportunity or reason to interact with him.

By the end of the meeting a specific plan has been developed, carefully describing the specific responsibilities of the one-to-one assistant. During mealtime she will pay close attention to Mark for any signs of choking, but she should encourage independent eating. During other times she will assist Mark in moving from one place to another when necessary, but she should also encourage his interactions with other children.

The plan is successful. Teachers and children get to know Mark better and enjoy him. Mark becomes more confident. By the end of the year he is beginning to walk independently, and he no longer chokes on his food. Perhaps even more importantly, Mark develops some good friends and playmates at the center and the one-to-one assistant starts to relax!

Read–Reflect–Discuss Questions

1. When a new one-to-one assistant is assigned to a child in your class, how would you orient this paraeducator to your classroom? What would your preference be in how the assistant would function in your classroom?
2. What steps would you take to clarify the roles and lines of communication for the one-to-one aide, yourself (the teacher), and mother?
3. How would you adapt the environment, activity or routine, materials and/or instruction in preparation to fade out the one-to-one assistant?

Key Terms

adaptive equipment
ambient noise
audiogram
deaf and hard of hearing (DHH) specialist
fine motor skills
fluency disorders
gross motor skills

inclusion support specialists
kinesthetic sensation
language disorders
orientation and mobility (O&M) specialist
proprioception
protective reflexes

speech production (articulation) disorders
trailing techniques
vestibular sensation
visual field
voice disorder

Helpful Resources

Working with the Intervention Team

Heron, T. E., & Harris, K. C. (2000). *The educational consultant: Helping professionals, parents and mainstreamed students* (4th ed.). Austin, TX: Pro-Ed.

Working with Paraeducators

Ashbaker, B. Y., & Morgan, J. (2013). *Paraprofessionals in the classroom: A survival guide*. Columbus, OH: Pearson.

Ashbaker, B. Y., & Morgan, J. (2015). *101 ideas for supervising your paraprofessional*. Amazon: Kindle Edition.

Causton-Theoharis, J., & Kluth, P. (2009). *The paraprofessional's handbook for effective support in inclusive classrooms.* Baltimore, MD: Paul H. Brookes.

Doyle, M. B. (2008). *The paraprofessional's guide to the inclusive classroom: Working as a team* (3rd ed.). Baltimore, MD: Paul H. Brookes.

Giangreco, M. F., Yuan, S., McKenzie, B., Cameron, P., & Fialka, J. (2005). "Be careful what you wish for...": Five reasons to be concerned about the assignment of individual paraprofessionals. *Teaching Exceptional Children, 37*(5), 28–34.

National Education Association. *Paraeducator Roles and Responsibilities.* Retrieved April 10, 2016 from www.nea.org/home/20783.htm.

Pickett, A. L., & Gerlach, K. (2003). *Supervising paraeducators in educational settings: A team approach.* Austin, TX: Pro-Ed.

Styer, C., & Fitzgerald, S. (2015). *Effective strategies for working with paraeducators.* Kirkland, WA: Styer-Fitzgerald Publishing, Inc.

Appendix A

Selected Questions from Commonly Asked Questions about Child Care Centers and the Americans with Disabilities Act (ADA)

For a complete list of questions see www.ada.gov/childqanda.htm

Q: What are the basic requirements of Title III (for private child care centers)?

- Centers cannot exclude children with disabilities from their programs unless their presence would pose a *direct threat* to the health or safety of others or require a *fundamental alteration* of the program.
- Centers have to make *reasonable modifications* to their policies and practices to integrate children, parents, and guardians with disabilities into their programs unless doing so would constitute a *fundamental alteration*.
- Centers must provide appropriate auxiliary aids and services needed for *effective communication* with children or adults with disabilities, when doing so would not constitute an undue burden.
- Centers must generally make these facilities accessible to people with disabilities. Existing facilities are subject to the *readily achievable* standard for barrier removal, while newly constructed facilities and any altered portions of existing facilities must be *fully assessable*.

Q: How do I decide whether a child with a disability belongs in my program?

- Child care centers cannot just assume a child's disabilities are too severe for the child to be integrated successfully into the center's child care program. The center must make an *individualized assessment* about whether it can meet the particular needs of the child without fundamentally altering its program. In making this assessment, the caregiver must not react to unfounded preconceptions or stereotypes about what children with disabilities can or cannot do, or how much assistance they may require. Instead, the caregiver should talk to the parents or guardians and any other professionals (such as educators or health care professionals) who work with the child in other contexts....

Q: Our center specializes in "group child care." Can we reject the child just because she needs individualized attention?

- No. Most children will need individualized attention occasionally. If a child who needs one-to-one attention due to a disability can be integrated without fundamentally altering the child care program, the child cannot be excluded solely because the child needs one-to-one care.... But the ADA generally does not require senders to hire additional staff or provide constant one-to-one supervision of a particular child with a disability.

Q: If an older child has delayed speech or developmental disabilities, can we place that child in the infant or toddler room?

- Generally, no. Under most circumstances, children with disabilities must be placed in their age-appropriate classroom....

Q: We diaper young children, but we have a policy that we will not accept children more than three years of age who need diapering. Can we reject children older than three who need diapering because of a disability?

- Generally no. Centers that provide personal services such as diapering or toileting assistance for young children must reasonably modify their policies and provide diapering services for other children needed due to a disability....

Appendix B
Skill Profile (0–72 Months)

	GROSS-MOTOR SKILLS CULMINATING ACTIVITIES	FINE-MOTOR SKILLS	PREACADEMIC SKILLS	SELF-HELP SKILLS —	MUSIC/ART/STORY SKILLS	SOCIAL SKILLS AND PLAY SKILLS	UNDERSTANDING LANGUAGE	ORAL LANGUAGE
0–12 MONTHS	Sits without support; crawls; pulls self to standing and stands unaided; walks with aid; rolls a ball in imitation of adult	Reaches, grasps, puts object in mouth; picks things up with thumb and one finger (pincer grasp); transfers object from one hand to other hand; drops and picks up toy	Looks directly at adult's face; tracks objects (follows them smoothly with eyes); imitates gestures—e.g., pat-a-cake, peekaboo, bye-bye; puts block in, takes block out of container; finds block hidden under cup	Feeds self cracker: munching, not sucking; holds cup with two hands, drinks with assistance; holds out arms and legs while being dressed	Fixes gaze on pictures in book	Smiles spontaneously; responds differentially to strangers and familiar people; pays attention to own name; responds to "no"; copies simple actions of others	Looks at people who talk to him; responds differentially to variety of sounds—e.g., phone, vacuum, closing doors; responds to simple directions accompanied by gestures—e.g., "come," "give," "get"	Makes different vowel sounds; makes different consonant–vowel combinations; vocalizes to the person who has talked to him; uses intonation patterns that sound like phrases—e.g., intonations that sound like scolding, asking, telling
12–24 MONTHS	Walks alone; walks backward; picks up object without falling; pulls toy; seats self in child's chair; walks up and down stairs with aid	Builds tower of three cubes; puts four rings on stick; places five pegs in peg board; turns pages two or three at a time; scribbles	Follows one direction involving familiar actions and objects—e.g., "Give me (toy)," "Show me (body part)," "Get a (familiar object)"; completes three-piece form board; matches similar objects	Uses spoon, spilling little; drinks from cup, one hand, unassisted; chews food; removes garment; zips, unzips large zipper; indicates toilet needs	Moves to music; looks at pictures in book, patting, pointing to, or naming objects or people; paints with whole arm movement, shifts hands, scrubs, makes strokes	Recognizes self in mirror or picture; refers to self by name; plays by self, initiates own play activities; imitates adult behaviors in play; plays with water and sand; loads, carries, dumps; helps put things away	Responds to specific words by showing what was named—e.g., toys, family members, clothing, body parts; responds to simple directions given without gestures—e.g., "go," "sit," "find," "run," "walk"	Asks for items by name; answers "What's that?" with name of object; tells about objects or experiences with words used together (two or three words)—e.g., "More juice"

(continued)

GROSS-MOTOR SKILLS CULMINATING ACTIVITIES	FINE-MOTOR SKILLS	PREACADEMIC SKILLS	SELF-HELP SKILLS	MUSIC/ART/STORY SKILLS	SOCIAL SKILLS AND PLAY SKILLS	UNDERSTANDING LANGUAGE	ORAL LANGUAGE
24–36 MONTHS Runs forward well; jumps in place, two feet together; stands on one foot, with aid; walks on tiptoe; kicks ball forward; throws ball, without direction	Strings four large beads; turns pages singly; snips with scissors; holds crayon with thumb and fingers, not fist; uses one hand consistently in most activities; imitates circular, vertical, horizontal strokes	Matches shapes; stacks five rings on peg, in order; demonstrates number concepts to two (i.e., selects set of one or two, can tell how many one or two are)	Uses spoon, no spilling; gets drink unassisted; uses straw; opens door by turning handle; puts on/takes off coat; washes/dries hands with assistance	Plays near other children; watches other children, joins briefly in their play; defends own possessions; engages in domestic play; symbolically uses objects, self in play; builds with blocks in simple lines	Responds by selecting correct item—big vs. little objects, one vs. one more object; identifies objects by their use—e.g., "Show me what mother cooks on" by showing stove or "Show me what you wear on your feet" by showing shoe	Asks questions; answers "Where is it?" with prepositional phrases—e.g., "in the box," "on the table"; answers "What do you do with a ball?"—e.g., "throw," "catch"; tells about something with functional sentences that carry meaning—e.g., "Me go store" or "Me hungry now"	Joins vocabulary words together in two-word phrases. Gives first and last name. Ask "what" and "where" questions. Makes negative statements (e.g., "Can't open it."). Shows frustration at not being understood. Sustains conversation for two or three turns.
36–48 MONTHS Runs around obstacles; walks on a line; balances on one foot for five seconds; hops on one foot; pushes, pulls, steers wheeled toys; rides (i.e., steers and pedals) trike; uses slide without assistance; jumps over 6-inch (15-cm)-high object, landing on both feet together; throws ball with direction; catches ball bounced to him	Builds tower of nine cubes; drives nails and pegs; copies circle; imitates cross	Matches six colors; makes tower of five blocks, graduated in size; does seven-piece puzzle; counts to five in imitation of adults; demonstrates number concept to three	Pours well from pitcher; spreads substances with knife; buttons/unbuttons large buttons; washes hands unassisted; cleans nose when reminded; uses toilet independently; follows classroom routine with minimum teacher assistance; knows own sex; knows own age; knows own last name; participates in simple group activity—e.g., sings, claps, dances; chooses picture books, points to fine detail, enjoys repetition; paints with some wrist action, makes dots, lines, circular strokes; rolls, pounds, squeezes, pulls clay material	Knows phrases of songs; listens to short simple stories (five minutes); painting—names own picture, not always recognizable; demands variety of color; draws head of person and one other part; manipulates clay materials—e.g., rolls balls, snakes, cookies, etc.	Joins in play with other children, begins to interact; shares toys, takes turns with assistance; begins dramatic play, acting out whole scenes—e.g., traveling, playing house, pretending to be animals; responds to "Put it in" and "Put it on"; responds to "Put it beside" and "Put it under"; responds to commands involving two objects—e.g., "Give me the ball and the shoe"; responds to commands involving two actions—e.g., "Give me the cup and put the shoe on the floor"; responds by selecting correct item—e.g., hard vs. soft objects; responds to "Walk fast" by increased pace, and to "Walk slowly" by decreased pace	Answers "Which one do you want?" by naming it; Answers "If . . . what/when" questions—e.g., "If you had a penny, what would you do?" "What do you do when you're hungry?"; answers questions about function—e.g., "What are books for?" Asks for or tells about with grammatically correct sentences—e.g., "Can I go to the store?" "I want a big cookie"	Talks in sentences of three or more words, which form agent-action-object ("I see the ball") or agent-action-location (Daddy sit on chair"). Tells about past experiences. Uses "–s" on nouns to indicate plurals. Uses "–ed" on verbs to include past tense. Refers to self using pronouns/or me. Repeats at least one nursery rhyme; can sing a song. Speech is understandable to strangers, but there are still some sound errors.

(continued)

GROSS-MOTOR SKILLS CULMINATING ACTIVITIES	FINE-MOTOR SKILLS	PREACADEMIC SKILLS	SELF-HELP SKILLS	MUSIC/ART/STORY SKILLS	SOCIAL SKILLS AND PLAY SKILLS	UNDER-STANDING LANGUAGE	ORAL LANGUAGE
48–60 MONTHS Walks backward heel-to-toe; jumps forward 10 times, without falling; walks up/down stairs alone, alternating feet; turns somersault	Cuts on a line continuously; copies cross; copies square; prints a few capital letters	Points to and names six basic colors; points to and names three shapes; matches related common objects—e.g., shoe, sock, foot; apple, orange, banana; demonstrates number concept to four or five	Cuts food with a knife—e.g., sandwich, celery; laces shoes; knows own city/street; follows instructions given to group	Sings entire songs; recites nursery rhyme; "reads" from pictures (i.e., tells story); recognizes story and retells simple facts; painting—makes and names recognizable pictures; draws a person with two to six parts	Plays and interacts with other children; dramatic play—closer to reality, attention to detail, time, and space; plays dress-up; builds complex structures with blocks	Responds by showing penny, nickel, dime; responds to command involving three actions—e.g., "Give me the cup, put the shoe on the floor, and hold the pencil in your hand"	Asks "How?" questions; answers verbally to "Hi!" and "How are you?"; tells about something using past tense and future tense; tells about something using conjunctions to string words and phrases together—e.g., "I have a cat and a dog and a fish"
60–72 MONTHS Runs lightly on toes; walks a balance beam; can cover 6 feet, 6 inches (2 m) hopping; skips; jumps rope; skates	Cuts out simple shapes; copies triangle; traces diamond; copies first name; prints numerals 1–5; colors within lines; has adult grasp of pencil; has handedness well established (i.e., child is left or right handed)	Sorts objects on one dimension—i.e., by size or by color or by shape; does 15-piece puzzle; copies block design; names some letters; names some numerals; names penny, nickel, dime, quarter; counts by rote to 10; can tell what number comes next	Dresses self completely; learns to distinguish left from right; ties bow; brushes teeth unassisted; crosses street safely; relates clock time to daily schedule	Recognizes rhyme; acts out stories; draws a person with head, trunk, legs, arms, and features; pastes and glues appropriately; models objects with clay	Chooses own friend(s); plays simple table games; plays competitive games; engages in cooperative play with other children involving group decisions, role assignments, fair play; uses construction toys to make things—e.g., house of Legos, car of rig-a-jig	See preacademic skills	Child will have acquired basic grammatical structures, including plurals, verb tenses, and conjunctions; following this developmental ability, the child practices with increasingly complex descriptions and conversations

The above items are selected from *The Sequenced Inventory of Communication Development*, University of Washington Press, 1975. This profile was prepared by the communication disorders specialists Linda Lynch, Jane Rieke, Sue Soltman, and teachers Donna Hardman and Mary O'Conor. The Communication Program was funded initially as a part of the Model Preschool Center for Handicapped Children by Grant No. OEG-072-5371 U.S. Office of Education, Program Development Branch, BEH: Washington, DC, at the Experimental Education Unit (WJ-10) of the College of Education and Child Development and Mental Retardation Center, University of Washington, Seattle, Washington

Appendix C
Sample Lesson Plan with Adaptations

The Very Hungry Caterpillar

by Eric Carle
Adapted Lesson Plan

Grade level: Preschool ages 3–5

Domain Areas: Language Art, Mathematics, Science, and Visual Performance

Topics: Insects; Foods; Counting (1 to 5); Life Cycle of the Butterfly

Behavioral Objectives (Goals):

- Students will retell the story.
- Student will name the insects and foods in the book.
- Student will count/recognize numbers 1 to 5.
- Student will create an art project.
- Students will identify the life cycle of a butterfly.
- Students will reflect on their own lives (what they know about insects and food).

Lesson Plan

Description of the Activities:

1. Introducing the book: Children will be introduced to the book by the front cover. There will be some prereading questions: "What do you think this book is about?" "What do you know about caterpillars and butterflies?"
2. Presenting the story to children on multiple days: Teacher reads the book in multiple ways by using the book alone, the flannel board story, and/or the hand puppets.
3. Reviewing the story: Teacher helps children to retell the story by using the book alone, the flannel board story, and/ or hand puppets.
4. Creating an art project (egg carton caterpillar):
   - Preparation: Teacher cuts one strip of six cups from the egg carton (before craft time).
   - Students paint the cups.
   - Let dry overnight then teacher pokes two holes in the top of the first cup.
   - Let students poke both ends of the pipe cleaner from inside the cup through the holes.
   - Glue the wiggly eyes on the head.
5. Completing a worksheet on the lifecycle of a butterfly:
   - Students cut out the four pictures of the lifecycle.
   - Students glue the pictures in sequential order (egg, caterpillar, cocoon, butterfly).

Materials Needed:

- *The Very Hungry Caterpillar* by Eric Carle
- Adaptive book, *The Very Hungry Caterpillar*, including pictures/icons of foods, numbers, caterpillar, cocoon, and butterfly
- Flannel board story of *The Very Hungry Caterpillar*
- Hand puppets for *The Very Hungry Caterpillar*

- Simple worksheet found online for life cycle of a butterfly with four sequence pictures (egg, caterpillar, cocoon, butterfly)
- Art project: cardboard egg cartoon, tempera paint, paintbrush, pipe cleaner, wiggly eyes, glue

Criteria for Evaluation:

- Students engage in listening to the story.
- Students respond to teacher's questions.
- Students retell the story.
- Students finish their art project.
- Students finish butterfly life cycle worksheet.

Activity Adaptations
Activities 1–3: Introducing, Presenting, and Reviewing the Book
Adapt the Environment:

- Have student sit at the front closer to the teacher or next to a good friend.
- Review circle time expectation before the activities.
- Give verbal/visual prompts for circle time expectations for children who get distracted.
- Recognize and encourage students who are on task and meeting circle time expectations—in other words, catch them being good.

Adapt Activity or Routine:

- Use sign language, pictures/icons, puppets or real objects for insects, foods, and numbers.

Adapt Materials:

- Use a big book.
- Use an adapted book with pictures/icons of the insects, foods, and numbers, which can give all students a picture/icon to help increase awareness, attention, and participation. Students can then give their picture/icon to the teacher when it is named.
- Provide adapted seating such cube chairs, stools, and Rifton chairs, especially for children who need postural stability.
- Give students who are easily distracted their own copy of the book so they may follow along.

Adapt Requirements of Instruction:

- Provide a fidget toy to help increase attention span.
- Provide instructions verbally and visually by using sign language and pictures/icons.
- Simplify questions and allow more time for students to respond.
- Allow children to respond in a variety of ways other than verbally—by pointing, using eye gaze, or giving a picture/icon, gestures, or sign language.
- Retell the story in a small group with fewer students to provide more opportunities to practice.

Activity 4: Art Project (egg carton caterpillar)
Adapt the Equipment:

- Use adapted chairs for correct posture.
- Provide footrests under chairs using books or a ream of paper to stabilize the student.
- Use a slant board with the egg carton taped to the board.

Adapt Activity or Routine:

- Allow students to stand up at the table instead of sitting down.
- Pair two children together to do the activity (one with disability and one without) to encourage peer interaction, sharing, and imitation.

Adapt Materials:

- Enlarge the paintbrush by building up the handle or using larger paintbrushes.
- Cut a hole in a large sponge so the paint cup fits inside—this stabilizes the paint cup so it does not tip over.

- Use individual space/boundaries at the table with a placemat or a tray.
- Stabilize the egg carton by taping it to the table or tray.
- Teacher enlarges the holes in the first cup to make it easier to place the pipe cleaner in.
- Enlarge the pipe cleaner by using a puffy/thicker pipe cleaner.
- Ask a student who gets overwhelmed to join the activity when there are less children at the table.

Adapt Requirements or Instruction:

- Make a picture mini-sequence for the art project (paint caterpillar, string pipe cleaner, glue eyes or paint, string, glue).
- Provide instructions verbally and visually by using sign language and pictures/icons.
- Use a first–then visual support for students who have difficulty maintaining attention, that is, *first* art project, *then* favorite toy.
- Decrease the number of steps, that is, have the student only paint the caterpillar.
- Teacher draws eyes on the head so the student has a visual of where to glue the eyes.
- Enhance the poked holes by drawing a black circle around them so students can better see where to place the pipe cleaners.
- Allow more time to complete the art project.

Activity 5: Worksheet of the Lifecycle of a Butterfly

Adaptive Equipment:

- Use adapted scissors such as spring-loaded scissors, loop scissors, push-down tabletop scissors (for using one hand).
- Use larger glue sticks to simplify a student's ability to grasp.
- Use smaller squeeze bottles for glue to simplify a student's ability to squeeze.
- Allow student to use a brush to apply glue.

Adapt Activity or Routine:

- For students who tire easily or who have difficulty attending, do the cutting one day and the gluing the next day.
- Demonstrate each step of the process by creating a model in front of the students.
- Use the model as a visual to help children sequence correctly.
- Draw the numerals 1, 2, 3, 4 in the blank boxes so students know how to sequence their pictures.
- Use a first–then visual support for students who have difficulty maintaining attention, that is, *first* worksheet, *then* favorite toy.

Adapt Materials:

- Enlarge the worksheet so students with a mild vision impairment can see the paper better.
- Print worksheet on heavier paper such as card stock to make it easier to hold and cut.
- Enhance the worksheet by outlining where the student should cut with a highlighter.

Adapt Requirements or Instruction:

- Allow more time for student to finish the worksheet.
- Make a picture mini-sequence for the worksheet (cut, put in order, glue).
- Provide instructions verbally and visually by using sign language and pictures/icons.
- Simplify by allowing student to match cutout pictures to the same picture—turns the activity into a matching activity instead of a sequence activity.
- For a student who is not able to continuously cut across the paper, give him a half-inch strip of paper so he can make individual snips. Then have the sequence already cut for him, and he can either match or place the pictures in order with glue.

(Original lesson plan from Betty Tseng, Early Childhood Special Education Teacher, Franklin McKinley School District, San Jose, California.)

Appendix D

Sample Individualized Education Program (IEP) and IEP Summary Form

The Individualized Education Program (IEP) is a written document that is developed for each eligible child with a disability. The Part B regulations specify, at 34 CFR §§300.320-300.328, the procedures that school districts must follow to develop, review, and revise the IEP for each child. The following document sets out the IEP content that those regulations require.

Student information:

Last name: Montgomery	First name: John	IEP Date 5/31/17
Birthdate: 5/31/13	Age: 4	Gender: Male
Native Language: English	Disability: Multiple Disabilities	

A statement of the child's present levels of academic achievement and functional performance including:

- How the child's disability affects the child's involvement and progress in the general education curriculum (i.e., the same curriculum as for nondisabled children) **or** for preschool children, as appropriate, how the disability affects the child's participation in appropriate activities. [34 CFR §300.320(a)(1)]

John's disability affects his pre-academic skills and communication language skills.

Strengths/Preferences/Interests: careful most of the time, persistent, likes to be independent, confident, and courageous; supportive family, follows rules he understands

Concerns of Parent Relevant to Educational Progress: academic skills, motor skills, self-help skills, communication skills, and increase attention span

Pre-Academic/Academic/Functional Skills: John is not yet matching objects by color, shapes, or size. His skills are at a 19-month level. John enjoys scribbling but does not yet draw a vertical or horizontal line or circular strokes—12- to 24-month level

Communication Development: Due to the difficulties with his mouth, John drools and has difficulty keeping his tongue in his mouth, which is a factor in his delayed speech sounds and poor understanding of what he says. He has 10–20 words and is hard to understand—16- to 20-month level

Gross/Fine Motor Development: John can walk up/down stairs independently. For fine motor skills, he can open doors, unscrew lid on the jar. He has difficulty opening and closing scissors and picking up small objects—16-to 20-month level.

U.S. Department of Education   **Model Form: Individualized Education Program**
Office of Special Education and Rehabilitative Services,
Office of Special Education Programs

> **Social Emotional/Behavioral:** When he doesn't want to do something, he usually shoves the item off the table and walks away. He gets mad rather quickly. But, parents seem to be able to calm him down quickly.
>
> **Adaptive/Daily Living Skills:** John uses the toilet when asked, washes/dries his hands, gets a drink by himself—23-month level. He has difficulty getting himself dressed due to his fine motor difficulties.
>
> **Health:** John has Apert syndrome, which affects the structure of his skull, face, his hands and feet (webbed), and his hearing. He failed a hearing test in November of this year and passed the vision test. He will be having surgery next month.

A statement of measurable annual goals, including academic and functional goals designed to:

- Meet the child's needs that result from the child's disability to enable the child to be involved in and make progress in the general education curriculum. [34 CFR §300.320(a)(2)(i)(A)]
- Meet each of the child's other educational needs that result from the child's disability. [34 CFR §300.320(a)(2)(i)(B)]

> **Area of Need: Receptive Language Goal 1:** By 5/31/18, John will correctly point to 60 named objects and pictures when presented with a chart with four pictures in four of five times correctly.
>
> **Area of Need: Expressive Language Goal 2:** By 5/31/18, John will spontaneously use verbal language or gestures to express his basic wants and needs in the classroom on four of five occasions.
>
> **Area of Need: Prewriting Goal 3:** By 5/31/18 John will be able to copy a vertical/horizontal lines and circle strokes with an adapted writing instrument on four of five occasions.
>
> **Area of Need: Oral Motor Skills Goal 4:** By 5/31/18 John will participate in activities designed to address muscle coordination with his face and mouth in four of five requests during a five-minute period of oral motor therapy.

For children with disabilities who take alternate assessments aligned to alternate achievement standards (in addition to the annual goals), a description of benchmarks or short-term objectives. [34 CFR §300.320(a)(2)(ii)]

> John will not take an alternative assessment.

A description of:

- How the child's progress toward meeting the annual goals will be measured. [34 CFR §300.320(a)(3)(i)]
- When periodic reports on the progress the child is making toward meeting the annual goals will be provided such as through the use of quarterly or other periodic reports, concurrent with the issuance of report cards. [34 CFR §300.320(a)(3)(ii)]

> **Goal 1-4:** Progress will be measured in November 2017, February 2018, and May 2018 through teacher observation and anecdotal records.

A statement of the <u>special education and related services</u> and <u>supplementary</u> aids and <u>services</u>, based on peer-reviewed research to the extent practicable, to be provided to the child, or on behalf of the child, and <u>a statement of the program modifications or supports</u> for school personnel that will be provided to enable the child:

- To advance appropriately toward attaining the annual goals. [34 CFR §300.320(a)(4)(i)]
- To be involved in and make progress in the general education curriculum and to participate in extracurricular and other nonacademic activities. [34 CFR §300.320(a)(4)(ii)]
- To be educated and participate with other children with disabilities and nondisabled children in extracurricular and other nonacademic activities. [34 CFR §300.320(a)(4)(iii)]

> **Service:** Inclusion preschool class. Provider: Special education staff: Group services.
>
> **Service:** Speech and language therapy. Provider: Speech and language pathologist. Individual and group Services

An explanation of the extent, if any, to which the child will not participate with nondisabled children in the regular classroom and in extracurricular and other nonacademic activities. [34 CFR §300.320(a)(5)]

> John will participate in the inclusive general preschool education classroom 100% of the time.

A statement of any individual appropriate accommodations that are necessary to measure the academic achievement and functional performance of the child on state and districtwide assessments. [34 CFR §300.320(a)(6)(i)]

> Adapted writing utensils and adapted scissors.

If the IEP Team determines that the child must take an alternate assessment instead of a particular regular state or district-wide assessment of student achievement, a statement of why:
- The child cannot participate in the regular assessment. [34 CFR §300.320(a)(6)(ii)(A)]
- The particular alternate assessment selected is appropriate for the child. [34 CFR §300.320(a)(6)(ii)(B)]

> John will take the DRDP (2015).

The projected date for the beginning of the services and modifications and the anticipated frequency, location, and duration of special education and related services and supplementary aids and services and modifications and supports. [34 CFR §300.320(a)(7)]

Service, Aid, or Modification	Frequency	Location	Beginning Date	Duration
Inclusion preschool classroom	5 times a week for 2.5 hours a day	Northwood Elementary School	5/31/2017	5/31/2018
Speech and language therapy	2 times a week for 30 minutes each	Northwood Elementary School	5/31/2017	5/31/2018

Student:		Strengths/Preferences/Interests:
Birthday:		
Age:		
Disability:		

Summary of Present Developmental Levels and Abilities:

Summary of Goals/Objectives:

Summary of Adaptations/Modification/Needs:	Important to Know/Other Information:

Questions or Items to Follow-Up On:

Appendix E
Blank Recording Forms

INCLUSION SUPPORT RECOMMENDATIONS		
Inclusion Observation Reporting Form*		
Child:	Center:	Date:
Teacher(s):	Inclusion Specialist:	
SCHEDULE	OBSERVATIONS (What facilitator observes?)	SUPPORTS/ADAPTATIONS (Suggestions for teachers that may help child be part of activities.)

*Note: Above form could be copied on NCR paper so copies may be left for parents and staff after each visit.

BEHAVIOR OBSERVATION CHART
ABC Analysis

Child: Observer:

DATE	ACTIVITY (Where, when, who, what?)	ANTECEDENTS (What happened immediately before behavior?)	BEHAVIOR (What actually happened?)	CONSEQUENCES (What happened immediately after behavior?)	COMMENTS

POSITIVE BEHAVIOR SUPPORT PLAN

Child: **Date:**

Team Members:

ANTECEDENTS/TRIGGERS	BEHAVIOR(S)	CONSEQUENCES

FUNCTION OF BEHAVIOR (hypothesis and possible communication)

PREVENTION	REPLACEMENT BEHAVIOR(S)	NEW CONSEQUENCES
		To Old Behavior: **To Replacement Behavior:**

ACTIVITY/STANDARDS INVENTORY

Child: **Date:**

SITUATION	PEER BEHAVIOR (How do peers participate?)	TARGET CHILD BEHAVIOR	BARRIERS TO PARTICIPATION	ADAPTATIONS

LEVEL OF PARTICIPATION IN DAILY ACTIVITIES

Child: **Week of:**

ACTIVITY	Monday	Tuesday	Wednesday	Thursday	Friday
Free play					
Circle					
Outside play					
Mealtime					
Toileting					
Centers					
Computers					
Good-bye					

A = Participated with assistance

I = Participated independently

W = Wandered around

D = Did not participate

INDIVIDUAL SUPPORT SCHEDULE

Child: **Date:**

Teacher: **Center:**

Inclusion Specialist:

SCHEDULE	SPECIFIC SUPPORTS/ADAPTATIONS (What staff will do for child that will help child be part of activities?)
Arrival	
Morning activities (free play)	
Cleanup	
Toilet/Hand Washimg	
Snack	
Circle time	
Small group (work time)	
Outside play	

OBJECTIVE BY ACTIVITY MATRIX

Child:

Date:

ACTIVITY	OBJECTIVE					

SPECIAL ACTIVITY PLAN

Child: | **Date:**

ACTIVITY	STRATEGIES
Description:	Peers:
Purpose & objective(s):	
	Adults:
Materials:	

EVALUATION

Outcomes:

Suggestions for future activities:

ROLES AND RESPONSIBILITIES FOR INCLUSION

Child: **Date:**

RESPONSIBILITIES	WHO IS RESPONSIBLE?			
	Child Care	Special Education Teacher	1:1 Aide (as needed)	Administrator
Developing child's goals				
Assigning responsibility and supervising 1:1 aide				
Adapting environment and/ or curriculum				
Implementing lesson plans				
Monitoring child's progress				
Communicating with families				
Consulting with other service providers				
Arranging and coordinating team meetings				
Other?				

CODE:

P = Primary responsibility   E = Equal responsibility

S = Secondary responsibility   I = Has input in decision-making process

Child: **Date:**

1. Describe the child's strengths and the things that he/she does well.

2. What improvements has the child made in school in his/her developmental skills and behaviors since we last spoke?

3. What concerns do you have about the child's development or behavior?

4. Based on question 3, what teaching strategies or adaptations have already been tried or are currently in place for the above concerns?

5. Based on question 3, what goals would you like to see to help the child make progress and improvement in these areas?

FAMILY PREPARATION FOR TEAM MEETING
Directions: Please fill out his paper in preparation for our meeting

Child: **Date:**

1. Describe your child's strengths and the things that he/she does well.

2. What improvements has your child made at home in his/her developmental skills and behaviors since we last spoke?

3. What concerns do you have about your child's development or behavior?

4. Based on your concerns with question 3, what goals would you like to see to help your child make progress and improvements in these areas?

5. How else can the staff help to support you, your child, and your family?

Glossary

AAC See *augmentative or alternative communication.*

A-B-C analysis Method of observation and evaluation of a challenging behavior that describes the *antecedent, behavior,* and *consequence.*

abnormal gag reflex The forward and downward movement of the tongue and extension of the jaw, often caused by hypersensitivity or by difficulty swallowing.

access All children will be able to utilize classroom materials and participate in learning centers and activities.

accommodations Assisting a child with special needs to allow for full access and participation in typical early childhood settings.

activity area Spaces within a classroom designed to facilitate different types of activities.

activity/standards inventory Analysis of the discrepancy between the participation of peers without disabilities and the participation of the child with special needs with identification of the barriers responsible for the lack of participation.

adaptations Special teaching techniques or equipment that enable a child with special needs to participate in an activity.

adaptive equipment Physical devices designed or modified to support the independence and participation of a child with special needs.

aided hearing Hearing that is augmented by amplification by wearing a hearing aid.

ambient noise Surrounding, extraneous sounds in an environment.

ambulatory Can walk unassisted.

Americans with Disabilities Act (ADA) Public Law 101-336 that assures full civil rights to individuals with disabilities, including access and accommodations in early education programs.

anecdotal record keeping Monitoring child behavior and progress by writing narrative descriptive notes.

anticonvulsant medication Drug that prevents or lessens seizure activity in the brain.

applied behavior analysis This teaching approach involves observation, assessment, task analysis, systematic teaching of skills, and ongoing data collection to monitor progress.

asymmetric tonic neck reflex (ATNR) A reflex in which turning the head to one side causes the arm and leg on that side to extend and the limbs on the opposite side to flex.

athetosis Slow, involuntary writhing movements typical of some types of cerebral palsy.

audiogram Graphic representation of an individual's hearing thresholds, plotted by pitch (frequency) and loudness (intensity).

auditory cues Speech or environmental sounds presented with, and which the child learns to associate with, specific events.

augmentative or alternative communication (AAC) Method of communicating that uses assistive devices or techniques, such as signs, picture boards, and computers.

auto symbolic play Pretend play.

aversive stimulus Unpleasant stimulus.

backward chaining Teaching the steps of a task in reverse order; teaching the last step in the chain first.

behavior chain A sequence of behaviors.

behavior modification Systematic, consistent efforts to modify a specific behavior by manipulation of antecedents and consequences.

behavior specialist A professional who assists teachers and parents in understanding effective techniques of managing challenging behavior.

cause and effect Understanding that specific actions create specific effects.

circle time Gathering children together in a group to share an activity directed by an adult, such as singing or listening to a story.

close-ended No flexibility; toy must be played with in a specific way.

cochlear implant A prosthetic device that electrically stimulates the cochlea via an electrode array surgically implanted in the inner ear.

collaboration Two or more coequal partners voluntarily working side by side with mutual respect and cooperation to reach a common goal through shared decision making.

collaborative consultation An interactive process that enables people with diverse skills to generate creative solutions to problems.

communication board Board displaying pictures that a child who is nonverbal can point to express wants and needs.

communication notebook Augmentative communication technique used with a child who is nonverbal in which picture cards depicting important communication topics and key words are arranged in a notebook. Can also refer to parent-teacher communication in which notes are written back and forth in a notebook that is sent home with the child each day.

communicative function Communicative value or purpose of a specific behavior.

conductive hearing loss Hearing loss caused by obstruction in the transmission of sound to the cochlea due to obstruction in the ear canal or the middle ear, which may result from otitis media or a perforated eardrum.

consequence What happens immediately following a specific behavior.

consultation Sharing of advice on effective instructional practices.

cortical visual impairment Visual impairment resulting from an inability of the occipital lobe of the brain to process visual stimuli.

co-teaching model A group of children without disabilities and their teacher are combined in the same classroom with a group of children who have disabilities and a special education teacher.

cutout cup A flexible plastic cup with a semicircular piece cut out of the rim.

data recording Recording, usually in writing, the frequency and/or duration of a specific behavior through direct observation.

deaf and hard of hearing (DHH) specialist Person trained to provide educational and communication services to individuals with hearing loss.

decibel Unit used to measure the intensity or loudness of sound.

deficit orientation Approaching families of children who have disabilities with the assumption that they are in difficult, disadvantaged circumstances, rather than the assumption that they have many strengths.

delayed reinforcement Responses are not given immediately following the behavior.

dialogic reading An adult helps the child tell the story when the adult is reading to the child. The adult becomes the listener, the questioner, and the audience for the child. It is an interactive, shared picture-reading process.

diplegia Weakness or paralysis, usually associated with cerebral palsy, which primarily affects the legs.

directed eye gaze The purposeful use of eye gaze as a communicative act by looking in the direction of a desired object or symbol.

direct services When a service provider interacts directly with the student.

discovery walk Early childhood activity in which a walking route is planned with the goal to discover and collect interesting things.

discrete trial approach Behavioral intervention approach that is highly structured and often uses tangible reinforcers for performance of specific behavior.

Down syndrome A condition caused by a chromosomal abnormality that results in unique physical characteristics and varying degrees of intellectual disabilities.

Dycem mat Piece of non-slip plastic material that is slightly sticky. Often used as placemat for dishes or other objects to keep them from sliding around on a table surface.

EESS Refers to making adaptations that Enlarge, Enhance, Stabilize, and Simplify with the goal of making it easier for a child to have access and participate.

epilepsy Recurrent seizures caused by abnormal electrical activity in the brain.

event sequence box A row of small boxes in which actual objects are placed to represent the sequence of activities of the day.

expatiation Caregiver responds to a child's utterance with a more complex version of the child's utterance with new information added.

extinction Reducing the strength or frequency of a particular behavior by eliminating the reinforcer following the behavior.

family systems approach The family is viewed as a dynamic interactive unit; what affects one family member affects all.

fine motor skills Skills, such as drawing and picking up small objects, that require the coordination of the small muscles, particularly muscles of the hands and fingers.

floor time A therapeutic approach that seeks to help children develop a sense of pleasure in interacting and relating to others, and done through play.

fluency disorders Speech disorders such as stuttering that affect the rate and rhythm of speech production; characterized by frequent repetitions, prolongations, and blocking of speech sounds.

food obsessions Craving of certain foods, often to the exclusion of most other foods.

food phobias Obsessive avoidance of certain foods or textures.

frequency Measurement of the pitch of sound in cycles per second extending from high to low.

functional behavior analysis Behavioral analysis technique that seeks to determine from the child's perspective the *function* or value of the behavior by carefully observing and recording the antecedents, consequences, and frequency of the behavior.

gastrostomy tube (G-tube) Feeding tube inserted directly into the stomach through a surgically created opening in the abdominal wall. Used when a child is unable to receive adequate nutrition orally or if the esophagus is blocked; may be temporary or permanent.

grief reactions Normal emotional processes in response to a loss, such as the death of a child or the birth of a child with a disability. Family members experience such reactions as shock, denial, anger, depression, and acceptance.

gross motor skills Skills that require the coordination of large muscles, such as sitting, walking, and throwing a ball.

hand-over-hand guidance Adult manipulates a child's hands to perform a task by putting a hand over that of the child.

hand-under-hand guidance Adult manipulates a child's hands to perform a task by putting a hand under that of the child.

hemiplegia Weakness or paralysis on one side of the body.

high-incidence disabilities The most common disabilities, including learning disabilities, speech and language disorders, and mild mental retardation.

high-preference inventory Identification of a child's most preferred and least preferred activities, objects, and people, determined through caregiver interviews and careful observation of child's likes and dislikes; information can be used to identify ways of motivating, engaging, and reinforcing a child who has a severe disability.

high-quality early childhood inclusion Has three defining features: access, participation, and supports.

hypersensitive Excessively sensitive.

hypertonic Characterized by increased tone or tension (stiffness) in the muscles.

hypotonic Characterized by decreased tone or floppiness in the muscles.

inclusion The movement toward, and the practice of, educating students with disabilities in general education classrooms alongside their peers without disabilities with appropriate supports and services provided as necessary.

inclusion support specialists Has a strong background, both in experience and in training, in both general and special early childhood education; works collaboratively with team members to ensure appropriate supports are provided to each child based on his/her goals and specific needs.

indirect services A specialist makes recommendations on effective instructional strategies to the adults responsible for the direct instruction.

intellectual disabilities Significantly subaverage intellectual functioning.

Individualized Educational Program (IEP) Written educational program for a child with special needs who qualifies for special education services.

Individualized Family Services Plan (IFSP) Written family plan of the child and family services needed to support an infant or toddler who has special needs during the first three years of life.

Individuals with Disabilities Education Act (IDEA) The laws and amendments governing the rights of children with disabilities after 1990.

insistence on sameness Term used to refer to tendency of many children with autism to become anxious when certain daily routines or features of the environment are changed.

internal state Individual's state of arousal or alertness, such as asleep, drowsy, quiet awake, or agitated.

itinerants Professionals who provide specialized services in a variety of settings, traveling from site to site; frequently use a consultation model of service delivery.

kinesthetic cues Movement cues that stimulate the child's *kinesthetic sensation,* the awareness of the movement and position of one's body or limbs in space.

kinesthetic sensation Awareness of movement of various parts of the body, including the contracting and stretching of muscles and compression of the joints.

language disorders Inability or difficulty with expressing, understanding, or processing language.

language skills Refers to the ability to learn vocabulary, to put words together into complete sentences, and to understand when others speak.

learned helplessness Development of a pattern of nonresponse or lack of effort because a lack of opportunity to experience the success and efficacy of one's own behavior and initiative.

learning disability Covers a wide range of neurologically based difficulties or *brain differences* that affect the ways in which a child processes and organizes visual and auditory information.

least amount of help Offering the least amount of help possible to encourage independence.

least restrictive environment (LRE) Most normalized environment in which the needs of a child with disabilities can be met appropriately.

low-incidence disabilities Refers to disabilities that occur fairly infrequently, including sensory impairments (visual impairment, hearing loss/deafness, and blindness), motor disability such as cerebral palsy, severe mental retardation, autism, and multiple disabilities.

low vision Covers a range from mild to severe vision loss; includes individuals who have some functional vision and who may be partially sighted or legally blind.

manipulatives Small toys and objects that encourage use of hands and development of fine motor skills.

manual approach Use of manual signs as opposed to speech production (oral approach); the mode of communication preferred by many deaf individuals. Most commonly preferred manual sign system is ASL, American Sign Language.

mapping language onto experience Language strategy in which the adult carefully uses words and sentences to describe the activities in which the child is engaged.

mastery motivation Intrinsic drive to master a skill or behavior.

mild to moderate disabilities More recent term used to refer to *high-incidence disabilities.*

mini-script Short sequences of events or actions.

mobility Ability to move about in one's environment.

modification Changing the curriculum goals in some way, such as changing the instructional level, content, or performance criteria.

most amount of help Generally refers to the offering of physical assistance.

motor control The ability to voluntarily engage muscles in purposeful movements.

movable soft areas Outdoor or indoor play surfaces and structures that are soft and portable; can be used to create play spaces for children with severe motor disabilities or for children who are developmentally young.

multitiered system of support A system of multiple tiers to support all children with academic concepts and behavior. The tiers include high quality teaching strategies and instruction first, targeted supports, and finally individualized interventions.

muscle tone A muscle's level of tension and resistance while at rest; abnormal muscle tone may be either *hypertonic* or *hypotonic.*

natural environment An environment where, to the maximum extent possible, children with disabilities are educated with children who do not have disabilities.

non-ambulatory One cannot walk without the assistance of a device such as a walker.

objectives Behaviors and skills the child will learn en route to the achievement of long-term goals. Objectives are specific and measurable.

objective-by-activity matrix Chart that displays each activity of the day and the specific IEP objectives to be addressed during each activity.

olfactory cues Cues that stimulate the sense of smell, such as encouraging a child who is blind to smell the paint before beginning an art activity.

one-to-one paraprofessional/aide An adult assigned to shadow a specific child and provide specific kinds of support, such as physical support and mobility assistance, behavioral management, or medical assistance as needed.

open-ended Flexible; no one right way to play with an open-ended toy.

oral approach Communication approach preferred by some individuals with hearing loss that focuses on auditory training and learning to understand and produce speech (as contrasted with the *manual approach,* which advocates for the primary use of signs).

orientation and mobility (O&M) specialist Professional who provides training in both orientation skills (such as the use of all available senses to help children who are blind orient themselves in relation to their environment) and mobility skills (use of aids such as a cane and strategies such as trailing).

orthopedic impairment A physical disability.

outcomes/ outcome statements Changes families want to see for their child or themselves as a result of services.

pacing The speed at which a caregiver performs an activity or moves from one activity to another; the rate of speech, and amount of time the child is given in which to respond.

parallel play Children play independently, beside one another.

parent-professional partnerships Collaborative relationships between parents and professionals.

parent-to-parent support Parent support model that links experienced parents of children with special needs to parents who are new to the experiences and services related to having a child with special needs.

partial sight Refers to an individual with *low vision.*

participation All children will be able to learn and be involved in all activities.

perceptual motor development The integration of the modalities used for processing information (usually visual or auditory) with a nonverbal response.

person-first terminology Use of terms that show respect and acceptance for all by placing the person first ahead of the disability.

phonemes The smallest units of speech sound that can be combined to produce words.

pica Craving to eat nonfood substances, such as dirt or chalk.

picture exchange communication system (PECS) System of communication training often used with children who have autism who do not use functional speech; they select a picture card representing a desired object or activity and hand it to an adult as a request.

picture sequence board Display of pictures (photos or drawings) representing the sequence of steps in a complex task.

Pivotal Response Teaching A systematical application of the principles of ABA to pivotal areas that lead to the development of social and educational skills needed to function independently in inclusive settings.

positive behavior support Behavioral technique that focuses on prevention of challenging behaviors and providing support for more positive behaviors by identifying the function of the challenging behavior and teaching the child a replacement behavior that is more acceptable.

postural control Ability to assume and maintain an upright balanced position; ability to control and stabilize the trunk.

Prader-Willi syndrome Chromosomal disorder associated with obesity, low tone, mild to moderate intellectual disability, and severe feeding disorder (food cravings).

pragmatics Ability to use language effectively in different situations.

Premack principle Children's performance can be enhanced by allowing them to engage in a highly reinforcing activity immediately following a less preferred or more difficult activity. For example, scheduling outdoor play immediately following story time would be beneficial for a child who has difficulty sitting quietly and maintaining attention.

problem-solving approach Generation of creative solutions to solve naturally arising problems.

progressive matching Matching the child's vocalization or word with a similar utterance, which is slightly more complex or elaborated. For example, if the child says "ba" for bottle the adult responds "bottle," if the child says "bottle" the adult responds "want bottle," and so on.

prompts Verbal, gestural, or physical cues given by an adult to help a child learn a skill or participate in an activity.

prone stander Padded board that enables a child with severe physical disabilities to be positioned upright.

proprioception Body's awareness of its position in space. Proprioceptors in the inner ear, muscles, and tendons provide feedback that supports posture and balance.

protective reflexes Automatic reactions to loss of balance, such as extension of arms and/or legs to protect oneself in a fall or extension of one arm to the side when sitting balance is lost.

pull-out model A specialist provide intervention outside of the child's classroom.

punishment Behavioral term referring to a negative consequence that decreases the strength of a behavior.

push-in model Services provided within the classroom.

quadriplegia Weakness or paralysis of both arms and both legs, usually involving the head and trunk as well.

receptive language The ability to understand the intent and meaning of someone's effort to communicate.

reflective listening Comments made by the listener that let the speaker know he or she has been heard and understood. Effective reflective listening gives back to the speaker both the ideas and the feelings perceived by the listener.

reinforcer Consequences of a behavior that increase the strength or frequency of a behavior.

relational bullying Acts such as snubbing, exclusion, or spreading rumors that are damaging about another child.

repetitive behavior Constant repetition of the same behavior.

replacement behavior Behavior that the child can be coached to use in place of an unacceptable behavior.

representational skills The understanding that a picture or symbol can represent reality and the ability to demonstrate such representation; for example, a dog can be represented by the spoken word *dog*, by a picture of a dog, or by the written word "d-o-g."

request-for-more strategy A simple, but effective, strategy for increasing the participation and initiation of a child with severe disabilities in which a pleasurable activity is interrupted and the child is taught to use a particular response to request the activity to resume (e.g., swinging) or to request more of something (e.g., a drink of juice).

residual hearing The degree of usable hearing without amplification.

scaffolding Adult's provision of just the right cues and supports necessary to assist children to perform a task they cannot yet do independently.

security object Familiar object with which a child seeks to maintain contact, particularly when experiencing stress or new situations.

self-stimulatory behavior Repetitive behaviors produced by a child that provide sensory stimulation to self-calm or to block out other stimuli, which the child experiences as painful or uncomfortable. Self-stimulatory behaviors include visual self-stimulation (e.g., spinning a wheel), tactile (twirling one's hair or head banging), kinesthetic (rocking), or auditory (constant humming).

semantic extension The extension of an idea or concept; modeling more complex language.

sensorineural hearing loss Hearing loss resulting from malfunctioning of the cochlea or auditory nerve.

sensory integration Ability of the central nervous system to receive, process, and learn from sensations, such as sights, sounds, movement, and the pull of gravity.

sensory integration therapy Therapy that seeks to get senses to work together to understand a sensory message and to translate the message into appropriate action.

separation Removal of a young child from or lack of access to an attachment figure.

service coordinator Individual identified in the IFSP who will be responsible for coordination of services specified in the individualized family service plan.

speech production (articulation) disorder Condition that interferes with the production of speech; includes articulation disorders (such as difficulty producing speech sounds or coordinating the oral musculature), fluency disorders (stuttering), or voice disorders (hoarseness).

speech skills The ability to produce sounds or phonemes that make up words.

spinal subluxation Partial dislocation of one of the upper spinal vertebrae that results in symptoms such as head tilt, increase in motor clumsiness, and weakness in one arm.

supports Any assistance that results in access and participation of children with disabilities in routine, daily activities within an educational setting.

tactile cues Signals provided by an adult that stimulate the sense of touch. Cues accompany or precede an event, such as touching the child's hand with a washcloth before washing the child's face or touching the spoon to the child's lips before beginning feeding; especially useful for children who are blind.

tactile defensiveness Abnormal sensitivity to touch and being touched resulting in a child's avoidance or resistance to being touched or to handling certain materials.

task analysis Breaking a task into a sequence of steps to determine which components of a task a child can already perform and which need to be taught. A task analysis also suggests the order in which steps should be taught.

task persistence The extent to which a child will persist at accomplishing a difficult task.

task sequencing The sequence of behaviors and events that make up an activity.

Teaching Pyramid Model A promotion, prevention, and intervention framework used to promote young children's social and emotional development while preventing and addressing challenging behavior.

threshold (auditory) The intensity (loudness) at which an individual can barely detect a sound.

time away Behavioral consequence when a child is removed from the group.

tongue thrust Strong reflexive protrusion of the tongue; interferes with eating and dental development.

tonic bite reflex Teeth clamp shut as a result of jaw closure, which occurs reflexively when gums or teeth are stimulated, often in children with cerebral palsy.

total communication approach Teaching approach that uses multiple modalities in communication, including facial expression, manual signs, finger spelling, lip reading, speech, writing, and AAC devices.

traffic management Arrangement of space and materials to encourage efficient movement of children from one area to another; avoids cross traffic, provides for access and mobility needs of children with disabilities, and places materials so they are accessible in the areas where they will be used.

trailing techniques Technique used to assist children who are blind with the development of independent mobility; involves following along a surface (such as a wall) or edge (such as the edge of a countertop) with the hand extended at a 45-degree angle to the side. For example, a preschool child may learn to trail along a wall to find the bathroom.

transformations Alterations.

transitions The process of moving from one event or activity to another (for example, from circle time to recess), from one setting to another (from home to a children's center), or from one program to another (from preschool to kindergarten).

trial-and-error exploration Typical behavior of a child in the sensorimotor stage of development, characterized by purposeful exploration of objects and search for novel effects by systematically engaging in trial-and-error manipulation. For example, a child seated in a high chair drops crackers from different angles and positions and watches where they land.

tunnel vision A condition in which the visual field is constricted, allowing only straight-ahead vision, an effect similar to looking through a tunnel.

vestibular sensation The vestibular system is located in the inner ear and responds to the position of the head in relation to gravity. This sensation enables people to maintain balance.

visual field Total area that can be seen while looking straight ahead, without moving the head or eyes.

voice disorder Conditions that affect the quality of the voice, such as pitch, loudness, and resonance; includes such disorders as hoarseness and excessive nasality.

zone of proximal development (ZPD) Level of ability or performance a child can exhibit while interacting with a significant adult but cannot perform independently.

References

Chapter 1

Department of Health and Human Services (HHS) & U.S. Department of Education (ED). (2015). *Policy statement on inclusion of children with disabilities in early childhood programs.* Retrieved from www2.ed.gov/policy /speced/guid/earlylearning/joint-statement -full-text.pdf.

Division for Early Childhood of the Council for Exceptional Children (DEC) & National Association for the Education of Young Children (NAEYC). (2009). *Early childhood inclusion: A joint position statement of the Division of Early Childhood (DEC) and the National Association for the Education of Young Children (NAEYC).* Chapel Hill, NC: University of North Carolina, FPG Child Development Institute.

Friend, M., & Cook, L. (2013). *Interactions: Collaboration skills for school professionals.* Upper Saddle River, NJ: Pearson.

Giangreco, M. F., Suter, J. C., & Doyle, M. B. (2010). Paraprofessional in inclusive schools: A review of recent research. *Journal of Educational and Psychological Consultation,* 20, 41–57.

Heron, T. E., & Harris, K. C. (2001). *The educational consultant: Helping professionals, parents, and students in inclusive classrooms.* Austin, TX: PRO-ED.

Hill, C. (2003). The role of instructional assistants in regular classrooms: Are they influencing inclusive practices? *The Alberta Journal of Educational Research,* 69(1), 98–100.

Richardson-Gibbs, A. M., & Klein, M. D. (2014). *Making preschool inclusion work: Strategies for supporting children, teachers and programs.* Baltimore, MD: Paul H. Brooks.

Chapter 2

Bruner, J. (1982). The organization of action and the nature of the adult/infant transaction. In E. Tronick (Ed.), *Social intercharge in infancy: Affect, cognition and communication* (pp. 23–35). Baltimore, MD: University Park Press.

DEC/NAEYC. (2009). Early childhood inclusion: A joint position statement of the Division for Early Childhood (DEC) and the National Association for the Education of Young Children (NAEYC). Chapel Hill, NC: The University of North Carolina, FPG Child Development Institute.

Luongo, S., & Kearns, K. (2015). *Adapting play materials* (video). Community Living Toronto. Retrieved from http://connectability.ca /Garage/wp-content/themes/connectability /plugin/si_workshops/adapted_materials /open_logo.htm.

Milbourne, S. A., & Campbell, P. H. (2007). *CARA's Kit: Creating adaptations for routines and activities.* Philadelphia, PA: Child and Family Studies Research Programs, Thomas Jefferson University.

Vygotsky, L. (1980). *Mind in society: The development of higher psychological processes.* Cambridge, MA: Harvard University Press.

Chapter 3

American Psychiatric Association. (2013). *Diagnostic and statistical manual of mental disorders* (5th ed.). Washington, DC: American Psychiatric Publishing.

Ayres, A. J. (2005). *Sensory integration and the child: 25th anniversary edition.* Los Angeles: Western Psychological Services.

Bird, G., & Buckley, S. (2001). *Reading and writing for infants with Down syndrome (0–5 years).* Down Syndrome Education. Retrieved from www.dseinternational.org/.

Buckley, S. (2002). *Reading and writing for individuals with Down syndrome.* Down Syndrome Education. Retrieved from www.down -syndrome.org/practice/152/.

Chen, D. (Ed.). (2014). *Essential elements in early intervention: Visual impairment and multiple disabilities.* New York: AFB Press.

Dotie-Kwan, J. (2000). Supporting young children with visual impairment. In M. D. Klein, A. M. Richardson-Gibbs, S. Kilpatrick, & K. C. Harris (Eds.), *Project support.* Los Angeles, CA: California State University.

Greenspan, S. I., & Weider, S. (2006). *Engaging autism: The floortime approach to helping children relate, communicate, and think.* Reading, MA: Perseus Books.

Hodapp, R. M., & Ly, T. M. (2003). Visual processing strengths in Down syndrome. A case for reading instruction. In S. Soraci & K. Murata-Soraci (Eds.), *Perspectives on fundamental processes in intellectual functioning: Visual information processing.* Stamford, CT: Ablex.

Hunt, N., & Marshall, K. (2012). *Exceptional children and youth.* Belmont, CA: Wadsworth, Cengage Learning.

Koegel, R. L., & Koegel, L. (2012). *The PRT Pocket guide: Pivotal Response Treatment for autism spectrum disorders.* Baltimore, MD: Paul H. Brookes.

Koegel, R. L., & LaZebnik, C. (2005). *Overcoming autism: Finding the answers, strategies, and hope that can transform a child's life.* New York, NY: Penguin Books.

Lynch, E. W., & Hanson, M. J. (2011). *Developing cross-cultural competence.* Baltimore, MD: Brookes.

MacDonald, R., Parry-Cruwys, D., Dupere, S., & Ahearn, W. (2014). Assessing progress and outcome of early intensive behavioral intervention for toddlers with autism. *Research in Developmental Disabilities,* 35 (12), 3632–3644.

Mesibov, G. B., Shea, V., & Schopler, E. (2004). *The TEACCH approach to autism spectrum disorders.* New York, NY: Springer Science and Business Media.

Roizen, N. (2013). Down syndrome (trisomy 21). In M. Batshaw (Ed.), *Children with disabilities* (pp. 307–318). Baltimore, MD: Paul H. Brookes.

Chapter 4

Helm, J. H., & Katz, L. G. (2010). *Young investigators: The project approach in the early years* (2nd ed.). New York: Teachers College Press.

Kuo, G., & Faber Taylor, A. (2004). A potential natural treatment for attention deficit hyperactivity disorder. Evidence from a national study. *American Journal of Public Health,* 94(9), 1580–1586

McManis, L. D., & Parks, J. (2011). *How to evaluate technology for early learners.* E-book and toolkit. Winston-Salem, NC: Hatch Early Learning. Retrieved from www.hatchearlylearning.com/events /how-to-evaluate-technology-for-early -learners/.

NAEYC & Fred Rogers Center for Early Learning and Children's Media. (2012). Technology and interactive media as tools in early childhood program serving children from birth through age 8. *Joint Position Statement.* Washington, DC: National Association for the Education of Young Children.

Nimmo, J., & Hallet, B. (2008). Childhood in the garden: A place to encounter natural and social diversity. Retrieved March 5, 2016 from *Young Children on the Web.* www.naeyc.org/files/yc/file/200801 /BTJNatureNimmo.pdf.

Sachs, N., & Vincenta, T. (2011). Outdoor environments for children with autism and special needs. *Implications,* 9(1). Retrieved January 31, 2016 from www.informedesign .org/_news/april_v09-p.pdf.

Spencer, K. H., & Wright, P. M. (2014). Quality outdoor play spaces for young children. *Young Children.* Retrieved January 31, 2016 from www.naeyc.org/yc /article/Quality_Outdoor_Play_Spaces _Spencer.

Taylor, A. F., Kuo, F., & Sullivan, W. C. (2001). Coping with ADD: The surprising connection to green play settings. *Environment and Behavior,* 33(1), 54–77.

Watson, A., & McCathren, R. (2009). Including children with special needs: Are you and your early childhood program ready? *Beyond the Journal,* Young Children on the Web. Retrieved January 30, 2016 from www.naeyc.org/files/yc/file/200903 /BTJWatson.pdf.

Chapter 5

Cipani, E., & Schock, K. M. (2011). *Functional behavioral assessment: Diagnosis and treatment* (2nd ed.). New York: NY: Springer Publishing Company.

Cook, R., Klein, M. D., & Chen, D. (2016). *Adapting early childhood curricula for children with special needs* (9th ed.). Boston, MA: Pearson.

Dunlap, G., Wilson, K., Strain, P., & Lee, J. K. (2013). *Prevent-teach-reinforce for young children: The early childhood model of individualized positive behavior support.* Baltimore, MD: Paul H. Brooks.

Fox, L., Dunlap, G., Hemmeter, M. L., Joseph, G. E., & Strain, P. S. (2003). The teaching pyramid: A model for supporting competence and preventing challenging behavior in young children. *Young Children, 58*(4), 48–52.

Santos, R. M., & Ostrosky, M. M. (2002). *Understanding the impact of language differences on classroom behavior.* Retrieved from http://csefel.vanderbilt.edu/briefs/wwb2.pdf

Chapter 6

Beukelman, D. R., & Mirenda, P. (2012). *Augmentative and alternative communication: Supporting children and adults with complex communication needs.* Baltimore, MD: Paul H. Brookes.

Cook, R. E, Klein, M. D., & Chen, D. (2016). *Adapting early childhood curricula for children with special needs* (9th ed.). Boston, MA: Pearson.

Chapter 7

Cohen, M., & Gerhardt, P. F. (2016). *Visual supports for people with autism: A guide for parents and professionals* (2nd ed.). Bethesda, MD: Woodbine House.

Cook, R., Klein, D., & Chen, D. (2016). *Adapting early childhood curricula for children with special needs* (9th ed.). Boston, MA: Pearson.

Murphy, K. (2011). Thinking through transitions. *Connections,* 20. Folsom, CA: California Association for the Education of Young Children.

Chapter 8

Gonzalez-Mena, J. (2007). *Diversity in early care and education: Honoring differences.* Columbus, OH: McGraw Hill Education.

Roopnarine, J., Shin, M., Jung, K., & Hossain, L. (2003). *Play and early development and education: The instantiation of parental belief systems.* In O. Saracho & B. Spodek (Eds.), *Contemporary perspectives on play in early childhood education* (pp. 115–132). Charlotte, NC: Information Age Publishing.

Sluss, D. (2015). *Supporting play in early childhood: Environment, curriculum, assessment.* Stamford, CT: Cengage Learning.

Chapter 9

Cook, R.E., Klein, M.D., & Chen, D. (2016). *Adapting early childhood curricula for children with special needs* (9th ed.). Boston, MA: Pearson.

Chapter 10

NAEYC & NCTM. (2002). *Early childhood mathematics: Promoting good beginnings.* Washington, DC: National Association for the Education of Young Children.

Premack, D. (1965). Reinforcement theory. In D. Levine (Ed.), *Nebraska symposium on motivation.* Lincoln, NE: University of Nebraska Press.

Chapter 11

Kuo, G., & Faber Taylor, A. (2004). A potential natural treatment for attention deficit/hyperactivity disorder: Evidence from a national study. *American Journal of Public Health, 94*(9), 1580–1586.

Lillemyr, O., Dockett, S., & Perry, B. (Eds.) (2013). *Varied perspectives on play and learning: Theory and research on early years education.* Charlotte, NC: Information Age Press.

Chapter 12

Eicher, P. S. (2013). Feeding and its disorders. In M. Batshaw, N. Roizen, & G. Lotrecchiano (Eds.), *Children with disabilities,* (7th ed., pp. 121–140). Baltimore, MD: Paul H. Brookes.

Haesler, R. M., & Mills, J. J. (2013). Nutrition and children with disabilities. In M. Batshaw, N. Roizen, & G. Lotrecchiano (Eds.), *Children with disabilities* (7th ed., pp. 107–120). Baltimore, MD: Paul H. Brookes.

Marotz, L. R. (2015). *Health, safety, and nutrition for the young child.* Stamford, CT: Cengage Learning.

Chapter 13

Bondy, A., & Frost, L. (2011). *A picture's worth: PECS and other visual communication strategies in autism.* Bethesda, MD: Woodbine House.

Cook, R., Klein, M. D., & Chen, D. (2016). *Adapting early childhood curricula for children with special needs* (9th ed.). Boston, MA: Pearson.

Hodgdon, L. A. (2011). *Visual strategies for improving communication: Practical supports for school and home.* Troy, MI: Quirk Roberts Publishing.

Sadao, K. C., & Robinson, N. B. (2010). *Assistive technology for young children: Creating inclusive learning environments.* Baltimore, MD: Paul Brookes

Zevenbergen, A., & Whitehurst, G. (2003). *Dialogic reading: A shared picture book intervention for preschoolers.* In A. van Kleeck, S. A. Stahl, & E. B. Bauer (Eds.), *On reading books to children* (pp. 177–183). Mahwah, NJ: Erlbaum.

Chapter 14

Bronte-Tinkew, J., Carrano, J., Horowitz, A., & Kimukawa, A. (2008). Involvement among resident fathers and links to infant cognitive outcomes. *Journal of Family Issues, 29,* 1211–1244.

Cook, R. E., Klein, M. D., & Chen, D. (2016). *Adapting early childhood curricula for children with special needs* (9th ed.). Boston, MA: Pearson.

Guthrie, A. C. (2000). Fathers' involvement in programs for young children. *Young Children, 59*(4), 75–79.

Hanson, M. J., & Lynch, E. W. (2013). *Understanding families: Supportive approaches to diversity, disability, and risk.* Baltimore, MD: Paul H. Brookes Publishing Company.

Klein, M. D., & Chen, D. (2001). *Working with young children from culturally diverse backgrounds.* Belmont, CA: Cengage Learning.

Lynch, E. W., & Hanson, M. J. (Eds.). (2011). *Developing cross-cultural competence: A guide for working with young children and their families.* Baltimore, MD: Paul H. Brookes.

Marsiglio, W., & Roy, K. (2012). *Nurturing dads: Social initiatives for contemporary fatherhood.* ASA Rose Monograph Series. New York: Russell Sage Foundation.

Raikes, H. H., Summers, J., & Roggman, L. A. (2005). Father involvement in Early Head Start programs. *Fathering: A Journal of Theory, Research and Practice about Men as Fathers, 3*(1), 29–58.

Turnbull, A., Turnbull, R., Erwin, E., & Soodak, L. (2015). *Families, professionals and exceptionality: Positive outcomes through partnerships and trust* (7th ed.) Upper Saddle River, NJ: Pearson.

Chapter 15

Ayres, A. J. (2005). *Sensory integration and the child: 25th anniversary edition.* Los Angeles: Western Psychological Services.

Cook, R., Klein, M. D., & Chen, D. (2016). *Adapting early childhood curricula for children with special needs* (9th ed.). Boston, MA: Pearson.

Heron, T., & Harris, K. C. (2000). The consultation process. In *The educational consultant: Helping professionals, parents and students in inclusive classrooms* (4th ed., pp. 1–36). Austin, TX: Pro-Ed.

Index